Chinese Capitalism in a Global Era

Chinese Capitalism in a Global Era examines the dynamic ways in which millions of ethnic Chinese in East and Southeast Asian economies organize their economic activities. It analyses how Chinese capitalism has changed under conditions of contemporary globalization and anticipates what the future holds for it.

The book challenges the conventional notion of Chinese capitalism as "crony capitalism", based around kinship networks and untouched by globalization. Yeung argues rather that key actors are capable of taking advantage of their participation in globalization processes to significantly transform the nature and organization of Chinese capitalism in East and Southeast Asia. He concludes that the system that is emerging is neither distinctively Chinese nor converging towards the Anglo-American form of capitalism, but a hybrid of both.

The book is comprehensive in its scope of analysis, interdisciplinary in its coverage of literature, and well grounded in a wide variety of empirical evidence that addresses different sectors and economies in Asia. It will be of interest to students and researchers in the areas of, international political economy, economics, Asian Studies, development studies, organization and management studies, economic geography, and urban studies.

Henry Wai-chung Yeung is Professor of Economic Geography at the Department of Geography, National University of Singapore. He was a recipient of the Commonwealth Fellowship, the Fulbright Foreign Research Award, and Residency at the Rockfeller Foundation's Bellagio Study and Conference Center . His previous publications include *Transnational Corporations and Business Networks* and *Entrepreneurship and the Internationalization of Asian Firms*.

Routledge Advances in International Political Economy

Chinese Capitalism in a Global Era

Towards hybrid capitalism

Henry Wai-chung Yeung

Routledge
Taylor & Francis Group

LONDON AND NEW YORK

First published in hardback 2004
First published in paperback 2006 by Rouledge
2 Park Square, Milton Park, Abingdon Oxon OX14 4RN

Simultaneously published in the USA and Canada
by Routledge
29 West 35th Street, New York, NY 10001

Routledge is an imprint of the Taylor & Francis Group

Printed and bound in Singapore by Markono Print Media Pte Ltd.

British Library Cataloguing in Publication Data
A catalogue record for this book is available from the British Library

Library of Congress Cataloging in Publication Data

ISBN 0-415-30989-1(hbk)
ISBN 0-415-40858-X (Taylor and Francis Asia Pacific paperback edition)

To Weiyu and Kay,
for their love, fun and company throughout my messy
writing of this book in three different continents

Contents

Figures

Tables

Preface

I want to start with a religious confession to reflect on my own positionality in the course of producing this book. Some ten years ago, I began my research and writing on Chinese capitalism as a half-baked 'culturalist' who quite believed in the intrinsic importance of *guanxi* or social relationships in explaining the economic organization of Chinese capitalism. I saw these cultural traits as shaping the behaviour and activities of ethnic Chinese firms, whether they are large or small, in manufacturing or service industries, and operating primarily locally and nationally or internationally. Ever since then, Chinese capitalism and its business organizations have been simultaneously fascinating and frustrating to me. I find the subject matter very fascinating simply because it is both close to my heart as an ethnic Chinese born in mainland China and to 'home' as a citizen in one predominantly ethnic Chinese economy (Singapore) and a permanent resident in another under the authority of the People's Republic of China (Hong Kong SAR). However, I feel increasingly frustrated to read more and more popular writings on Chinese capitalism (many wrongly called 'overseas Chinese business') that are nothing more than ethnic stereotypes or, worst, racist caricatures. The popularity and prominence of such triumphant characterization of Chinese capitalism as 'bamboo networks', '*guanxi* capitalism' or 'Confucian capitalism' has contributed to an essentialist idea that all ethnic Chinese in East and Southeast Asia share similar Confucian worldviews bounded within their traditional social and cultural values. Chinese capitalism has therefore been seen as static and self-contained in peculiar social and political contexts in East and Southeast Asia. Prompted by these readings, I often wonder whether I am indeed an 'overseas Chinese' – overseas to where and what? Am I a believer in Confucianism? I am probably as 'confucied' (or confused?) as you are. Do I know and practise *guanxi* as all Chinese are allegedly expected to do? So the story and its mischief goes on and on in these essentialist writings. You will find my critical opinions on some of these works in this book.

Is there then something wrong with my research and thinking? After some introspection, I doubt it. During the course of this decade-long research into Chinese capitalism, what has apparently changed in me is not the subject of my intellectual pursuit, but rather my thinking and reasoning about it. Perhaps this change has something to do with growing age and maturity in my intellectual capacity. But more significantly, I believe this change in my beliefs about Chinese capitalism is positively correlated with the dramatic pace at which globalization tendencies have transformed the world economy and the dynamic integration of Chinese capitalism into these tendencies. My fatherly mentor, friend and collaborator, Peter Dicken, calls the change 'global shift'. I believe there is a concomitant shift in the nature and economic organization of Chinese capitalism in association with this global shift of economic activities.

And it is this story of change and transformation in Chinese capitalism that I really want to unfold in this book. Going back to my confession, I ask for forgiveness and would like to claim that I am no longer interested in being a 'culturalist' who explains Chinese capitalism primarily in relation to cultural norms and practices. Indeed, a lot more has recently been said about how Chinese capitalism and its core feature, the Chinese family firm/business, have been so institutionalized through Chinese culture that nothing will really change it. All these studies have primarily focused on identifying and explaining the dominant features of Chinese capitalism and show how they are different from a variety of capitalisms elsewhere. This accumulation of culturalist and institutionalist interpretations of Chinese capitalism is fine in so far as they contribute to the first wave of intellectual enquiry into the changing nature and organization of Chinese capitalism. After all, we have to start with something before any rethinking and further development may be possible.

However, as I shall argue in this book, a second wave of research on Chinese capitalism must go beyond its almost permanent characterization and fixation in time and space. Instead, we must begin to examine how such core attributes of Chinese capitalism may change and evolve and the underlying processes that account for the changes. This more dynamic approach is necessary because Chinese capitalism is not a kind of cultural artefact that is forever cast in stone (like those you see in museums of history). Rather, Chinese capitalism is lived as a peculiar set of spatial-temporal outcomes, though highly institutionalized, of immense struggles and contestation by social actors through their discursive strategies and material practices. Taking such an actor-oriented approach, I think it is time to move on with our intellectual agenda to examine Chinese capitalism in a global era (the title of this book). This move, however, should not be about throwing 'culture' (the baby) out with the popular writings on the 'overseas Chinese business' (the bathwater). It is instead about seeing culture as a set of practices that change with circumstances and contexts and about paying more attention to social actors in enabling this change and transformation.

As such, I urge readers to think of Chinese capitalism not as iron-cast blocks of structures and systems that defy change and transformations. By reinterpreting and retheorizing its dynamics in a global era, I believe Chinese capitalism is increasingly becoming a form of hybrid capitalism that reflects both the influence of globalization tendencies on nationally or supra-nationally organized economic systems and the impact of significant participation of key actors from those economic systems in globalization tendencies. As a form of hybrid capitalism, Chinese capitalism embodies the interpenetration of culturally and institutionally specific dynamics at the local and regional scales, and the growing influence of flows of people, capital, technology and knowledge on the global scale.

In undertaking such a major project as writing this book, I am truly indebted to numerous organizations and individuals. To begin, the idea of writing this book quite literally woke me up one early morning during my stay in a Geneva hotel in late May 2001. I was participating in an expert workshop on the *World Investment Report 2001* sponsored by the United Nations Conference on Trade and Development (UNCTAD). Since then I have never looked back and this book ends up as the product of that morning dream. Thanks to UNCTAD for the kind invitation that indirectly made this book possible.

Many individuals must be acknowledged here for contributing, in one way or another, to the completion of this book. To begin, this book is about the social actors in Chinese capitalism whose collective effort makes the system work (and change). While I do not wish to name specific individuals for their help, I must thank all those hundreds of interviewees and informants throughout East and Southeast Asia who generously shared their wisdom and views on Chinese capitalism with me over the past decade. I hope this book has not in any way misrepresented their ingenious initiatives to create a better future for themselves and their families.

Among many individuals, I must thank specifically Kris Olds, my long-time friend and research collaborator. Our joint research into Chinese capitalism over the past six or so years has underpinned many of the key ideas in this book. So although I credit him for the good ideas, if any, presented in this book, I must relieve him from any responsibility for errors and inadequacies. His kind permission for me to use materials from our joint publications is much appreciated. I am also very grateful to two of my former students, Chi-Zhi Tan and Tse-Min Soh, whose work has contributed to some of the empirical evidence presented in this book. Moreover, I must thank my editor at Routledge, Heidi Bagtazo, and the two anonymous Routledge reviewers who offered very encouraging and constructive comments on my book proposal that no doubt have shaped its final content and trajectory. I apologize if I have failed to take all their comments into account.

At my academic home in Singapore, the National University of Singapore (NUS) thoughtfully granted me sabbatical leave (June 2002–June 2003) during which much of the writing was done. NUS also funded much of my research on Chinese capitalism (RP960045 and RP970013), and Wan Menghao and Elen Sia provided wonderful research assistance. My gratitude must also be extended to two sponsoring organizations and two host institutions that made my sabbatical possible and fruitful. The Association of Commonwealth Universities (UK) and the Department of State and Council for International Exchange of Scholars (USA) kindly awarded me a Commonwealth Fellowship (June–December 2002) and a Fulbright Foreign Researcher Award (January–April 2003), respectively. The geography departments at the University of Manchester, UK, and the University of Washington in Seattle, USA, were fantastic hosts for productive intellectual work. I thank J.W. Harrington, Chair of Geography at the University of Washington, for offering some resources to produce the final manuscript for publication. During my stay in these two places, I received very helpful inputs and ideas from various friends and colleagues, in particular Peter Dicken, Neil Coe, Martin Hess in Manchester, and Gary Hamilton, Katharyne Mitchell, Matthew Sparke and Kam Wing Chan in Seattle.

While on sabbatical, I presented the core arguments of this book in various seminars and colloquiums at the University of Manchester (UK), the University of Washington, Seattle (USA), the University of California, Davis (USA), Ohio State University, Colombus (USA), the University of Wisconsin, Madison (USA), the University of California, Los Angeles (USA), and the University of British Columbia, Vancouver (Canada). Some of these trips were made possible by the generous invitation and support of the following individuals and their institutions: Robert Feenstra (UC Davis), Gerry Pratt (UBC), Larry Brown (OSU), Kris Olds (UW-Madison) and Cindy Fan and Thomas Gillespie (UCLA). I would like to thank the seminar participants for their critical and insightful comments, in particular David Bachman, Trevor Barnes, Bill Beyers, Michael Bradford, Larry Brown, Noel Castree, Kam Wing Chan, Kevin Cox, David Edgington, Nancy Ettlinger, Robert Feenstra, Jim Glassman, Gary Hamilton, J.W. Harrington, Cole Harris, Dan Hiebert, David Ley, Edward Malecki, Becky Mansfield, Morton O'Kelly, Paul Robbins, Fiona Smith, Matt Sparke, Kevin Ward and Susan Whitings.

As it stands, parts of the book are based on theoretical and empirical materials I have earlier published in various refereed journals and book chapters. I have nevertheless made a determined effort to integrate these materials and rewritten most of them to present a coherent and, hopefully, compelling stream of arguments and evidence. The availability of book-length space also allows for a more theoretically grounded discussion of Chinese capitalism that goes well beyond the sum of all published articles. So I strongly encourage you to read this book from cover to cover in order to get a full sense of what I have argued and illustrated. I acknowledge the following publishers and copyright holders for generously granting me permissions to use my earlier work for this book:

© Blackwell Publishing, UK (*International Journal of Urban and Regional Research*, 1999, Vol. 23, No. 1, pp. 103–27), © Center for International Business Education, University of Michigan Business School, US (*Journal of Asian Business*, 2000, Vol. 16, No. 1, pp. 95–123), © Palgrave Macmillan Publishers, UK (Yeung, Henry Wai-chung and Olds, Kris, 'Globalizing Chinese firms', in *Globalization of Chinese Firms*, 2000, Macmillan, pp. 1–28; Yeung, Henry Wai-chung, 'The dynamics of the globalization of Chinese firms', in *Globalization of Chinese Firms*, 2000, Macmillan, pp. 75–104), © Pion, UK (*Environment and Planning A*, 2000, Vol. 32, No. 2, pp. 191–200 and *Environment and Planning D: Society and Space*, 1999, Vol. 17, No. 5, pp. 535–55), © Sage Publications, UK, and © ISA: International Sociological Association, Spain (*International Sociology*, 2000, Vol. 15, No. 2, pp. 269–90), © Taylor & Francis, UK (Yeung, Henry Wai-chung, 'Managing traditional Chinese family firms across borders', in *Rethinking Chinese Transnational Enterprises: Cultural Affinity and Business Strategies*, 2001, Curzon, pp. 184–207; Yeung, Henry Wai-chung, 'Transnational entrepreneurship and Chinese business networks', in *Chinese Entrepreneurship and Asian Business Networks*, 2002, Curzon, pp. 184–216), © Taylor & Francis Journals, UK (*Economy and Society*, 1999, Vol. 28, No. 1, pp. 1–29 and *Review of International Political Economy*, 2000, Vol. 7, No. 3, pp. 399–433), © The Family Firm Institute, USA (*Family Business Review*, 2000, Vol. 13, No. 1, pp. 55–70). Where possible in the book, I have made explicit references to these earlier publications. Every effort has been made to trace copyright holders, but in a few cases this has not been possible. Any omissions brought to the publisher's attention will be remedied in future editions.

Last but certainly never least, my wife Weiyu and daughter Kay have been patiently watching the progress of this book project from its inception to its completion. It is indeed pretty hard to write and live in three different cities, particularly when there is so much to do in Manchester and in Seattle. Their physical presence throughout the entire writing process has certainly kept me in good spirits and on track. As a compensation for their many forgone trips to the beautiful English landscape and the serene American wilderness, I can only offer this book.

Henry Yeung
Singapore, Manchester and Seattle

1   Hybrid capitalism

Demystifying Chinese capitalism

[handwritten: deeply rooted in cultural norms]

Unpacking Chinese capitalism

For several centuries, tens of millions of ethnic Chinese people in East and Southeast Asia have engaged in a distinctive form of economic organization through which an informal array of Chinese entrepreneurs, traders, financiers and their closely-knit networks of family members and friends came to dominate the economic sphere of the very host economies they later considered 'home'.[1] While deeply rooted in the cultural norms and social values of the traditional Chinese society in mainland China, this *[handwritten: heuristic device]* form of economic organization has evolved and adapted to dramatically different institutional contexts and political-economic conditions in the host Asian economies. In this book, I use the term 'Chinese capitalism' as a heuristic device to describe this historically and geographically specific form of economic organization that refers to the social organization and political economy of the so-called 'overseas Chinese'[2] living outside mainland China, particularly in East and Southeast Asia (i.e. Hong Kong, Macau, Taiwan, Singapore, Indonesia, Malaysia, the Philippines, Thailand and Vietnam; see Figure 1.1).[3] Chinese capitalism is a dominant mode of economic organization in East and Southeast Asia because of not only its economic significance in the host economies, but also its complex and yet intricate social organization and authority systems. The sheer diversity and prowess of economic activities controlled and coordinated by these ethnic Chinese have enabled some of them to become the very foundations of the Asian economies in which they primarily reside and operate. For example, Hong Kong-based Li Ka-shing, whose empire controlled about 16 per cent of Hong Kong's stock exchange index in 1998 (up from 12.7 per cent in 1988 reported in Redding, 1990: Table 7.4), caused the index to fall by 1.6 per cent on 23 December 1998 with his remarks about the unfriendly business environment in Hong Kong (*The Straits Times*, 23 and 24 December 1998). In another example, Wee Cho Yaw, the second-generation banker from Singapore and his family-controlled United Overseas Bank succeeded in taking over the fourth-largest Singapore bank (Overseas Union Bank, OUB) on 26 October 2001. After the acquisition, the

Figure 1.1 Map of Asia.

Wee family held controlling stakes in at least 14 public companies listed on the Singapore Exchange (10 per cent of all listed Chinese family firms). UOB became the largest bank in Singapore, with an international network comprising 273 offices in 18 countries in the Asia-Pacific region, Western Europe and North America.

Sceptics, nevertheless, may question the independent existence and coherence of this phenomenon known as Chinese capitalism. Building on the important contributions of Redding (1990), Hamilton (1991a, 1996a,

1999a, 2004), Whitley (1992, 1999) and others (see below), I believe that there is a concrete phenomenon, known as Chinese capitalism, to be described and explained. As this book will demonstrate, although this form of capitalist economic organization is changing in a global era, it is logical and reasonable to start an inquiry into Chinese capitalism by assuming it to be a relatively distinct and coherent phenomenon. This is indeed the underlying logic of Redding's (1990: 9) seminal work *The Spirit of Chinese Capitalism* in which he

changing in a global era

> begins with an assumption that there is a distinct and bounded phe-
> nomenon to be explained, that it is the culmination of a set of
> processes which need to be seen historically, and that the beliefs and
> values of businessmen have a part to play in the understanding of it.

In fact, such an assumption about capitalism's distinctiveness and coherence has been made since Max Weber's [1930] (1992) controversial treatise on the spirit of modern capitalism. In his 1920 introduction to the work, Weber [1930] (1992: xxxiv) argued that 'in modern times the Occident has developed, in addition to this [political capitalism through wars and acquisitions], a very different form of capitalism which has appeared nowhere else: the rational capitalistic organization of (formally) free labour. Only suggestions of it are found elsewhere'. Instead of subscribing to Karl Marx's view of capitalism as the valorization of capital through the exploitation of labour on a contractual basis (see also Screpanti, 2001), Weber [1920] (1983a: 41) believed that '[w]here we find that property is an object of trade and is utilised by individuals for profit-making enterprise in a market economy, there we have capitalism'. He went on to describe and explain this distinct form of modern capitalism in the Occident in relation to a peculiar ethos of accumulating wealth continually for its own sake, the rational utilization of labour and the rise of modern rational organizations (see also Andreski, 1983; Berger, 1986; Saunders, 1995; Silk and Silk, 1996). The spirit of modern industrial capitalism, Weber [1930] (1992: 27, 31) described, refers to 'that attitude which seeks profit rationally and systematically . . . Where it appears and is able to work itself out, it produces its own capital and monetary supplies as the means to its ends'.

What then distinguishes Chinese capitalism from other forms of economic organization at the beginning of the twenty-first century? My interest does not rest with comparing the success and failure of different varieties of capitalism, a difficult question to which not many scholars other than Weber can provide tentative answers. Rather, I seek to describe and explain in this book the changing dynamics of Chinese capitalism in relation to globalization and how these changes and transformations have led to the emergence of Chinese capitalism as a form of hybrid capitalism. To conduct such a dynamic analysis, however, I need to start *embedded – not easily isolated*

with a 'template' of what Chinese capitalism might be, as we know it today. This is an equally difficult task because Chinese capitalism, if it exists at all, is embedded within particular political and socio-economic contexts that cannot be easily isolated. As Berger (1986: 16) cautioned in his influential account of the capitalist revolution, 'it is not easy to excise the capitalist phenomenon from this wider context and look at it [capitalism], as if holding it with pincers under a lens, in any kind of "pure" form'. I do not assume the existence of a 'pure' form of capitalism – in its Anglo-American, German or Japanese genres – with which Chinese capitalism can be compared and contrasted. I also recognize the continuously evolving character and transformative power of these diverse genres of modern capitalism. To distinguish Chinese capitalism as a distinct mode of economic organization in East and Southeast Asia today, it is thus reasonable to identify it with a set of common denominators so that subsequent changes and transformations can be discerned. As pointed out by Block (2002: 224),

continuously always

> [i]t is not enough to say that capitalism is a constructed system. The task is to illuminate how it is constructed; to see how a diverse and often contradictory set of practices are welded together to produce something that has the appearance of being a natural and unified entity.

Broadly speaking then, Chinese capitalism has four key defining attributes that, taken together, might satisfy the simple definition of capitalism as 'production for a market by enterprising individuals or combines with the purpose of making a profit' (Berger, 1986: 19; emphasis omitted). First, Chinese capitalism refers to an institutionalized mode of economic organization that, until recent decades, has operated largely outside mainland China. It is rationalized and represented by a particular kind of economic institution: the Chinese family firm. This predominance of the family firm, however, is clearly not unique to Chinese capitalism. In fact, more than 75 per cent of all registered companies in the industrialized economies today remain family businesses and a third of listed companies in the *Fortune 500* list have families at their helm (Becht *et al.*, 2003). Forty-three of Italy's top 100 companies are family-owned and 26 of France's and 15 of Germany's are also family-owned. In the UK where ownership rapidly dispersed throughout the twentieth century, Franks *et al.* (2003) found that founding families retained board control well beyond the sale of their ownership stake (see also Chandler, 1990). According to a recent study of corporate ownership around the world (La Porta *et al.*, 1999: 481), even the Microsoft Corporation can be classified as a family-owned firm, with 23.7 per cent controlled by Bill Gates.

In Chinese capitalism, the family firm serves as the key organizational platform or 'mode of organizing', in the words of Hamilton (2000), for the continuous accumulation of wealth by ethnic Chinese families that in turn defines the rationality of Chinese capitalism, albeit in culturally specific ways. As Weber [1930] (1992: xxxi–xxxii; original italics) reminded us, '[modern] capitalism is identical with the pursuit of profit, and forever *renewed* profit, by means of continuous, rational, capitalistic enterprise'. While historically such 'rational' capitalistic enterprises might not have been developed in mainland China, Chinese capitalism, as I define it here, is organized around a particular social system of economic action and business activities that manifests itself through complex webs of family networks and personal relationships. It is embedded in a peculiar form of political economy in which the ethnic Chinese rule the host economy and leave the political sphere to the reign of indigenous ethnic groups or colonial masters. Chinese capitalism is thus organized and coordinated via neither market relations nor hierarchies of 'rational' firms (Williamson, 1975, 1985; Powell, 1990). Rather, it encompasses both markets and hierarchies and configures these capitalist institutions through an informal system of social relationships and family obligations (see Hamilton, 2000). Gordon Redding (1990: 3), a leading proponent of Chinese capitalism, thus observed that:

> the Overseas Chinese [*sic*] have developed one particular form of organization – the family business – and kept to it. Admittedly there are refinements to it, a wide range of sizes and technologies in use, a great variety of products, services, and markets, and an adventurous set of new variations on how to spin it out to larger and larger size, but certain common denominators seem never to be departed from. It remains in essence a family fortress, and at the same time an instrument for the accumulation of wealth by a very specific set of people. It is guarded against incursions from outside influence, and its workings are not publicly known. It is usually run nepotistically, with a benevolent paternalism throughout. Much of its effectiveness derives from intense managerial dedication, much of its efficiency from creating a working environment which matches the expectations of employees from the same culture. It is, in a very real sense, a cultural artifact.

Similarly, Brown (2000: 6) concurred that

> [t]he major institution within Chinese business has been the family. The family was the source of funds, contacts and managers. The primacy of the family has been maintained in recent decades, despite rapid diversification and international expansion. In many cases, the Chinese firm had no distinct existence outside the family.

Second, Chinese capitalism is not a mode of economic organization bound within specific territorial boundaries of nation-states. It is indeed a 'stretchable' form of capitalism that is embedded, but not limited by, the institutional contexts of the 'home' economies. As noted by Hamilton (1996b: 337), 'Chinese capitalism is not confined to a political space the way many other forms of capitalism have been. Rather, Chinese capitalism fills an economic space'. He further argued that 'instead of equating it with national economies, capitalism is best conceptualized in terms of the organized economic activities and institutional conditions that constitute it, and countries are best conceptualized as locations where specific activities occur' (Hamilton, 1999b: 4). Brown (2000: 171) also recognized that 'the rapidly changing economic and geographical expansion of Chinese firms in Southeast Asia means that a description of Chinese capitalism must jump between different countries, as Chinese businesses jumped'. Defined in this way, Chinese capitalism has no clear-cut political boundaries. Rather, it can only be delimited by the geographic extent and spread of its economic activities. This attribute poses a peculiar problem to the analysis of comparative capitalism and business systems in economic sociology and international political economy because most studies in these two fields focus on the development and institutionalization of different 'varieties' of capitalism in distinctive national contexts (e.g. the US and the UK compared with Germany and Japan). Thus, Chinese capitalism should be conceived as a supra-national form of economic organization. This flexible territoriality of Chinese capitalism partly explains why several leading sociologists of Chinese capitalism (e.g. Wong, 1988; Redding, 1990; Whitley, 1992, 1999; Hamilton, 1996a, 1999a, 1999c; Orrù *et al.*, 1997) tend to focus on Hong Kong and Taiwan (instead of Southeast Asian countries) as their primary geographical target of analysis because ethnic homogeneity in these two economies tends to facilitate the analysis of the emergence of a distinctive business system and an economic organization of capitalism. Even in these two ethnic Chinese economies, however, the issues of national sovereignty and territorial boundedness remain highly contested and questionable. Examining the impact of cultural globalization in Taiwan, Hsiao (2002: 52) recently observed that a distinctively Taiwanese business system is infused with influences from all sorts of management styles and practices.

> Despite the globalizing of Taiwan's economy and its businesses over the past few decades, it is clear that neither American nor Japanese management models have supplanted Taiwan's indigenous business practices. Instead, there is significant fusion of management styles in many of the multinationals operating in Taiwan as well as in many of the local companies that compete in world markets. As a result, there is no pure American, European, Japanese, or Taiwanese-Chinese management model that can best characterize the actual business culture of today's Taiwan.

Third, Chinese capitalism has achieved some degree of structural coherence and rationality – or 'spirit' in the words of Weber [1930] (1992) – through centuries of distinctive cultural practices and social organization originating from then imperial China. This identifiable association of the geographical origin of cultural practices in Chinese capitalism with China as the Middle Kingdom in its historical times differentiates Chinese capitalism from the economic organization of other diaspora groups such as the Jews. As noted by Hwang (1987: 968),

> Historically and, to an extent, even in modern contexts, many Chinese have lived in encapsulated communities that are hierarchically organized, with major economic and other resources controlled by a few power figures who could arbitrarily allocate resources. In these settings, it has been imperative to be sensitive to one's social position and to the kinds of resources that one could elicit and be forced to give up through obligations incurred over long periods of time.

These cultural practices serve as the underlying logic for distinctive economic behaviour and social action among ethnic Chinese. In many ways, most ethnic Chinese identify with this structural coherence and rationality that in turn legitimizes their very socio-economic behaviour. In short, there is a kind of economic culture, defined by Berger (1986: 24) as 'structures of consciousness', that constitutes Chinese capitalism. Put in another way, this cultural coherence and legitimation in Chinese capitalism is akin to Storper and Salais's (1997: 18) idea of the economy as a hybrid object constituted through a diversity of conventions and worlds of production in which actors organize and legitimize their action and behaviour.

> The processes by which actors interpret their situations and then enter into pragmatic forms of coordination with other actors constitute the work of constructing the economy. Actors select and build meaningful courses of action in production by engendering routinized, largely implicit forms of coordination, which we call conventions. It is in generating conventions, and then drawing on them in practical activity, that the creative, out-of-equilibrium pathways of development are constructed. There is a great diversity of possible conventions for organizing productive activity, and also a great diversity of possible, conventionally agreed-upon economic tests of whether an activity is economically viable or 'efficient'.

The world of conventions in which Chinese capitalism is situated can be best described as the interpersonal world, whereby economic activities are conducted and legitimized through interpersonal relationships and networks.

Fourth, unlike its Anglo-American counterpart analysed in the new institutionalism literature (DiMaggio and Powell, 1991; Orrù *et al.*, 1997; Whitley, 1999; Guillén, 2001a), Chinese capitalism is actor-centred rather than institution-specific. Whitley (1999: 25) argued that 'units of economic decision-making and control vary considerably in their constitution and organization across capitalist economies . . . "Firms" are by no means the same sorts of economic actors in different economies'. In the absence of formal legal structures and political systems that are unique to ethnic Chinese outside mainland China, social actors such as families and their business groups have become the primary driving force in Chinese capitalism. To a certain extent, this actor-specific constitution of Chinese capitalism is related to the 'geopolitical anxiety' of ethnic Chinese in East and Southeast Asia.[4] Their geographical dispersal during the past two centuries and their lack of political power in the host economies of Southeast Asia have greatly increased their geopolitical anxiety that in turn legitimizes their reliance on family-based actors rather than host-country institutions to coordinate their social and economic activities. While these actors are influenced by the formal rules and regulations of their host economies (e.g. property rights and ownership requirements), their capacity to transcend territorial boundaries enables them to exploit inherent advantages embedded in different formalized regulatory systems throughout East and Southeast Asian economies. Although Hong Kong and Singapore no doubt have very similar historical legacies and geographical advantages, their political economies differ very significantly (laissez-faire compared with developmental state) and Chinese family firms from both economies operate in broadly similar ways (Yeung, 2002a; Chapter 6 below). This observation of realized similarities in Chinese family firms from two contrasting economies characterized by distinctive political-economic structures thus runs contrary to Whitley's (1999: 44) qualification that:

> Even where norms and values are reproduced by families and ethnic communities which are both subnational and international, as in the case of the overseas Chinese [*sic*] and many migrant communities, the significance of these informal social organizations for systems of economic organization remains dependent on the structures and policies of states and political economies more generally.

This contradiction in the lack of dependence of Chinese capitalism on state structures and policies is largely explained by the key role of social actors rather than institutional structures in coordinating the economic organization of Chinese capitalism.

While Chinese capitalism continues to evolve in East and Southeast Asia, however, there is much misunderstanding and mystification of Chinese capitalism in the popular literature and mass media. Before the

1997–8 Asian economic crisis, much of the literature and media reports perpetuated an essentialist reading of Chinese capitalism. The popularity and prominence of such optimistic characterizations of Chinese capitalism as 'bamboo networks', '*guanxi* capitalism', the 'Chinese commonwealth' and the 'Chinese global tribe' had contributed significantly to the emergence of an essentialist idea that all ethnic Chinese in East and Southeast Asia hold similar worldviews bounded within their traditional social and cultural values. In what Aihwa Ong (1997: 195) referred to as a process of self-orientalization, Chinese capitalism was seen as static and self-contained within peculiar social and political contexts in East and Southeast Asia. During and after the crisis, this misreading of Chinese capitalism and its social practices contributed to the widely circulated crony capitalism argument that guided much of the rescue efforts by such international organizations as the World Bank and the International Monetary Fund. It is therefore timely to revisit and, in the process, demystify the nature and dynamics of Chinese capitalism in East and Southeast Asia.

In his polemical *Harvard Business Review* article published over a decade ago, John Kao (1993) concluded that Chinese capitalism and its 'worldwide web' will become a major force in the global economy of the twenty-first century. In another popular book *Tribes*, Joel Kotkin (1992: 9) was seemingly pushing for a similar appraisal of Chinese capitalism by noting that 'the Chinese global tribe likely will rank with the British-Americans and the Japanese as a driving force in transnational commerce'. Despite the 1997–8 Asian economic crisis, it appears that current thinking in international political economy reveals a serious reappraisal of the economic potential of Chinese capitalism and its associated organizations and institutions. Once established in their host economies, ethnic Chinese and their firms begin to extend their operations and networks across borders to form increasingly seamless webs of Chinese capitalism on a regional and, sometimes, global scale. No longer bounded by what Hwang (1987: 968) called 'encapsulated communities that are hierarchically organized', the participation of these firms and actors in the wider globalization processes has led to some fundamental changes in the ways in which they organize economic activities and social life. As the central theme of this book, these emergent developments thus underscore the significance of a relatively recent phenomenon in Chinese capitalism: the gradual transformations in the *modus operandi* and economic institutions of Chinese capitalism towards a more open and flexible form of capitalism. I refer to this reshaped form of Chinese capitalism as hybrid capitalism that is defined by its incomplete, partial and contingent transformations towards an evolving set of capitalist norms, institutions and structures. My argument on Chinese capitalism thus complements Hamilton's (1999b: 4) idea that

> capitalism is not a stable and readily identifiable configuration that, like a flower, suddenly bursts forth in bloom. Instead, capitalism is

merely a term that covers an extremely wide range of diverse economic activities organized in the context of competitive markets and whose institutional conditions include private ownership and non-state decision making.

In such a conceptualization of Chinese capitalism, we are beginning to witness the rise of a peculiar mode of hybrid capitalism characterized by the infusion of a variety of disembedded economic logics and social organizations that defy easy identification and simple analysis. As argued by Gibson-Graham (1996: 15–16),

> a capitalist site (a firm, industry or economy) or a capitalist practice (exploitation of wage labor, distribution of surplus value) cannot appear as the concrete embodiment of an abstract capitalist essence. It has no invariant 'inside' but is constituted by its continually changing and contradictory 'outsides'.

The very transformative nature of hybrid capitalism also implies that there is no definite end-state and form because political and economic outcomes of transition depend very much on complex interactions among social actors and their embedded institutions. The fact that Chinese capitalism is not bounded within distinctive national economies also contributes to its emergent hybridity, because multiple forces and conditioning factors shaping its structures and trajectories are at work. The key attributes of Chinese capitalism identified earlier are more prone to changes and transformations than those embedded in distinctively national business systems (e.g. US, British, German and Japanese). Nonini and Ong (1997: 20) called this hybridized Chinese capitalism 'ungrounded empires' that refer to

> the new deterritorialized and protean structures of domination that span the Asia Pacific and within which diaspora Chinese act – empires that constantly change shape, being constituted by Chinese transnational practices in the ether of airspaces, international time-zones, migrant labor contracts, mass media images, virtual companies, and electronic transactions, and operating across all recognized borderlines.

More crucially in understanding hybrid capitalism, we have to pay analytical attention to its dynamics of transformation, not its equilibrium features and structures. The concept of culture in Chinese capitalism, for example, needs to be reconceptualized as a repertoire of historically contingent and geographically specific practices that respond and adapt to changing local, regional and global circumstances rather than as permanently fixed mental and organizational structures that resist challenges and pressures to change (Hwang, 1987; Yang, 2002). This perspective on Chinese capitalism as hybrid capitalism is particularly relevant as Chinese capitalism undergoes dynamic transformations and increases in its economic and organizational complexity throughout different East and Southeast Asian economies.

In the remaining part of this chapter, I first describe the realities of Chinese capitalism and review its discursive constructions in the academic and popular literature. I then offer a critical assessment of this literature, pointing out in particular its failure to address the changing dynamics of Chinese capitalism in a global era. In the final section, I introduce the core theoretical arguments of this book and explain how a dynamic perspective can allow us to understand better Chinese capitalism as a form of hybrid capitalism. Four core dimensions contributing to this hybridity in Chinese capitalism are explained.

The myth of Chinese capitalism: realities and discourses

The economic significance of ethnic Chinese in East and Southeast Asia

Ethnic Chinese have had a significant presence in East and Southeast Asia for a very long time (see Figure 1.1). The commercial influence of ethnic Chinese merchants overseas dates back at least to the third century AD when official missions were despatched to countries in the then South Seas (*Nanyang*). These missions were followed by Buddhist pilgrims and, later during the Sung dynasty, by traders (Hodder, 1996: 1). After Chinese trade from Fujian and Guangdong to the south was legalized and licensed in 1567, stable and distinct Chinese communities became a historical feature of Southeast Asia (Reid, 1997: 41). In the mid-seventeenth century, there were communities of 3,000–5,000 Chinese in the major port cities of Java, Siam and Vietnam. By 1700, ethnic Chinese were unrivalled as the pre-eminent commercial minority in Southeast Asia and were 'the quickest to exploit the opportunities of the new commercialism because they were uninhibited by feudal tradition or landholding and because they had the necessary international contacts to move capital and goods across boundaries' (Reid, 1997: 43). These ethnic Chinese made a major contribution to the Southeast Asian region long before the nineteenth century (Dixon, 1991; Chan and McElderry, 1998; Ma and Cartier, 2003). Some of them became immensely powerful with both colonial and indigenous governments in Southeast Asia then: Thio Thiau Siat in Sumatra and Penang, Tan Seng Poh in Singapore, Loke Yew in Kuala Lumpur, Khaw Soo Cheang in South Thailand and Oei Tiong Ham in Java (Reid, 1997; Gomez and Hsiao, 2001). Chinese capitalism was thus international from its inception and has remained so throughout the centuries. Its dominant forms of economic organizations have always been adapting to changing circumstances in the regional and host economies, though arguably such adaptation has been greatly accelerated in recent decades.

As shown in Table 1.1, there were 32.8 million ethnic Chinese living outside mainland China in 1997. This figure excludes those ethnic Chinese in Hong Kong SAR (6.9 million in 1999), Macau SAR (0.5 million in 1999) and Taiwan (21.8 million in 1999) (World Bank, 1999). If we include these ethnic Chinese in the so-called Greater China, there are now over 60 million ethnic Chinese living outside mainland China. Despite the growing influx of Chinese migrants into North America and Western Europe in the period 1980–2000, the majority of these ethnic Chinese (90 per cent) are still living in Asia. Table 1.2 offers a detailed breakdown of the distribution of ethnic Chinese in East and Southeast Asia in 1995. Measured in absolute terms, Taiwan and Indonesia have the largest number of ethnic Chinese population. In terms of ethnic distribution, Taiwan, Hong Kong and Singapore exhibit the largest concentration of ethnic Chinese population. These ethnic Chinese contribute considerably to the dynamic economic locomotive of Asia and serve as a catalyst for regional economic growth. The World Bank estimated that the combined economic output of ethnic Chinese outside mainland China was about US$400 billion in 1991 and up to US$600 billion by 1996 (quoted in Weidenbaum and Hughes, 1996: 25). Through family, clan and dialect ties, they have virtually created a nation without borders that generates a GDP only fractionally less than that of mainland China (Asia, Inc., 1996; see also Table 1.2). Up to the mid-1990s, the collective funds of these ethnic Chinese in the region (excluding Hong Kong and Taiwan) were conservatively estimated at US$400 billion (Hodder, 1996: 3).

In terms of their ownership of economic assets in the host economies,

Table 1.1 Distribution of ethnic Chinese outside mainland China in 1963, 1985 and 1997

Region	Ethnic Chinese population ('000s)			Total ethnic Chinese population (%)		
	1963	*1985*	*1997*	*1963*	*1985*	*1997*
Asia[1]	12,147.7	19,108.0	·25,515.0	95.8	86.9	77.7
America	434.0	2,045.4	4,738.7	3.4	9.3	14.4
Europe	20.2	580.2	1,937.9	0.02	2.6	5.9
Africa	40.0	50.7	120.3	0.03	0.02	0.4
Oceania (including Australia)	34.6	207.4	528.2	0.03	0.09	1.6
Total	12,676.5	21,991.7	32,840.1	100.0	100.0	100.0

Source: Ma (2003: Table 1.1; 13-16).

Note
1 Excluding Hong Kong SAR, Macau SAR and Taiwan.

Table 1.2 Ethnic Chinese in East and Southeast Asia, 1995

Country/Economy	Population (million)	Total population (%)	Contributions to GDP (US$ billion)	Total GDP (%)
Taiwan	21	99	255	95
Hong Kong	6	98	120	80
Singapore	2	76	62	76
Malaysia	6	32	48	60
Thailand	6	10	80	50
Indonesia	8	4	98	50
Philippines	1	1	30	40
Vietnam	1	1	4	20

Source: *The Economist* (9–15 March, 1996: 12).

ethnic Chinese have emerged to be a class on their own. Table 1.3 presents some financial statistics of the 500 largest local public companies controlled by ethnic Chinese in seven Asian economies in 1994. Although the figure might have changed somewhat after the 1997–8 Asian economic crisis, it is still very indicative of the significance of ethnic Chinese in East and Southeast Asia. Taken together, these ethnic Chinese controlled some 500 of the largest public companies with total assets amounting to more than US$500 billion. Based on data from local stock exchanges in Southeast Asia between 1994 and 1998, Brown (2000: 3) estimated that ethnic Chinese business conglomerates accounted for an overwhelming majority of market capitalization in Indonesia (73 per cent), Malaysia (60 per cent), the Philippines (50 per cent), Singapore (81 per cent) and Thailand (90 per cent). These estimates confirm broadly the 1996 figures in Table 1.4 that demonstrates the enormous corporate and economic power of Chinese families and their ownership of public companies in East and Southeast Asian economies. In all seven stock exchanges, the share of families in total market capitalization varies from

Table 1.3 Financial statistics of the 500 largest public companies in East and Southeast Asia controlled by ethnic Chinese, 1994

Country/Economy	No. of companies	Market capitalisation (US$ billion)	Total assets (US$ billion)
Hong Kong	123	155	173
Taiwan	159	111	89
Malaysia	83	55	49
Singapore	52	42	92
Thailand	39	35	95
Indonesia	36	20	33
Philippines	8	6	8
Total	500	424	539

Sources: Wu and Duk (1995: Table 3); Weidenbaum and Hughes (1996).

Table 1.4 Family ownership of publicly listed firms and GDP in East and Southeast Asian economies, 1996

Country/ Economy	Year of stock exchange establishment	Total no. of listed firms	Market capital (US$ million)	No. of sample firms (% of total)	Share of total market capital (%)	% owned by families (20% cut-off)	Family control weighted by market capital (%)	Total market capital by top 5 families (%)	Total market capital by top 15 families (%)	Share of GDP by top 15 families (%)
Hong Kong	1891	583	449,258	330 (56.6)	78	66.7	71.5	26.2	34.4	84.2
Taiwan	1962	382	273,608	141 (36.9)	66	48.2	45.5	14.5	20.1	17.0
Indonesia	1977	253	91,016	178 (70.4)	89	71.5	67.3	40.7	61.7	21.5
Malaysia	1964	621	307,179	238 (38.3)	74	67.2	42.6	17.3	28.3	76.2
Philippines	1965	216	80,649	120 (55.6)	82	44.6	46.4	42.8	55.1	46.7
Singapore	1910	266[1]	153,234	221 (83.1)	96	55.4	44.8	19.5	29.9	48.3
Thailand	1975	454	99,828	167 (36.8)	64	61.6	51.9	32.2	53.3	39.3

Source: Claessens et al. (2000: Tables 2, 6, 9).

Note
1 Main board listing only.

64 per cent in Thailand to 96 per cent in Singapore. Assuming the majority of those families reported in Table 1.4 were ethnic Chinese, the extent of market capitalization and share of GDP accounted for by the top 15 ethnic Chinese families in 1996 is astonishing. It ranges from over 50 per cent in total market capitalization in Indonesia, the Philippines and Thailand and over 40 per cent in GDP share in Hong Kong, Malaysia, the Philippines and Singapore. Other estimates also reported that ethnic Chinese controlled up to 80 per cent of Indonesia's corporate assets (and running 160 of the 200 largest businesses), 40–50 per cent of Malaysia's corporate assets, 90 per cent of Thailand's manufacturing and 50 per cent of Thailand's services (Wu and Duk, 1995; Weidenbaum and Hughes, 1996). In 1995, every reported Indonesian billionaire was ethnic Chinese. In Thailand, ethnic Chinese controlled the four largest private banks of which Bangkok Bank was the largest and most profitable in the region. In the Philippines, ethnic Chinese controlled over one-third of the 1,000 largest corporations (Weidenbaum and Hughes, 1996: 25). Focusing only on public companies controlled by ethnic Chinese and their families, these statistics have excluded many more privately controlled Chinese firms throughout the Asian region. If we include this substantially larger quantity of private ethnic Chinese firms, the economic landscape of Chinese capitalism in East and Southeast Asia will indeed look highly uneven and concentrated.

The economic muscles of business conglomerates controlled by ethnic Chinese and their extensive networks across the region have soon propelled the outward movement of firms and capital from their 'home' economies to form intricate webs of cross-border investments in Asia and beyond. Louis Kraar (1993: 87), *Fortune's* Asia editor from 1983 to 1988, wrote in the early 1990s that '[t]he strongest overseas Chinese [*sic*] have huge conglomerates with global reach. This is not some quaint ethnic side-show; the overseas Chinese are increasingly the main event in Asian business today'. More than that, these ethnic Chinese are seemingly recreating an ancient empire outside mainland China, this time as a twenty-first-century economic superpower. Similarly, Asia, Inc. (1996) concluded that 'they have become merchant mandarins, parlaying for peace and prosperity. And, in the process, rebuilding an ancient empire'. This observation may not be too exaggerated if we look at the extent of foreign direct investment (FDI) by these Chinese business conglomerates. In mainland China since the beginning of the open-door policy in December 1978, for example, ethnic Chinese from abroad invested more than US$50 billion in their 'motherland' by the mid-1990s, accounting for about 80 per cent of total realized FDI. From 1979 to 1995, they formed more than 100,000 joint ventures in China (Weidenbaum and Hughes, 1996: 27). These figures are very significant since during the entire 1990s mainland China emerged as the largest recipient of FDI to all developing countries. UNCTAD (2002: Table B.1) reported that at US$44.2 billion and US$46.8 billion respectively in 1997 and 2001, inward FDI to China accounted for 9.2 per cent and 6.4 per cent (US$478 billion and US$735 billion) of total global FDI and 23.1 per cent and 22.8 per cent of total FDI (US$191 billion and US$205 billion) into developing countries.

The globalization of ethnic Chinese firms involves, therefore, many such firms spanning their activities across different countries and regions as well as more integration of these activities for strategic and efficiency reasons (Yeung, 1999d; Yeung and Olds, 2000a; Mathews, 2002). Ethnic Chinese-owned and controlled firms from three of the four 'Asian dragons' (Hong Kong, Taiwan and Singapore) and other Southeast Asian countries (Indonesia, Malaysia, Thailand and the Philippines) are increasingly entering into the regional and global marketplace in a significant way. As shown in Table 1.5, 14 Chinese firms were among the top 50 transnational corporations (TNCs) from emerging economies in 1995. In 2000, there were 13 Chinese firms on the same list. Interestingly, Hutchison Whampoa from Hong Kong was also ranked 14th-largest TNC in the world by foreign assets in 2000 (US$41.9 billion). Data in Table 1.5 show that these 13 large ethnic Chinese TNCs originated mostly from Hong Kong, Singapore, Malaysia and Taiwan. Merely two decades earlier, however, not a single ethnic Chinese TNC from these economies made it to Heenan and Keegan's (1979: 104) list of the top 33 TNCs from developing countries ranked by sales in 1977. Table 1.6 presents further information on some of the leading ethnic Chinese business actors from East and Southeast Asia. According to the *Forbes* ranking, several of them (Li Ka-shing, the Kwok brothers and Lee Shau-kee from Hong Kong, Tsai Wan-lin from Taiwan and Robert Kuok from Malaysia) were among the world's top 100 richest billionaires in 2000 and 2003 in spite of the 1997–8 Asian economic crisis. Lever-Tracy (2002: 515) also reported that on the eve of the Asian economic crisis in June 1997, *Forbes* listed 29 ethnic Chinese among its world total of 200 working billionaires (i.e. about 15 per cent). In recent years, these ethnic Chinese entrepreneurs have been actively globalizing their domestic operations and posing themselves as a global competitor in such diverse business fields as electronics and garment manufacturing, property development, financial services, hotel chains and so on.[5] It is likely that they will continue to grow further and compete head-on with major TNCs on a global basis. One may wonder about the foundations of these giant Chinese business conglomerates and their remarkable role in the economic success of Chinese capitalism in East and Southeast Asia. To answer this question, I turn to the existing research on the so-called overseas Chinese capitalism.

Explaining Chinese capitalism: three competing discourses

Although the 'overseas Chinese' have been a subject of study for a long time (Wang, 1981, 1991, 2000; Lim and Gosling, 1983; Suryadinata, 1997;

Yen, 2002), academic studies of 'overseas Chinese capitalism' are relatively recent, originating in the mid-1980s and detailed in Table 1.7. Today Chinese capitalism has become an important subject for multi-disciplinary research. Here, I briefly summarize three key themes of this vast literature and evaluate their discursive origins and assumptions. These themes are: the spirit of 'overseas Chinese' capitalism; Chinese business systems; and political-economic alliances in Southeast Asian countries (Yeung and Olds, 2000b). It must be noted that these themes are often interrelated and by no means exhaustive. I ground these three research themes in discussions of evolving but dominant conceptions of Chinese capitalism and Chinese business networks, both historical and contemporary.[6] These business networks are often perceived to be, according to most (but not all) of the literature, as predominantly constituted by actors of ethnic Chinese origin and/or the domestic (i.e. national) institutional contexts that Chinese actors find themselves situated in. This discussion of traditional conceptions of 'Chinese' business networks and Chinese capitalism lays the ground for the subsequent actor-network informed analysis of the reshaping of Chinese capitalism in a globalizing era, an account that better recognizes the enhanced role of non-Chinese actor-networks in the process.

The spirit of overseas Chinese capitalism

The complex and extensive interpenetrations of ethnic (overseas) Chinese business networks and entrepreneurs among various Asian countries have been well recorded in the existing literature.[7] Chinese capitalism has been argued to be a predominant mode of economic organization in Asia that has spearheaded the rapid diffusion of economic activities and intra-regional investment flows among various Asian economies in which ethnic Chinese have significant control in the economic realm. One of the most influential approaches in the literature is to consider overseas Chinese capitalism as an alternative economic institution that differs from Anglo-American capitalism. This is the so-called culturalist explanation of the East Asian economic miracle. Redding (1990), for example, argued that overseas Chinese capitalism is essentially an economic culture characterized by a unique capacity to cooperate (see also Haley *et al.*, 1998; Mackie, 1998; Clarke *et al.*, 1999; Crawford, 2000, 2001 for this culturalist view of Chinese capitalism). The overseas Chinese are united by their deep sense of being ethnic Chinese who have not psychologically left China or some ideal and romanticized notion of Chinese civilization (Redding, 1990: 2). Overseas Chinese capitalism is not based on an elite system (like Japan), nor does it rest on an explicit legal-political system (like the US and the UK), but rather is predicated on a household economy that is well adapted only to its socio-cultural milieu. The spirit of overseas Chinese capitalism is therefore a 'set of beliefs and values which

Table 1.5 Leading Chinese firms among the top 50 transnational corporations from emerging economies ranked by foreign assets, 1995 and 2000

Ranking (foreign assets)		Name of TNC (founder or family)	Home economy	Industry	Foreign assets (US$ million)		Total assets (US$ million)		Foreign sales (US$ million)		Total Sales (US$ million)		Foreign employment		Total employment		Trans-nationality index[1]	
1995	2000				1995	2000	1995	2000	1995	2000	1995	2000	1995	2000	1995	2000	1995	2000
7	1/14[2]	Hutchison Whampoa (Li Ka-shing)	Hong Kong	Diversified	2,900	41,881	11,699	56,610	1,632	2,840	4,531	7,311	16,115	27,165	29,137	49,570	38.7	50.3
19	6	New World Dev't (Cheng Yu-tung)	Hong Kong	Diversified	1,161	4,578	12,396	16,412	471	565	2,159	2,633	33,550	800	45,000	23,530	35.2	15.8
4	17	First Pacific (Liem Sioe Liong)	Hong Kong	Diversified	3,779	2,116	6,821	2,322	4,694	652	5,250	809	33,467	8,511	45,911	8,560	72.6	81.4
20	18	Citic Pacific (Larry Yung)	Hong Kong	Diversified	1,070	2,076	5,094	4,022	694	981	1,401	2,058	7,900	7,118	11,500	11,354	46.4	48.6
28[3]	21	Orient Overseas International (Tung family)	Hong Kong	Transport	1,256	1,819	1,306	2,155	1,718	2,382	1,882	2,395	3,396	3,792	4,030	4,414	90.6	80.9
25	29	Fraser and Neave (Lee family)	Singapore	Food and beverages	957	1,318	3,199	4,211	1,066	944	1,809	1,551	8,190	7,826	10,064	10,750	56.7	49.5
26	33	Acer Group (Stan Shih)	Taiwan	Electronics	665	1,143	3,645	3,956	2,494	1,447	5,825	4,760	4,324	3,554	15,352	12,300	31.7	26.5
37[4]	34	Amsteel (William Cheng)	Malaysia	Diversified	209	1,143	1,459	3,453	80	544	1,066	1,416	7,800	37,094	28,200	50,218	16.5	43.6
–	40	WBL (Lee family)	Singapore	Electronics	–	879	–	1,106	–	338	–	534	–	12,467	–	13,374	–	70.8
–	43	Berjaya Group (Vincent Tan)	Malaysia	Diversified	–	832	–	3,352	–	954	–	2,052	–	5,500	–	21,783	–	29.0

Rank	Rank	Corporation (principal individual/family)	Economy	Industry	Foreign assets	Total assets	Foreign sales	Total sales	Foreign employment	Total employment	TNI (%)
–	44	Hongkong Electric Holdings (Li Ka-shing)	Hong Kong	Utilities	811	6,622	–	1,456	300	2,366	8.9
–	45	Great Eagle Holdings (Lo Ying Shek)	Hong Kong	Business services	751	3,755	196	372	601	3,004	27.8
–	50	Hume Industries (Quek Leng Chan)	Malaysia	Construction	593	1,178	931	1,341	6,536	12,545	51.6
31	–	Tatung Co Ltd (T.S. Lin and family)	Taiwan	Electrical equipment	813	2,929	1,083	3,100	9,543	27,254	32.6
35	–	Genting Bhd (Lim Goh Tong)	Malaysia	Properties	692	2,283	62	982	–	–	18.3
37	–	Wing On Intl Ltd (Guo brothers)	Hong Kong	Retailing	576	1,344	40	366	1,435	4,006	29.9
42	–	Creative Technology (Sim Wong Woo)	Singapore	Electronics	405	661	1,175	1,202	2,048	4,185	69.3
43[4]	–	Evergreen Marine (Chang Yung-fa)	Taiwan	Transport	117	1,678	80	1,152	91	1,298	7.0
47	–	Formosa Plastics (Wang Yue-che)	Taiwan	Chemicals	327	2,326	241	1,650	–	3,449	10.4

Sources: UNCTAD (1996: Table I.13; 1997: Table I.8; 2002: Table IV.10).

Notes

The table excludes government-linked corporations in Singapore (e.g. Neptune Orient Lines, Singapore Telecom and Keppel Corporation) and Taiwan (e.g. Chinese Petroleum and United Microelectronics).

1 The index of transnationality is calculated as the average of foreign assets to total assets, foreign sales to total sales and foreign employment to total employment.

2 Data refer to the ranking among the world's top 100 TNCs.

3 Data refer to 1996.

4 Data refer to 1994.

Table 1.6 Major ethnic Chinese and their transnational corporations from East and Southeast Asia, 1997, 2000 and 2003

Company/Group name	Major shareholder (ethnic Chinese)	Economy of origin	Estimated net worth (US$ billion) and Forbes world's richest billionaires ranking[1]						Major worldwide operations
			1997	Rank	2000	Rank	2003	Rank	
Cheung Kong Holdings	Li Ka-shing	Hong Kong	11.0	19	11.3	20	7.8	28	Husky Oil and Pacific Concord (Canada), Hutchison Whampoa (Asia)
Pacific Century CyberWorks (PCCW)	Richard Li (son)	Hong Kong	NA	NA	4.3	97	1.0	427	PCCW (worldwide)
Sun Hung Kai Group	Kwok brothers	Hong Kong	12.3	12	9.0	26	6.6	42	Sun Hung Kai Group (Asia)
Henderson Land Group	Lee Shau-kee	Hong Kong	14.7	9	8.6	28	3.7	88	Henderson Land Asia
Johnson Electric Group	Patrick Wang	Hong Kong	NA	NA	4.5	88	2.6	137	Johnson Electric (worldwide)
Li & Fung Group	Fung brothers	Hong Kong	NA	NA	2.3	184	NA	NA	Li & Fung Trading (worldwide)
Cathay Life Insurance	Tsai Wan-lin	Taiwan	11.3	16	6.7	44	3.7	88	Cathay Life (China)
Fubon Financial Holdings	Tsai Wan-tsai	Taiwan	NA	NA	NA	NA	1.8	222	Fubon group
Formosa Plastics	Wang Yue-che	Taiwan	5.5	49	4.3	100	1.9	209	Formosa Plastics (worldwide)
Evergreen Group	Chang Yung-fa	Taiwan	NA	NA	1.7	229	NA	NA	Evergreen Marine (worldwide)
Hong Leong Group	Kwek Leng Beng	Singapore	5.8	45	2.0	207	1.7	236	CDL Hotels
	Quek Leng Chan	Malaysia	2.9	112	1.8	224	1.5	278	Guoco (HK)
Goodwood Park Group	Khoo Teck Puat	Singapore	3.9	78	2.7	171	2.6	137	Goodwood Park Hotel Group (Asia)
Far East Organisation	Ng Teng Fong	Singapore	7.0	33	3.4	143	1.7	236	Sino Land (HK)
Sina Mas Group	Oei Widjaja	Indonesia	5.4	50	3.2	151	NA	NA	Asia Pulp and Paper and Asia Food
Salim Group	Liem Sioe Liong	Indonesia	4.0	75	1.0	312	NA	NA	First Pacific Group (HK)
Lippo Group	Mochtar Riady	Indonesia	1.8	183	NA	NA	NA	NA	Lippo Banks (worldwide)
Kalimanis Group	Bob Hasan	Indonesia	3.0	106	NA	NA	NA	NA	–
Kerry Group	Robert Kuok	Malaysia/HK	7.0	33	4.6	84	3.4	97	Shangri-la Hotels and TVB (Asia)
YTL Group	Francis Yeoh	Malaysia	1.6	193	1.2	281	NA	NA	YTL Construction (Asia)
Charoen Pokphand Group	Dhanin Chearavanont	Thailand	1.7	184	1.2	281	1.3	329	CP Pokphand (Asia), Telecom Asia (Asia)
Fortune Tobacco	Lucio Tan	Philippines	NA	NA	2.1	201	1.9	209	Eton Properties (HK)

Note
1 Source: http://www.forbes.com, accessed on 1 March 2003.

lies behind the behavior of Chinese businessmen' (Redding, 1990: 79). In this line of culturalist explanation, ethnic Chinese are described as placing great values on relationships with one another. In classical Confucian thought, a man exists only in relation to others. There is no one-man society as such. The key to the Chinese socialization process is to achieve harmony and balance through good interpersonal relationships (or *guanxi*). Good relationships are based on cooperative behaviour among members of the community (Silin, 1976; King, 1991). To highlight the importance of cooperation in Chinese social thought, Hamilton (1991b: 51) contrasted Western philosophical thoughts that 'the economic conception of a self-interested rational economic actor is not universal fiction; it is a European fiction, entirely a product of Western enlightenment thought that was enacted through political legislation and embodied in economic institutions'.

According to its leading proponents (Redding, 1990, 1996; Wong, 1988; Hefner, 1998; Gomez and Hsiao, 2001), these beliefs and values have a significant impact on the nature and practices of 'overseas Chinese' capitalism, as follows.

1 Certain values surrounding authority in Chinese culture (e.g. Confucianism) foster the stability and adaptiveness of the family firm.
2 Chinese values legitimize a distinct form of cooperation between organizations.
3 Chinese values retain long-term legitimacy because of their grounding in Chinese ethics.
4 Economic exchange and growth is enhanced by intra-organizational stability and inter-organizational cooperation.
5 There is no tight linkage between a set of state-supported institutions and the organizational principles of business.
6 Kinship relationships are very important in Chinese organizations.

In particular, the family provides the central foundation on which Chinese social organizations and institutions are constructed. The family becomes the central unit of social thought and the worldview among the Chinese, because of the teaching of Confucianism that maintains the role of family, compliance and social order. This phenomenon among the overseas Chinese is known as familism, referring to the centrality of the family as a fundamental unit of social and economic organization among ethnic Chinese. Some scholars of Chinese capitalism have thus argued that familism gives the overseas Chinese a sense of 'Chineseness'. This culturalist approach explains the success of overseas Chinese capitalism through the role of familism and the Chinese socialization process.

Other recent studies of Chinese capitalism, however, cast doubt on this culturalist view of Chinese capitalism (Nathan, 1993; Greenhalgh, 1994;

Table 1.7 Multi-disciplinary research into Chinese capitalism

Disciplines	Key authors	Analytical categories	Key explanations
Business and economics	• George/Usha Haley • John Kao • Linda Lim • Victor Limlingan • Thomas Menkhoff • Gordon Redding • Murray Weidenbaum • Richard Whitley	• worldwide web of Chinese business • Chinese business strategies • spirit of Chinese capitalism • bamboo networks • Chinese business system	• increasingly stretching beyond their Confucian-style family ventures • low cost, low profit margin and high turnover volume strategies for competition • Chinese values and beliefs lead to a strong tendency towards cooperation • the role of bamboo networks in facilitating the creation of a new economic superpower in Asia • the role of institutional foundations of Chinese family firms • different business recipes and different characteristics of business systems
Geography	• Rupert Hodder • You-tien Hsing • Wei Li • Katharyne Mitchell • Kris Olds • Henry Yeung • Yu Zhou	• the Chineseness • globalization of Chinese firms • the changing role and configurations of Chinese business networks • the role of the state and political-economic alliances	• no such thing as Chineseness because definitive components of Chinese culture are not peculiar or unique to overseas Chinese • the role of political connections in facilitating Chinese firms in China • personal relationships and business networks are necessary mechanisms of transnational operations by Chinese firms • cross-border operations of Chinese firms within the context of globalization • Chinese business networks being reshaped by non-Chinese international actors in a globalizing era

Discipline	Authors	Key concepts	Key arguments
History	• Raj Brown • Wellington Chan • Stephanie Chung • Arif Dirlik • Edmund Gomez • Liu Hong • Anthony Reid	• Chinese institutions and organizations • family business • Chinese capitalism	• the historical antecedents of Chinese institutions and organizations • the social role of family business as a socialization process • Chinese capitalism is a localized, not a generalized, phenomenon • Confucian discourse and cultural explanation of East Asian economic miracle are driven by political ideologies
Sociology and anthropology	• Kwok Bun Chan • Susan Greenhalgh • Gary Hamilton • Constance Lever-Tracy • Donald Nonini • Aihwa Ong • Alan and Josephine Smart • Tong Chee Kiong • Noel Tracy • Wong Siu-lun • Mayfair Yang • Souchou Yao	• overseas Chinese capitalism • familism • business networks and personal relationships • social capital and social construction	• Chinese capitalism is socially organized, centred on the family firm • business networks as important institutional forms to circumvent hostile host-country environments and support economic success • Chinese networks as a form of social capital • strong entrepreneurial tendency of Chinese business

Ong, 1997; Yao, 1987, 1997, 2002; Ma, 2003). They suggest that the recent interest in and discourse on Chinese capitalism as an alternative paradigm of development is little more than an invention of a new post-socialist and post-revolution discourse on global capitalism:

> Chineseness is no longer, if it ever was, a property or essence of a person calculated by that person's having more or fewer 'Chinese' values or norms, but instead can be understood only in terms of the multiplicity of ways in which 'being Chinese' is an inscribed relation of persons and groups to forces and processes associated with global capitalism and its modernities.
>
> (Nonini and Ong, 1997: 3–4)

Dirlik (1997: 308), for example, argued that the characteristics of Chineseness might be the effect of the development of global capitalism. The detailed attention described on pages 9–15 by business media and financial analysts must also be seen in the context of a decade or more of attention in the popular media and in a variety of academic disciplines on the East Asian miracle, *guanxi* capitalism, the overseas Chinese and overseas Chinese capitalism, the Asian family firm and business networks in East and Southeast Asia. In this dominant intellectual and discursive context, a consistent discourse on the nature of Chinese capitalism (and Asian business networks more generally) is emerging. This discourse is blossoming in newspaper articles, journal articles, books, workshops and conferences (especially in Australia, Canada, Hong Kong, Singapore and the US). Indeed, Dirlik (1997: 305) critically examined this proliferation of attention, material and events, and concluded that Chinese capitalism is an ideological and instrumental invention, an idea that was born not in any Chinese society, but in the US. There were two conditions, both global in significance, that gave birth to it: the retreat from socialism in mainland China and the apparent regression in Anglo-American capitalism against evidence of unprecedented growth in East and Southeast Asian societies. As Arif Dirlik (1997: 304) put it, 'the discourse on Chinese capitalism does not merely describe; more importantly, it may be a discourse creating its object', much as the Asia-Pacific/Pacific Rim can be viewed as an invention, an ideational construct that projects 'upon a certain location on the globe the imperatives of interest, power, or vision of these historically produced relationships' (Dirlik, 1992: 56). Similarly, Ong (1997: 182) critiqued that:

> [s]uch discourses, produced in a circuit that migrates from political centers to entrepreneurs' circles, constitute a new regime of truth about a distinctive Chinese capitalism. The power of such an East Asian narrative derives in part from defining Chinese business activities as a kind of moral economy based on Confucian ideals.

Dirlik (1997) further suggested four reasons why the prevailing culturalist discourse on Chinese capitalism might go wrong. First, the notion of Chineseness is rather vague and contestable (Hodder, 1996; Wang, 1999; Yao, 2002; Ma, 2003). There are different self-images among the various Chinese populations in East and Southeast Asia. Those individuals are presented and treated in analysis as a uni-dimensional phenomenon, the Chinese. This line of thought is particularly problematic because 'it creates and legitimizes the notion of "the Chinese" as a distinct entity which can be explained by the implicit application of laws and forces which are presumed to exist' (Hodder, 1996: 12–13). To Wang (1999: 119), 'Chineseness is of little interest unless it is changing or is forced to defend itself against change. And underlying the changes that have been the most meaningful for them [Chinese in mainland China] this past century are the forces of modernization'. Second, the Confucian revival in East Asia (such as in Taiwan and Hong Kong) and Southeast Asia (Singapore) represents a 'Weberizing' of Confucianism (Tu, 1996). The dominant discourse suppresses the dark side of Confucianism (such as authoritarianism and gendered exploitation). As Hsing (2003: 232) pointed out so perceptively,

> The characteristics of the Chinese Confucianism, loyalty and hierarchy, in Max Weber's work, for example, are seen as the reason for the lack of capitalism in China at the beginning of the twentieth century. But the same characteristics are seen as the reason for the economic miracle in [the] 1970s in East Asia. Thus the same conduct and characteristics in these two cases led to opposite consequences. To put it plainly, good or bad, capitalism or no capitalism, it is because they are Chinese and they are Confucianists. It does not really avoid the trap of essentialism, while at the same time assigning a causal relationship to coexisting phenomena.

Third, kinship ties are not unique to ethnic Chinese. As argued by Maurice Freedman some years ago (cited in Wong, 1988: 132), the crucial distinction between Chinese and Western economic behaviour is not that of kin and non-kin, but is personal and impersonal. Chinese individuals tend to personalize their economic relations and kinship is just one of the possible bases for this solidarity. Finally, business networks among ethnic Chinese may be a transitional strategy that is more pertinent in some circumstances (such as a hostile host environment).

Whether you agree with Dirlik or not,[8] there is apparently no immediate solution to this fundamental epistemological difference in the conception of Chineseness and therefore the nature of overseas Chinese capitalism. Granted some validity in both sides of the arguments, I examine here the extent to which ethnic Chinese actors and their firms are culturally unique in their globalization strategies and processes and how this uniqueness, if any, evolves and changes with their global reach beyond the Asian region. The focus is not on whether Chinese capitalism is distinctively Chinese, but rather on whether and in what ways it evolves in a global era towards a kind of hybrid capitalism defined earlier in this chapter. This theme therefore represents a new direction of research on Chinese capitalism, because I now examine whether and how Chineseness can operate across national boundaries in Asia and beyond. This brings us to the second theme in the multi-disciplinary literature on Chinese capitalism and its business systems.

Chinese business systems

Whitley's (1992, 1999) business systems approach offers a potentially fruitful avenue for understanding the nature and organization of Chinese capitalism. Whitley (1992: 13) defined business systems as

> distinctive configurations of hierarchy-market relations which become institutionalized as relatively successful ways of organizing economic activities in different institutional environments. Certain kinds of activities are co-ordinated through particular sorts of authority structures and interconnected in different ways through various quasi-contractual arrangements in each business system. Thus, what resources are organized by differently structured hierarchies and markets varies between these systems, as do preferred ways of developing businesses and making choices. They develop and change in relation to dominant social institutions, especially those important during processes of industrialization. The coherence and stability of these institutions, together with their dissimilarity between nation states, determine the extent to which business systems are distinctive, integrated and nationally differentiated.

To him, business systems are distinctive and enduring ways of structuring market economies that are wide-ranging and long-term in nature. He argued that 'different kinds of business and market organization develop and dominate different market economies as a result of major variations in social institutions and constitute distinctive business systems' (Whitley, 1992: 7). As such, the focus is not so much on culture *per se*, but rather on the institutional structures of particular business systems that are socially constructed over time (and space, according to Hamilton, 1996b). The organization of Chinese firms, as a result, is largely shaped by these institutional structures (Hamilton and Biggart, 1988; Hamilton and Kao, 1990; Hamilton, 1996c).

Perhaps the best-known attribute of Chinese business systems is the role and extensive penetration of business networks or bamboo networks.[9] Personal relationships or *guanxi* are an important mechanism of implementing cooperative strategies in Chinese business networks, although their importance changes over time and in different places (Guthrie, 1998, 1999; Tsang, 1998; Dunfee and Warren, 2001; Fan, 2002). The reliance on personal relationships and business networks, however, is not restricted exclusively to the business practice of ethnic Chinese only (Björkman and Kock, 1995; Lewis, 1995; Windolf and Beyer, 1996; Lane and Bachmann, 1998; Olds and Yeung, 1999; Zang, 1999, 2000). Fan (2002: 559) thus described the paradox that 'B2G [business to government] *guanxi*, which is widely condemned in China, obtained its popularity in the western business literature, and is on the way to becoming a new fad in international business'. Hodder (1996: 52) also argued that '*Guanxi* (or reciprocity) is not a "thing", or "variable" or "channel". It does not characterize "the Chinese", nor is part of a cultural mantle by which individuals can be identified as Chinese'. This strand of literature argues that unlike their Western counterparts in which cooperative relationships are based on firm-specific business strategies (Beamish and Killing, 1997; Gulati *et al.*, 2000; DiMaggio, 2001a; Gnyawali and Madhavan, 2001; Thompson, 2003), cooperative relationships in Chinese capitalism are largely embedded in business networks. Interpersonal relationships serve as the foundation of cooperative relationships in Chinese capitalism.

Another important characteristic of Chinese business systems is the entrepreneurial tendency of ethnic Chinese (Mackie, 1992; Chan and Chiang, 1994; Hamilton, 1999c; Menkhoff and Gerke, 2002). Entrepreneurship is defined as a pro-business quality of undertaking calculated ventures under reasonable risks and uncertainty. Historically and culturally, imperial China was frugal and self-centred in its economic relations with the outside world. The contemporary Chinese, however, are experienced migrants and tend to form socially organized networks to provide emotional and personal support. To a Chinese entrepreneur, setting up an overseas venture is very challenging, but the social significance of network exploration and formation makes the venture attractive in its own right. This argument applies to those investments based on ethnic links by Chinese businesspeople, particularly in their hometowns in mainland China. Another element of Chinese entrepreneurship lies in their greater likelihood of internalizing external markets. The overseas Chinese psyche has a deep-seated and culturally embedded desire for self-ownership and autonomy in decision-making (Bond, 1986; Wong, 1988; Redding, 1990; Brown, 1994). Although the family serves as a significant binding and centripetal force, Chinese entrepreneurs prefer to be their own boss. There is a famous Chinese proverb: 'Better be the beak of a cock than the rump of an ox' (Wong, 1988: 101). It is not surprising that the overseas Chinese are well known for their entrepreneurial spirit. A rule of thumb in Chinese entrepreneurship is that a senior (sometimes former employer) is obliged to help a junior to set up his/her own business if the latter is proven to be entrepreneurial enough. This unwritten cultural rule is unthinkable in Anglo-American capitalism because of culturally embed-ded individualism and competitive behaviour (Hamilton, 1991b).[10]

In short, the business systems approach to the study of Chinese capital-ism has provided us with a useful contingency model for understanding the dynamic characteristics of Chinese firms when they cross national boundaries. The challenge of this approach is to understand how Chinese business systems are reshaped by different institutional structures when their leading firms globalize among different economies and countries. This is a critical issue for our understanding of the impact of globalization on actor-specific practices in Chinese capitalism. It also has important implications for examining the transferability of Chinese business systems to countries or regions with fundamentally different institutional and/or cultural structures. It is imperative, for example, to evaluate the success of Chinese firms in managing business networks and relationships over space. This manageability of cross-border business networks will deter-mine the strategies and processes of their globalization and the success or failure of Chinese capitalism in an era of accelerated globalization (Yeung and Olds, 2000a).

Political-economic alliances in East and Southeast Asia

Related to the business systems explanation of Chinese capitalism is a strand of literature that focuses on the ways in which the overseas Chinese and their firms integrate themselves into the host economies. This approach takes into account the local specificities of host economies and examines how ethnic Chinese successfully assimilate into local cultural and institutional environments.[11] The empirical focus of this literature is the hostility and discrimination faced by ethnic Chinese in many South-east Asian countries and their political-economic coping strategies.[12] These studies of cross-border flows of ethnic Chinese capital from main-land China to East and Southeast Asia combine both cultural and institu-tional perspectives to arrive at a coherent explanation of the economic success of the overseas Chinese in Southeast Asia. Their main argument is that ethnic Chinese in East and Southeast Asia are able to overcome host-country hostility through kinship-based cooperation and political-economic alliances with host-country powerbrokers (i.e. patron–client relationships).

Host-country hostility contributes as much to situations of imperfect competition as to the deep-seated sense of self-protection and closely-knit social organization among ethnic Chinese in Southeast Asia (Lynn, 1998). Historically, dynasties in imperial China did not provide security to indi-viduals' livelihoods because of the belief in the family as the central unit of the Chinese social structure. Thus the family has become the ultimate source of support and resources. For centuries a strong sense of coopera-tion has been developed in Chinese economic organization, in particular along the family and kinship structures. With their massive outward exodus in the late nineteenth and early twentieth centuries, the ethnic Chinese faced one of the greatest dilemmas in their social life: how to overcome formidable hostility in host countries. Naturally, these ethnic Chinese, particularly in Southeast Asia, turned to their inward-looking mode of social and institutional support: family and business networks based on cooperative and particularistic ties. These particularistic ties function as a means to achieve closure to outside competitors and to overcome their peculiar form of insecure psyche known as the siege mentality (Yoshihara, 1988; Redding, 1990) or the trader's dilemma (Menkhoff, 1993).

Closely-knit family and business networks provide one of the best solutions to overcome these institutional barriers and the personal psyche of fear and insecurity, a form of geopolitical anxiety. These networks are based on personal relationships, centred particularly on the family and its immediate circle of social actors (such as close friends). Family members command the absolute trust vital to survive the formative years of living abroad in hostile host countries (Wong, 1991; Menkhoff, 1993; Landa, 1994; Braadbaart, 1995; Pyatt and Redding, 2000; Chung and Hamilton, 2001). Apart from falling back on trusted family members, ethnic Chinese in Southeast Asia are said to rely on family business as a natural extension of the entrepreneur's strategies of 'family-ization' (Chan and Chiang, 1994: 297) through which outsiders are socialized into the family to form an exclusive and elitist inner circle of relations:

> Clear boundaries are drawn between those business members who are in the family, and therefore are more trusted, from those who are not, and therefore cannot be totally or readily trusted but must be co-opted *gradually* by the family-ization process and through marriage alliances.
>
> (Chan and Chiang, 1994: 354; original italics)

Because of this strategy of 'family-ization', individuals or states in host countries perceive ethnic Chinese as building a strong fortress through networks of personal and business relationships against possible hostile actions. This mode of social organization is sometimes criticized as inward-looking, particularly from the viewpoint of host countries (Mahathir, 1970). But it is also seen as one of the strongest competitive advantages of Chinese business in an era of economic turbulence and structural change.

Ethnic Chinese in Southeast Asia have responded to ethnic-biased economic policies in two major ways: establishing political-economic alliances and diversification through internationalization. First, many ethnic Chinese in Southeast Asia have entered into patron–client relationships with ruling military and political leaders. It is commonly acknowledged that the rise of Liem Sioe Liong in Indonesia, Robert Kuok in Malaysia,

Lucio Tan in the Philippines and Chin Sophonphanich in Thailand can be attributed to their close relationships with key politicians and military leaders in respective countries. They were often offered either privileged access to monopolized markets and resources or outright political protection against the tide of discriminatory practices at the state level. They therefore benefited from these political-economic alliances by establishing themselves quickly in key domestic industries (e.g. banking, property development, manufacturing).[13] Brown (2000: 42) concluded:

> the cultural embeddedness of Chinese capitalism is a product of historical cultural factors. Chinese capitalism in Southeast Asia, despite its heterogeneity, is not competitive. The accumulative, predatory tendencies of Chinese capitalism should not be mistaken for competitiveness. The Chinese links with the state, indigenous merchants, local elites and native technocrats, have varied from co-opting elites onto the boards of Chinese companies, to raising equity from indigenous sources, government capitals, to operating joint ventures with the state and with foreign multinationals and seeking technological alliances with foreign multinationals. The state has ranged from patron to partner, from investor to executor.

She further argued that 'links with the state and the exploitation of Chinese networks ensured the survival of Chinese family enterprises, irrespective of whether they were in labour intensive industries or in capital intensive sectors. Competition was not a determining factor in the survival of Chinese family enterprises' (p. 100).

Second, upon consolidating themselves in their domestic economies by the 1980s, many Chinese firms in Southeast Asia began to diversify their operations abroad in search of new investment opportunities that are denied to them in their 'home' economies as a result of state regulation. This represents a new phase of development in the business history of ethnic Chinese firms, when they increasingly operate across national boundaries to become diversified TNCs. Well-known examples are the Salim Group from Indonesia, the Kerry Group from Malaysia, the Charoen Pokphand (CP) Group from Thailand and the Fortune Tobacco Group from the Philippines (see Table 1.6). In doing so, their strategies and processes of globalization are also shaped by the changing configurations of Chinese business systems and institutional structures of their 'home' economies as well as the increasingly global competitive environment (see also Chapter 3).

A critical assessment

Although these multi-disciplinary studies have helped us understand better Chinese capitalism in East and Southeast Asia, they are largely concerned with the nature of Chinese capitalism and economic activities in relatively narrow socio-cultural and geographic (domestic/host) contexts. As such, many (not all) of them tend to suffer from four general weaknesses: static analysis; bias towards small family firms; lack of attention to capital sourcing; and structural determinism. First, most studies see the organization and behaviour of ethnic Chinese actors and their firms as a somewhat static product of cultural adaptation, an inward-oriented defence strategy in order to survive host country hostility, or of institutional structuring, a fixed and predetermined outcome of Chinese business systems. Once established, such actors and their firms are perceived to exhibit little internal and external transformations, but rather continue to exist as relatively closed (albeit evolving) socio-cultural formations, often anchored in one national or regional base. There are no provisions for change and transformations among these Chinese actors and firms within the same 'home' economies and across different Asian economies. It is as if they have a particular fate or destiny, depending very much on their cultural origins and/or institutional structures that almost leave a permanent imprint on these capitalist organizations. Such a static analysis in the literature tends to obfuscate the dynamic nature of Chinese capitalism, emphasizing instead its fixity, permanence and inertia.

As hinted earlier in this chapter, this tendency towards static analysis in the literature on Chinese capitalism, particularly in the culturalist perspective, has much to do with its Weberian origins. The *modus operandi* in these implicitly Weberian studies usually follows several standard methodological steps. Beginning with contrasting mainland China, Chinese societies and people with the Occident or the 'West', these studies often proceed to describe their differences in belief systems, rationalities and institutions. They then use these differences to explain their different developmental outcomes as if they must conform to a single superior trajectory of industrial capitalism, or what Weber called 'rational capitalism' (see also Hamilton, 2000). Chinese capitalism is conceived in an Orientalist manner without regards to its dynamics and change over time and space. Weber, for example, had argued that the significant influence of Confucian values in Chinese social thought was detrimental to the development of a rational instrumentalism essential to the rise of modern capitalism in North America and Western Europe:

> The patrimonial nature of administration and legislation created a realm of unshakeable sacred tradition alongside a realm of arbitrariness and favouritism. These political factors impeded development of industrial capitalism, sensitive to the lack of rational and calculable administration and law enforcement, whether in China, India, Islam, or elsewhere ... Capital investment in industry is far too sensitive to such *irrational* use of authority and too dependent upon the possibility of calculating in advance the steady and rational operation of the state

machinery to emerge under a government of this type. But the decision question is, why did this administration and judiciary [in Imperial China] remain so *irrational* from a capitalist point of view? . . . Rational industrial capitalism, which in the Occident found its specific locus in manufacturing, has been handicapped not only by the lack of a formally guaranteed law, a rational administration and judiciary, and by the ramifications of a system of rights to collect revenue, but also, basically, by the lack of *spiritual* foundations. Above all it has been handicapped by the attitude rooted in the Chinese 'ethos' and peculiar to a class of officials and aspirants to office.

(Weber, [1920] 1983b: 82–4; my emphasis)

In his 1976 introduction to Weber's *The Protestant Ethic and the Spirit of Capitalism*, Anthony Giddens (1992: xv) summarized succinctly Weber's view that Confucian values

set as an ideal the harmonious adjustment of the individual to the established order of things . . . An ethic which stresses rational adjustment to the world 'as it is' could not have generated a moral dynamism in economic activity comparable to that characteristic of the spirit of European capitalism.

If Weber was right about the Confucianism-related conditions inhibiting the development of modern industrial capitalism in the then imperial China, the success and dynamism of Chinese capitalism in East and Southeast Asia, as we know it today, must have a lot to do with its antithesis: the entrepreneurial tendencies of ethnic Chinese unleashed in host economies free from patrimonialism in administration and legislation, but equally lacking in rational legal and judiciary systems. In short, how do ethnic Chinese in these host economies succeed in building a form of capitalism known as Chinese capitalism, if their cultural beliefs and social ethos are so 'irrational'? In my view, their entrepreneurial tendencies are more than static cultural adaptation to different host institutional conditions; they are indeed important dynamics of Chinese capitalism itself. Changes and transformations are thus endemic to Chinese capitalism such that capitalism-inhibiting beliefs in one time-space context (e.g. Confucianism in imperial China) might be strategically modified and deployed in another context (e.g. entrepreneurialism in East and Southeast Asia today) to overcome their own internal limits to capitalist development. Sympathetic to Weber's views on capitalism in general, Berger (1986: 28) thus noted that 'very probably, Weber was quite wrong in his view of the modernity-inhibiting character of Confucianism and other East Asian traditions'. The communalistic behaviour of actors in Chinese capitalism, for example, should not be held to invalidate its existence. As Peter Saunders (1995: 93) aptly pointed out, a capitalist society can be either individualistic or communalistic in its culture, and there is nothing in the character of capitalism itself which necessarily generates one rather than the other. There is a 'pervasive, powerful and persistent' belief that capitalism and individualism are inherently related, even though they originated separately and at different times.

As a set of historically specific cultural practices, families, networks and communities in Chinese capitalism are continuously evolving in response to different challenges and circumstances. Thus, Yang (2002: 469; original italics) argued that 'it is better to treat *guanxixue* [the practice of relationships] not as an innate timeless given of Chinese culture, but as a historically situated set of cultural practices whose features and discourse have different meanings and different deployments in given historical moments and political contexts'.

Although small and medium-sized family firms continue to receive most of the attention from researchers, few resources have been devoted to the analysis of the growth of large Chinese business conglomerates with public listed arms (Yeung, 1998a, 2003a; Gomez, 1999; Zang, 1999, 2000; Brown, 2000; Yeung and Soh, 2000). These large business conglomerates are certainly more than the methodological proxy that 'distinguishes any particular variety of capitalism' (Whitley, 1999: 65). As shown in Tables 1.5 and 1.6, they are indeed the prime movers and shakers in the economic organization of Chinese capitalism such that they cannot be simply analysed as outcomes of abstract cultural norms and institutional structures in a post hoc manner. Instead, these conglomerates must be analysed as an integral and critical constituent of Chinese capitalism. My analysis is therefore of how these conglomerates are interactively changing the nature and organization of Chinese capitalism. I am less interested in how Chinese capitalism is shaping the characteristics and attributes of Chinese firms, an approach commonly adopted in the literature on the 'spirit' of Chinese capitalism and Chinese business systems. As two *Business Week* editors recognized,

> [a]s more and more Chinese network builders popped up each year in *Forbes'* list of billionaires [see Table 1.6], there came a point when they began to shake their stigma of being 'ersatz capitalists.' Western investment bankers and consultants who learned more about the inner workings of a Dhanin Chearavanont, Li Ka-shing, Mochtar Riady, or Peter Woo found that these were serious business empires. They were men with a love for big deals who controlled powerful intelligence networks that gave them an inside track on deals'.
>
> (Clifford and Engardio, 2000: 74)

Even in Taiwan where the small and medium-sized enterprises (SMEs) have been hailed as the backbone of the burgeoning economy (Hamilton and Kao, 1990; Shieh, 1992; Hamilton, 1997; Hsing, 1998), recent studies have shown an increasing concentration of corporate power in the hands of the largest business groups, most of which are owned and controlled by ethnic Chinese families and are listed on Taiwan's stock exchange. Amsden and Chu (2002: Table 2-1; 27), for example, found that the share of sales/GNP by Taiwan's top 100 business groups grew from 32.3 per cent in 1973 to 33.8 per cent in 1988 and a staggering 54 per cent in 1998. A similar trend towards corporate concentration in sales, equity and assets also occurs in other economies dominated by ethnic Chinese firms.

There are few studies on the changing nature of capital sourcing for the business expansion of ethnic Chinese in Asia. This is a significant weakness in the context of the spread of global production networks driven by TNCs throughout the Asia-Pacific region and the growth of regional equity and bond markets. Such regional equity and bond markets are heavily dependent upon the operation of Chinese-controlled conglomerates, and they (via digital technologies) provide real-time links between Chinese family firms and the skein of global financial centres. Thus, while Karl Fields' (1995) study devoted a substantial chapter to corporate finance among Taiwanese firms before the 1990s, little substantial and quantitative data were provided to illuminate the nature of corporate finance. Instead, he conceded:

> no comprehensive study of *guanxiqiye* [related enterprises] financial sources has been attempted. Nor can such a study be carried out as long as such financial information remains confidential. In fact, one of the motives for choosing the informal, 'related enterprise' mode of organization has been to facilitate unmonitored financial flows to the groups and among group firms.
>
> (Fields, 1995: 145)

In another study of corporate networks among a sample of 107 Chinese firms listed on the Stock Exchange of Singapore in 1992, Zang (1999: 864–5) found that 'in the big Chinese business sector in East and Southeast Asia, the interlocking directorate has replaced traditional informal networks and has performed the function of co-ordination and control in the market place. It is a modern form of maintaining personal relationships in the Chinese business community and embodies a class alliance among Chinese capitalists'. He also found that family firms are more likely to network than non-family firms, and family ownership has a positive effect on interlocking directorates (Zang, 2000). But he fell short of describing and explaining corporate finance and performance among these Chinese family firms. In brief, the study of how Chinese family firms mobilize global capital via domestic and international financial markets remains extremely limited (see, however, Shikatani, 1995; Olds and Yeung, 1999; Yeung and Olds, 2000b; Carney and Gedajlovic, 2002a).

Earlier studies of Chinese capitalism tend to privilege broader structural influences at the expense of real actors. Many characteristics of Chinese capitalism are explained by the cultural and institutional structures from which Chinese family firms emerge. These institutional structures can be the imperial system in China or the discriminatory structures in Southeast Asia. As such, actors in Chinese capitalism are allowed little power and autonomy to negotiate these deterministic structures. In the business systems approach, for example, macro-economic structures and institutions at the societal level are the focus of analysis, making it extremely difficult to refute the often highly generalized observations on Chinese capitalism. For example, consider the following argument by Whitley (1992: 255):

> Taiwanese businessmen, for instance, have not adopted US business practices even though they depended heavily on the US market. Thus, business systems develop and change in response to institutional pressures and to dominant ways of doing things in their international markets.

Although it is virtually impossible to prove the validity of the first observation, the subsequent conclusion is also so generalized that empirical testing is quite absurd. In fact, empirical analysis or testing of actor behaviour is not the main concern in Whitley's (1992, 1999) work. Another main problem with such a systems-level analysis of capitalist dynamics is that *a priori* assumption of divergence and difference tends to overshadow a genuine analysis of the diverse possibilities of change/endurance and convergence/divergence occurring at the same time. Consider the following basic assumption of the comparative business systems approach in Whitley (1999: 5; my emphasis):

> [It] seeks to explain how and why forms of economic organization *diverge* in specific ways, and to identify the factors involved in their *change.* It assumes that economic relationships and activities are socially constituted and institutionally *variable*, such that the ways competitive processes operate, and the nature both of the actors engaged in them and of their outcomes, *vary* significantly between societal contexts. The logics governing economic decision-making and actions are *inherently structured* by dominant institutions, and so are *variable* between different conventions and 'rules of the game'.

This assumption of variability and divergence in the business systems approach has virtually precluded any analysis of dynamics of change in which both divergence and convergence can occur in such interesting ways that a new hybrid form of capitalism may emerge.
It is precisely for these reasons that we need to look at how key actors in

Chinese capitalism negotiate change in an era of volatile globalization by connecting (or being connected to) actor-networks that are embedded within much wider geographical and organizational spaces. As noted by Ong and Nonini (1997b: 326–7), 'Chinese transnationalists show that their identities are increasingly diaspora-based rather than land-based. Furthermore, the transformation of identities through capital's global mobility recasts class, gender, race, and nationality differences in new ways'. Here, global actors (and the actor-networks they are embedded in) play a fundamental role in helping to (re)shape Chinese capitalism. This state of affairs is set to continue, if not accelerate, due to development processes in East and Southeast Asia. It is also important to recognize that the most influential actor-networks (re)shaping Chinese capitalism are those associated with an international business and finance dimension. This is because international business actor-networks have the capacity to enrol relevant Chinese and non-Chinese actors in their actor-networks, forging changes in some business practices while also reinforcing other socio-economic norms. At the most basic of levels though, the (re)shaping of Chinese capitalism and its economic organization has been and is being driven by the desire of large Chinese firms to access the financial resources that flow through the global financial system. That such a situation should arise is not surprising given the nature of profits that have been generated from the development process in the Asia-Pacific region in the period since 1980 that in turn contribute to the hybridization of Chinese capitalism in a global era.

Hybrid capitalism: what remains of Chinese capitalism in a global era?

Globalization and the dynamics of Chinese capitalism: the core issue

It is common for researchers in international political economy to argue that there are distinctive ways of organizing economic institutions in different parts of the world. This stability in capitalist organizations and patterns of economic relationships often persists in the face of rapid political-economic change external to the societies concerned. Together, these patterns of social and organizational structuring form different business systems that refer to a phenomenon of relatively stable and enduring patterns of business practices in specific localities and societies. Once established in particular institutional contexts, these business systems may develop considerable cohesion and become resistant to major changes. Even such powerful changes as internationalization and globalization are deemed to have only limited effects on the nature of business systems (Whitley, 1994, 1998, 1999). Even after they are transformed, these distinctive systems of economic organization would 'bear the marks of conflicts between opposing conceptions of capitalism and their allied

Central
analytical question

institutional arrangements and interest groups' (Whitley, 1998: 447). Their evolutionary trajectories are seen as dependent on pre-existing configurations of domestic social, economic and political institutions (Whitley and Kristensen, 1996, 1997; Grabher and Stark, 1997; Guillén, 2001a; Hall and Soskice, 2001a). As noted earlier, this business systems perspective is particularly relevant in analysing the political economies of the Asia-Pacific region where business systems are socially and institutionally embedded. In the words of Backman (1999: 365), '[o]ld habits are hard to break' in the context of opaque and corrupted business systems in some Asian economies. To some observers, these business systems in Asia are characterized by the differentiated role of inward-looking inter-firm networks, excessive reliance on personal relationships in business transactions and the strong intervention of the state in business and economy. These qualitative differences in business systems constitute a mosaic of distinct political economies in Asia.

The central analytical question I want to pursue is whether Chinese capitalism and its allegedly distinctive business systems can be as stable and enduring in today's context of accelerated globalization. Taking a transformative view of globalization similar to that of Held *et al.* (1999) and Dicken (2003a), I define globalization as a set of dialectical processes that simultaneously create a functionally interdependent world economy and accentuate the importance of all kinds of differences in societies and space (Yeung, 1998b, 2002b). These processes include global flows of materials (e.g. people, goods) and intangibles (e.g. capital, technology, information and services). My core argument is that in assessing the impact of globalization tendencies, it is important to distinguish between business systems as enduring structures of capitalism and key social actors in these systems as agents of change. The lack of explicit attention to actors and their strategies and behaviour as agents of organizational and system change is a major lacuna in the business systems perspective and related approaches in studies of comparative capitalism (Hall and Soskice, 2001a; Clegg and Redding, 1990). Indeed, Whitley (1996: 414) offered an auto-critique that his perspective

how does this fit?

> tends to downplay the significance of particular firms' actions in favour of the more general logic of particular institutional systems ... [It] has not paid a great deal of attention to international forms of economic organization, or how the growing cross-national interdependence of some firms and markets has affected national business systems.

He suggested that future studies should address the ways in which 'the growing internationalization of economic activities has affected interdependencies between firms and their domestic business environments' and the mechanisms by which the roles of economic actors 'become institutionalized and reproduced ... as well as the circumstances in which they are liable to change' (Whitley, 1996: 423). Sharing the same vision for organization studies, Gereffi (1996: 437) concluded that 'traditional boundaries between nations, firms, and industries are being reconfigured, and organization theory as well as development theory need to find ways of encompassing all the relevant actors within a single framework'.

Through detailed empirical analysis of qualitative case studies and quantitative surveys of Chinese firms presented in this book (see Appendix for methodology), I aim to specify how globalization tendencies can transform the dynamics of Chinese capitalism and, subsequently, its nature and organization. While such transformations are brought about by these globalization tendencies, I do not purport that a new cross-national form of economic organization will replace existing configurations in Chinese capitalism by virtue of its superior efficiency and that radical changes in Chinese capitalism will occur rapidly and in a single direction. In this sense, I share Whitley's (1999: 118) caveat that globalization's 'significance and consequences for the different varieties of capitalism ... remain to be clarified. In particular, the conditions under which these changes are likely to result in a qualitative transformation of distinctive forms of economic organization require more detailed specification' (see also Redding, 2000). To specify these conditions of transforming Chinese capitalism in a global era, I argue that the dialectical tendencies of globalization towards homogenization and differentiation have differential impacts on the configurations and dynamics of Chinese capitalism and its constituents. In Figure 1.2, I outline the organizing framework for this book. Although the literature on Chinese capitalism has examined

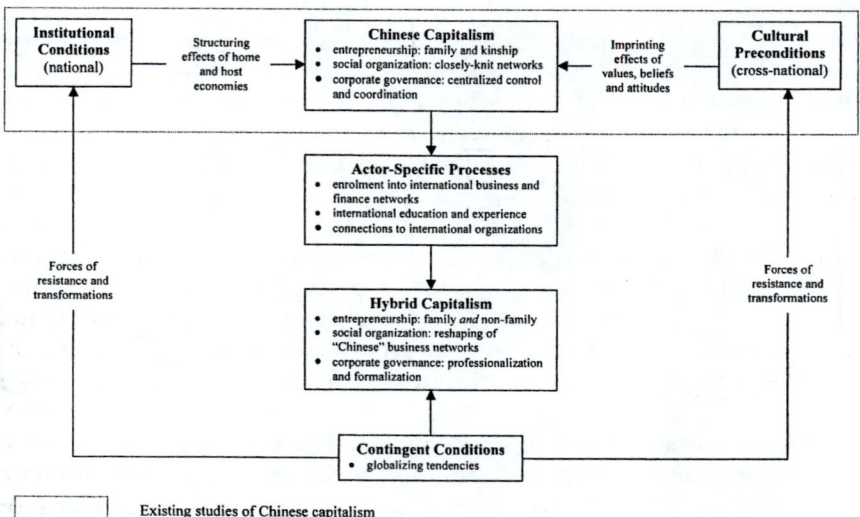

Figure 1.2 The hybridization of Chinese capitalism in a global era.

the imprinting effects of culture and the structuring effects of institutional conditions on the nature and organization of Chinese capitalism, we have little knowledge about how actor-specific processes in an era of globalization have contributed to the emergence of a hybrid form of Chinese capitalism.

This book thus aims to demonstrate that globalization tendencies are undermining certain social and institutional foundations of Chinese capitalism while accentuating the need for transformations in its traditional dimensions. Today, key actors in Chinese capitalism increasingly face the dilemma of succumbing to the pressures of transparency in order to secure global finance while preserving their traditional practices of network reliance and complex family ownership and/or control. In this globalizing context, there are fewer competitive advantages derived from the reliance on personal relationships on the basis of intra-regional business networks. Instead, the spatiality of business networks has been relegated from the intra-regional scale to the global scale, so that global actor-networks are increasingly influencing the nature and organization of Chinese capitalism (see Chapter 2). Globalization has made possible the complex interpenetration of global actor-networks into Chinese capitalism. Globalization tendencies also continue to reinforce local differences in business conducts and discursive practices. This tendency towards local differentiation is also a process of creating and reforming hierarchies and structures of national economies. The local embeddedness of Chinese firms remains a key source of competitive advantage. This localization process enables Chinese capitalism to retain some core attributes in a global era, thus contributing to its growing hybridity in form and organization. The dynamics of Chinese capitalism depend critically on globalization tendencies as a major transformational force in the global economy today.

While, as argued by their proponents, Chinese capitalism tends to be enduring over time because of historical legacies and institutional embeddedness, key actors and their firms emerging from this distinctive mode of economic organization may be much more susceptible to changes brought about by globalization tendencies. This is because key actors in these ethnic Chinese firms are increasingly participating and enrolled into global actor-networks that, in turn, reshape how these actors conceive and operate their own firms and networks (see Figure 1.2). Although Chinese capitalism is structurally embedded in specific national social organization and political-economic institutions, its key actors are significantly more mobile and receptive to change. It is possible that globalization has only limited effects on Chinese capitalism at the structural level and yet a significant transformative impact on its key organizational entities – ethnic Chinese and their firms – at the level of key actors. The nature and degree of enrolment by key ethnic Chinese actors into the global economy therefore explains the dynamics of Chinese capitalism and its differential impact on specific actors and their embedded business systems. Facilitated by globalization, this enrolment process enables actors to experience different organizational behaviour and business practices worldwide. It also allows these actors to transform their own firms and networks, subject to some binding effects of their own distinctive business systems. When these dynamic changes occur collectively among ethnic Chinese firms in a clearly defined business system, fundamental institutional changes may be forthcoming and this may result in significant changes in the dominant forms and organization of Chinese capitalism itself. In this way, Chinese capitalism must be conceived as an open system and subject to dynamic changes from within, at the level of actors themselves. Interestingly, Whitley (1992, 1999) has pre-empted this argument:

> the open nature of social systems means that markets and firms can change as the result of learning and altered perceptions thus modifying the efficacy of previously successful structures and practices ... Social systems are open because they can develop emergent properties and powers as a result of reinterpretations of social and material realities which alter the nature of the social world. The meaningful and concept-dependent nature of social relations and institutions means that *internal* learning and changing perceptions as a result of *external* events can alter significantly and system outcomes become quite different. Thus, when enough people in an organization change their perception of what is going on and redefine its nature, its structure and procedures will alter.
>
> (Whitley, 1992: 5–6; my emphasis)

But his distinction between internal learning and external events is not really meaningful in my analysis of how key actors in Chinese capitalism enrol and participate in global actor-networks. He has also not pursued the argument further in his empirical analysis of business systems in East Asia. In Chapter 2, I elaborate on these complex interactions between actor-networks in Chinese capitalism and dynamic business systems in the context of contemporary globalization. Working from the varieties of capitalism perspective similar to Whitley's business systems approach, Hall and Soskice (2001b: 5) argued that such strategic interaction is 'central to economic and political outcomes, the most important institutions distinguishing one political economy from another will be those conditioning such interaction, and it is these that we seek to capture in this analysis'. They proposed 'a firm-centered political economy that regards companies as the crucial actors in a capitalist economy. They are the key agents of adjustment in the face of technological change or international competition whose activities aggregate into overall levels of economic performance' (Hall and Soskice, 2001b: 6).

This book's focus on ethnic Chinese actors and their enrolment in global networks at different spatial scales is therefore highly important for at least three reasons. First, this bottom-up approach examines the dynamics of globalization and Chinese capitalism that operate at the level of actor-networks. This contrasts with and complements the overwhelming top-down approach in much of the literature on globalization and the political economy of business systems (Mittelman, 2000). Second, whereas firms and their strategies may be conceived of as agents of economic change at the structural level, it is clear that these firms are controlled and managed by specific social actors (Yeung, 1998a, 2002a). By focusing on the action and behaviour of these social actors (e.g. their enrolment into global actor-networks), we are better able to unpack the monolithic view of the firm as a coherent and stable feature of capitalist economies. The actor-network perspective in this book helps us to appreciate the differentiated strategies and behaviour of firms as deliberate responses by social actors to the changing contexts of globalization and dynamic processes in business systems. Third, while my analysis is rooted in the historical evolution of Chinese capitalism, it pays serious attention to more recent trends and events in the global economy. The dynamics of the global economy, particularly those encapsulated in globalization tendencies, are conceived of as critical to the changing nature and transformations in Chinese capitalism. In this sense, time, expressed through changing contexts, does play a major role here, albeit not in a linear and unidirectional manner. On this issue of time, I beg to differ from Redding's (1990: 4) argument that:

> The Chinese family business has had plenty of time to develop new forms. Sophisticated Chinese organizations have flourished both in and out of China for as long as Western organizations, perhaps longer. They have interacted with powerful markets for just as long and have been accessible to modern managerial technology had they wished. The fact remains that a traditional form of control is retained, and a particular form of legitimacy seen as appropriate.

His view is predicted on Chinese family business in mainland China before the communist takeover in 1949, where the institutional structuring of norms and cultural practices was highly powerful in its historical context. It does not take into account the more recent changing contexts and circumstances with which Chinese family firms outside mainland China are confronted (Wong, 2000). After all, these firms in East and Southeast Asian economies have recent origins and formations in the 1950s and the 1960s. They have not had the luxury of 'plenty of time' to develop their organizational forms because they have been preoccupied with either surviving hostile host economies (e.g. Indonesia and Malaysia) or participating in nation-building processes (e.g. Taiwan and Singapore). Although they have carried with them distinctive cultural norms of control and forms of legitimacy from mainland China – centripetal authority exercised through the family – these Chinese family firms are by no means cultural artefacts resistant to changes and transformations in view of new competitive contexts arising from globalization tendencies. In fact, one might argue that the recent rediscovery of network forms of organizations in advanced industrialized economies has had a lot to do with the changing competitive context in the global economy. As DiMaggio (2001b: 23; my emphasis) explained in his introduction to *The Twenty-First-Century Firm,*

> [j]ust as Western observers first found the Japanese employment system exotic, but then, once they adjusted their conceptual lenses to take account of what they observed, began to perceive elements of it in their own societies, so the discovery of complex interfirm alliances in Japan and the 'little tigers' of East Asia led Westerners to perceive *for the first time* the presence of *networks* in their own economies.

In this sense, changing contexts matter a great deal to our understanding (and rediscovery) of key elements of capitalist economic organizations across different economies and societies.

Conceived as such, Chinese capitalism has a certain degree of systemic endurance and yet is subject to dynamic transformations over time through its agents of change. I argue that such a gradual process of transition and transformation leads to a form of hybrid capitalism that is open and fluid in nature (see Figure 1.2). Through this process of hybridization, Chinese capitalism simultaneously converges towards certain norms and rules in Anglo-American capitalism – the dominant form of global capitalism today (itself changing of course) – and yet diverges from its key institutions and structures, reflecting context-specific dynamics and the uneven impact of global flows of capital, information, discourses and technologies. At any given time, this hybrid form of capitalism evolves through the strategic interactions of key actors with globalizing forces; its hybridity represents the outcomes of these complex interactions in globalizing actor-networks. My conception of hybrid capitalism implicitly recognizes variety and divergence, but does not preclude the possibility of some degree of convergence. The notion also allows for dynamic and open analysis. It acknowledges diversity in the face of globalization tendencies and still conceptualizes these changes as transitory and hybrid. This approach to the hybridization of Chinese capitalism is thus characterized by its non-essentialist view of capitalism (the debate on Chineseness), its non-static view of capitalist economic organization (Chinese capitalism as a cultural artefact) and its recognition of the co-existence of some elements of the past and new entities brought about through changes and transformations.[14] As Berger (2002: 10) has recently commented on the rapid transformation of Chinese capitalism, hybridization represents a deliberate effort to synthesize foreign and native cultural traits . . . The development of an overseas Chinese [*sic*] business culture, combining the most modern business techniques with traditional Chinese personalism, is a very important case of this [hybridization], given the great economic success of the Chinese diaspora throughout the world (see also Redding, 2000).

Hybrid capitalism: four dimensions of Chinese capitalism

In the empirical chapters of this book (3–6), I focus on four major dimensions of this emerging hybridity of Chinese capitalism in a global era (see Figure 1.2): the internationalization of actor-networks; transnational entrepreneurship; transformations in social organization; and changing corporate governance and strategic management. To begin, dynamic transformations in the dominant form of Chinese capitalism cannot take place without some external influences and pressures on institutionalized business practices and social action. These are unlikely to be found in domestic operating contexts precisely because the institutionalization of capitalist structures often takes place in these domestic contexts and political economies. This external influence is likely to emerge when key actors in Chinese capitalism experience differential norms and rules in contrasting operating contexts during their internationalization processes. Through internationalization, these key actors are also more likely to develop new linkages and to enrol into actor-networks elsewhere. Chapter 3 explains how key actors in Chinese capitalism (i.e. leading firms) participate in globalization processes. It describes the nature and organization of this internationalization process and examines how internal conditions (home/host economy) and external/global factors contribute to the global reach of Chinese capitalism.

Another dimension of the hybridization of Chinese capitalism refers to the changing nature of entrepreneurship that operates across borders. Ever since Joseph Schumpeter's (1934) seminal work, entrepreneurship is virtually synonymous with capitalist economic development. As the invisible force behind the Schumpeterian notion of creative destruction, entrepreneurship is what drives the capitalist system via the formation of new forms and/or the sustainable development of existing business organizations. By inference, entrepreneurship is also what changes and transforms capitalism. Within institutionalized business systems, it is not surprising to expect a certain preconfigured and stable set of entrepreneurial traits. As described above, much research on Chinese capitalism has focused on its entrepreneurial tendencies in hostile domestic environments in Southeast Asia. A major missing link in this research into Chinese capitalism is how key actors in Chinese capitalism develop and exhibit different repertoires of entrepreneurial tendencies and practices when they internationalize in different host economies. Focusing on this notion of transnational entrepreneurship among ethnic Chinese actors, Chapter 4 describes how specific actors in Chinese capitalism have not only internationalized their activities, but also brought about dynamic changes in Chinese capitalism. Their social and business practices have transcended traditional practices identified in the literature on Chinese capitalism.

Hybrid capitalism is also shaped by transformations in the social organization of economic activities. This dimension of Chinese capitalism, however, is particularly difficult to reconfigure because of its embeddedness in particularized cultural norms and belief systems. As described in the review of the literature above, Chinese capitalism is socially organized around the family firm, *guanxi* relationships and business networks. These attributes of social organization provide the institutional foundation where Chinese capitalism crystallizes. What then happens to this foundation when key actors in Chinese capitalism are increasingly engaged with actor-networks on a global scale? Are globalization tendencies sufficiently powerful to shake it up, so to speak? In this era of global business and finance, what will remain in the reconfigured and hybridized form of Chinese capitalism? Chapter 5 demonstrates that the bamboo network is no longer exclusively based on *guanxi* relationships among ethnic Chinese in East and Southeast Asia. The social organization of Chinese capitalism is changing in the context of globalization tendencies. More non-Chinese and non-family actors are now enrolled in Chinese business networks that were previously described as inward-looking and closely-knit, based on family ties. The main mechanisms through which these transformations in the social organization of Chinese capitalism are brought about are outlined.

The final, but perhaps most important, dimension of Chinese capitalism is the changing pattern of corporate governance and strategic management among its leading firms. Defined as the ownership structures and management control systems that arbitrage capital, production and market exchanges, corporate governance represents the *genius loci* of any form of modern capitalism, irrespective of whether they are liberal market economies or coordinated market economies (Shleifer and Vishny, 1997; La Porta *et al.*, 1999; Franks *et al.*, 2003). In short, it is concerned with 'the exercise of power over the direction of the enterprise, the supervision of executive actions, the acceptance of a duty to be accountable and the regulation of the corporation within the jurisdiction of the states in which it operates' (Tricker, 1990: 188). In fact, Chandler's (1977, 1990) work has clearly shown the emergence of managerial capitalism in the US through the separation between ownership and management control of modern corporations. Earlier research on Chinese capitalism, particularly in the culturalist school, has pointed to the existence of a distinctive set of authority structures and coordination systems based on the integration of ownership and management control within the Chinese family firm.

Although I accept the predominance and continual significance of small family firms among ethnic Chinese in East and Southeast Asia, large business conglomerates controlled by ethnic Chinese are increasingly broadening their corporate governance structures to meet the competitive challenges of globalization. If globalization tendencies can exert a major impact on the transformation of Chinese capitalism, such an impact is most likely to be evident in changing corporate governance among Chinese firms. As such, the hybridization of Chinese capitalism can be characterized by both the continuing existence of Chinese family firms and the growing professionalization of management and governance structures in large Chinese business groups. Chapter 6 shows how corporate governance among Chinese firms, particularly those family-owned, is converging to a certain extent towards the Anglo-American model of managerial capitalism. Although this convergence process is neither complete nor fully accepted internally among actors in Chinese capitalism, there is strong evidence that the process has already started and is unlikely to be reversible in the near future.

This book endeavours to show how globalization tendencies have transformed the nature and organization of Chinese capitalism into a form of hybrid capitalism. Contrary to many previous studies of Chinese capitalism, I am less interested in describing and explaining certain essentialized attributes (or the spirit) of Chinese capitalism as if they were permanent fixtures. Instead, I aim to describe and explain how (Chinese) capitalism is a dynamic set of norms, beliefs and institutions that simultaneously structure economy and society and is transformed by these changing economic and societal trends. The final chapter examines how Chinese capitalism is (re)shaped in the context of the recent 1997–8 Asian economic crisis, but not why the crisis happened in Asia. Instead, I explain how the crisis has influenced and speeded up the ongoing development of the future trajectories of Chinese capitalism in East and Southeast Asia. Some implications for the future of Chinese capitalism in the face of global capitalism are offered.

2 The dynamics of Chinese capitalism

Globalization and actor-networks

Globalization and the dynamics of capitalism

In this chapter, I theorize the complex interactions among actor-networks, Chinese capitalism and dynamic business systems in the context of contemporary globalization. As the conceptual core of this book, the chapter goes beyond static and essentialist interpretations of Chinese capitalism and its business systems. I argue that key actors in Chinese capitalism are capable of taking advantages of globalization tendencies to bring about dynamic changes in their business systems. This process occurs when these actors both participate in globalization processes and are influenced by global material and immaterial flows. Social actors are therefore key agents of change in contemporary capitalism. The chapter begins by theorizing the role of globalization tendencies in reshaping capitalist dynamics. The second section describes the existing configurations of Chinese capitalism as a peculiar business system. The final section examines the various mechanisms through which Chinese capitalism is reconfigured in a global era. In particular, I focus on the globalization of actor-networks through which ethnic Chinese actors are increasingly involved in a diverse range of economic practices and business activities beyond their traditional concerns. I argue that these globalizing actor-networks serve as the key mechanism through which the hybridization of Chinese capitalism takes place.

To date, an overwhelming body of literature has been devoted to globalization, both as a contested set of discourses and as a transformative force in the global economy. As a set of discourses, globalization encapsulates certain political agenda, in particular neoliberalism, to create its own conditions of existence (Yeung, 1998b, 2002b; Kelly, 1999). As a set of material processes, globalization is constituted by intensified flows of tangible and intangible forms across societies on a global scale. It is, however, beyond the scope of this chapter to review this huge body of literature.[1] Here one critical dimension of globalization is emphasized: its dialectical nature towards both spatial integration (a result of the globalization of economic activities) and spatial disintegration (an outcome of the localization of these very activities). This is an important point because it has often been assumed in the ultra-globalist literature that globalization represents a single and unidirectional socio-spatial logic that will cause movement towards the homogenization of social organization and economic practices. These enthusiastic proponents of globalization envisage an end-state perspective in which a borderless and homogenous 'global' world emerges (Ohmae, 1990, 1995; O'Brien, 1992; Horsman and Marshall, 1994). The critics of these ultra-globalists, however, have taken too seriously this end-state view of the homogenization of national economic and institutional structures that are collectively known as business systems. This group of scholars argues that despite globalization processes, differences in economic organization between capitalist economies continue to create different 'varieties' of capitalism.[2] They view ultra-globalists as adhering to a form of economic functionalism that 'assumes that market competition inevitably replaces inefficient economic systems by more efficient ones, and that global competition will produce a new transnational system which will out-compete the many current varieties of capitalism' (Whitley, 1998: 447). Couched in a similar tone, Guillén (2001a: 3) rejects the modernist and flat-earth view of globalization. He asserts strongly that

> [c]ountries and organizations do not gravitate toward a supposedly universal model of economic success and organizational form as they attempt to cope with globalization. Rather, the mutual awareness that globalization entails invites them to be different, namely to use their unique economic, political, and social advantages as leverage in the global marketplace.

These two opposing views of globalization – one of homogenization and another of continual differences – obfuscate the dialectical and transformative nature of globalization. We are left with an either/or choice when it comes to how to grapple with the problem of understanding the complex impact of globalization on the forms and structures of economic organization in different societies. One has to believe either in the powerful role of globalization in homogenizing different business systems and varieties of capitalism or in the stubborn resistance of these capitalist structures of economic organization to changes brought about by globalization. I believe that these dichotomous views of globalization are false because they are based on static premises and fail to acknowledge the dynamic nature of both globalization and capitalist systems of economic organization. More specifically, the ultra-globalists are clearly guilty of forming a singular and unidirectional end-state logic of a borderless global world in which national differences cease to exist. They fail to recognize that the very logic of globalization itself is highly contested and negotiated in a reflexive manner by multiple actors (e.g. individual elites, firms, nation-states, international organizations and so on) at different spatial scales (e.g. local, regional, national and global). Indeed, this multiplicity of contestation and negotiation strategies provides the central dynamic of the complex interaction between globalization and contemporary capitalism. There is, for example, no convincing reason to expect a firm to follow the same globalization logic as a nation-state. In the case of Chinese capitalism in East and Southeast Asia, it is clear that ethnic Chinese firms often operate on the basis of such actor-specific motives as familism and personal relationships, rather than state-specific rationality such as ethnic redistribution in Indonesia and Malaysia and nation-building in Singapore and Taiwan (see below). As such, globalization is embodied in a set of complex and conflicting tendencies, the outcomes of which often cannot be predicted a priori.

On the other hand, the globalization critics have overemphasized the distinctiveness of national business systems and institutional structures and caricatured globalization as necessarily eroding national differences. Although national business systems are strongly embedded in domestic social and economic institutions and exhibit certain defining norms and characteristics, they are surely not organizational blueprints that are forever cast in stone. Instead of asking what the new forms of global capitalism are (themselves subject to changes and represent a moving target) and how they replace existing national systems of capitalism, the appropriate question should be concerned with what constitutes the central dynamics of existing systems of capitalism and how this dynamics can be unleashed under different contextual circumstances (see also Chapter 1). Globalization helps to create one such changing circumstance that has been particularly powerful since the late twentieth century. In an era of accelerated globalization, it becomes imperative for us to consider the reconfiguring of capitalist business systems as open, rather than closed and static, systems.

In so far as we view globalization as a set of highly contested tendencies and processes, the consideration of reconfiguring business systems needs not be contingent upon the arrival of a globalized world or the complete satisfaction of certain stringent conditions for the establishment of global forms of economic organization. Whitley (1999: 120) has specified some of these conditions for globalization to work itself through transformations in nationally based business systems, as follows.

1   A large number of leading firms engage in international trade and production alliances.
2   These alliances form a major part of their activities for some considerable time.
3   These alliances are mostly with partners from the same kind of foreign business system.
4   The practices being changed are not closely connected to powerful domestic agencies and institutions.

As will be shown throughout this book, most of these conditions have been breached by the enrolment of leading actors from Chinese capitalism in globalizing actor-networks in international business and finance. Many actors in Chinese capitalism have now engaged in internationalization and cross-border activities for at least ten years (see Chapter 3). Interestingly, they have now been enrolling non-Chinese (foreign) actors in their alliances and networks. They have also actively participated in globalizing actor-networks that are not necessarily connected to a particular kind of business systems. As such, the transformations and hybridization of Chinese capitalism are not necessarily dependent on the arrival of a globalized world. The real analytical challenge rests with the processes of reconfiguration rather than the end product itself (e.g. the demise of national business systems and the emergence of one dominant form of global capitalism). This, I believe, is a very important point missed by critics of globalization. Given the dialectical and contested nature of globalization, one wonders whether such an end-state view of either a dominant form of global capitalism or a mosaic of nationally distinctive business systems is really meaningful. I believe it is imperative for us to focus on the dynamic processes of change and reconfiguration that underpin the hybridization of different varieties of capitalism.

So far I have not unpacked what I mean by the dialectics of globalization. I can only briefly outline the key transformations of globalization tendencies (Dunning, 1993; Held *et al.*, 1999; Hirst and Thompson, 1999; Dicken, 2003a). There is no doubt that the global economy today has become much more functionally integrated and interdependent than ever. To a large extent, this increasing integration and interdependence of national economies on a global scale is explained by the cross-border activities of TNCs and their associated flows of FDI. In 1997 the value of international production, attributed to some 53,000 TNCs and their 450,000 foreign affiliates, was respectively US$3.5 trillion (measured by cumulative FDI stock) and US$9.5 trillion (measured by estimated global sales) (UNCTAD, 1998: 2). By 2001 there were 65,000 TNCs controlling more than 650,000 foreign affiliates that contributed to one-tenth of world GDP and one-third of world exports. Their combined FDI stock and global sales were respectively US$6.6 trillion and US$19 trillion, almost doubling the figures in 1997 (UNCTAD, 2002: xv). This rapid globalization of international production has invariably led to greater competition among leading firms embedded in different business systems. As the rules of competition have been altered (Best, 1990, 2001; Porter, 1998), leading firms in global industries have begun to innovate relentlessly and to adopt strategically selected practices of their global competitors. This process has been viewed by both camps of globalization as homogenizing national business systems towards a more 'efficient' model of global capitalism and global competition (Dicken, 2003b; Gertler, 2003).

What is missing in this interpretation is the possibility for the emergence of new organizational forms among firms in global competition. Instead of producing a global economy based on the Anglo-American model of competitive capitalism, globalization has generated rather different and pluralistic modes of organizing economic and social life connected by global spaces of flows (Peck and Yeung, 2003). One of the central mechanisms through which these spaces of flows are interconnected is the rise of the so-called 'network society' (Castells, 1996) and 'spaces of network relations' (Yeung, 1998a; Dicken *et al.*, 2001). The 1990s have witnessed the emergence of the 'connected corporation', 'differentiated network', 'global production networks', 'alliance advantage' and 'alliance capitalism' (Lewis, 1995; Gomes-Casseres, 1996; Dunning, 1997; Nohria and Ghoshal, 1997; Doz and Hamel, 1998; Henderson *et al.*, 2002). These terms refer to significant qualitative changes in the economic organization of firms, business systems and capitalism. There is now a greater tendency in most capitalist economies to form strong intra-firm networks to exploit firms' core competencies and to form differentiated inter-firm networks through equity and non-equity arrangements (Contractor and Lorange, 1988; Buckley, 1994; Yeung, 1994a, 1998c; Beamish and Killing, 1997; DiMaggio, 2001a; Thompson, 2003). In organizational terms, globalization has led to both convergence and divergence in the mechanisms and institutions of economic coordination and control. While certain organizational forms (e.g. mass production) continue to exist, other new organizational forms (e.g. strategic alliances and flexible specialization) emerge to become important modes of economic coordination and control.

Although globalization is defined by the greater integration of the spatial organization of economic activities, it also accentuates differences when actors from different business systems interact together. Mutual awareness and appreciation promoted through globalization processes creates de facto diversity and differences in norms, views and practices that reinforce the hybridity of different forms of capitalism. I am not arguing that capitalism does not change at all, for this line of reasoning will risk being accused of structural determinism. Rather, I argue that capitalism changes in highly unpredictable directions that result in hybrid forms and structures of economic organization in different economies and societies. These differences are further exacerbated by the highly uneven nature of globalization processes, in which territorial differences and geographical unevenness remain endemic (Yeung, 2002b). To compete successfully in the global economy, actors in different business systems and capitalist structures try to interpret each other's best practices and incorporate them strategically in their own firm-specific routines and organizational processes. This transfer of best practices between firms in different business systems, however, is highly problematic because of very differentiated contexts. Even in the most celebrated example of this spatial transfer of best practices (e.g. Japanese automobile transplants in the US: see Mair *et al.*, 1988; Kenny and Florida, 1993), there are serious limitations whether these practices can work easily in different capitalist systems (see also Gertler, 1995, 2003; Gertler *et al.*, 2000).

Actors in different systems of capitalism also engage in significant efforts to outdo each other through continuous innovations and changes. This iterative process of organizational adoption and change defines the dialectics of globalization because it both creates pressures for the homogenization of business systems at certain points in time and space, and reinforces their continual differences and hybridity at other points. Concluding his comparative institutional analysis of globalization and organizational change in Argentina, South Korea and Spain, Guillén (2001a: 228) argued that

> [t]he enhanced possibilities for networking in a global world make it easier for individuals, communities, firms, and labor unions to bypass brokers [e.g. the state and other powerful institutions], to look around by themselves, to adopt the patterns of economic action and organizational form that they find most appealing. (See also Mathews, 2002.)

It is thus impossible to specify a priori a singular logic and power relation for the interaction between the dialectical imperatives of homogenization and differentiation. This is because the realization of such dialectical tendencies is very much contingent on pre-existing trajectories and legacies of organizational patterns and the multiple contexts of change (see also Figure 1.2). Since these organizational trajectories are highly institutionalized in specific territorial formations (e.g. a nation-state), their scales and scopes of change are differentiated at an abstract level through differential relations between capital and state. In addition, the contexts of change vary from one capitalist system to another. This variability in contexts complicates the specification of the timing of change and its outcomes. As such, we have to pay special attention to historically contingent and geographically specific processes that account for organizational change and the dynamics of different forms and structures of capitalism. To sum up, the dynamics of capitalism in a global era depends not just on the continual endurance of its social organization and institutional structures, but also more importantly on the dialectics of globalization. How then does globalization influence the configurations and dynamics of capitalism such that a hybrid form of capitalism emerges? This is the key theoretical question.

Varieties of capitalism and the configurations of Chinese capitalism

Varieties of capitalism and the institutional structuring of business systems

Although the literature on different varieties of capitalism and their business systems is enormous, it is useful to point out that variations in institutional structures and business systems can significantly explain the sources and variations of resource and capability endowments enjoyed by social actors and economic agents from different economies. These divergent forms of capitalism can be explained by their differential configurations of institutional structures and their differential institutional structuring of organizational forms (Yeung, 2002a: 19–25). An example is the late twentieth-century British economy that had strong international capabilities in financial services and architecture, but weak ones in complex assembly manufacturing and construction. Another similar example is the strength of the Japanese economy in complex assembly manufacturing (e.g. automobiles and electronics), but less strength in precision engineering (e.g. Germany) or media businesses (e.g. the US). Whitley (1999: 7–8) has offered a concise summary of Lazonick's (1991) account of economic development and competitiveness, in which three varieties of capitalism are highlighted in accordance with their variations in the configurations of economic institutions and competitive strategies: proprietary (e.g. the UK), managerial (e.g. the US) and collective (e.g. postwar Japan).

In proprietary capitalism, vertically and horizontally specialized firms are the dominant economic agents. They coordinate their inputs and outputs through market contracting (see also Sako, 1992) and have little distinctive organizational capacity to pursue innovative strategies. They typically delegate control over labour processes to skilled workers. In comparison, large vertically integrated and often horizontally diversified firms dominate managerial capitalism. Professional and salaried managers run these firms that are in turn organized into authority hierarchies (Chandler, 1977, 1990; Gabor, 2000; Best, 1990; Sabel and Zeitlin, 1996). Having developed their own innovation capabilities through R&D activities, they competed for much of the early twentieth century through innovation-based strategies for mass consumer markets. They also exerted strong managerial control over work processes through formal rules and procedures and mechanization, the hallmarks of Fordism or mass production. High levels of managerial integration in such firms, however, did not extend to the manual workforce or to suppliers and customers. Among the three varieties of capitalism, collective capitalism has the highest level of organizational integration of economic activities through extensive long-term collaboration between firms in business groups and networks, both within sectors and across them. This is because loyalty and commitment between employer and employee extend further down the hierarchy than in the proprietary or managerial variants. This cooperative labour process is crucial to the development of innovative organizations because it encourages employees to improve products and processes on a continuing basis (Storper and Salais, 1997).

How then do these different configurations of capitalism shape the organization of economic coordination and control systems? This diverse institutional structuring of organization systems is evident in the substantial variations in ownership patterns, business formation and coordination, management processes, and work and employment relations across countries and/or regions. For example, the ways in which industrial capitalism developed in the UK, Denmark and Germany differ significantly as a result of variations in their political systems and the institutions governing agricultural production and distribution. To a large extent, the structure and practices of state agencies, financial organizations and labour-market actors in these countries continue to be divergent and to reproduce distinctive forms of economic organization (Whitley, 1999; Hall and Soskice, 2001a). This institutional structuring of organization systems has four distinctive dimensions. First, ownership patterns of firms in particular countries can be significantly structured by pre-existing institutions in those countries, which may control sources of capital and other initial inputs to production in ways that either promote or discourage private entrepreneurship and private ownership of business establishments. Late industrializing countries, for example, typically have poorly developed capital and stock markets. The lack of capital and other inputs to production (e.g. human resources) has often led to strong involvement by the state in financing early industrialization in these countries (Amsden, 1989, 2001; Wade, 1990; Hamilton-Hart, 2002). In other industrialized economies, however, significant variations in state policies and industrialization processes may shape the behaviour of national firms in terms of their corporate financing (e.g. reliance on capital markets) and corporate governance patterns (Shleifer and Vishny, 1997; La Porta *et al.*, 1999; Franks *et al.*, 2003). American firms, for example, have significantly shorter-term shareholding and higher reliance on capital markets than Germany and Japanese firms. Biggart and Guillén (1999: 725) argued that:

> organizing logics vary substantially in different social milieus. For example, in some settings it is 'normal' to raise business capital through family ties; in others, this is an 'inappropriate' imposition and fostering ties to banks or to foreign investors might be a more successful or legitimate fund-raising strategy.

Second, institutional arrangements may influence the patterns of business formation and co-ordination. In countries with highly competitive markets institutionalized through specific deregulation policies and the establishment of market procedures, firms are usually established by private entrepreneurs on the basis of their perceived benefits from new combinations of production, marketing and distribution methods. Recent empirical studies in technological innovations based on patent data have shown that the conditions of home countries influence the levels and trends of R&D activities and technological innovations in national firms. The technological activities of global corporations are firmly rooted in home countries, as indicated by the location and nature of R&D activities. These firms derive their firm-specific technological advantages from home-country institutional environments (Cantwell, 1989, 1995; Lundvall, 1992; Patel, 1995; Niosi, 1999). In terms of business coordination, firms in competitive market economies are more likely to engage in arm's-length transactions and to hold adversarial relationships with customers and suppliers. This is a story well told in transaction costs economics (Williamson, 1975, 1985). It is interesting, however, that there are still substantial variations in these business coordination and control mechanisms even among competitive economies in the world today (Hamilton and Feenstra, 1995; Biggart and Guillén, 1999; Feenstra *et al.*, 1999; Guillén, 2001a; Yeung, 2002a). In countries where the ownership and control of firms are more interconnected, firms cooperate as well as compete and are able to share risks with financial partners, it becomes highly difficult and problematic to define precisely the boundaries of firms (or hierarchies) and markets. This apparently disorganized institutional structuring of markets and hierarchies (e.g. in Europe) contrasts strongly with their counterparts from the Anglo-American world (Whitley, 1999). In other economies that are significantly dominated by state involvement, business coordination and control evolve through the forms of business groups, conglomerates and networks (Granovetter, 1995; Shiba and Shimotami, 1996; Keister, 2000; Carney and Gedajlovic, 2002b, 2003). These organizational forms and processes are characterized by cooperative relationships with customers and suppliers based on trust and social ties.

Third, different configurations of home-country institutional arrangements have important implications for intra-firm management and/or entrepreneurial processes. The institutionalization of capital markets in the US, for example, has put tremendous pressure on top management to seek short-term returns and to practise finance-centred corporate strategies (Shleifer and Vishny, 1997). Under this form of capital market discipline, strategic management tends to be much tighter in resource allocation within the firm. Long-term investments in productive and/or innovative activities may be discouraged. Financial management becomes the primary instrument of intra-firm management in most American companies. In contrast, in countries practising cooperative capitalism, stable and enduring relationships between banks, firms and the state encourage strategic behaviour and long-term investments by corporate managers. More resources can be devoted to those activities that promise to generate returns. Intra-firm management is less based on financial returns *per se* and more managerial autonomy is granted except during financial (or other) crises.

Fourth, enduring patterns of institutional arrangements in some countries may shape work and employment relations (capital-labour relations) so as to have serious implications for entrepreneurship. Sociological models of ethnic entrepreneurship (misfit and disadvantage models) are highly powerful in their explanations of the structural outcome of entrepreneurial activities among ethnic immigrants and groups in the host countries (Yeung, 2002c). Work and employment relations here refer to the extent and mode of owner control, the delegation of work control to skilled workers and the location of organizational segmentation boundaries (Whitley, 1999). In the case of the UK, this segmentation occurs primarily between generalist top managers and managerial specialists as well as between skilled maintenance workers and unskilled operatives (Braverman, 1974; Thompson, 1989). In the US, it remains concentrated between college-educated managers and manual workers. In Japan, it occurs between male, core employees and female, temporary workers, as well as between large firms and their subcontractors. In addition, the extent of organizational integration of employees and long-term interdependence between employers and employees has been used to explain variations in private and corporate entrepreneurship and business culture (Tiessen, 1997; Daly, 1998).

Existing configurations of Chinese capitalism: towards structural instability?

The nature of different business systems in Asia has already received much attention in the literature.[3] In the case of Chinese capitalism, the different institutional structures of the host economies have contributed to the various configurations of economic organization summarized in Table 2.1 (Yeung, 2000f). Here the focus is on three core characteristics in the existing configurations of Chinese capitalism: the formation of intra- and inter-firm business networks, the reliance on family relationships and strong state-business relations. As will be argued below, these three dimensions of Chinese capitalism have been significantly reconfigured through the participation of key actors in globalization. Family firms, for example, are the archetypal example of Chinese capitalism in Hong Kong. Their origins are complex, but can be broadly linked to cultural factors (Wong, 1988; Wang and Wong, 1997; Chiu, 1998) as well as colonial state practices. With hindsight, the latter factor is perhaps most critical, because the bias of the colonial government in Hong Kong against ethnic Chinese capital, particularly in the industrial sector, provided the institutional condition for the emergence of networks of small and medium-sized family-controlled firms (Table 2.1). These Chinese family firms could not

Table 2.1 Institutional and ideological structures of selected Asian economies with a significant presence of ethnic Chinese

	China	Hong Kong	Taiwan
Institutional structures			
Political institutions	• communism: one-party rule • strong state planning and control • limited political reforms • member of APEC	• liberal state, limited democracy • efficient civil service • limited state influence in the economy • member of APEC	• developmental democracy: authoritarian control until the early 1990s • strong bureaucracy, a legacy of Japanese colonial influence • significant influence of business families in politics • limited participation in international relations
Economic institutions	• declining state-owned enterprises (SoEs) • rapid growth of town and village enterprises (TVEs) • strong reliance on *guanxi* or personal relations in economic exchange • limited labour movements	• family-based corporate organization • networks of small- and medium-sized firms • strong interpersonal relationships and business networks • limited labour movements	• family-based corporate organization intertwined with giant state-sponsored national champions • strong networks of SMEs • strong interpersonal relationships and business networks • limited labour movements
Dominant economic ideology	• socialism	• free-enterprise liberalism • familism	• familism • developmentalism

Changes since the 1990s	• economic reform towards more market-based system • more economic liberalization • limited impact of the 1997–8 crisis • recent opening of western regions	• rapid integration into the Chinese economy • reversion to Chinese rule in 1997 • limited direct election of chief executive • growing state intervention • badly hurt by the 1997–8 crisis	• increasing democratization • less state influence in large business • rise of pro-independence movements and antagonism with China • stock market crash in the mid-1990s and devaluation of the New Taiwan dollar • unscathed by the 1997–8 crisis
Industrial structures and firm strategies **Direct investment**	• limited outward FDI by SOEs • largest recipient of FDI among developing economies and top three globally • large inflows of FDI by ethnic Chinese in Asia	• extensive outward FDI: China and Southeast Asia • large inward FDI: mainly in service industries • launch-pad for FDI into China	• limited outward FDI until relaxation during the mid-1980s • large FDI presence in China, particularly Fujian and Guangdong provinces • some inward FDI in R&D-intensive sectors
Intra-firm trade	• limited: export-oriented production • restrictions on local sales of foreign firms	• limited within Hong Kong • large among firms with outward-processing arrangements in China • Hong Kong as the major transshipment point for China trade	• moderate • well-developed and integrated production networks in some high-tech industries, e.g. electronics

continued

Table 2.1 continued

	China	Hong Kong	Taiwan
R&D	• low, but recent growth • historical concentration in military and heavy industries • strong influence of foreign firms	• low, despite recent emphasis • product adaptation • customer-based innovation • strong managerial knowledge	• high in key sectors, e.g. electronics • product adaptation • customer-based innovation • world leader in PCs, semiconductors, shoes
Corporate governance	• long-term shareholding by state institutions at various levels • managers appointed by the state and the party • introduction of the responsibility system	• long-term shareholding • risk-seeking, financial-centred strategies • control within family members • constrained by family ideology • strong influence of capital markets	• long-term shareholding • control within family members • constrained by family ideology • more reliance on network capital
Corporate financing	• state funding: importance of off-budget financing • recent rise in bank and private funding • limited capital markets • highly price-sensitive	• diversified funding from personal networks and capital markets (local and international) • capital from international bond and equity markets • high price sensitivity	• diversified, network funding • high price sensitivity
Industrial structure	• large SOEs, but declining in number and output • rapid growth of TVEs: mostly small and medium-sized • large contribution from export-oriented industries; mostly foreign-funded firms • large presence of the agricultural sector • highly concentrated industrial development in coastal provinces • large pool of surplus labour	• powerful influence of a few business families • reliance on financial services and property development • large presence of SMEs • highly flexible production systems • massive hollowing out of labour-intensive manufacturing, mainly to China • segmented and unsaturated labour markets	• large presence of SMEs • highly flexible production systems • massive hollowing out of labour-intensive manufacturing, mainly to China • saturated skilled-labour markets

Institutional structures

	Singapore	Indonesia	Malaysia	Thailand
Political institutions	• developmental democracy: domination of the People's Action Party • strong bureaucracy • reciprocal consent between state and foreign firms • member of APEC and ASEAN	• authoritarian state until election of Democratic Party-Perjuangan in 1999 • weak bureaucracy, but dense state regulation • strong influence of the military • member of APEC and ASEAN	• social democracy: domination of the UMNO • weak bureaucracy • ethnicity-biased political system • constitutional monarchy • member of APEC and ASEAN	• constitutional democracy: unstable coalition • weak bureaucracy, but dense state regulation • strong influence of the military • member of APEC and ASEAN
Economic institutions	• large presence of government-linked companies (GLCs) and statutory boards • very well-developed capital and financial markets • strong presence of foreign firms in major sectors • state-sanctioned labour movements	• economic organization based on ethnicity • state involvement in *pribumi* firms • strong patron–client relationships • some powerful Chinese family groups • limited labour movements	• economic organization based on ethnicity • state involvement in *bumiputra* firms • strong patron–client relationships • certain domestic markets nationalized: petroleum and automobile • limited labour movements	• economic organization based on nationalism • limited state involvement in national firms • strong patron–client relationships • limited labour movements
Dominant economic ideology	• developmentalism • survivalism	• ethnicity-biased and nationalistic developmentalism	• ethnicity-biased developmentalism	• nationalism

continued

Table 2.1 continued

	Singapore	Indonesia	Malaysia	Thailand
Changes since the 1990s	• more consultative-style of governance • high-tech and high value-added development strategies • massive state-directed programme to internationalize domestic firms • limited impact of the 1997–8 crisis on the manufacturing sector	• continual concentration in resource extraction and labour-intensive industries • large-scale liberalization and deregulation of foreign borrowing • massive property boom • badly hurt by the 1997–8 crisis: IMF assistance needed	• large-scale state projects, e.g.Multimedia Super Corridor • more opening of the economy to FDI • emergence as a major manufacturing centre in some industries, e.g. electronics • badly hurt by the 1997–8 crisis due to large domestic debt	• emergence as a major manufacturing centre in some industries, e.g. electronics and automobile assembly • large-scale liberalization and deregulation of foreign borrowing • massive property boom • badly hurt by the 1997–8 crisis: IMF assistance needed
Industrial structures and firm strategies Direct investment	• limited outward until the early 1990s (regionalization programme) • concentration of outward FDI: Malaysia and, recently, China. • high dependence on inward FDI	• limited outward FDI by ethnic Chinese • severe competition from inward FDI in some industries	• limited outward FDI by ethnic Chinese • large inward FDI among LDCs: historical influence of UK and recent favour of Japan	• limited outward FDI by ethnic Chinese • severe competition from inward FDI in some industries

Intra-firm trade	• limited among domestic firms • very high among foreign firms in Southeast Asia • limited local linkages of foreign firms	• limited among both domestic and foreign firms	• large among foreign-controlled regional production networks	• large among foreign-controlled regional production networks
R&D	• low until the 1990s, steady growth • high-tech in a few key sectors: electronics, chemicals and, recently, biomedical sciences	• low	• low, but recent growth	• low
Corporate governance	• stable shareholders, particularly GLCs • top management of GLCs from professionals and former civil servants • some influence of capital markets	• state/*pribumi* firms: important role of ethnicity and political connections • Chinese firms: control within family members and constrained by family ideology	• state/*bumiputra* firms: important role of ethnicity and political connections • Chinese firms: control within family members and constrained by family ideology	• Thai firms: important role of ethnicity and political connections • Chinese firms: control within family members and constrained by family ideology
Corporate financing	• diversified, global funding • capital from influential state holding company • high price sensitivity	• state/*pribumi* firms: reliance on government projects and funding • Chinese firms: reliance on family sources and capital markets • high price sensitivity	• state/*bumiputra* firms: reliance on government projects and funding • Chinese firms: reliance on family sources and capital markets • high price sensitivity	• Thai firms: reliance on government projects and funding • Chinese firms: reliance on family sources and capital markets • high price sensitivity

continued

Table 2.1 continued

	Singapore	Indonesia	Malaysia	Thailand
Industrial structure	• domination of foreign firms and GLCs in most sectors • weak SMEs • reliance on financial services and electronics • segmented and saturated skilled-labour markets	• domination of Chinese firms in SMEs • reliance on labour-intensive industries • large presence of agricultural sector in certain commodities, e.g. pulp and paper and forestry products • large pool of surplus labour	• domination of Chinese firms in SMEs • national firms in strategic sectors • reliance on labour-intensive industries • large presence of the agricultural sector in certain commodities, e.g. palm oil and rubber • saturated labour markets	• large presence of SMEs • reliance on labour-intensive industries • large presence of the agricultural sector, e.g. rice cultivation • large pool of surplus labour

rely upon state support and had to resort to family and business networks for capital, labour and other critical resources to support flexible production arrangements (Sit and Wong, 1989; Chiu *et al.*, 1997; Eng, 1997; Enright *et al.*, 1997; Yeung, 2000b; 2002a).

The role of the state and its apparatus in shaping economic institutions in Asia is also critical. This perspective originates from the literature on the developmental state that first made its impact in development studies during the early 1980s (Johnson, 1982, 1995; Deyo, 1987; Amsden, 1989; Wade, 1990; Ungson *et al.*, 1997). In much of this literature the empirical focus is on how the state in Japan and several of the Asian newly industrialized economies (South Korea, Singapore and Taiwan) have actively and directly shaped national developmental trajectories through the establishment of economic planning agencies, the pursuit of strategic industrial policy and the promotion of 'national champions'. These champions are private firms in highly promising industries and export-oriented sectors. They are strongly encouraged by the state through loans, grants and subsidies, monopoly rights, tax holidays and import protection. The inevitable outcome of the strong involvement of the state in industrial development is the formation of strong state-business relations. In Taiwan (see Table 2.1) the state-business relationship is evolving from a family-centred industrial organization to one in which large firms have much better access to state resources and subsidies (see Mathews, 1997, and Mathews and Cho, 1998 for a case of the semiconductor industry). Faced with the lack of competitiveness vis-à-vis large firms, small and medium-sized Taiwanese firms have to leverage their strategic advantages of flexibility and adaptability through informal networks and subcontracting relationships (Chow, 2002). Some of these small firms have even brought their networks across national borders into mainland China (Hsing, 1998) and Southeast Asia (T.-J. Chen, 1998). Buck (2000) examined the growth, disintegration and decentralization of Taiwan's industrial networks in the context of the state-led land reform programme, redistributive agricultural policies and conservative financial policies since the mid-1960s. He argued that the rapid proliferation of small-firm networks in Taiwan was driven by the contingent actions of rural household entrepreneurs that culminated in tremendous rural industrialization, a phenomenon commonly found in mainland China today (Lin, 1997; W. Chen, 1998; Marton, 2000). These industrial and business networks organized by small and medium-sized firms are thus the unintended consequences of state policies rather than a creation by state-led development (Hsu and Cheng, 2002).

The case of Singapore (see Table 2.1) points to a radically different empirical situation in which the developmental state has actively developed the island economy into a major node in the global spaces of flows (Rodan, 1989; Huff, 1994; Perry *et al.*, 1997; Low, 1998; Yeung and Olds, 1998; Yeung, 2002a). Instead of developing industrial networks constituted exclusively of local firms, the state favours the development and deepening of global-local linkages through which Singapore can gain from the influx of foreign high-tech investments, and these global corporations can benefit from Singapore's evolving local supplier networks (for a case study of Singapore's electronics industry see Perry and Tan, 1998; Chew and Yeung, 2001). The state is also highly active in developing an external wing for the national economy through the regionalization of domestic firms (Yeung, 1998d, 1999a, 2002a; see also Chapter 4). This process of outward orientation of the national economy has again been spearheaded by statutory boards and government-linked companies. The unique configuration of state-business relationships in Singapore provides an institutional foundation for the emergence of a business system significantly different from its typical counterparts in other economies of Chinese capitalism (e.g. Hong Kong and Taiwan).

In other Southeast Asian countries, it appears that political-economic alliances based on patron–client relationships have taken precedence over state-driven industrial and business networks in these still developing economies (see Table 2.1). This preference for political connections is particularly important in the context of the state's ethnic-biased redistributive economic policies through which indigenous capitalists (known as *pribumi* in Indonesia and *bumiputra* in Malaysia) have been given special rights and privileges. An unfortunate outcome is the rise of so-called ersatz capitalism in these Southeast Asian economies (Yoshihara, 1988; McVey, 1992; Brown, 2000; Yeung, 1999b; 2000c). Here Chinese capitalism is embedded in the political-economic alliances of the host Southeast Asian economies. Whereas some ethnic Chinese have consolidated and strengthened their intra-ethnic group networks to overcome hostile business and institutional constraints in the host countries, other more pragmatic ethnic Chinese have engaged in patron–client relationships with indigenous Southeast Asian capitalists (see Gomez, 1999 for the case of Malaysia). This process of network juxtaposition has resulted in a hybrid network structure in Southeast Asia comprising both family networks and political-economic alliances. Still, other ethnic Chinese have chosen an exit strategy by internationalizing their business operations in other parts of Asia and beyond (see Chapter 3). In their internationalization processes, these ethnic Chinese from Southeast Asia have once again leveraged their transnational networks of personal and business relationships (Yeung, 1998e, 1999c; Yeung and Olds, 2000a).

To sum up, the existing configurations of Chinese capitalism are characterized by the formation of intra-firm networks through vertical and horizontal integration and inter-firm networks through embeddedness in social and business relationships. While cultural affinity and historical legacies may partially explain some of these complex network relationships among social actors and firms, national institutional structures are also important mechanisms for the (re)production of these distinctive modes of economic organization in Chinese capitalism. In most Asian countries, these national institutional structures have been actively shaped by the developmental policies of nation-states and, in some cases (e.g. Hong Kong), by their colonial predecessors. In a globalizing era in which the nation-state has allegedly been made increasingly powerless (Weiss, 1998), one wonders whether globalization is fundamentally reshaping the institutional foundations of Chinese capitalism.

Globalizing actor-networks and the reconfiguring of Chinese capitalism

A key driving force behind the ongoing process of economic globalization is the internationalization of capital and firms and the rapid diffusion of authority to an array of non-state and supra-state agents (Sassen, 1996, 1999; Strange, 1996). Together, they make up the increasingly powerful international business and finance sphere. For example, capital, in its portfolio and direct investment forms, plays a much more significant role in global economic integration today. To some observers (e.g. Ohmae, 1990, 1995; O'Brien, 1992), the rise of stateless capital has become a defining characteristic of contemporary global capitalism where financial capital shapes business practices and organizations through market discipline. An increasingly integrated, digitized and securitized global financial system is decoupling and disembedding from the global production system (Helleiner, 1994). With capital and money markets separated from industry, 'money has been commodified' (Martin, 1994: 255) and given stealth-like qualities. Other observers of the global financial system argue, however, that money, the international financial system and international financial centres have simply been '"detraditionalized" over the last 30 years or so . . . because of the breakdown of state authority and its replacement by more diffuse sources of governance', such as international credit rating agencies (Thrift and Leyshon, 1994: 301). This detraditionalization is accentuated by the enormous task of understanding, managing and communicating about global economic change in a more reflexive manner. This is a style of understanding, managing and communicating that draws a broader array of actors into playing a significant (albeit variable) role in materially and discursively constructing the multiple economic systems that make up the global economy (Thrift, 1996, 2000). The governance (in the broadest sense) of the global economic system, therefore, depends not only on the activities of the nation-state, but increasingly on actors in the international business sphere (economists representing credit rating agencies, security analysts representing investment banks, business reporters representing the international business media industry and officials representing supra-state institutions like the International Monetary Fund). These are actors who govern through intermediaries including technology, texts, the visual media, other humans and money itself. Taken together, such actors, their institutions and their intermediaries generate heterogeneous network relations that could be deemed actor-networks (Law, 1994; Thrift and Leyshon, 1994; Law and Hassard, 1999; Dicken *et al.*, 2001). Actor-networks are thus simultaneously 'an actor whose activity is networking heterogeneous elements' of humans and non-humans, and 'a network that is able to redefine and transform what it is made of' (Callon, 1987: 93).

Here the underlying processes that drive key actors in Chinese capitalism to engage with actor-networks associated with the international business and finance sphere, what I call 'globalizing actor-networks', are examined. I argue that although familism and *guanxi* relationships continue to provide the institutional foundations of Chinese capitalism (even in large listed conglomerates), the concept of 'Chinese'[4] business networks needs to be reconfigured to recognize the enhanced constitutive nature of a range of non-Chinese actor-networks. This is because globalizing actor-networks play fundamental (albeit uneven) roles in (re)shaping the social organization and business practices of Chinese capitalism and in particular the practices of large Chinese conglomerates. Although I recognize that the majority of Chinese firms are small family-owned enterprises that are not listed on various stock exchanges, it is important to focus on large Chinese business conglomerates (that have listed arms) and their lead firms because they play an increasingly powerful role in spurring on development processes in the Asia-Pacific (including regionalization), in acting as catalysts for smaller Chinese family firms that may be linked into these conglomerate-driven production and financial networks and in acting as key sources of capitalization in major Asian stock markets. In short, these large ethnic Chinese conglomerates constitute and are capable of (re)shaping the very institutional foundations of Chinese capitalism itself.

My argument is underscored by both globalization tendencies (e.g. the globalization of both capital and knowledge about capital) and the changing nature of Chinese capitalism (to be analysed in Chapters 3–6), for instance the internationalization of leading Chinese firms, their interactions with non-Chinese actors, the professionalization of Chinese firms and the issue of family succession. The increasing linkages and interconnections that are formed with non-Chinese actor-networks also underlie the dynamics of some of the most powerful Chinese firms in a globalizing era (see Chapter 1, especially Tables 1.5 and 1.6). These linkages and interconnections can provide new sources of competitive advantage for large Chinese firms in the global economy, while also enhancing risk and generating new forms of interdependencies.[5] In taking such an actor-network perspective, this book should contribute to the evolving literature on Chinese capitalism (and Asian and ethnic capitalism more generally) in two main ways. First, the relational perspective underpinning this book has the potential to enhance our understanding of the changing forms and capacities of Chinese capitalism, because the focus is on the actor-networks that shape Chinese capitalism. Chinese capitalism is thus not treated as 'the carriers of events but rather as a set of *effects* arising from a whole complex of network relations' (Thrift, 1996: 24, original italics; see also Emirbayer, 1997; Dicken *et al.*, 2001). In other words, Chinese capitalism is a 'process' before it becomes hybridized as a 'result' (Callon, 1986: 224). Such a relational perspective on Chinese capitalism as a form of hybrid capitalism draws us away from the more traditional concern with Chinese capitalism in its distinctive cultural contexts (see Chapter 1). Actors in Chinese capitalism, through their engagement with a variety of powerful globalizing actor-networks, are exhibiting more complex identities and orientations; these are multiple identities increasingly shaped by the forces of globalization. This perspective complements a variety of non-essentialist approaches to Chinese identity at the individual and the group level (Nathan, 1993; Dirlik, 1997; Nonini and Ong, 1997; Olds, 2001; Yao, 2002). However, it is important to reinforce the point that in the process of engaging with globalizing actor-networks, actors in Chinese capitalism also contribute to reshaping the nature of global capitalism.

Second, the issue of enhanced geographical scale in our understanding of Chinese capitalism is addressed. Historically, ethnic Chinese business in Southeast Asia was predominantly confined to local and regional scales of operations, whether they were large conglomerates or small family firms. Sources of operational capital for such firms were derived from actors and institutions from within the region for the most part, actors and institutions that tended to be of the same (or similar) ethnic background (Brown, 1995a; Hodder, 1996; Brook and Luong, 1997; Yeung, 2003a). In short, Chinese capitalism was bounded by the socio-geographical specificities in which it was embedded. Such specificities also included institutional constraints (in places like Indonesia and Malaysia) and unique state-business relationships (in places like Singapore and Taiwan). Today, however, virtually all large ethnic Chinese business conglomerates have widened and deepened their geographical scales of operations and their sources of operational capital in particular. They are expanding their operations and networks across national boundaries and are drawing on resources from global equity and bond markets via the process of public listing, offering and placement. This process of internationalization leads to the enrolment of Chinese business groups into diverse and overlapping non-Chinese actor-networks that span the globe, linking Chinese firms based on the Asia-Pacific area to such global cities as New York, London, Tokyo and Washington, DC. Their incorporation into globalizing actor-networks facilitates the reshaping of Chinese capitalism, lessening its distinctive Chinese character in an organizational and structural sense, though often (and somewhat ironically) consolidating its Chinese character in a discursive sense (Dirlik, 1997; Ong and Nonini, 1997a; Yang,

2002). The remainder of this section develops some conceptual tools for analysing the changing configurations and hybridization of Chinese capitalism in a global era. I focus on the emergence of multiple flows and networks amongst increasingly interdependent actors, groups and institutions. I examine the role of three forms of globalizing actor-networks (the international business media, international finance and multilateral agencies) in the material and discursive reconstitution of Chinese capitalism. The aim of such an endeavour is to develop a broader (and hopefully less essentialist) understanding of a form of hybrid capitalism that has received significant attention from academics, businesspeople and policy-makers since 1980 (see Chapter 1).

Despite the claims of the varieties of capitalism approach and the business systems approach, it is fair to recognize that there are indeed significant transformations in the institutional governance and organizational structures of the global economy today. Even though it may not fundamentally reconfigure capitalist business systems, globalization has at least made apparent multiple possibilities and opportunities through actors' enrolment and participation. This increasing awareness of and involvement in globalization is particularly important for key actors and elites in Chinese capitalism who are being enrolled into globalizing actor-networks and thereby are connected as actors and through practices in drastically different modes of capitalist economic organization. From an evolutionary perspective, these emerging changes can lead to dynamic changes in the social organization and institutional structures of a particular mode of capitalism, if the equilibrium of existing parameters is punctuated by sudden and unexpected events. In the case of Chinese capitalism under globalization, certain emerging changes at the level of key actors may disrupt the equilibrium of its business systems. This punctuated equilibrium of Chinese capitalism has been particularly apparent during and after the 1997–8 Asian economic crisis (see also Baer *et al.*, 1999; Henderson, 1999; Yeung, 1999b, 2000a, 2000c). Ethnic Chinese actors are defined as political, social or business elites who are capable of effecting institutional changes at a very high level – often national. In Figure 1.2 there are at least three interrelated mechanisms through which this enrolment in globalizing actor-networks becomes possible: first, engaging with international business actor-networks; second, gathering knowledge and experience through international educational institutions; and third, connecting with international organizations and multilateral institutions. Although these mechanisms are by no means equal in their theoretical and practical importance, it is hard to ascertain empirically their relative importance. I believe that the first mechanism is particularly relevant to the strategic behaviour of Chinese firms, whereas the remaining two mechanisms are important to ethnic Chinese elites in gaining access to knowledge elsewhere and in legitimizing their economic power and dominance in their 'home' economies.

Engaging international business actor-networks

The emergence of Asia as a major global economic powerhouse is linked to both the globalization of non-Asian firms in Asia and the globalization of Asian firms in non-Asian host economies. Whitley (1996, 1998, 1999) argued that the consequences of these globalization tendencies for capitalist business systems and firms are limited, although he provided no convincing empirical evidence beyond some a priori and stringent theoretical conditions. He outlined the following six major and necessary conditions if the internationalization of East Asian firms were to change the distinctive characteristics of their home-country business systems (Whitley, 1999: 189).

1   A high proportion, probably over a half, of their key assets, employees and sources of profits would have to be located abroad.
2   These overseas assets would have to be concentrated in host-economy contexts both very different from their domestic ones and highly similar to each other.
3   These host economies would need to be politically, economically and technologically at least as advanced and powerful as their home economies.
4   The host business systems would have to be as cohesive and integrated in their characteristics as the postwar East Asian ones, and to be as closely connected to equally integrated and mutually reinforcing societal institutions.
5   These East Asian firms would need to integrate their overseas operations tightly with domestic ones so that, when adapting to foreign institutions, the changes influence how they do business at home.
6   Any changes that internationalizing firms may implement as a result of their overseas commitments would be largely peripheral to their core characteristics, which are closely associated with dominant institutions and interest groups in their domestic economies.

As anyone might imagine, these conditions are not only very stringent, but also extremely difficult to be substantiated empirically. Without providing this evidence, Whitley (1999: 183) merely asserted that 'it is not at all clear that the growth of outward FDI by East Asian firms, and of intra-regional trade, has been sufficient to meet the conditions required for large-scale transformations of prevalent business systems'. As this book demonstrates, it is by no means clear that these alleged limited effects of globalization do not represent a long-term process associated with the changing dynamics of Asian business systems in general and Chinese capitalism in particular. The two-way globalization of firms between Asia and other regions implies that key actors in Chinese capitalism are compelled to learn new management and business practices from their competitors, suppliers, customers and so on. At the same time, these same actors need to undo some of their previous learning and practices in order to compete effectively against foreign competitors in Asia as well as in their home turfs (i.e. North America and Western Europe). It is true that business contacts between East and West occurred long before, e.g. during Meiji Japan in the late nineteenth century (Westney, 1987; Hamilton, 1997) and during the early modernization of mainland China at the turn of the twentieth century (Godley, 1981). But the sheer scale, scope and speed of these contacts today make them highly influential in the changing dynamics of Chinese capitalism.

The process of organizational learning through international business actor-networks occurs in several ways. First, ethnic Chinese actors may appoint non-Asian actors to manage their diverse operations both in Asia and in host countries outside Asia. These global managers often have significant experience in managing transnational operations in national economies embedded in different business systems. Their involvement in leading Chinese firms may reshape the norms and practices in these organizations. Hong Kong's Li Ka-shing, for example, has a track record for appointing non-Asian managers to top executive positions in his flagship company, Hutchison Whampoa, that was ranked the top TNC from emerging economies and the top 14th TNC in the world in 2000 (see Table 1.5). Olds (2001: 65) documented that two former managing directors of Hutchison Whampoa were British expatriates: John Richardson (chairman: 1980–4) and Simon Murray (1984–94). They subsequently joined Barclays Bank and Deutsche Bank as their heads of Asia-Pacific affairs for an obvious reason: their extremely deep knowledge of and embedded relationships with leading actors in Chinese capitalism. Ethnic Chinese actors may also pick up new organizational knowledge and practices in non-Asian host countries through transnational operations (e.g. see Mathews and Snow, 1998; Mathews, 2002 for the case of Taiwan's Acer Group). Such knowledge and practices can originate from their intensive interaction with customers and suppliers in the host countries or from their previous employment in foreign firms. Actor-networks are formed between ethnic Chinese actors and their customers, suppliers and competitors on a global scale, facilitating interpersonal information and knowledge flows and organizational adaptation. Examining the international human resource management practices of Singapore companies in mainland China, for example, Tsang (1999a, 1999b, 2002) found that expatriation has an important function of knowledge transfer and training. Similarly Guthrie (1999: 5) in his sociological study of mainland China's transitional economy, observed that '[c]ontact with foreign firms, via joint ventures, and the feeling of being set adrift by the central government – and thus the need to mimic firms from developed market economies – predict which firms will adopt Western practices'. Mainland Chinese firms are increasingly adopting Anglo-American economic and management practices 'not for reasons of efficiency but for reasons of legitimacy' (p. 6).

Second, globalizing actor-networks in international finance represents one of the most influential mechanisms for effecting dynamic changes in Chinese capitalism. Even proponents of enduring national business systems have recognized this influence:

> The effects of internationalizing financial flows on business-system characteristics could be considerable under certain conditions. If, for instance, most of the leading firms in credit-based financial systems were to raise the bulk of their external finance from international capital markets instead of relying on their usual business partners, this could alter the strategic priorities of these firms and eventually affect the nature of their domestic business system.
>
> (Whitley, 1999: 129)

This is indeed happening in Chinese capitalism, a mode of hybrid capitalism that does not stay inside particular national boundaries and is not bound by particular national legal and financial systems (see Chapter 1). In the context of financial globalization and the desire to access large-scale flows of capital to fund development projects, many of the largest Chinese conglomerates in Asia are faced with new challenges. Indeed, the goal of securing new forms of financial resources represents one of the most critical factors that lead to the reshaping of Chinese capitalism. An increasing number of ethnic Chinese firms are now seeking capital resources beyond their immediate social and ethnic networks to finance their development objectives. Gordon Wu of Hong Kong's Hopewell Holdings, for example, spent much of the first half of the 1990s trying to raise capital in financial markets in London, New York and Tokyo to finance his mega-infrastructure projects in China, Indonesia and Thailand (*Far Eastern Economic Review*, 9 December 1993: 71–2). By 1994, his efforts to woo global investors had finally paid off when he successfully raised US$776 million by spinning off his power plants in Asia into a new company, Consolidated Electric Power Asia (Clifford and Engardio, 2000: 58). Olds (2001: 119) reported that, through the sharing of important information and contacts and the formation of joint ventures, Hong Kong's Li Ka-shing had developed long-term relations with such global investors as Paul Reichmann, Rupert Murdoch, George Soros and the Bronfman family. Reducing the reliance on internal (predominantly ethnic) capital within Chinese capitalism is attractive in an era of global competition where investment outlays are becoming significantly larger and financial leverages have become the norm in most competitive industries. The threats of hostile takeovers and acquisitions in deregulated Asian markets have also forced Chinese firms to secure external finance to strengthen their financial positions (see more detailed empirical analysis in Chapters 5 and 6).

This shift from informal networks of credits and loans towards stock and capital markets in financing Chinese capitalism is not a recent phenomenon, though its extent has been significantly underestimated in the literature (see Chapter 1). Examining the consolidated balance sheets of Hong Leong (Malaysia and Singapore), Tan Kah-kee, Yeo Hiap Seng and Bangkok Bank, Brown (2000: 30) estimated that:

> Before 1945, [these] Chinese firms relied on retained earnings and profits for more than 60 per cent of their total finance, with bank loans accounting for a further third. After 1960, stocks accounted for a third of the total finance and dependence on retained earnings fell to less than 40 per cent.

She also found that Thailand's CP Group has increasingly used capital markets and offshore banks for financing.

> In the early years, more than half of CP's working capital was borrowed from banks. In 1991 this amounted to US$33.3 billion but then fell in the next year to US$16.4 billion. The decline was a consequence of increased exploitation of the stock market and of the restructuring of subsidiaries to accumulate capital. The profits accumulated through speculation on the stock market and on real estate also provided long term finance between 1992 and 1996.
>
> (Brown, 2000: 158)

CP also issued corporate bonds and syndicated loans for its infrastructural projects. It floated US$1 billion bonds in the US in October 1992 and launched the Far East Fund in Japan in November 1993 to raise another US$1 billion (Brown, 2000: 157–8). In February 1994 CP launched another issue of US$150 million floating rate notes to finance its agribusiness in China. The issue was secured in Luxembourg and guaranteed by a consortium including Standard Chartered Asia and NatWest Markets (Brown, 2000: 237).

For those ethnic Chinese firms and/or countries in search of financial resources from outside their 'home' economies and/or regions, it is important to secure the consent and recognition from global financiers for comparable standards of corporate governance and return to investments. These global financiers are leading bankers, fund managers, brokers and so on, who are often based in major global cities that in turn serve as their command-and-control centres of global investments (Sassen, 1991). The successful enrolment of ethnic Chinese actors in these global financial actor-networks is imperative in an era of more intensified competition, greater financial requirements for expansion and investments, and higher risks associated with excessive reliance on domestic finance. Revisiting the example of John Richardson, the former chairman of Li Ka-shing's Hutchison Whampoa during 1980–4, he subsequently worked for Barclays Bank and BZW to manage their Asia-Pacific portfolios. As Richardson recalled, these global financial houses often suffered from the 'tyranny of distance' in the sense that they were afraid of making large commitments to unfamiliar regions. In January 1995 Barclays was the lead arranger for a HK$2.4 billion syndicated loan (originally planned at HK$1.5 billion) to Henderson Land, the flagship property development company of a prominent Chinese family firm from Hong Kong founded by Lee Shau-kee (see Table 1.6). Richardson recalled how he had managed to convince the London office to arrange for the syndicated loan, thereby effectively connecting Lee to Barclays' actor-networks in global finance:

> I have known Lee Shau Kee for 20 years. London was cautious, but I told them: 'If we can't do a deal with this guy then we can't do business in Asia'. That's where I see my role: trying to steer us on a sensible course. Happily London supported us.
>
> (Quoted in Olds, 2001: 65)

To ensure that global financial elites are comfortable with their financial positions and obligations, key actors in ethnic Chinese firms are required to follow certain accounting standards and business norms in global capital markets (see more empirical evidence in Chapter 6). As early as 1992, for example, Peter Woo, the successor to one of Hong Kong's most powerful Chinese family conglomerates, the Wharf Group, pronounced that '[t]here are no friends in finance. The world has changed. They [old style Chinese entrepreneurs] need to realize we are in a world market and need an international culture' (quoted in Clifford and Engardio, 2000: 70). He received his MBA from Columbia University (New York) and developed his early career in the Chase Manhattan Bank, so that his attitude to the traditional norms in Chinese capitalism is not entirely surprising. The necessity for securing global finance provides a key force to effect dynamic changes in Chinese capitalism. The 1997–8 Asian economic crisis has only made these changes even more apparent and necessary. Recent empirical studies in financial economics (Schmukler and Vesperoni, 2001; Mitton, 2002), for instance, identified significant positive relationships between improved corporate governance (e.g. establishing credible investor protection provisions and appointing Big Six auditors) and the lower cost of capital. The potential improvement in corporate governance is particularly welcome in developing economies in which many Chinese family firms thrive and shareholder protection and judicial efficiency are clearly inadequate. Klapper and Love (2002) found that good corporate governance mattered a lot more in countries with weak shareholder protection and poor judicial efficiency. Schmukler and Vesperoni (2001) also reported that firms from emerging economies could benefit from accessing international bond markets by securing long-term financing and extending their debt maturity structure (see a case study of Richard Li in Chapter 5).

Raising capital in international financial markets, however, requires ethnic Chinese (family) firms to become increasingly credible and transparent in their management practices and systems of financial control (as defined by the gatekeepers of the global financial system) (Ridding and Kynge, 1997). This pressure for credibility and legitimacy in corporate governance and organizational practices has also been exerted on foreign investment in mainland China. As described by Guthrie (1999: 174), 'investors situated in highly institutionalized (in a rational-legal sense) environments are pushing for institutions that make them comfortable with the prospect of investing in a developing system such as China's'. These new business practice standards prove to be some of the most daunting challenges to ethnic Chinese firms that have historically been pooling resources from other members in their ethnic-centred business networks, while remaining opaque to all but the closest of family members. The main tension is between losing personal or family control over knowledge and decision-making, and having access to substantial and perhaps cheaper financial resources via global equity and bond markets. While actor-networks centred in on cutting through finance, the media, credit ratings agencies, multilateral institutions and other fields (e.g. academia) all play a role in reshaping Chinese capitalism, it is important to recognize their uneven power relations. As Massey (1994: 148–9) pointed out in relation to the global space of flows, different actors need 'differentiating socially' as 'different social groups [and actor-networks] have distinct relationships to this anyway differentiated mobility: some people are more in charge of it than others; some initiate flows and movement, others don't; some are more on the receiving end of it than others; some are effectively imprisoned by it'. In terms of these uneven power relations vis-à-vis the reshaping of Chinese capitalism, the first group of actors representing international finance has the greatest capacity to exert power (see case studies in Chapter 5). Again, power in this sense is 'the ability to bind other actors and intermediaries into knowledge-producing networks' in a manner that leads to assent and adherence (Bridge, 1997: 619). For example, financial institutions can create a discourse of valid business practices (including transparency) that puts pressure on ethnic Chinese firms to enrol in their globalizing actor-networks, thereby generating assent and adherence.

There are different aspects to this exercise of power via globalizing actor-networks with an international finance dimension. Financial analysts may require specific forms of information before they can make a recommendation on whether to buy, hold or sell. Their capacity to make such decisions enrols ethnic Chinese firms in finance-directed actor-networks because these firms have little choice but to supply information on their operations. Moreover, finance-directed actor-networks are bound via telecommunications systems to global fund managers who make decisions about investing in global equity and bond markets. In a reciprocal manner, such a situation drives Chinese firms to enrol in these finance-directed actor-networks (so they have an opportunity to access this capital), just as it drives financial analysts to enrol in the actor-networks guided by ethnic Chinese firms (so analysts can access accurate and timely information). In both cases though, it is the finance-directed actor-network that has the 'the strongest powers of translation' because they effectively reshuffle 'other's interests and goals', while 'becoming indispensable such that others must flow through the practices established in the network' (Bridge, 1997: 620). In this case, ethnic Chinese firms become the others in this globalizing actor-network of international finance.

Third, this quest for global finance requires actors in Chinese capitalism to come to terms with actors in international media and research institutions on business activities. This is because today's global financial system is increasingly characterized by a broader array of actors beyond just bankers and financiers (Harmes, 1998). Actors in international media and research houses play an increasingly critical role in producing reflexively texts, information and knowledge about Chinese capitalism that can significantly hinder or facilitate ethnic Chinese actors' access to global finance (see case studies in Chapter 5). For example, top international financial newspapers (e.g. *The Financial Times* and *The Wall Street Journal*), magazines (e.g. *Fortune* and *Forbes*) and media (e.g. CNN and CNBC), credit-rating agencies (e.g. Moody's and Standard & Poor's), stockbroking firms and other research houses (e.g. Morgan Stanley) regularly produce reports on ethnic Chinese (family) firms (and, sometimes, their 'home' economies). The consumers of these texts are key actors in the global financial industry and international business, including investment bankers, fund managers, brokers and so on, along with a host of other economic and political elites in global cities. These agencies, as witnessed in Asia during the 1997–8 economic crisis, have the capacity to enrol nation-states and firms of all sizes in their actor-networks (Sassen, 1996; Olds and Yeung, 1999). They do this through their capacity to make what are perceived to be valid judgements, their inscription of these judgements in text and digital forms and the dissemination of this information throughout global financial networks on a near real-time basis. High credit ratings of Chinese firms, for example, allow them to issue project-specific bonds in international capital markets so that they can retain de facto control rather than diluting ownership via the issue of new shares in the stock markets.

The successful enticement of these global actors into making favourable assessments of ethnic Chinese firms in turn requires these Chinese actors to enrol themselves in globalizing actor-networks in international media and research activities. Not only are ethnic Chinese firms participating in producing such texts (and counter-texts) through setting up their own credit-rating firms, stockbroking houses and so on, some of them are also opening their doors to welcome global actors to inspect their operations. Such reciprocal processes of enrolment and enticement have major implications for the changing norms and practice of these ethnic Chinese firms and, perhaps eventually, the nature and organization of Chinese capitalism itself. Global flows of information demand a global media strategy. Chinese firms attempting to operate at a multitude of geographical scales increasingly seek to draw upon economic resources via global capital flows. They must therefore structure their activities to facilitate favourable business media coverage. Furthermore, this media coverage must be handled by a small number of elite translators of global economic knowledge (e.g. *Asiamoney, Euromoney* and *The Financial Times*). Developing a global media strategy is a practice subject to continual planning among Chinese business groups, though usually in association with trusted public relations firms that often have global appeal and experience. It is also dependent on nurturing effective social relations with key sources working in the global media sector. The formation of these relations is also a goal for representatives of global media since their business includes describing and analysing relevant information on the activities of highly capitalized ethnic Chinese firms.

Gathering knowledge and experience through international educational institutions

Another important trend in Chinese capitalism today is that most key actors have spent time during their educational life in institutions in North America, Western Europe and Australia. Most significantly, the globalization of business knowledge is linked to the emergence and domination of top business schools located in North America and Western Europe (Thrift, 1998, 1999; Wenger, 1998, 2000; Berger and Huntington, 2002). Key actors in Chinese family businesses now face the challenge of professionalizing their management and business practices (see Chapters 4–6). Other ethnic Chinese actors in non-family businesses are also active in organizational re-engineering and management restructuring to prepare for global competition. This process of professionalizing Chinese capitalism is driven by both internal and external factors. Internally, more patriarchs in Chinese family firms have allowed and encouraged their heir-apparent to be educated in top business schools abroad. Exposed to professional management training in these business schools, the eventual return of these successors to Chinese family businesses contributes to the changing dynamics of Chinese capitalism in two ways. Personal contacts and relationships developed by these successors abroad potentially widen the social and geographic scope of Chinese/Asian business networks when external non-Chinese members (often MBA classmates or former colleagues of sons and nephews) are brought or socialized into Chinese capitalism and its business networks. Key Chinese actors thus not only are enrolled in globalizing financial actor-networks with their friends and acquaintances from business schools, but also sometimes actively entice these actors into their own networks in Asia. This two-way process of enrolment and enticement infers that the concept of exclusive Chinese capitalism should be broadened to a larger degree to include non-family and non-Chinese members (see case studies in Chapters 4 and 5).

The return of professionally trained family heirs represents an important step towards the professionalization of Chinese family business. DiMaggio and Powell (1983: 152) have termed this process 'normative isomorphism' through which '[u]niversities and professional training institutions are important centers for the development of organizational norms among professional managers and their staff'. When the heir eventually takes over the family business, he/she is likely to adopt a much more open view towards the involvement of professionals in the management of the Chinese family firm (Fung, 1997; Magretta, 1998 for the case of Victor Fung from Hong Kong's Li & Fung). Well trained in top business schools elsewhere and often equipped with considerable international business and industry experience, these professional managers are key players in an emerging transnational community of business elites who are not only transferable in terms of their managerial skills, but also much more difficult to be controlled in the traditional Chinese way of work management. Sklair (2000) has coined the term 'transnational capitalist' to describe this group of highly powerful executives. As Whitley (1999: 97) noted, 'this mobility has become frequently based upon the possession of a general management credential such as the MBA degree ... [And] "management" is seen more as a generalizable set of skills and competences than as a set of industry-specific functions linked to more technical competences'. In many high-tech sectors in which ethnic Chinese actors are playing an increasingly important role, this professionalization of business practices and strategic management becomes even more pronounced (see Hsu and Saxenian, 2000 for the case of Taiwanese high-tech entrepreneurs). This professionalization of Chinese firms is certainly not the same phenomenon as predicted in the existing literature on Chinese family firms in which paternalism, nepotism, personalism and fragmentation are widely believed to be the key characteristics of their organizational rigidities (see the empirical analysis in Chapters 4 and 6). In post-reform mainland China, there is also strong evidence that new Chinese business elites are increasingly professional in their management mindsets and practices, although their cultural beliefs remain traditional. Yan (2002: 23–4) has referred to them as a new type of 'Confucian merchant', a term that implies that 'a businessperson is also a scholar who has mastered the essence of traditional Chinese culture, is devoted to the promotion of scholarship and cultural affairs, and maintains close ties with the political elite'.

Many Chinese family firms are driven to professionalize their businesses and networks because of severe problems with succession and the need to stay competitive. First-generation Chinese family firms are often fully controlled by the founders. Top decision-making is often directive, centred on the founder, rather than consensual among the corporate board members. Over time, however, at a certain stage of its expansion, the patriarch of the family firm becomes overloaded with information and decision-making responsibility. There may also be a shortage of able or competent family heirs to take over some corporate decision-making and responsibilities. As Fukuyama (1995: 64) argued, 'a single family, no matter how large, capable, or well educated, can only have so many competent sons, daughters, spouses, and siblings to oversee the different parts of a rapidly ramifying enterprise'. An inevitable result of this succession problem is that most of the large Chinese family businesses today are stacked with professional managers. A fund manager, for example, told *The Financial Times* that 'many of the people who actually run Robert Kuok's businesses are not linked to the family empire. Obviously he has to trust these lieutenants, but he is prepared to delegate' (5 March 1998). Instead of reproducing 'highly personal and direct control over work processes and limited employer-employee trust' (Whitley, 1999: 93), we begin to find more competent professional managers being socialized into Chinese capitalism such that over time they become insiders and movers in this reshaped form of hybrid capitalism. In Tsang's (2001) detailed case study of one Chinese family firm from Singapore, he found that a small team of mobile local executives in China was developed to resolve the problem of succession.

Another external factor reshaping 'Chinese' capitalism emerges from the nature of global competition itself. The global economy today is generating fiercer competition between firms and industries. Many of Asia's largest Chinese business conglomerates have built their empires in regulated or monopoly markets. Some of them have also benefited tremendously from rent-seeking behaviour during the early phase of development in many Southeast Asian countries (Yoshihara, 1988). Secure franchises, as with Robert Kuok's position in sugar and flour in Malaysia or Liem Sioe Liong's monopoly rights in cement and commodities in Indonesia, used to guarantee reliable profit streams and thus the disincentives to secure access to global finance. Recent deregulation in these Southeast Asian countries, however, has intensified competition and increased the pressure on profitability. To strengthen their competitiveness, some Chinese firms from Southeast Asia have internationalized into new markets and business fields (see Chapter 3). The stigmatization of Chinese entrepreneurs as essentially deal-makers seems increasingly outdated in an era of global competition. Citing Redding's (1990) work, however, Whitley (1999: 107) remained convinced that 'many Chinese family businesses diversify *only* into fields, such as property development, where dealing skills are more important than detailed technical knowledge of products and processes'. As shown in the case of Richard Li (second son of Hong Kong's Li Ka-shing) in Chapter 5, venturing into high-tech industries by members of leading Chinese family businesses is no longer a misnomer these days. In so doing, these Chinese entrepreneurs and/or technopreneurs depend as much on professional managers as their counterparts in Silicon Valley do. Other Chinese firms have also actively sought new management and financial resources. The change in the global business environment, for example, has rendered market conditions more competitive and shifted management skills away from those highly personalized relationships developed by their founders. One Hong Kong consultant was quoted as saying that 'the growth of the companies and sharper competition requires delegation, financial controls and man management [in Chinese capitalism]. It might well be that the founder is not best equipped to deal with this' (*The Financial Times*, 5 March 1998). As reported by two *Business Week* editors,

> If these businessmen needed technology, they knew they could buy it. If they needed expertise and management help, they could find a joint-venture partner or hire expatriate executives. If a company founder had no formal business schooling or couldn't speak English, the sons and daughters invariably had engineering degrees of MBAs from the U.S. Indeed, many of East Asia's next-generation business leaders were as comfortable in the languages and cultures of the West as they were in those of Malaysia, Taiwan, or Guangdong. In that regard, they were more cosmopolitan and global-minded than were chief executives in America, Europe, and Japan.
>
> (Clifford and Engardio, 2000: 60–1)

Connecting with international organizations and multilateral institutions

An increasingly important group of globalizing actor-networks endowed with the capacity to reshape Chinese capitalism runs through international organizations and multilateral institutions. Ethnic Chinese elites are now more connected with international organizations and multilateral institutions than ever. These powerful supra-national economic organizations and financial institutions include the IMF, World Bank, OECD, APEC and UNCTAD, which engage in private and public debate over economic reform at a national and sectoral level and occasionally participate in the development of specific economic restructuring programmes in the Asia-Pacific region. Representatives of these multilateral institutions implement diffuse forms of governance that have significant effects in shaping the business practices of Chinese firms, in particular through recommendations (and pressure to implement) on the systemic reform of nationally regulated legal and financial systems (including banking and stock markets). This is important given that the ethnic Chinese control large proportions of national economic activity in the Asia-Pacific, in particular Southeast Asia (see case studies in Chapter 5).

These dynamic changes in Chinese capitalism brought about by international organizations, however, cannot be effective without the consent and involvement of ethnic Chinese elites. The issue of power relations becomes paramount because any big changes to the existing configurations of Chinese capitalism imply a concomitant demise of certain interest groups (e.g. cronies and rent-seekers) and the emergence of other groups (e.g. supporters of democracy and transparency). Why then would key actors in Chinese capitalism participate and enrol in these globalizing actor-networks of multilateral institutions? Some ethnic Chinese actors are clearly opportunists who participate in these globalizing actor-networks in order to ride on the new wave and secure their own legitimacy in business and politics. Other Chinese actors find the past legacies of Chinese capitalism impossible to transform without significant external pressures. Enrolling in globalizing actor-networks helps them to advance their ideas of reforming and transforming Chinese capitalism. These enrol in networks of international organizations in order to promote global understanding and interaction. It is unlikely that this would lead to the wholesale demise of Chinese capitalism in favour of a new cross-national economic coordination system. What is clear, however, is that this process of enrolling ethnic Chinese actors in the global networks of international organizations and multilateral institutions has a potential long-term impact on the dominant forms and organizations of Chinese capitalism. This transformation of Chinese capitalism into hybrid capitalism must be understood in relation to the participation of ethnic Chinese actors in globalizing actor-networks.

Globalization is therefore transforming the governance and authority systems of Chinese capitalism (see Chapters 5 and 6). There is an increasing and important shift from the paternalistic governance of Chinese family firms based on personal relationships and owner management to network governance based on decentralization, financial performance and corporate board decisions. This shift depends on the geographical scale and scope of ethnic Chinese firms and their globalizing actor-networks. There are at least three types of actor-networks among Chinese firms: global networks, national networks and national/international networks. Through linkages developed by globalization, these actors in Chinese capitalism are enrolled in actor-networks at different spatial scales and complexities. As a consequence, the empirical reality of Chinese capitalism is made up of a diverse mosaic of characteristics attributable to several varieties of capitalism. Influenced by globalization, Chinese capitalism is becoming much more messy in its dominant forms and organizational structures in a movement towards a form of hybrid capitalism.

This shift towards network governance structures is most pronounced among ethnic Chinese firms enrolled in globalizing actor-networks. These firms are more likely to be very active in globalizing their operations (see empirical analysis in Chapter 3). They are also more likely to invoke and implement organizational changes, for two reasons. First, the paternalistic governance structure creates formidable organizational obstacles to successful globalization because of the centralization of control and information and the replication of headquarters characteristics in foreign subsidiaries. Globalizing Chinese firms may find it difficult to develop new sources of ownership-specific advantages in non-Asian host countries because rules of competition there are much more transparent and established. Paternalism is not very favourable towards unleashing the potential and entrepreneurial tendencies of local managers in these host countries (Birkinshaw and Hood, 1998a). A shift towards network governance is possible when key actors in these ethnic Chinese firms realize the potential of enrolling in actor-networks in host countries (e.g. recruiting top management executives from host countries). This transformation in strategic management allows ethnic Chinese firms to tap into synergies of 'differentiated networks' because diverse subsidiaries operate in distinct national environments and therefore may potentially reap different advantages embedded in these environments (Nohria and Ghoshal, 1997). Different attributes of a globalizing Chinese firm can be explained in terms of selected attributes of the external network within which it is embedded. These differences in the external network are related to the institutional context of the globalizing Chinese firm.

Globalization is beginning to transform domestic institutional contexts in which paternalistic governance structures are embedded. As the market organization and political-economic structures in Asian economies are changing gradually (see Chapter 3), the monopolistic advantage and/or state subsidies often enjoyed by some typical ethnic Chinese firms dissipate quite quickly. Globalization is changing the rules of the game in Asia in favour of competence-based competition rather than the monopolistic competition that prevailed during the early phase of Asia's industrialization. This revision of competitive rules and institutional contexts means that the paternalistic governance structures of ethnic Chinese firms are no longer very effective in securing and accumulating resources for expansion. It becomes important for these ethnic Chinese firms and their key actors to develop competitive advantages based on organizational competence rather than monopolistic licences or political favours. These latter advantages will not disappear overnight. But key actors in ethnic Chinese firms, particularly those enrolled in globalizing actor-networks involving international organizations and multilateral institutions, have made serious attempts to pre-empt these transformations of domestic institutional contexts and the arrival of global competition. They are more susceptible to organizational change towards a governance structure based on their enrolment in globalizing actor-networks. Their performance and successes are more dependent on their linkages to other actors in global networks than their domestic institutional structures.

This chapter has set up some conceptual apparatuses for subsequent empirical analysis. My theorization of the complex interactions between globalizing actor networks and Chinese capitalism calls for more analytical and empirical attention to the diverse ways in which Chinese capitalism becomes increasingly hybridized in a global era. It shifts the intellectual concern away from the inherently distinctive elements of Chinese capitalism, as described in Chapter 1, to a more fluid and flexible account of how Chinese capitalism evolves and interacts with globalization. This conceptualization of Chinese capitalism as a hybrid mode of economic organization contingent on the ways in which its key actors enrol and participate in globalizing actor-networks places a significant emphasis on changes and transformations as the central dynamics of contemporary capitalism. It does not assume a priori that these will lead to the wholesale convergence or the continual divergence of different modes of capitalist economic organizations. Instead, it specifies some of the underscoring key mechanisms that allow for a more detailed empirical analysis. This actor-network framework for analyzing the dynamics of Chinese capitalism goes beyond the dogmatic views of globalization in both the ultra-globalist account and its critics. It assumes no predetermined outcomes of the complex interactions between Chinese capitalism and globalizing actor-networks; it allows for both convergence and divergence; and it celebrates dynamic processes rather than enduring structures.

In the next four empirical chapters, I attempt to substantiate these theoretical ideas on the hybridization of Chinese capitalism with a variety of evidence. My empirical task is not about proving the existence of Chinese capitalism as a hybrid form of capitalism, for this approach will further propagate structures at the expense of agency. Rather, I seek to shed light on different aspects of the ongoing hybridization process that reshapes Chinese capitalism. In particular, I show how the internationalization of Chinese capitalism has taken place through the participation of key Chinese actors in globalization processes (Chapter 3); how the transnational entrepreneurial activities of these actors have transcended traditional practices and norms (Chapter 4); how significant transformations in the social organization of Chinese capitalism have been brought about by globalizing actor-networks (Chapter 5); and how corporate governance and strategic management in Chinese capitalism have increasingly been moving away from the traditional model of familism and relationship networks (Chapter 6). Taken together, these chapters provide some useful evidence to reassess the nature and organization of Chinese capitalism in a global era.

3 The internationalization of Chinese capitalism

Introduction

To begin our empirical investigation into the hybridization of Chinese capitalism, it is logical to examine how key actors in Chinese capitalism are involved in globalization tendencies through their cross-border economic activities. This initial step helps us to understand not only why transformations in Chinese capitalism may occur, but also the origins of these transformations. As theorized in Chapter 2, significant transformations in Chinese capitalism are unlikely to occur in response to pressures from within Chinese business systems, but rather more in response to new learning, experience and knowledge accumulated through enrolment in actor-networks beyond the confines of Chinese capitalism. The internationalization of key actors in Chinese capitalism, particularly Chinese firms, is therefore a necessary precondition for subsequent changes, transformations and hybridization (Yeung, 1999c, 2000a, 2000e). It must be noted, however, that these firms are generally not the same firms as their predecessors a few decades ago. During their early existence in the twentieth century, Chinese firms in East and Southeast Asia focused predominantly on domestic operations. Their business strategies and management structures were very much influenced by traditional modes of social practices and economic organization transferred then from mainland China. This was the time when Chinese capitalism was mostly inward-looking and closely knit in predominantly family-based networks. Most studies of Chinese capitalism reviewed in Chapter 1 have confirmed the organizational capabilities and cultural specificities of these firms in establishing themselves in their domestic settings.

The broader political and institutional contexts in which these firms and their actor-specific strategies were embedded nevertheless are by no means static. Rather, the changing configurations of the global competitive context and domestic politics, together with the continual evolution and transformation of Chinese capitalism in East and Southeast Asia, have set in motion a centrifugal process through which these firms are increasingly establishing themselves beyond their domestic economies. As such, the understanding and explanation of this recent global reach of Chinese capitalism cannot be achieved without considering changes in the broader contexts of global competition and political economies. As argued by Dirlik (1997) and Smart (1997), it is impossible to understand the dynamics of Chinese capitalism without the dynamics of global capitalism because 'the contemporary discourse on a Chinese capitalism is an integral aspect of the discourse on Global capitalism' (Dirlik, 1997: 308). Many ethnic Chinese firms from East and Southeast Asian economies have ventured into different locations in the Asia-Pacific region and beyond. They are rapidly becoming major players in the region. Recently, some of them have even begun to globalize their commercial and manufacturing operations to become global competitors in such business fields as electronics and garment manufacturing, telecommunications, property development, financial services, hotel chains and so on. The internationalization of Chinese capitalism has thus become more a reality than a myth (cf. Redding, 1990).

This chapter examines the changing nature of the internationalization of Chinese capitalism. Spearheaded by its leading firms, it can be explained by an amalgamation of multi-dimensional dynamic processes and therefore cannot be narrowed down to any single factor. We need to pay as much attention to the firm-specific strategies as to the changing contexts in which Chinese firms are embedded and their strategies implemented. As such, a comprehensive explanation of this internationalization needs to examine the changing configurations of its operating contexts and the internationalization strategies of its specific actors, Chinese firms. Another important point is that some of these configurations of contexts and strategies are historically contingent and geographically specific. They are historically contingent because the internationalization of Chinese capitalism is very much a recent phenomenon (Kao, 1993; Yeung and Olds, 2000a); they are geographically specific in that Chinese firms are largely associated with ethnic Chinese and their geographical concentration in East and Southeast Asian economies (see Chapter 1). The peculiar configurations of explanatory contexts and strategies for the internationalization of Chinese firms therefore may not be applicable to the internationalization of other firms and their capitalist systems.

More specifically, some core features of these internationalization strategies can be highlighted here: sectoral specialization through vertical integration, diversification into unrelated businesses, and family ownership and management. These strategies are prompted by increasing pressure from the accelerated globalization of economic activities because they are facing more competition from global players entering their domestic markets, their domestic markets are becoming more saturated, their 'home'-based competitive advantages are dissipating quickly through privatization and deregulation, and their family successors are becoming more outward-looking in business practices and opportunity-seeking.

It can be argued that through their international business activities, Chinese firms from East and Southeast Asia are becoming an increasingly important force in the regional and the global economy. Through these processes, the very nature of Chinese capitalism is itself being transformed. A hybrid mode of Chinese capitalism is emerging that manifests elements of traditional social practices and economic organization and yet incorporates new norms and behaviour through the enrolment of ethnic Chinese actors in globalizing actor-networks.

Chinese capitalism goes international: changing global and regional contexts

Emerging global and regional opportunities for actors in Chinese capitalism

As noted in Chapter 2, the globalization of economic activities is a recent phenomenon. Since the 1960s, the global economy has become increasingly interdependent through cross-border flows of capital, goods and people. The role of TNCs in these cross-border activities is particularly important. The outcomes of this accelerated process of globalization are manifested in the increasing global interdependence of national economies and Triadization. In the former case, the economic fortunes of countries are intertwined with the global shift of economic activities (Dicken, 2003a). In the latter, three distinct regions have emerged as the leading centres of the global economy: North America, Western Europe and Asia (Ohmae, 1985, 1995; Lévy, 1995). In the Asia-Pacific region ethnic Chinese and their groups of firms have made a notable head start in the internationalization of their diverse range of activities, particularly since the 1980s. Their dynamics is supported not only by the emergence of global firms *per se*, but also by the changing market structures and institutional configurations in their 'home' economies and regions.

The opening of mainland China in the late 1970s and the regionalization of markets in North America and Western Europe in the 1980s both prompted and accelerated the internationalization of Chinese firms. Since the inauguration of its open-door policy in December 1978, mainland China has experienced remarkable economic growth. Meanwhile, its two immediate ethnic Chinese neighbours, Hong Kong and Taiwan, also grew tremendously during the 1980s. The late 1980s witnessed the emergence of a Greater China zone in which cross-border investments contributed to greater subregional integration between Hong Kong and Taiwan on the one hand and southern China on the other (La Croix *et al.*, 1995; Chang, 1995; Lever-Tracy *et al.*, 1996; Ng and Tuan, 1996; Clarke *et al.*, 1999). Ethnic Chinese actors and their business conglomerates from Hong Kong, Taiwan and Southeast Asian countries are the leading force behind this process of subregional integration. Through their participation in global production networks with both material and knowledge flows connected to North America and Western Europe (X. Chen, 1994; Christerson and Appelbaum, 1995; Magretta, 1998; Appelbaum, 2000), these firms have increasingly spearheaded cross-regional learning and production activities. The opening of mainland China and the subsequent emergence of the Greater China economic zone have therefore facilitated the regionalization of ethnic Chinese firms in the Asia-Pacific, in particular those from Hong Kong (Smart and Smart, 1991, 1998; Leung, 1993), Taiwan (Luo and Howe, 1993; Hsing, 1996, 1998; Huang, 1998), Singapore (Tan and Yeung, 2000a, 2000b; Tsang, 2001, 2002) and Thailand (Brown, 1998, 2000).

Another important trend in the global economy is the regionalization of markets in North America and Western Europe. The formation of the North American Free Trade Area (NAFTA) and the Single European Market in the early 1990s has created unprecedented opportunities for Chinese firms from Asia to tap into emerging regional markets and centres of technological innovation in these regions. As these ethnic Chinese firms have consolidated their foothold in Asia, they have begun to penetrate into markets in North America and Western Europe through international production and investment rather than international trade. This represents an important strategic change in the nature of Chinese capitalism because many Chinese firms have grown out of the export-oriented platforms through which industrialization in their domestic economies took place. In today's interdependent global economy, it is no longer sufficient for leading firms to rely on exports in order to serve foreign markets. Customers are becoming more demanding and markets more volatile than before. This is especially the case for matured and developed markets in North America and Western Europe because of intense competition from domestic and global firms. Transnational operations as a strategic tool have become one of the most important competitive strategies for these firms to secure a place in global competition. This increasingly outward orientation of its leading firms and actors has also contributed to the subsequent reconfiguration of Chinese capitalism towards a mode of hybrid capitalism. In addition, one of the most significant competitive disadvantages of Chinese firms has been their lack of technological and managerial sophistication. In their drive to become a major competitive player in the global economy, for example, both Singapore and Taiwan have been very keen on developing the technological and managerial capabilities of their national firms (see Mathews, 1997, 1999, 2002). These predominantly ethnic Chinese firms in both these newly industrialized economies (NIEs) are compelled to internationalize their manufacturing, services and trading operations in the Triad regions in order to secure access to intangible technology, managerial know-how and business opportunities. Why are these ethnic Chinese-based economies so keen on internationalizing their domestic firms? One of the answers comes from their changing domestic institutional configurations (see Chapter 2).

Changing institutional configurations and organizational restructuring in Asia

Institutional configurations of firms refer broadly to the enduring relationships between state institutions, business systems and individual firms. In explaining the behaviour of individual firms, we have to examine not only their firm-specific motives and rationality, but also the broader institutional contexts in which these firms are embedded (Hodgson, 1988, 2000; Granovetter, 1991). Understanding these institutional contexts becomes even more important when the firm is involved in internationalization and faces more institutional constraints (Whitley, 1994, 1998). The changing institutional configurations of business systems thus provide an important nexus through which the internationalization of Chinese capitalism can be understood. In his study of the institutional influences on the development of Chinese firms, Whitley (1992: 198) noted that the distinctive characteristics of Chinese family firms 'stem from the patrimonial nature of pre-industrial China and the dominant forms of commercial organization that developed there.' Some aspects of this patrimonial system included the lack of local power centres, the emphasis on moral worth as the basis of authority, the low integration of vertical royalties, considerable merchant insecurity, patriarchal authority in families and equal inheritance. The subsequent industrialization patterns and institutional environment in Taiwan and Hong Kong further influenced the evolution of these Chinese family firms and therefore the nature and organization of Chinese capitalism itself (see also Chapter 2, particularly Table 2.1). Some of these institutional influences consisted of: a dominant and exclusionary state (e.g. Taiwan); a distant state and low risk-sharing (e.g. Hong Kong); a weak labour movement; and the establishment of trading and business networks. The aggregate result of these institutional influences on leading Chinese family firms was manifested in their distinctive organizational characteristics as follows:

1 Strong personal owner control.
2 Managerial specialization and entrepreneurial diversification.
3 Risk management by minimizing commitments and maximizing flexibility.
4 Limited inter-firm commitments.
5 Personal links between firms.
6 Highly personal authority and low formalization of procedures.
7 Limited commitment to and low dependence on employees.
8 Centralized decision-making and control and weak middle management.

9 A paternalist and aloof management role. (See Chapter 6 for my empirical analysis of changing corporate governance in Chinese capitalism.)

These traditional management practices, organizational structures and capital formation in Chinese capitalism were enduring and remained basically the same despite new challenges posed by the influx of foreign trade, technology and imperialism at the turn of the twentieth century in mainland China (Chan, 1982, 1992; Chan and McElderry, 1998). This strong inertia in organizational change resulted in a low internationalization of Chinese firms in their early stage of development (see below). Large Chinese firms, whether having transnational operations or being oriented exclusively towards the domestic economy, existed as loose groups of affiliated companies throughout their early phases of organizational development. Typically, these affiliated companies were linked through family relationships and interlocking directorates. The holding-company format used to consolidate the ownership and control of large Chinese business groups did not become a reality until after 1949, mainly in Hong Kong, Taiwan and Singapore (Chan, 1995: 89). Business networks became the predominant mode of organizing Chinese firms in their domestic institutional contexts throughout much of the twentieth century (Hamilton, 1991a, 1996a; Yeung, 1998a; Chan, 2000). These networks also served as the institutional foundation of the early internationalization of leading firms in Chinese capitalism during the first half of the twentieth century. This phenomenon in turn explains why much of the literature on Chinese capitalism tends to focus on the so-called *guanxi* networks in organizing the socio-economic activities of ethnic Chinese in East and Southeast Asia (see Chapter 1).[1] Thus, Hodder (1996: 68) argued that 'social networks founded upon reciprocity and its soft-framed institutions may be constructed as an end in themselves, but they may also be directed towards the extension and institutionalization of trade'.

During their internationalization journey, however, ethnic Chinese firms necessarily experience different configurations of business systems and institutional influences in both host and 'home' economies. The role of ethnic Chinese *guanxi* and business networks may diminish when Chinese firms move beyond the Asia-Pacific region and venture into foreign markets. As Brown (1995b: 9) observed, '[t]he importance of the Chinese networks still endures, but the complex changes they have undergone are crucial'. In globalizing their operations, many Chinese firms are increasingly linked with non-Chinese global corporations and host-country national firms that grow out of very different configurations of business systems and institutional contexts. Their business practices and organizational processes are often based on professional management, formal contracts, price competition, arm's length inter-firm relationships and so on. Chandler (1977, 1990) described these norms and practices as constituting a form of managerial capitalism in which there is a distinct separation between ownership and management in modern corporations. A growing number of ethnic Chinese firms from Hong Kong and Singapore, for example, have professionalized their management; their foreign subsidiaries have also been given substantial autonomy in decision-making and control (see Chapter 6). There is thus a tendency towards the hybridization of different forms of capitalism and their dominant modes of economic organization when actors from different firms are increasingly participating in globalizing actor-networks (see Whyte, 1996; Olds and Yeung, 1999).

In their domestic context, however, the role of *guanxi* and business networks in the regionalization of Chinese firms in the Asia-Pacific region may still be pervasive and indeed further reinforced when they enter into all sorts of cooperative arrangements with global corporations eager to make a presence in the region. Ethnic Chinese firms can play a very significant role in the globalization of North American and Western European firms in the Asia-Pacific by providing vital business contacts, reducing economic risks and uncertainty, identifying the initiatives of nation-states and pooling capital and appropriate technology. For example, these firms were important 'gatekeepers' in the privatization of major public-sector industries in Indonesia, Malaysia and Thailand during the 1980s and the 1990s. In their study of the privatization of Thailand's telecommunications industry, Priebjrivat and Rondinelli (1994) found that Chinese firms played a vital mediating role between state political and military elites and foreign giant telecommunication corporations (see also Brown, 2000 on the CP Group). This multi-faceted role of *guanxi* and business networks indicates that Chinese firms may pursue hybridized management and organizational practices during their internationalization processes: first, increasing incorporation of international management practices and organizational structures in host countries outside the Asia-Pacific region; and second, the continual exploitation of the role of *guanxi* and business networks within the Asia-Pacific region. Over time, these two sets of practices are likely to be mutually influential and thereby create new possibilities for the emergence of a hybrid form of economic organization in Chinese capitalism.

Apart from restructuring business systems and institutional contexts in Asia, the changing priorities and concerns of their 'home' economies also significantly shape the internationalization of Chinese capitalism. International business studies have shown that the globalization of firms is to a large extent related to the changing conditions in and competitive advantage of their home countries (Dunning, 1993, 1997). As the domestic economies of ethnic Chinese firms go through different stages of economic development and political change, it becomes necessary for them to respond to changing circumstances in their 'home' economies by engaging in cross-border operations in Asia and beyond. One of the most important driving forces from their 'home' economies is the limit to future growth that arises from either discriminatory state regulation or market saturation. The former condition is applicable to many Southeast Asian countries in which ethnic Chinese capital has dominated the domestic economy rather than the polity, for example Indonesia, Malaysia, the Philippines and Thailand (see also Table 2.1). Since the late 1970s, many Southeast Asian countries experienced unprecedented growth in their domestic economies until the 1997–8 Asian economic crisis. This rosy picture of economic growth in Southeast Asian countries, nevertheless, masks some important undercurrents that have been prompting the outward orientation of Chinese firms in recent years. Some of these contextual issues of before the Asian economic crisis are summarized in Table 3.1.

Despite rapid growth in domestic economies, the lack of sizeable domestic markets free from state intervention and monopolistic domination has hindered the further growth of many Chinese firms. Late industrialization in many developing Southeast Asian countries has limited the scale and size of domestic markets, making it almost impossible to take full advantage of scale economies in many industries, including cement, automobiles and even home appliances (Suehiro, 1985, 1993; Brown, 2000). In these countries ethnic Chinese capital has been subject to discriminatory regulation and constraints imposed by host-country states (Mackie, 1988; Yoshihara, 1988; McVey, 1992; Hodder, 1996; Brook and Luong, 1997; Hefner, 1998). Ethnic-biased economic policies aimed at improving the economic positions of the *pribumi* in Indonesia and the *bumiputra* in Malaysia have inadvertently forced many ethnic Chinese firms to reconsider their growth strategies. In so far as they have grown to a certain size and organizational complexity, many of these firms in Southeast Asia begin to internationalize in overseas markets in search of new investment opportunities that are denied in their 'home' economies as a result of state regulation. In doing so, their strategies and processes of internationalization have also been shaped by the changing configurations of Chinese capitalism in their 'home' economies (see case studies on pages 103–6). During the 1980s and the 1990s, there was a policy shift towards a more open and competitive environment in Southeast Asia (Yoshihara, 1994; Barlow, 1999). Many countries began to pursue export-oriented industrialization and to attract foreign investment from North America and Western Europe. As domestic markets were increasingly open to foreign investment and privatization and deregulation policies were being pursued, the monopolistic advantage and subsidies often enjoyed by some leading ethnic Chinese-controlled conglomerates in these countries dissipated fairly quickly. In response, these conglomerates diversified into overseas operations by establishing new ventures and/or acquiring existing operations complementary to their domestic operations.

More crucially, anti-Chinese sentiments have remained strong and pervasive in the political cultures and public discourses of many Southeast Asian countries. In much post-independence Southeast Asia, anti-foreign and anti-Chinese sentiment has been an important force in shaping the nature and organization of Chinese capitalism (Mackie, 1988; Yoshihara, 1988, 1994; McVey, 1992; Lim, 1996). During the 1950s and the 1960s, almost all Southeast Asian countries were in their embryonic stage of post-colonial industrialization. Anti-Chinese sentiment was deeply rooted in Indonesia and the Philippines (Robison, 1986; Mackie, 1988; Suryadinata, 1988). The 1970s saw the emergence of major ethnic backlashes in Indonesia and Malaysia. The regulatory regimes became much more restrictive. Domestically, pressure was exerted to enable indigenous people to acquire a greater share of national economic wealth. In Malaysia, for example, the New Economic Policy (NEP) was launched in 1970 with two prime objectives (Jesudason, 1989, 1997; Gomez and Jomo, 1997): to eradicate poverty in general and to achieve better ethnic economic parity. From the 1980s the attitudes of these Southeast Asian countries changed towards a more vigorous promotion of inward investments. The ethnicity issue did not disappear completely, but it was supplemented by an increasing influx of foreign capital. Ironically, a large proportion of this originated from ethnic Chinese economies outside mainland China – Hong Kong, Taiwan and Singapore. Uneven development continues to be a prominent feature in the contemporary economic landscapes of many Southeast Asian countries (Jomo, 1988; Yoshihara, 1988; Jesudason, 1989; Kelly, 2000). Ethnic riots targeting ethnic Chinese in Indonesia in May 1998, for instance demonstrate that ethnic inequality remains central to the stability and continued growth of many Southeast Asian countries.

Market saturation is emerging as a compelling condition in ethnic Chinese-dominated NIEs, particularly Singapore, Taiwan and Hong Kong, where the leading Chinese firms have more or less outgrown their domestic economies. The search for foreign markets has become the only feasible economic strategy to sustain their continuous capital accumulation and growth (Yeung, 1994b, 1999d; Dicken and Yeung, 1999; Hamilton *et al.*, forthcoming). With the exception of Hong Kong (Castells *et al.*, 1990; Yeung, 2000b), the state has a high degree of influence over their developmental trajectories (Amsden, 1989; Wade, 1990; Appelbaum and Henderson, 1992). In Singapore the corporatist state has depended on the influx of foreign capital to sustain its economic growth since independence in 1965 (Rodan, 1989; Huff, 1994; Low, 1998). This economic strategy has not been abandoned, but the state launched a major regionalization drive in 1993 to develop an external wing of the economy. This was deemed necessary if Singapore were to succeed in growing beyond the limits of its domestic market and in capturing the emerging markets of the Asia-Pacific region (Yeung, 1998d, 1999a, 2002a).

In contrast, the phenomenon of state-driven outward investment by

Table 3.1 National contexts of Chinese business firms from Southeast Asia before the 1997–8 Asian economic crisis

Country	Growth and market potential	Presence of Chinese business	Policy towards Chinese business	Leading ethnic Chinese TNCs
Indonesia	• high growth since 1987 • weak domestic market • many protected industries	• small Chinese population (~5% of total) • long history of Chinese business • presence in virtually all industries	• ethnic-biased *pribumi* policy • political patronage with Suharto	• Salim Group controlled by Liem Sioe Liong • Lippo Group controlled by Mochtar Riady
Malaysia	• high growth since 1987 • emerging domestic market • some protected industries	• large Chinese population (~30% of total) • long history of Chinese business • significant presence in property and financial sectors	• ethnic-biased *bumiputra* policy • New Economic Policy since 1969 • political patronage with Malays	• Kerry Group controlled by Robert Kuok • Hong Leong Group controlled by Quek Leng Chan
Philippines	• unstable growth since 1985 • weak domestic market	• small Chinese population (~1.5% of total) • recent history of Chinese business • limited presence in industries	• ethnic-biased industrial policy • political patronage with Marcos	• Fortune Tobacco controlled by Lucio Tan

Singapore	• high growth since 1987 • small domestic market • large presence of foreign firms and government-linked companies	• large Chinese population (~78% of total) • long history of Chinese business • significant presence in commerce and property sectors	• no ethnic-biased policy • strong role of the state and its institutions	• Hong Leong Group controlled by Kwek Leng Beng • Far East Organization controlled by Ng Teng Fong
Thailand	• high growth since 1987 • emerging domestic market • some protected industries	• significant Chinese population (~14% of total) • long history of Chinese business • significant presence in commerce and industries	• ethnic assimilation policy • political and military patronage	• Charoen Pokphand Group controlled by Chearavanont family • Bangkok Bank controlled by Sophonpanich family

Source: Yeung (1999c: Table 2).

Chinese firms occurred in Taiwan during the mid-1980s when the state relaxed its foreign exchange and foreign investment regulations (Chen, 1986; T.-J. Chen, 1998; Hsing, 1998; Chow, 2002). Before that the Taiwanese government had actively promoted the emergence of formidable national champions in certain industrial sectors (e.g. Formosa Plastics in chemicals and Acer in computers; see Table 1.5), through granting subsidies and incentives, providing R&D infrastructure and protecting key domestic markets (Amsden, 1989; Wade, 1990; Mathews, 1997, 2002). Since 1985 the state has also been actively encouraging national firms to relocate their low-cost production facilities to other countries in the region and to secure strategic access to foreign technology in North America and Western Europe (T.-J. Chen, 1992, 1998; X. Chen, 1996; Chen and Chen, 1998; Hsu and Saxenian, 2000; Hsu and Cheng, 2002). In that respect, Chinese firms from Taiwan have been successful in internationalizing their operations beyond their national boundaries. From 1952 to 1988, Taiwan's cumulative approved outward investment stood at US$704 million, of which 61 per cent went to the US (Taiwan Ministry of Economic Affairs, 1996). By 1995 the figure had increased very substantially to US$10.2 billion, of which 27 per cent was destined for the US. Much of this investment in the US by Taiwanese firms went into high-tech industries that in turn contributed to the globalization of Taiwan's IT hardware firms.

By 1998 Taiwanese IT firms had secured a large share in global markets for computer hardware and peripherals, ranging from 33 per cent in CD-ROM to 85 per cent in scanners (see Table 3.2). Although many of these IT firms remain family-owned and controlled (see Microsoft, described in La Porta *et al.*, 1999), it is important to point out that there is a high degree of professional management and organizational competencies in these firms. The culturalist stereotype of these dynamic IT firms as small-scale Chinese family firms is unable to account for their rapid emergence and transformations. Mathews (2002), for example, argued for the fundamental importance of organizational innovations, not merely technological change, in underscoring the success of what he called 'dragon multinationals'. These Taiwanese firms are therefore the embodiment of an emerging hybrid form of Chinese family firms that combine the virtues of family ownership and the dynamism of professional management and technological competencies. The sheer volume and intensity of US–Taiwan flows of management and technical personnel during the 1990s, a phenomenon well documented in Hsu and Saxenian (2000) and Saxenian and Hsu (2001), has undoubtedly speeded up this process of hybridization.

The internationalization of Chinese firms from Hong Kong, the epicentre of Chinese capitalism, is prompted not so much by any coherent state action, but rather by the changing political climate and inherently small size of the domestic market. It is true that these firms have long been

Table 3.2 Market concentration and globalization of Taiwan's IT hardware firms, 1998 and 1999

Product	Industry concentration[1] (number of firms in parenthesis) (%)		Offshore production (by Taiwan firms) (%)	Value of production (US$ million) (Taiwan and offshore)	Global market share (%)
	1998	1999	1999	1999	1998
Video card	95 (4)	95 (4)	18	33	40
Sound card	87 (2)	90 (3)	65	78	49
Desktop PC	84 (3)	62 (5)	88	7,188	–
SPS	83 (5)	89 (5)	91	1,744	65
Notebook PC	74 (5)	72 (5)	0	10,198	39
CD-Rom	72 (5)	–	60	1,740	33
Keyboard	64 (3)	77 (5)	91	512	65
Mouse	62 (3)	62 (4)	89	155	60
Scanner	57 (5)	76 (5)	38	925	85
Motherboard[2]	55 (5)	58 (5)	38	4,854	66
Monitor	45 (5)	47 (5)	71	9,330	58
Graphics card	40 (5)	53 (5)	65	848	–
			57 (weighted average)	39,881 (total)	

Source: Amsden and Chu (2002: Table 2.2; 28).

Notes
1 Measured in terms of sales. Concentration data are for the second half of 1998 and 1999.
2 Excluding those sold as part of a PC system.

operating in Southeast Asia (Yeung, 1998a). But the drive towards globalization did not become a serious consideration until the so-called 1997 question surfaced in the period leading to the 1984 Sino-British Joint Declaration that stipulated the return of Hong Kong to mainland China on 1 July 1997. Since that date many of these firms have stepped up their globalization process in response to ongoing industrial restructuring in Hong Kong and political uncertainty (Ho, 1992; Chiu *et al.*, 1997; Yeung, 1998a, 2002a; Meyer, 2000). Many local manufacturing firms relocated their manufacturing activities to nearby locations in mainland China, whereas their parent firms in Hong Kong remained as the management centre to coordinate increasingly complicated networks of production and activities. This process of industrial hollowing took place from the early 1980s and intensified after 1987 when the Pearl River delta and other special economic zones were opened in mainland China (Sung, 1991; Tuan and Ng, 1995a; Kwok and So, 1995; Ng and Tuan, 1996; Lin, 1997). This resulted in a drastic decline in manufacturing industries and the emergence of service activities in Hong Kong.[2] Tuan and Ng (1995b: 72), for example, found that 'Hong Kong has substituted exports from its cross-border operations for exports from local enterprises. A service-dominated economy with industrial management of plants crossing the border as a core of its manufacturing sector seems to be a fact today'. By 1980 and 1998, the share of the two sectors in GDP had increased respectively to 45 per cent and 50 per cent (Yeung, 2002a: Table 2.1). In the same years, manufacturing's share in GDP declined to 16 per cent and 6.2 per cent. By 2001 manufacturing accounted for only 5.2 per cent of Hong Kong's GDP at current factor cost, compared with trade (26.7 per cent) and financial services (22.6 per cent) (http://www.info. gov.hk/censtatd, accessed on 28 March 2003). Over a period of almost 30 years, both trade and financial services have emerged as the two leading pillars of Hong Kong's economy, enabling it to become an important global metropolis (Meyer, 2000; Schenk, 2001).

Some high-tech manufacturing Chinese firms from Hong Kong have also ventured into the Triad countries in order to penetrate the highly competitive marketplace (Yeung, 1998a: Box 7.1 for some case studies). Services Chinese firms from Hong Kong are also globalizing to diversify their political risks. For example, such firms from Hong Kong were very active in cross-border mergers and acquisitions as early as 1992, involving some US$78 billion and ranked third worldwide after the US and France (*Economic News*, 2 February 1993). Many leading Hong Kong property firms have bought into hotel chains in the US and Western Europe. Other Hong Kong firms are involved in high-profile acquisitions of foreign companies in telecommunications (Microtell in Canada and formerly Orange plc in the UK), oil and gas (Husky Oil in Canada), electronics (Sansui Electric in Japan), and retail and distribution (Harvey Nichols in the UK and the Singer Co. in the US). Like Taiwan, Chinese capitalism in Hong Kong has undergone significant changes and transformations during the past 20 years in relation to globalization. The assumption that the Chinese business system in Hong Kong remains enduring and intact in the face of these dynamic transformations is simply unrealistic, though it is by no means clear that these transformations are replacing Chinese capitalism with a distinctively new mode of capitalism based on the Anglo-American model. The changing contexts of Chinese capitalism, therefore, must be seen as infusing diverse and hybrid forms of organizing economic activities rather than imposing a predetermined trajectory of change. Before providing more detailed empirical evidence to support this observation, it is useful to offer a general analysis of the processes of the internationalization of these Chinese firms and their firm-specific strategies.

Modelling the internationalization of Chinese firms

Although the previous section explained the dynamic contexts in which ethnic Chinese firms are rapidly internationalizing in today's global economy, it is insufficient to explain this in terms of their dynamic contexts alone. To understand fully the behaviour of these firms, we need also to examine their firm-specific strategies that constitute the *raison d'être* of their globalization. I propose a heuristic model of the geographic expansion of these firms in their drive towards globalization, which is used to map their geographic expansion during the twentieth century. This is not as a universal explanation in its own right. In fact, most Chinese firms would not go through all stages of the model, thereby defying its inevitability. Instead, we will find a mixture of these firms in every stage of the model, depending on the historical and geographical circumstances of their formations and transformations, so the model is at best a summary of the diverse experiences of globalizing Chinese firms during the past two centuries (Yeung, 2000e).

An evolutionary model of the geographic expansion of Chinese firms

In his seminal paper on the evolution of TNCs, Perlmutter (1969) observed that they evolve in three stages: from ethnocentric to polycentric, to region-centric and geocentric (see also Malnight, 1995). Put in simple terms, the TNC starts as a domestic firm having one centre of activities. It serves the global market through exports and licensing (ethnocentric stage). Over time, it grows beyond its national boundaries and establishes multiple centres of activities (polycentric stage). At this stage, however, its different centres of activities are not integrated with the headquarters and are largely decentralized. Each foreign subsidiary is run as a stand-alone operation. It is only at the final stage that the regional and global operations of the TNC are integrated within coordinated networks. There is no longer any trace of parent-subsidiary relationships. The TNC is now fully integrated globally and is equipped with global scanning capabilities and intra-firm coordination and control of international production (Bartlett and Ghoshal, 1989; Nohria and Ghoshal, 1997; Doremus *et al.*, 1998; Dicken, 2003b). Although Perlmutter's model is simplistic and idealized, it can be applied to the internationalization of Chinese firms, albeit with some modifications and context specification. Weidenbaum and Hughes (1996: 4–5) have constructed a three-stage model of the internationalization of Chinese firms, as follows.

- Stage one: Chinese firms quite literally went from rags to riches when 'families created their own businesses, and in the process developed much of the modern private business sector throughout Southeast Asia' (Weidenbaum and Hughes, 1996: 4). This was indeed the early phase of firms' formation and expansion.
- Stage two: This phase is known as 'the duplication of the House of Rothschild phenomenon' (Weidenbaum and Hughes, 1996: 4), when Chinese firms internationalized their operations throughout the region based on common grounds in family ties, language, culture and ethnicity. These were particularly important institutional means

for internationalization in a region where formal business agreements were difficult to establish, let alone enforce. Weidenbaum and Hughes (1996: 5) noted that 'it is common for the father-CEO stationed in Hong Kong or Bangkok or Singapore to send one son to Shanghai, another to Taipei, a son-in-law to Manila, and a nephew to Kuala Lumpur'.

- Stage three: Chinese firms have engaged in massive investment and rapid penetration in mainland China and have completely surpassed their counterparts from North America and Western Europe.

It should be noted that Weidenbaum and Hughes's (1996) model is based on the experience of ethnic Chinese firms investing in mainland China. The model is therefore historically contingent and geographically specific. In order to ensure the relative generality of the model, it is necessary to add further stages to account for the globalization of Chinese firms into other destinations outside the Asia-Pacific region.

- Stage four: This is characterized by the internationalization of Chinese firms beyond the Asia-Pacific region. At this stage, their worldwide operations are not fully integrated and their organizational structures remain largely polycentric. Their emerging capabilities are embedded in their 'home' advantages and their ability to learn from partnership with global corporations in Asia.
- Stage five: The emergence of the global networks of Chinese firms when they begin to integrate their worldwide operations through sophisticated organizational networks. At this stage, the firms are increasingly transnational in that they no longer have a particular home origin. They are no longer purely Chinese because they draw capital and finance from the global networks of Chinese and non-Chinese capital. Their decision-making is no longer personalized by the patriarch of the family, but is rather dependent on the collective consensus of global executives from the various centres of activities within the network.

In reality, Chinese firms from different 'home' economies may enter the model at different stages because of their locational advantages and disadvantages (e.g. Hong Kong compared with Malaysia). The early stages of the model are more applicable to traditional Chinese firms, and the later stages are more relevant to newcomers from the Asian NIEs. To date, only a selected number of Chinese firms have reached Stage four when they manage to globalize their operations. Acer Computer from Taiwan is perhaps one of the best examples (Mathews and Snow, 1998; Mathews, 2002). It is now one of the top ten global manufacturers of personal computers. Its worldwide operations span some 35 countries in the Triad regions, enabling it to become one of the top 50 TNCs from emerging economies (see Table 1.5). However, 66 per cent of its profits in 1995 still came from Asia (*The Straits Times*, 26 March 1996). Having said that, there are actually very few true TNCs, irrespective of their countries of initial origin (Hu, 1992; Doremus *et al.*, 1998; Dicken, 2003b). To Hu (1992: 111), 'there is no doubt that a company like Siemens is German, a company like IBM is American, or a company like Toyota is Japanese'. Even in the case of Nestlé, the Swiss law allows Swiss companies to exclude foreigners from holding registered shares that carry voting rights. Nestlé thus limits non-Swiss voting rights to 3 per cent of the total. It is certainly a national (Swiss) rather than global corporation. It is even more difficult to find an ethnic Chinese firm that has fully transnationalized its operations. It will take many more decades of globalization for Chinese firms to reach stage five of the model.

Mapping the historical geography of Chinese firms

The historical geography of the globalization of Chinese firms is extremely interesting in that four distinct phases of globalization can be identified.

1 Early internationalization from China to other Asian countries from the late nineteenth century to the 1940s.
2 Capital flows from China to Hong Kong/Taiwan and Southeast Asia during the late 1940s.
3 Two-way investments between Hong Kong and Southeast Asia between the 1950s and the 1980s.
4 The globalization of Chinese firms from Hong Kong, Taiwan and Southeast Asian countries during the 1980s and the 1990s.

The word 'phase', instead of 'stage', is used because I want to situate the globalization of these ethnic firms in their historical and geographical contexts, although each of them may be at different stages of the evolutionary model. During the first phase, internationalization occurred either when some ethnic Chinese capitalists established operations outside mainland China or when ethnic Chinese invested in mainland China, then their home country (Godley, 1981). An example is the Wing On Group, now based in Hong Kong (Chan, 1995). At the turn of the twentieth century, both Hong Kong and Shanghai experienced new challenges as the mainland Chinese economy was buffeted by many new forces: rapid population growth, imported technology, foreign trade and Western imperialism among others (Chung, 1998). Chan (1995: 80) observed that 'by learning new managerial techniques, by planning out new strategies and by setting up appropriate organizations, [the Wing On Company] was one of the very small number of Chinese enterprises which responded successfully to these challenges'.

The Wing On Company's early success in internationalization can be explained by its multi-product marketing approach and its multi-unit organizational structure that provided critical support through access to new markets and sources of supply, a control mechanism to ensure consistency of quality and an efficient distribution network. The first company of the Wing On Group, Wing On Fruit Store, was established in Sydney in August 1897 by Guo Luo (1874–1956), one of the two founding brothers of the Wing On Company from a relatively wealthy peasant family in the Zhongshan county in southern China (Chan, 1995: 82). Guo Luo pursued a strategy of expansion through backward integration and diversification. He first secured his sources of fruit supply by setting up his own banana plantations on one of the Fiji islands. He diversified into trading other products such as dried coconuts, seashells, dried sea slugs, leather, plywood and other Chinese native products. By the early 1910s Chan (1995: 83) said that, 'the company owned some eighteen plantations covering over 2,000 acres of land and employing more than 1,200 workers, as well as other banana plantations, almost 1,000 acres in size, in the Charters Towers area of Queensland, Australia'.

The return of the Guo brothers to Hong Kong and Shanghai was prompted by revolutionary ideas in the 1900s (Chan, 1995). They wanted to bring in modern management practices to revolutionize traditional Chinese business practices in China. First, they decided to establish a modern department store in Hong Kong. The Wing On department store was opened for business in Hong Kong in August 1907, supported by a well-planned internal organization headed by family members. The department store existed as a separate affiliate or associated corporation of the Wing On Fruit Store in Sydney. The Company then expanded swiftly to found the Jinshanzhuang in Sydney (1907), the Wing On Native Bank in Zhongshan county (1910), a chain of Great Eastern Hotels in Guangzhou city (1914), Hong Kong and Shanghai (1918), the Wing On Warehouse (1916) and the Wei Sun Knitting Factory in Hong Kong (1919). There were also several new affiliates, each with its own corporate charter and independent sources of capital: the Wing On Fire and Marine Insurance Co. Ltd of Hong Kong (1915), the Wing On Co. Ltd of Shanghai (1918), the Wing On Textile Manufacturing Co. Ltd in Shanghai (1921), the Wing On life Assurance Co. Ltd in Hong Kong (1925) and the Wing On Commercial and Savings Bank Ltd in Hong Kong (1933). There was no single holding company to consolidate control and ownership of this diverse group of Wing On companies. But by the early 1920s the Guo brothers 'had fashioned out a complex multi-unit organization that bound its subsidiaries and affiliates together through the use of interlocking directorships and inter-company loans whenever they were needed' (Chan, 1995: 89). The case of the Wing On Group indicates that before the communist takeover of mainland China in October 1949, some Chinese firms had already been actively involved in cross-border investment within the Asian region, although these firms operated largely within Perlmutter's (1969) polycentric mode of international operations.

The second phase of internationalization coincided with the civil war and the communist takeover in mainland China during the late 1940s. This was the time when major disruptions in mainland China caused massive outflows of capital to Hong Kong, Taiwan and Southeast Asia. In landmark studies of the role of these emigrant entrepreneurs and capital flows in Hong Kong's industrialization, Wong (1988, 2000) examined how political chaos during the 1930s and the founding of the People's Republic of China in October 1949 led Shanghai's industrialists to seek a safer location for their businesses. This is a phase of 'involuntary internationalization' in Chinese capitalism, when ethnic Chinese capital fled in response to deteriorating domestic conditions rather than that business opportunities emerged from host countries. They also carried with them many cultural imprints and social norms that later became the hallmarks of Chinese capitalism, as defined in the literature critically reviewed in Chapter 1. Many of these emigrant entrepreneurs from Shanghai and elsewhere in China, in particular those owners of cotton mills, chose to re-establish themselves in Hong Kong where they found a favourable setting for the development of modern Chinese firms. One example is the Rong family that created the Shen Xin textile empire and dominated the Chinese textile industry. The eldest son of the family, Rong Hong-yuan, left Hong Kong in 1948 to set up the Bangkok Cotton Mill in 1950. But severe restrictions by the Thai government caused the mill to run into bankruptcy after a short period of operation (Wong, 1988: 21–2). These emigrant entrepreneurs played a major role in the subsequent industrialization of Hong Kong and contributed significantly to the importance of today's Hong Kong as a global textiles and garments coordination centre (Berger and Lester, 1997; Enright *et al.*, 1997; Yu, 1997; Meyer, 2000).

The third phase of internationalization witnessed significant two-way investments between Hong Kong and Southeast Asia throughout the following 30 years (Yeung, 1996, 1998a, 2002a). After more than a decade of industrialization in Hong Kong, by the end of the 1950s the textile industry had become one of the vital pillars of the economy. Hong Kong was one of world's largest exporters of textile products. The same period, nevertheless, saw the imposition of quota constraints on Hong Kong's cotton textile products (Lau, 1991). Many textiles Chinese family firms began to consider seriously their growth strategies. Transnational operations seemed to be one of the most viable solutions to circumvent quota restrictions. Chinese firms in the textiles industry began to internationalize their operations in search of alternative non-quota production and domestic markets. For example, as early as 1951, Nanyang Cotton Mill Ltd had built a 10,000-spindle spinning mill in Argentina where no Chinese had ever owned a factory, although the mill was eventually sold in 1960 (Hong Kong Cotton Spinners Association, 1988: 92). By the 1970s nearly all those Chinese textiles firms controlled by the Shanghainese entrepreneurs in Hong Kong had diversified their investments into Southeast Asia, Canada, Latin America and parts of Africa (Wong, 1988: 39).

Another Shanghainese entrepreneur, Frank Tsao, pioneered the first textile venture in 1958 in Malaysia, known as the Textile Corporation of Malaya, with several Hong Kong friends. The venture was established primarily for two reasons. First, Malaysia could be an alternative production site to circumvent quota restrictions imposed on Hong Kong by industrialized countries in Europe and America which at that time did not impose any quota restrictions on textile products imported from Malaysia. Second, Tsao himself had extensive personal and family connections in Malaysia. At a personal level, the Textile Corporation had industrial and financial support from several other leading Shanghai industrialists from Hong Kong and Malaysia, for instance Chow Wen-hsien and Chow Chung-kai from Winsor Industrial Group in Hong Kong and Robert Kuok in Malaysia. Tsao was also a personal friend of Mahathir Mohamad, the longest serving prime minister of Malaysia since its independence (*Capital*, June 1994: 80). Since then, Tsao's textile and garment empire in Malaysia has expanded further to include Malayan Weaving Mills, Textile Corporation and Malacca Textile. Tsao's main business, however, was not in textiles, but in shipping. Together with Robert Kuok, Tsao helped the Malaysian government to set up its Malaysian International Shipping Corporation (MISC) in the late 1960s. In the process, Tsao was invited to be a shareholder of this national shipping line, albeit with a small share of only 4 per cent. For his distinctive contribution to the Malaysian shipping industry, Tsao was conferred Tan Sri, a knighthood, by the king of Malaysia. He had a much higher shareholding in the Thai national shipping line, at an estimated 70 per cent in the early 1990s, which he had also been helping to establish since 1965 (*Singapore Business*, February 1989: 21; July 1994: 28; *Forbes*, August 1992: 41). During the 1980s and early 1990s Tsao was heavily involved in developing Singapore's largest private property development, the Suntec City Convention Centre. The billionaire club, which he chaired, received strong financial and personal support from many leading Hong Kong businessmen, including property magnates such as Li Ka-shing, Lee Shau-kee and Cheng Yu-tung (see Table 1.6) and eminent industrialists such as Li Dak-sum and Anthony Yeh. The Suntec project was primarily a transnational project based on personal friendship and cooperative strategies among leading Chinese businessmen from Hong Kong (Yeung, 1998a).

In the fourth phase of geographic expansion during the 1980s and the 1990s, Chinese firms from Hong Kong, Taiwan and Southeast Asian countries began to globalize their commercial operations to almost every corner of the world. Perhaps the largest geographical destination of these cross-border investment flows from Chinese firms was mainland China itself. Since its open-door policy was instituted in December 1978, mainland China has become one of the largest recipients of global investment flows (see Chapter 2). There is no doubt that this wave of foreign investment has been substantially sustained by ethnic Chinese capital (East Asia Analytical Unit, 1995; Weidenbaum and Hughes, 1996). By 1994 the amount of cumulative realized foreign capital surpassed US$100 billion. This was spread across more than 167,500 foreign-invested enterprises, including wholly owned companies, joint ventures and cooperative enterprises. As shown in Table 3.3, ethnic Chinese firms have out-invested the US, Japan and the European Union, contributing well over 80 per cent of both the number of projects and investment between 1979 and 1993 (East Asia Analytical Unit, 1995: 197). A large amount of these flows of ethnic Chinese capital from Taiwan and Southeast Asian countries to mainland China have apparently been channelled through Hong Kong and Singapore, the twin capitals of Chinese capitalism (Wu, 1997; Low *et al.*, 1998).

Among the largest ethnic Chinese investors, in terms of capital invested and the number of companies they control in mainland China, is the Sino-Thai agribusiness group, the Charoen Pokphand (CP) Group. The CP Group controls more than 70 operations in mainland China, including its core agribusiness activities and Shanghai real estate development. Koike (1993: 368) noted that:

> agribusiness is attracting renewed interest as a highly promising field, although for it to further develop, the region's agricultural infrastructure needs to be drastically improved. Ethnic Chinese business groups in Southeast Asia will continue moving into agribusiness for some time to come, particularly in view of the potential of the mainland Chinese market.

Table 3.3 Sources of foreign capital in China, 1979–93

Source country/ economy	Number of enterprises	%	Foreign investment (US$ billion)	%
Hong Kong	106,769	63.7	47.5	69.1
Taiwan	20,612	12.3	6.4	9.3
Macau	4,188	2.5	1.9	2.8
Singapore	3,037	1.8	1.5	2.2
Thailand	1,361	0.8	0.8	1.2
Other	75	0.1	–	–
Sub total	136,042	81.2	58.1	84.6
United States	11,554	6.9	3.7	5.4
Japan	7,096	4.2	3.3	4.8
Other	12,808	7.7	3.6	5.2
Total	167,500	100.0	68.7	100.0

Source: East Asia Analytical Unit (1995: Table 10.1).

The group set up its first China venture, Conti Chia Tai, in Shenzhen in 1981 and was an early entrant into the China market. By 1993 it had operations in 26 of China's 30 provinces, indicating its broad interests in mainland China and geographic coverage. The group's total assets in mainland China were estimated at US$1.3 billion in 1993 (East Asia Analytical Unit, 1995: 324) and US$5 billion in 1995 (Brown, 2000: 207). Its China investments were mainly conducted through its Hong Kong subsidiary, CP Pokphand, which in 1993 controlled 36 very diversified businesses in China.

The CP Group was founded over 80 years ago in 1921 by two ethnic Chinese brothers, Chia Ek Chor and Chia Seow Whooey (last name Chia subsequently changed to Chearavanont), who arrived in Thailand in 1919 from the Shantou region of Guangdong (East Asia Analytical Unit, 1995: 323–6; Hamilton and Waters, 1995: 104–5; Weidenbaum and Hughes, 1996: 30–4; Brown, 2000: 86–91). The group started in the farm-seed business and moved into animal feeds and then into chicken farming and processing with initial technical support from the US poultry giant, Arbor Acres, in 1970. Its subsequent globalization strategy was premised on diversification into manufacturing industries to reduce excessive dependence on its agribusiness (Brown, 2000; Goss *et al.*, 2000; Pananond, 2001). As explained by its executive vice-president, Veerawat Kanchanadul,

> CP executives had realized the globalization trend even 20–25 years ago, not just now. Moreover, we also started to realize our capability to absorb new technological skills from our joint venture partner and to apply those skills to developing countries. That was the reason why we diversified into industries other than agriculture. We realized that the growth in agricultural sectors was slowing down. No matter how big you are, if you operate in a declining industry, you won't grow.
>
> (Quoted in Pananond and Zeithaml, 1998: 175)

Although the group's interests have extended to petrochemicals, motorcycle and automotive parts, real estate and telecommunications, 60–70 per cent of its revenue is still derived from agribusiness. Despite the 1997–8 Asian economic crisis, CP's agribusiness worldwide continued to be highly profitable and constituted 70 per cent of its revenues. In 1998 CP's total revenues were US$7 billion, a 40 per cent increase on 1993 (Brown, 2000: 91). During the 1980s the group became Asia's biggest exporter of processed and frozen chickens, mainly to Japan, China and Brazil. One of its largest ventures outside its agribusiness core was its stake in Telecom Asia, a joint venture with the US telecommunications giant Nynex. By the early 1990s the CP Group controlled more than 280 affiliated companies, of which only 14 were listed on stock exchanges worldwide (see Table 3.4). In 1993, the group officially reported US$5 billion in revenues and had 200 affiliated companies and 70,000 employees worldwide (Brown,

Table 3.4 Listed members of the Charoen Pokphand Group from Thailand, 1994

Name of company	Stock exchange	Market capitalization November 1994 (US$ million)	Net profit 1993 (US$ million)	CP stake (%)
1 EK Chor China Motorcycle	New York	360	20	72
2 CP Pokphand	Hong Kong, London	622	44	56
3 Hong Kong Fortune	Hong Kong	107	0	64
4 Orient Telecom and Technology	Hong Kong	896	12	51
5 CP Indonesia	Jakarta	234	13	71
6 CP Prima	Jakarta	198	6	92
7 CP Enterprise	Taipei	132	2	30
8 Shanghai Dajiang	Shanghai	141	17	44
9 CP Feedmill	Bangkok	839	48	39
10 CP Northeastern	Bangkok	60	3	59
11 Bangkok Produce Merchandising	Bangkok	49	3	37
12 Bangkok Agri-Industrial Products	Bangkok	118	4	73
13 Telecom Asia	Bangkok	9,030	23	29
14 Siam Makro	Bangkok	875	6	15

Sources: East Asia Analytical Unit (1995: Table A7.1); Brown (2000).

2000: 87). By 2002 its total revenue had increased to US$13 billion, its employees numbered over 100,000 and the geographical coverage of its 250 affiliates extended over more than 20 countries (http://www.cpthai-land.com, accessed on 14 March 2003). At its peak in 1995, the Cheara-vanont family's wealth was estimated at US$5.5 billion, making it the 25th wealthiest Chinese families in the world (Shikatani, 1995: Table 4.1). As shown in Table 1.6, the wealth of Dhanin Chearavanont, the fourth son of co-founder Chia Ek Chor, remained relatively unscathed after the 1997–8 Asian economic crisis, enabling him to stay on *Forbes'* list of the world's richest billionaires throughout the 1997–2003 period.

Another critical geographical indication of the extent of the globaliza-tion of Chinese firms is the flow of ethnic Chinese capital to the Triad countries in North America and Western Europe. We begin to observe an emerging spatial division of investment: ethnic Chinese capital in these Triad countries originates largely from Chinese firms based in Hong Kong, Singapore and Taiwan (see Sim and Pandian, 2003), whereas most Chinese firms from Southeast Asian countries engage in intra-regional investment. Some of the high-profile investments in North America and Western Europe by ethnic Chinese firms from Hong Kong are Li Ka-shing's property development projects in Vancouver (Olds, 2001; Chapter 4), his inroads into the telecommunications industry in the UK (via former Orange plc), and the acquisitions of hotel chains by property-based Chinese firms (see Yeung, 1998a, 2000d). As evident in the case of Singapore's Hong Leong Group (see Chapter 5), some of these property Chinese firms are increasingly interested in expanding their corporate empire by acquiring hotels throughout the world (Go and Pine, 1995). In bringing their entrepreneurial and deal-making expertise to North America and Western Europe, they not only showcase distinctive cultural practices in Chinese capitalism to their counterparts in the host regions, but more importantly they also learn how to enrol in and benefit from globalizing actor-networks in the international business and finance spheres. In turn, their globalization trails serve as an organizational platform through which new management norms and financial practices are introduced back into their 'home' economies. This process of hybridizing Chinese capitalism is therefore arguably more associated with the recent geographic expansion of key Chinese actors since the 1980s.

Strategies and modes of successful internationalization

The changing global context of competition and local configurations of Chinese capitalism have provided favourable conditions for the internationalization of ethnic Chinese firms from East and Southeast Asia. In their globalization drive, Chinese firms may face severe competition in different markets and constraints in different institutional contexts. Table 3.5 summarizes the operating contexts and strategies of internationalization among the leading Chinese firms from East and Southeast Asia. How do they overcome these difficulties and constraints? What are their strategies for growth in order to capture globalization benefits? Three strategies clearly emerge: sectoral specialization, diversification and control strategies.

Sectoral specialization

Sectoral specialization through forward and backward integration is a common strategy adopted by ethnic Chinese conglomerates in their internationalization process. This strategy is applicable to both manufacturing and non-manufacturing Chinese firms when specialization takes place in different segments of the value chain. For manufacturing firms, sectoral specialization refers to focusing on certain core manufacturing capabilities to achieve scale economies and cost advantages (Porter, 1985). The Taiwanese firm Acer's backward integration into R&D facilities in the US and forward integration into PC sales services is a good example (see also Mathews, 2002). For non-manufacturing firms (e.g. finance and property development firms), sectoral specialization often means continuous expansion of the corporate group to establish a significant presence in different markets. Both Robert Kuok from Malaysia and Kwek Leng Beng from Singapore are good examples of how they have expanded their hotel operations throughout Asia and beyond (via respectively Shangri-la Hotels Ltd and Millennium and Copthorne Hotels plc). In the property sector, Li Ka-shing from Hong Kong has made significant investments in the property market in Canada, particularly Vancouver, and in Singapore (see a case study in Chapter 4).

Market access becomes a key concern to most of these giant Chinese conglomerates. In this regard, transnational operations have become a means through which they consolidate their competitive position in particular business fields and to extend their value-added activities across borders. Most Chinese firms from East and Southeast Asia, however, tend to specialize in niche markets within particular sectors and industries. They are unable to produce sophisticated products with a strong brand name (like Acer). Rather, most firms prefer to operate in the interstices of the trading and subcontracting world. Many of the SMEs in Hong Kong, Singapore and Taiwan specialize in parts of the production chains and international subcontracting networks that are essentially controlled by giant global corporations from the Triad regions (Appelbaum, 2000; Chew and Yeung, 2001; Sim and Pandian, 2003). These SMEs may venture into other Asian countries in order to secure access to low-cost production sites and to meet the demand of their principal customers. Much of cross-border investment from Hong Kong and Taiwan is of this sort of origin. To a certain extent, their cross-border activities represent at best some degree of regionalization rather than globalization, because they have yet to make a global presence and to integrate their worldwide operations.

Diversification strategies

In their globalization process, some large Chinese conglomerates have particularly favoured diversification strategies. They tend to diversify from their core businesses that are often property development (e.g. Cheung Kong Holdings from Hong Kong), finance (e.g. the Hong Leong Group from Malaysia and Singapore), agribusiness (e.g. the CP Group from Thailand) and primary resources production (e.g. the Salim Group from Indonesia and the Kerry Group from Malaysia). Two factors account for their diversification strategies. First, many Chinese firms had gained their wealth and capital base through investments in real estates and trading businesses. They subsequently became cash-rich and needed to reduce their risks associated with excessive dependence on return to investments in these two volatile sectors. Diversification into other business fields posed as an attractive option to hedge their risks (see the case studies of Richard Li's PCCW and Kwek Leng Beng's Hong Leong Group in Chapter 5). Another reason for risk diversification was the pervasive threat of host-country governmental expropriation and ethnic discrimination

Table 3.5 Operating contexts and internationalization strategies of leading Chinese firms from East and Southeast Asia

Company name (in order of appearance in text)	Major shareholder (ethnic Chinese)	Major operations abroad	Operating contexts	Strategies of internationalization
Acer Computers (Taiwan)	Stanley Shih	• Acer Computers (worldwide)	• strong domestic government support • first-mover advantage in low-cost PC • high leverage on organizational innovations	• sectoral specialization and vertical integration in the IT industry • R&D facilities in the US
Kerry Group (Malaysia)	Robert Kuok	• TVB Group (HK and Asia) • Shangri-la Hotels (Asia)	• sugar monopoly in the domestic economy • successful presence in Hong Kong • long experience in hotel ownership and management	• sectoral specialization in hotel development • recent acquisitions in the media and cultural industries
Charoen Pokphand Group (Thailand)	Chearavanont family	• CP Pokphand (HK and China) • Telecom Asia (Asia)	• huge market for agribusiness in China • first Thai conglomerate moving into China (1981) • privatization of telecom industry in Thailand	• sectoral specialization and vertical integration in agribusiness • acquisitions of Telecom Asia to jump-start

Group	Key individual	Companies	Notes
Cheung Kong Holdings (Hong Kong)	Li Ka-shing family	• Hutchison Whampoa (worldwide) • Vodaphone (worldwide) • PCCW (worldwide)	• saturation in domestic property markets • leading positions in several domestic sectors (property, electricity, port and telecom) • high market capitalization in domestic stock exchange • sectoral specialization in property and port development abroad • acquisitions of the former Orange plc in the UK (subsequently acquired by Vodaphone plc, UK)
Hong Leong Group (Singapore)	Kwek Leng Beng	• CDL Hotels (worldwide)	• saturation of property development in Singapore • experience in running hotels in Singapore • large capital from property development and financial arms of the group • recent acquisitions of Millennium and Copthorne Hotels plc (UK) • local listing of hotels, e.g. CDL on Hong Kong Stock Exchange and M&C plc on London Stock Exchange
Salim Group (Indonesia)	Liem Sioe Liong	• First Pacific Group (HK) • KMP Group (Singapore)	• capital accumulation through political patronage in Indonesia • threat of ethnic backlash in Indonesia • deregulation and competition in Indonesia since the mid-1980s • diversification into unrelated businesses through First Pacific Group in Hong Kong • greenfield investment to set up KMP in Singapore

described on pages 90–1. Second, the diversification of Chinese firms into different business activities was often driven by opportunities arising from their diverse networks of personal and business relationships. As a result, the diversification of Chinese firms into different fields was sometimes determined by social relationships, not by strategic necessity (Hamilton, 2000). For example, although the diversification of Thailand's CP Group from feed mills to poultry farming is rather predictable, it is much more difficult to work out why it diversified into motorcycle manufacturing and telecommunications joint ventures. This unwieldy diversification led to severe losses in these new businesses during the 1997–8 Asian economic crisis, even though its core agribusiness remained profitable enough to cross-subsidize its losses (Brown, 2000: 91).

The internationalization of Indonesia's Salim Group has also been closely linked to ongoing expansion and diversification of its domestic operations (see Table 3.5). Sato (1993) has identified several phases in the development of the Salim Group. Founded in 1953, Liem Sioe Liong's group of companies focused on trading in important commodities. From the late 1960s to the mid-1980s, the former President Suharto's government pursued import-substitution policies and promoted such industries. Liem was one of the main beneficiaries of this policy. The group's total capital during 1970–85 grew at an average annual rate of 46 per cent. By 1985 it had reached US$550 million, a 300-fold increase since 1970 (Sato, 1993: 413). This process of rapid expansion and diversification can be divided into four major phases: entry into manufacturing (1968–74); setting up banking (1975–8); expanding the cement business (1977–81); and conglomerate diversification into unrelated businesses (1981–5). During the first phase (1968–74), the Salim Group focused on developing domestic manufacturing operations in Indonesia (e.g. textiles, flour milling and automobile assembly). However, it was only during the second phase (1975–8) that the group began to engage in overseas operations. Established in 1957, Bank Central Asia (BCA) underwent significant restructuring during this period under the management of Mochtar Riady, who was appointed its president in May 1975. In order to compete with other domestic private banks in Indonesia by raising low-cost funds needed for low-interest-rate lending, Liem and Mochtar jointly set up a deposit-taking company, the Central Asia Capital Corporation in Hong Kong in May 1975 (Sato, 1993: 416).

The Salim Group established another significant presence in Hong Kong during the fourth phase (1981–5), when it acquired the First Pacific Group in May 1982 and listed it on the Hong Kong Stock Exchange in 1983. Establishing subsidiaries in Hong Kong (and later in Singapore) has enabled the Salim Group to take advantage of lower taxation, to hedge against business risks, to facilitate financial operations and information collection and, perhaps most importantly, to disguise the real ownership of assets by the group in anticipation of hostile public sentiment in

Indonesia. Until recently, the First Pacific Group was synonymous with the Salim Group's overseas operations. Its four main lines of business used to be the distribution and sale of consumer goods, finance and banking, real estate, property and telecommunications. Through First Pacific, the Salim Group successfully acquired the long-established Dutch trading company Hagemeyer NV, the Thai trading company Berli Jucker Co. Ltd and Metro Drugs Inc. of the Philippines. Hagemeyer had an extensive network of overseas operations spanning at least 21 countries in Europe and Asia. More interestingly, the First Pacific Group posed as an important corrective to the common perception of Liem Sioe Liong's family business as the highly authoritative and hierarchical empire that characterizes Chinese capitalism. Since the early 1990s, professional managers have been managing the First Pacific Group. These managers have enormous international business experience. As a former group financial controller remarked,

> We are very unusual for a Hong Kong company in that the shareholders do not involve themselves actively in the management of the company. So if you look at Cheung Kong or Hutchison that are Li Ka-shing companies, or Wharf, you have Peter Woo or many other companies, their shareholders and management are quite closely related. I think First Pacific is virtually the only company which you don't have that. Obviously in the Hongkong and Shanghai Bank, the maximum shareholding of one company in the Bank can be 1 per cent. So there is no controlling family. Or in the Swire Group, where the family still has an influence in Swire, it's not the management; Jardine also or whatever. But First Pacific is very distinctive. We have in Hong Kong this head office; we don't have any Indonesians at all. There is not one Indonesian involved in the operations. So there is a real divorce between management and ownership.
>
> (Author's interview in Hong Kong, 28 February 1994)

The executive chairman in 2003, Manuel V. Pangilinan, was in charge of American Express's Asia-Pacific operations before joining First Pacific in 1993 as its managing director (author's interview in Hong Kong, 28 February 1994; http://www.firstpacco.com, accessed on 14 March 2003). After he took over the company from members of the Liem family, he strengthened the group through product diversification rather than focusing on its major core financial interests in Hibernia Bank and United Savings Bank (USA) in California and First Pacific Bank in Hong Kong (Brown, 2000: 253–4). Although the group faced a US$3 billion debt as a result of the 1997–8 Asian economic crisis, Pangilinan managed to turn the group round by selling its stake in Hagemeyer in January 1998 for US$1.7 billion, and divesting from its telecommunications units for another US$2 billion and the banking operations in California and Hong Kong. As evident in Table 1.5, the First Pacific Group remains highly ranked as the top 17th TNC from emerging economies in 2000, with foreign assets of US$2.1 billion and total employment of 45,911.

Control strategies

In order to compete for growth over time, Chinese firms must pursue certain control strategies that facilitate globalization. One key nexus of these managerial strategies in Chinese firms is the control and coordination of their overseas subsidiaries (see more detailed analysis in Chapter 6). Control and coordination are important in sustaining the competitive advantage of TNCs and their overseas operations because of the difficulties in transferring their competitive advantage from home countries to host countries (Hu, 1995). If appropriate control and coordination are not exercised in the management of foreign affiliates, a TNC may eventually find its firm-specific advantages being eroded in an era of global competition. In Chapter 1, it was noted that the patriarch of the family often exercises tight control and coordination of his family firm. This is possible because of sheer proximity of different business units within the same 'home' economy or the presence of networks of personal and business relationships. One explanation is that these firms are still inexperienced in internationalization. Internalization of management and control therefore provides a better safety net for these firms to protect their firm-specific advantages and to maximize their benefits from network relationships with other firms abroad. Typically, a Chinese firm from East and Southeast Asia prefers centralization through family owner-ship and control. The ownership structure often develops into very intric-ate intra-group shareholdings, often known as pyramid shareholding structures, that reflect the patriarch's desire to keep the whole group under control with minimum investment of their own and maximum mobilization of external resources (see also La Porta *et al.*, 1999; Claessens *et al.*, 2000). Palanca (1995: 198) pointed out that:

> [d]espite the exposure of the younger generation to modern types of business and the increase in connections with the other elite groups of society, the modern Chinese still preferred to keep their core busi-ness links within the family. Although there are partnerships with Fil-ipino and foreign counterparts, the control remained within the family.

When these Chinese family firms globalize their operations, it is question-able whether the patriarch can still exercise the same extent of control and coordination over foreign subsidiaries (see more detailed empirical analysis in Chapters 4 and 5). There is not just the issue of geographic dis-tance, but also the confrontation of new business environments. When these firms from Asia try to venture into unfamiliar marketplaces in North

America and Western Europe, acquisitions are preferred because the open business environment does not give these Chinese firms the significant competitive advantage that they enjoy in the opaque Asian business environment. These open business fields in the developed regions of the global economy intensify competition and accentuate the importance of economies of scale and expertise, particularly to those new entrants from Asia. Acquisitions of existing operations in these Triad countries facilitate risk minimization and the accumulation of experience, both of which pave ways for subsequent major investments in the host countries. Some of these new business environments, such as North America or Western Europe, may not justify tight control and coordination of local subsidiaries by their parent Chinese firms in Asia. Faced with direct competition and open business fields, many foreign subsidiaries of Chinese firms need to respond quickly and be able to adapt their organizational structures to allow for more local autonomy and decision-making. Professional managers with extensive international business experience are thus managing most of the transnational operations in North America and Western Europe of the six leading Chinese family-owned conglomerates in Table 3.5, such as Kwek Leng Beng's Millennium and Copthorne Hotels plc in the UK, Li Ka-shing's stake in the UK's Vodaphone and Liem Sioe Liong's First Pacific in Hong Kong. Such leading Chinese firms can also take in more local expertise through local partners and joint ventures, thereby building up new sources of competitive advantage to compete in the regional and global marketplace (Lee and Chen, 2003).

Firm-specific advantages also play an important role in explaining the choice of internationalization modes by Chinese firms. If a particular firm's key internationalization strategy is to secure technology and market share in order to overcome its lack of firm-specific competitive advantage, it may choose to directly acquire existing foreign operations. Taiwanese and Singaporean electronics firms particularly favour this approach when they internationalize into the US market. For example, as part of a strategy to reduce its dependence on OEM sales and to build up its market position in the US, Acer acquired Counterpoint, a start-up firm that built a powerful minicomputer using multiple microprocessors, in 1987 for US$6 million (Hu, 1995: 85). In 1990 Acer paid US$94 million for Altos Computer Systems Inc., a Silicon Valley firm that has an extensive network of distributors, to improve its distribution and market presence in America (Yeung, 1994a: 43). When a Chinese firm has gained sufficient firm-specific competitive advantage in its domestic countries, it may pursue a beachhead strategy for internationalization, where it may first engage in joint ventures with foreign firms to test the water. The foreign joint venture operation also serves as a unit for marketing and gathering information and intelligence to prepare the parent firm for the eventual establishment of wholly owned subsidiaries in the host countries.

Conclusion

This chapter has provided a fairly broad and general analysis of the changing dynamics of the internationalization of ethnic Chinese firms from East and Southeast Asian economies. In particular, it has examined the changing structural and institutional contexts in which these firms are embedded. In an era of accelerated globalization of economic activities, these firms continue to evolve from ethnocentric firms to large conglomerates capable of competing in the regional and global economy. Today, the unique configuration of institutional and organizational contexts that explains the early characteristics of Chinese capitalism and its key actors has certainly been changed. As the domestic economies of these firms enter into different stages of economic development and political change, these ethnic-based firms also move into different stages of their geographic expansion. In their drive towards globalization, these firms tend to prefer acquisitions and joint ventures as the main vehicles of foreign market entry. This preference can be explained by their relative lack of firm-specific competitive advantage (e.g. technology and managerial know-how) and their unfamiliarity with host-country business environments. After all, many of these firms have grown out of protected institutional environments in which information flows are limited and monopolistic advantages are maintained by patron–client relationships. Moreover, many of these firms choose to specialize in specific niche segments of the value chain because of the same reasons. For those with large capital base because of monopolistic positions in their 'home' economies, they exist in the form of giant conglomerates with diverse business interests and hundreds of affiliated companies. They prefer to diversify rather than to consolidate their business interests, in view of the inherent risk factor in the Asian institutional environment. As their business horizons are increasingly global in scale and their operations diversified in scope, the organizational characteristics of these firms are likely to become more diverse and dynamic. This dynamic process of change has brought about fundamental transformations in the nature of Chinese capitalism to a mode of hybrid capitalism in which a diverse mixture of capitalist norms and structures coexists.

4 Transnational entrepreneurship

Transnational entrepreneurship: the missing link of research on Chinese capitalism

Internationalization and its associated activities have become one of the most transformative dimensions of Chinese capitalism in today's globalizing world economy (see also Figure 1.2). When leading actors in Chinese capitalism extend their economic operations across borders, they are often entering into host business environments that are fundamentally different from their 'home' economies in terms of institutional and market structures, industrial organization, social relations and cultural practices. To overcome these barriers to internationalization, or what is commonly known in the management literature as 'the liability of foreignness' (Zaheer, 1995; Matsuo, 2000), leading Chinese firms require actors who are creative, proactive, adaptive and resourceful in different countries and regions; these are all critical aspects of transnational entrepreneurship, the ongoing process of calculated risk-taking and foresight in foreign business venturing (see Yeung, 2002a, 2002c). Sometimes these ethnic Chinese actors are the owners or founding entrepreneurs themselves. They often participate actively in the establishment and management of foreign operations. More commonly, those who spearhead the transnational operations of Chinese firms are 'intrapreneurs' or professional managers. They are neither founders nor owners; they may not even be ethnic Chinese hired on the basis of their personal relationships to the founders or owners. This new breed of actors in Chinese capitalism are given much autonomy to manage transnational operations. They may be equally entrepreneurial in their approach to managing cross-border operations. Examining the nature, *modus operandi* and performance of these entrepreneurs and intrapreneurs is therefore vital both to understanding the successful internationalization of these firms and to unpacking the changing dynamics of Chinese capitalism itself.

In this empirical chapter first I will discuss unpacking transnational entrepreneurship, a key missing link in much of the existing research on Chinese capitalism. As reviewed briefly in Chapter 1, previous studies of Chinese capitalism have almost exclusively emphasized the domestic entrepreneurial tendencies of ethnic Chinese in individual East and Southeast Asian economies and explained them in relation to cultural and/or institutional factors.[1] Entrepreneurship in Chinese capitalism has been construed in these studies as strongly embedded in uniquely Chinese cultural practices that serve as the organizational foundations to overcome ethnic-biased discriminatory political agenda in some Asian economies or state-driven economic development processes in others. Couched in these narrow terms, it is not surprising that Chinese capitalism has been recognized in the literature as largely a passive and static form of economic organization reacting primarily to domestic pressures in East and Southeast Asia economies. In a globalizing era, however, transnational entrepreneurship, a phenomenon much less acknowledged in the literature, plays an increasingly important role in the internationalization of Chinese firms from East and Southeast Asia and in opening up new horizons for cross-border learning and experiences. Many attributes of domestic entrepreneurship can be fruitfully exploited across borders to become transnational entrepreneurship. In Chinese capitalism, this interconnection between domestic and transnational entrepreneurship is even more pronounced and important because of the extensive interpenetration of Chinese business networks throughout the Asian region. The success of regional Chinese businesses can be attributed to the transformation of the entrepreneurial skills of Chinese entrepreneurs from predominantly domestic foundations to increasingly regional (and global) orientations. Thus these entrepreneurs are capable of transferring their skills and goodwill from their 'home' economies to the host countries and, in the process, filling various gaps in economic spaces (see case studies below). In this process of internationalization the leading actors also encounter different operating contexts and modes of organizational practices that require them to 'disembed' from the coping strategies (e.g. patron–client relationships) and entrepreneurial practices (e.g. family-oriented management) of their domestic contexts. This disembedding process brings out significant transformations in the nature and organization of Chinese capitalism to an increasingly hybridized mode of economic organization.

My second objective in this chapter is to offer some important theoretical and empirical correctives to the 'three-generation model' of Chinese capitalism. Previous studies of domestic entrepreneurship in Chinese capitalism have assumed not only the foundational importance of the family, but also the failure of the family firm to extend beyond three generations (see Wong, 1985, 1988; Yeung, 2000g, 2001). The universalization of this 'three-generation model' may be appropriate in Chinese capitalism in its domestic settings primarily because of fairly enduring organizational and institutional contexts that provide little incentive for different generations of family members to change and transform the family firm. Stagnation and decline may be the dominant features after the second generation of many Chinese family firms in East and Southeast Asia. When we consider the dynamics of Chinese capitalism in a global era, however, it becomes clear that the new generation of ethnic Chinese taking charge of their family firms is often endowed with different sorts of entrepreneurial tendencies from their fathers or even grandfathers. As noted in Chapter 2, this new generation has developed much better access to diversified globalizing actor-networks in international business and finance. Their complex repertoires of knowledge and skills are also likely to be much wider in relation to their international education and management experience. They are capable of bringing their traditional family firms across borders to tap into new economic opportunities. They can succeed their parents and grandparents in terms of not only family succession, but also of business performance and management practices. Internationalization, an underdeveloped theme in the existing literature on Chinese capitalism, thus provides both an important mechanism for the further growth of traditional Chinese family firms and a critical medium through which the new generation of family members can practise and extend their entrepreneurial tendencies in a transnational context.

In the next section, I briefly examine the nature of transnational entrepreneurship in Chinese capitalism as a precursor to the two subsequent empirical sections. In the third section, I provide an empirical analysis of the role of transnational entrepreneurship in the regionalization of Chinese family firms from Singapore and Hong Kong, and how entrepreneurs from these firms are able to capitalize on a diverse range of actor-networks beyond simply their family networks as predicted in the culturalist analysis of Chinese capitalism (see Chapter 1). There follows two case studies of Chinese family firms to showcase their succession through internationalization and the professionalization of management: Li Ka-shing and his son, Victor Li, from Hong Kong, and the Eu Yan Sang family from Singapore. These case studies serve to challenge the predominant three-generation model of the Chinese family firm. The last section introduces a revised model of the Chinese family firm in a globalizing era and offers some general lessons for understanding the changing dynamics of Chinese capitalism.

Transnational entrepreneurship and Chinese capitalism

Ethnic Chinese in East and Southeast Asia are well known to be exceptionally entrepreneurial in their domestic economies (see Chapter 3). Many of them have formed formidable business networks embedded in particularized family and social ties as well as political-economic alliances. Business networks are constituted not only of fellow Chinese entrepreneurs, but sometimes also of political figures (e.g. Taiwan and Thailand) and non-Chinese business people (e.g. Hong Kong and Singapore). Since the 1970s it has become clear that ethnic Chinese entrepreneurs are increasingly spreading their business networks across countries and also regions. This process represents a significant development in the business history of Chinese capitalism because transnational operations demand more than just traditional modes of social norms and economic practices to secure competitive advantage and to ensure the business success of these Chinese entrepreneurs in their 'home' economies (see also Chapter 3). Kao (1993: 32) may be right in arguing that 'cross-border investments alone are responsible for turning the de facto network of loose family relationships into today's Chinese commonwealth'. But he offers little to explain why and how such a transformation in the spatial organization of Chinese business networks takes place. Transnational entrepreneurship plays a critical role not only in spreading these business networks abroad, but also in transforming them into significant business opportunities.

What exactly then is the nature of transnational entrepreneurship? I have defined it elsewhere as a learning process because transnational entrepreneurship evolves from experience and learning gained through progressive involvement in foreign operations (Yeung, 2002a, 2002c). Through these cross-border operations, transnational entrepreneurs not only learn how to deal with unexpected contingencies in the host countries, but also develop a deeper understanding of their realities. Strong transnational entrepreneurship also requires taking certain risks. Of course, not all risk-taking is good, at least from a firm's point of view. But transnational entrepreneurs must have certain inherent capabilities to absorb calculated risks, that is, the right kind of risks, the sort that generate potential gain. This capability is particularly critical because operations in a foreign land are often filled with uncertainties and potential business risks. In fact, the capacity will increase with his/her experience with the host countries. A critical factor is the informal information and peer support he/she receives from the host country. The actor-network system becomes important here because strong social and business networks, albeit no longer exclusively 'family' and 'Chinese', may serve as the institutional foundations for transnational entrepreneurship. Social and political institutions significantly shape the attitudes of individual entrepreneurs and intrapreneurs. Transnational entrepreneurs are therefore conceived as creative individuals embedded in wider cross-border business networks and social and political institutions. These provide the necessary strategic infrastructure to enable the success of the entrepreneurs. Intrapreneurs are professional managers who are empowered to manage transnational operations. The empowerment may come from the founding entrepreneurs themselves through a prolonged process of socialization. It may also be institutionalized within the organization itself when top management from headquarters delegates power and control to professional managers abroad. This is known as an intra-firm network that facilitates headquarters' control and coordination of overseas subsidiaries through corporatized mechanisms (see case studies below).[2]

Another attribute defining transnational entrepreneurship is foresight in foreign ventures, which is important at least from the perspective of strategic management (see also case studies in Chapter 5). Foresight distinguishes domestic entrepreneurship from transnational entrepreneurship.

An entrepreneur is often well entrenched in his/her domestic economy and may have a strong sense of inertia towards venturing abroad, given his/her comfortable 'home' market share. But a transnational entrepreneur needs to possess vision and foresight in order to position the future of his/her (family) firm in an era of global competition (e.g. Acer from Taiwan in Mathews, 2002; and Li & Fung from Hong Kong in Fung, 1997; Magretta, 1998). Though often assisted by professional analysts and strategists, he/she must be able to identify market opportunities abroad and tap into them. This relentless search for direct investments in foreign markets is important in today's global economy because market presence remains the fundamental drive for an entrepreneur to venture abroad, whether he/she runs a manufacturing or a service firm. If successful, this entrepreneur will enjoy first-mover advantages unavailable to other firms and their actors. Every foreign venture, therefore, may appear as a new business start-up, synonymous with the process of new firms' formation so well documented in most entrepreneurship studies (McDougall *et al.*, 1994; Brush, 1995; McDougall and Oviatt, 1996, 2000; Yeung, 2002c, 2003b). The difference here, though, is that once a foreign venture is established, a transnational entrepreneur must continue to resolve operational and management problems in an operating context very different from his/her domestic economy. Transnational entrepreneurship is important in international business environments primarily for two reasons: foreign ventures are full of risks and uncertainties; and vision and foresight can help diversify one's business portfolios beyond the domestic economy.

How then does this concept translate into business practices in the context of Chinese capitalism and how does it enhance the internationalization of Chinese firms? Three attributes are particularly key in facilitating the transnational operations of Chinese firms: their greater opportunities for internalizing overseas markets, their trust and goodwill in host countries and their enrolment in transnational social and business networks. First, these entrepreneurs exhibit a greater tendency to internalize foreign markets through direct investments and other forms of equity investments (see also Chapter 3 for evidence on acquisitions). In cross-border operations, the drive towards ownership and control implies that transnational Chinese entrepreneurs are more willing to venture into possibly opaque business environments (e.g. mainland China), because once established, such ventures are less risky under the direct control and management of the entrepreneurs and their trusted managers. The entrepreneurs are also more likely to take a personal approach to these foreign ventures through direct participation in negotiation and more frequent visits. These aspects of transnational entrepreneurship are particularly useful in host countries with opaque business environments and ineffective corporate governance systems. Direct ownership in highly competitive and open business environments (e.g. North America and Western Europe) requires both transnational entrepreneurship and significant competitive advantages (e.g. brand names, proprietary technology, management expertise and so on). It also necessitates the strategic enrolment of Chinese transnational entrepreneurs in globalizing actor-networks in these host regions (see the case of Victor Li below).

Second, although developing ethnic-centric trust and goodwill forms an integral part of traditional business practices in Chinese capitalism, its strategic deployment during the internationalization of Chinese firms must be acknowledged. For aspiring transnational Chinese entrepreneurs, having strong trust and goodwill in the host countries (often Asia) certainly helps to open doors and gain better acceptance by the host business and political communities. Thus there is less need for complex and detailed contracts to be negotiated, because verbal guarantees by such an entrepreneur, well known for his/her trustworthy behaviour, are better than many contracts that lay out all contingencies. This reliance on trust and goodwill rather than just formal contracts is much less common in Anglo-American capitalism (see Chapter 1). Trust and goodwill are important not only for penetrating difficult host countries in Asia, but also for establishing themselves successfully in highly competitive business environments. Some of today's transnational Chinese entrepreneurs are increasingly globalizing into North America and Western Europe (Yeung and Olds, 2000a). It must be stressed that trust and goodwill, in their strategic and discursive modes, can be a significant source of competitive advantage that enables these key actors in Chinese capitalism to receive support from powerful non-Chinese bankers and financial analysts and therefore gain access to global capital markets. Strategically, trust and goodwill can be accumulated through improvement in corporate governance and incorporation of professional management (see Chapter 6). Discursively, trust and goodwill can be constructed through the enrolment of media reporters and financial analysts in Chinese business networks. The access to global capital and finance thus enables a widening of traditionally Chinese business networks to enrol strategically non-Chinese actors who function as bridges for transnational Chinese entrepreneurs to enter these globally competitive markets (see case studies in Chapter 5). Although they may prefer to own and control foreign ventures, transnational Chinese entrepreneurs do not always take an authoritarian approach to these ventures. They often delegate responsibilities to trusted members of their inner circles who are often non-Chinese. Traditionally, these members would be kin of the entrepreneurs. In a globalizing era, however, they are more likely to be non-family members who have been socialized into the entrepreneur's family through a process of family-ization (Chan and Chiang, 1994: 297). Some foreign ventures are established to provide opportunities both for developing family succession and for internalizing enterprising employees. Over time, more competent professional managers are socialized into Chinese capitalism such that they become trusted insiders in this reshaped hybrid capitalism.

Third, transnational Chinese entrepreneurs often rely on their social and business networks to facilitate foreign ventures, although (as argued in Chapter 2), these networks are no longer exclusively 'Chinese' in terms of their ethnic constituency. Studies of ethnic Chinese entrepreneurs from Hong Kong have revealed the importance of personal history and embedded interests in their transnational operations (e.g. Siu and Martin, 1992; Yeung, 1998a, 2002a). Contemporary Chinese are experienced migrants and form socially organized networks to provide emotional and personal support. Sometimes these networks are constituted almost exclusively of family and clan members. As Kao (1993: 24) argued, 'for many generations, emigrant Chinese entrepreneurs have been operating comfortably in a network of family and clan, laying the foundations for stronger links among businesses across national borders' (see case studies on pages 134–7). In other circumstances, transnational Chinese entrepreneurs may rely on their trusted friends and employees to develop business networks across borders. These strong personal relationships with key employees often result in the growth of transnational intrapreneurs who are empowered by their owners to develop foreign ventures. Such ethnic Chinese entrepreneurs therefore need to take significant risks and possess foresight in the selection and delegation of the transnational intrapreneurs. These three dimensions of transnational entrepreneurship offer a new horizon for us to examine the changing nature and organization of Chinese capitalism in a global era. While they do not necessarily imply the complete withering away of traditional cultural values and norms of Chinese capitalism, they certainly provide some useful analytical clues to understand the emergence of a hybrid mixture of entrepreneurial tendencies that characterize Chinese capitalism today.

Capitalizing on actor-networks abroad: the regionalization of Chinese family firms from Singapore

Before presenting some empirical findings from my survey of Chinese family firms in Singapore, it is useful to examine very briefly the developmental context of Singapore since its independence in 1965. Since then, the PAP-led (People's Action Party) state has planned and implemented several national development strategies to create and sustain Singapore's competitiveness in the face of accelerated global competition (Yeung, 2002a). While the state was able to pursue a labour-intensive export-oriented manufacturing platform for industrialization in the 1960s and the 1970s, the strategy met favourable global conditions when major American and European manufacturers were looking for alternative low-cost production sites to relocate their labour-intensive operations (an early process of economic globalization). By the late 1970s and early 1980s, Singapore was no longer competitive in attracting low-cost manufacturing assembly investment because cheaper production locations could be found throughout the world, notably in neighbouring Asian developing countries. Singapore then faced a competitiveness crunch in the changing international division of labour. To regain its competitiveness in the global space of flows, the state revised its national development strategies in favour of promoting high-tech and high-value-added manufacturing and business services (Rodan, 1989; Huff, 1994; Chiu *et al.*, 1997; Low, 1998). This strategy worked quite well during the 1980s when Singapore became an attractive location for clusters of global corporations in computer and chemical industries (see Wang and Yeung, 2000). In the mid-1980s, the state also introduced competitive packages of incentives to attract global corporations to locate their regional offices or regional headquarters in Singapore. The idea of promoting the control and coordination functions of global corporations fitted well into the new concept of world city formation through which Singapore aimed to be a major international business hub of the region (Perry *et al.*, 1998a, 1998b; Yeung *et al.*, 2001).

By the early 1990s Singapore had been transformed into a regional coordination centre capable of significant R&D activities and management functions (Perry and Tan, 1998; Mathews, 1999; Chew and Yeung, 2001; Phillips and Yeung, 2003). Although it had secured a niche in the competitive global economy, Singapore was still very much dependent on global capital and its major markets in North America and Western Europe. To consolidate further its national competitiveness and to enable the expansion of domestic capital, the state initiated the regionalization programme in 1993 through which Singaporean companies, in the forms of government-linked companies, family-owned firms or diversified shareholding companies, were encouraged to venture abroad. By building up its external wing, the state believed that Singapore not only could tap into the opportunities of the regional economy, but also could ride out economic crisis in the domestic economy. The Singapore Department of Statistics (1991a) estimated that at the end of 1976 FDI from Singapore was slightly above S$1 billion. This figure grew rapidly to S$1.7 billion in 1981, S$13.6 billion in 1990, S$70.6 billion in 1997 and S$91.9 billion in 2000 (http://www.singstat.gov.sg; accessed on 17 March 2003). I have examined elsewhere different aspects of the political economy of Singapore's regionalization programme (Yeung, 1998d, 1999a, 2000h, 2000i, 2002a): first, the regionalization of government-linked companies (GLCs) and other companies set up by statutory boards; and second, 'political entrepreneurship', through which the state opens up overseas business opportunities for private capitalists and negotiates the institutional framework for such opportunities to be tapped by Singaporean firms. During the 1990s the public sector and GLCs accounted for about 60 per cent of Singapore's GDP (Singapore Ministry of Finance, 1993: 39; Singh and Ang, 1998).

It must be emphasized that private capital from Singapore, predominantly ethnic Chinese capital, has a much longer history of regionalization, particularly in Malaysia (see Yeung 1998e), Hong Kong and mainland China. In 1997 these three destinations were among the largest recipients of outward

FDI from Singapore. For example, the earliest government-led investment in mainland China was in 1984 with the incorporation of Chiwan Petroleum Supply Base Co. Ltd in Shekou, near Hong Kong. The Chiwan base was a joint venture between China's Nanshan Development Company and a consortium of Singapore's leading GLCs.[3] But at least two of the 54 Chinese family firms from Singapore in my sample (see Appendix for methodology) set up manufacturing operations in mainland China during the 1970s.[4] Hock San Yuen Food Manufacturing invested in Qingdao as early as in 1975 to manufacture food and beverages. Sunwa Construction & Interior Pte Ltd (formerly Siew Yong Garments) established a garment factory in Guangzhou in 1979 and subsequently moved it to Shenzhen in 1981. Another Chinese family firm, Eu Yan Sang Ltd, set up its first Chinese medicine shop in Hong Kong as early as 1910 (see a full case study below).[5]

Table 4.1 shows the historical geography of these 54 Chinese family-owned TNCs from Singapore, which shows that their internationalization occurred well before the 1993 launch of Singapore's regionalization programme. In fact, their subsidiaries in Hong Kong, Indonesia, Malaysia and other regions (e.g. South America and Africa) were mostly established before 1985. In terms of their geographical spread, these 54 TNCs were operating mainly in Asia, in particular mainland China and Malaysia, which respectively attracted some 59 per cent and 74 per cent of them. Very few of them were indeed global in their geographical scope of operations. Of the four having operations in Europe, only two had operations in North America and Asia. In terms of the number of subsidiaries, the same geographical pattern emerges. Some 87.5 per cent of all 216 subsidiaries

Table 4.1 Historical geography of Chinese family firms from Singapore

Region/Country/Economy	Mean year of establishment	No. of operating TNCs (%)	No. of subsidiaries
Total Southeast Asia	–	–	91 (42.1)
Indonesia	1982	15 (27.8)	16 (7.4)
Malaysia	1983	32 (59.3)	55 (25.5)
Thailand	1988	7 (13.0)	7 (3.2)
Philippines	1994	6 (11.1)	6 (2.8)
Others	1994	7 (13.0)	7 (3.2)
Total East Asia	–	–	98 (45.4)
China	1991	40 (74.1)	77 (35.6)
Hong Kong	1981	14 (25.9)	17 (7.9)
Others	1993	4 (7.4)	4 (1.9)
Europe	1991	4 (7.4)	4 (1.9)
North America	1989	6 (11.1)	6 (2.8)
Other regions	1985	6 (11.1)	17 (7.9)
Sample total	NA	54 (100)	216 (100)

Source: Author's survey (see Appendix for methodology).

were located in Asia, in particular Malaysia (55) and mainland China (77). On average, each Chinese family-owned TNC from Singapore in my sample owned and controlled at least four subsidiaries abroad.

Given the long historical roots of ethnic Chinese investments from Singapore in other Asian countries, transnational entrepreneurs in these Singaporean Chinese family firms managed to extend their business operations across borders. The main focus here is on their capabilities in exploiting diverse actor-networks at regional and, sometimes, global levels (see theoretical explanations in Chapter 2). As shown in Table 4.2, among the 54 Chinese family firms from Singapore, 37 transnational entrepreneurs had some forms of connections/network relationships with the host countries before the establishment of transnational operations. This empirical finding conforms to the incremental model of internationalization well developed in the international business literature (Andersen, 1993; Buckley and Ghauri, 1993; Chryssochoidis *et al.*, 1997; Eriksson *et al.*, 1997; Blomstermo and Sharma, 2002), where TNCs are shown to engage in international business activities incrementally through the accumulation of foreign learning and experience, which happens through developing prior network relationships with foreign customers, suppliers, trading partners and so on (Lee and Chen, 2003).

In Table 4.2 prior connections of Chinese family firms from Singapore were particularly focused on business connections (37) rather than family networks (15), implying a more diversified nature of business networks among Chinese family firms. These prior business activities may be conducted at arm's-length or through introduction by other friends and business contacts. Once the transnational entrepreneurs have gained more experience with the host-country business environments, direct investments become much more attractive because of reduced risks and uncertainties. Good trust and goodwill relationships with host-country trading and business partners (mean score = 1.5) and personal contacts in host countries (mean score = 1.9) were cited as most important in facilitating these transnational operations. My previous research on 73 Chinese firms from Hong Kong also shows a similar pattern of much greater emphasis on business networks than family networks (Yeung, 1997a, 1997b, 1998a). As shown in Table 4.2, although almost 80 per cent of these Chinese firms (58) from Hong Kong had prior business connections with the host economies, only 30 per cent of them (22) had family connections with these host economies. Both sets of empirical findings point to the declining significance of family networks when Chinese firms from Hong Kong and Singapore operate across borders. They also point to the broadening of the scope and diversity of actor-networks among Chinese firms that engage in international business activities.

Transnational Chinese entrepreneurs from Singapore were clearly capable of capitalizing on prior actor-network relationships with host countries, particularly business connections, in order to venture into those

Table 4.2 A typology of prior connections of Chinese family firms from Hong Kong and Singapore

Types of connections	Hong Kong			Singapore		
	Frequency	%	Average importance[1]	Frequency	%	Average importance[1]
Business connections	58	79.5	–	37	68.5	–
• personal contacts	15	20.5	1.8	37	68.5	1.9
• trading and business partners	22	30.1	1.8	17	31.5	1.5
• industrial and commercial associations	2	2.7	5.0	12	22.2	2.6
• customers, suppliers and subcontractors	17	23.3	2.3	21	38.9	2.3
Political connections	4	5.5	–	15	27.8	–
• personal contacts with government officials	3	4.1	1.3	23	42.6	1.8
• special access to government grants/concessions	1	1.4	2.0	11	20.4	1.8
• contracts from host governments	–	–	–	8	14.8	2.1
Family connections	22	30.1	–	15	27.8	–
• relatives	4	5.5	2.5	9	18.5	1.9
• close friends	6	8.2	2.2	9	18.5	1.9
• kinship and clan associations	–	–	–	5	9.3	2.4
Social connections	3	4.1	–	10	18.5	–
• ethnic groups	2	2.7	2.0	9	18.5	2.0
• religious groups	–	–	–	3	5.6	3.3
Total sample size	73	100.0	–	54	100.0	–

Sources: Author's surveys.

Note
1 The scale of importance ranges from Very Important [1] to Not Important At All [5].

countries. My respondents in Singapore voted for three most important network advantages: easier coordination with local headquarters (mean score = 1.4); access to local information and knowledge (mean score = 1.9); and access to new distribution channels and markets (mean score = 2.0). Apparently, these three advantages are all related to better chances of penetrating into the host markets. In that sense, successful foreign ventures by transnational Chinese entrepreneurs from Singapore depend on their ability to exploit actor-network advantages. It is important, however, to caution that these network advantages are neither static in their relevance nor culturally predetermined in all circumstances. Instead, transnational entrepreneurs are expected to develop these ongoing connections when venturing abroad, irrespective of their host economies (see the case of Victor Li in Vancouver below). My respondents identified five key ingredients in enhancing these ongoing network relationships: high trust (25.2 per cent); prior personal or family relationships (17.4 per cent); prior transactional relationships (14.8 per cent); involvement in established networks (12.2 per cent); and strong reputation and creditworthiness (10.4 per cent). These five ingredients accounted for 80 per cent of all responses, indicating that while prior relationships are important in extending emerging actor-networks when venturing abroad, transnational entrepreneurs are expected to demonstrate their trust and credit worthiness through the cross-border operations. Trust relationships and cross-border operations are therefore mutually reinforcing. A Chinese entrepreneur with low-level trust relationships in the host countries finds it more difficult to venture abroad and the lack of success also reduces further his/her trust and creditworthiness in the host countries.

Some of these mutually reinforcing problems and their solutions are presented in Table 4.3, which shows that they are highly uneven across different regions. The lack of home-country government support is a major problem confronting all Chinese family firms in my Singapore sample, irrespective of their host regions of operations. For those operating in East and Southeast Asia, host-government regulation represents one particularly chronic problem. This is not surprising since most host countries in Asia have rather opaque rules and restrictive regulations on foreign investors, whose implementation is also often unpredictable and subject to the likes of host-country governments (see Chapter 3; Backman, 1999). For host developed countries in Europe and North America, the nature of the problems is quite different from Asia. Here the main problems are the lack of personal experience (Europe) and the lack of sufficient financial assets (North America). The open competitive business environments in these regions means that to penetrate the market successfully, transnational Chinese entrepreneurs need to build up substantially their experiential and financial capital bases, a strategic requirement that causes significant pressures to be applied to Chinese capitalism to change and adapt (see the case study of Hong Leong in Chapter 5). In order to resolve these

Table 4.3 Major problems faced and solutions by transnational entrepreneurs from Singapore by host regions

Problems/Solutions	Southeast asia	East Asia	Europe	North America	Other regions
Problems (mean score)[1]					
1 High costs of operations	3.7	3.2	2.8	3.6	3.8
2 Lack of technological edge	4.1	3.9	4.0	4.7	3.8
3 Problems with local partners	3.3	3.4	5.0	5.0	4.0
4 Lack of market information	3.8	3.3	3.3	4.4	3.8
5 Lack of special connections with host countries	3.6	3.4	3.5	4.0	3.8
6 Lack of personal experience	3.4	3.1	2.0	3.8	3.5
7 Labour force problems	3.4	2.9	3.3	4.5	4.0
8 Government regulations	2.9	2.5	3.0	4.0	3.5
9 Lack of sufficient financial assets	3.8	3.3	3.3	2.8	3.8
10 Lack of home government support	1.9	1.9	2.0	–	2.0
Solutions (cases)					
1 Reliance on local partners/connections	11 (18%)	32 (44%)	–	–	–
2 Sending trusted executives from Singapore to manage	2 (3%)	–	–	–	–
3 Asking local government for help	–	9 (12%)	1 (20%)	–	–
4 Closing down the operations/downsizing	8 (13%)	12 (16%)	1 (20%)	–	–
5 Personal involvement of top executives/entrepreneurs	9 (15%)	6 (8%)	–	1 (33%)	3 (50%)
6 Established procedures	12 (20%)	2 (3%)	–	–	2 (33%)
7 Encourage higher worker productivity/training of local staff	4 (7%)	3 (4%)	–	–	–
8 Adopt local practices/conform to local culture	11 (18%)	4 (5%)	1 (20%)	2 (67%)	–
9 Dismiss local staff/change local partners	3 (5%)	5 (7%)	1 (20%)	–	1 (17%)
10 Compensate with better products and customer servicing	–	–	1 (20%)	–	–
Total cases (multiple answers allowed)	60 (100%)	73 (100%)	5 (100%)	3 (100%)	6 (100%)

Source: Author's survey (see Appendix for methodology).

Note
1 The scale of importance ranges from Very Important [1] to Not Important At All [5].

problems in foreign ventures, transnational entrepreneurs in my sample take different approaches in different host regions. For their Asian operations, the entrepreneurs are much more comfortable with reliance on local partners and connections and adopting local practices in resolving operational problems, in particular in mainland China. Their capabilities in exploiting network advantages ensure the success of their foreign ventures in Asia. When asked for the key attributes of entrepreneurship in overcoming the problems of venturing abroad, most of my respondents chose one or more of the following interrelated attributes of transnational entrepreneurship: personal experience and expertise (25 per cent); strong vision and accomplishment (17 per cent); risk-taking (15 per cent); high motivation and independence (12 per cent); and well-connected and resourced (10 per cent). These five attributes of transnational entrepreneurship constituted an overwhelming 80 per cent of all responses.

Although transnational Chinese entrepreneurs have been spearheading the internationalization of Chinese firms from Singapore, we are also witnessing an increasing professionalization of Chinese family business and the emergence of transnational intrapreneurs in these formerly ethnocentric organizations. Very often, transnational Chinese entrepreneurs are unable to manage all their operations abroad. They have to co-opt more professional and trusted managers who are then socialized into the corporate family. Here the extent of transnational entrepreneurship among professional managers who are managing the foreign operations of Chinese family firms from Singapore is considered. First, on examining the survey data to find out how many of the 54 respondents in my sample considered themselves as entrepreneurs, it turned out that 31 of them (57.4 per cent) agreed that they could be considered entrepreneurs. twenty-eight respondents were either chairmen or CEOs/managing directors of Chinese family firms. Almost all of them were the patriarchs or the patriarchs' family members. Seventeen of these 28 respondents (60.7 per cent) claimed to be entrepreneurs. However, among the other 26 respondents who were not family members, only 14 (53.8 per cent) considered themselves as entrepreneurs. When asked about the ingredients of entrepreneurship in their view, there seemed to be a divergence in perception between family and non-family members. Those chairmen, CEOs and managing directors who considered themselves as entrepreneurs cited 'abilities to capitalize on opportunities' as the most important attribute of transnational entrepreneurship (18.4 per cent). Receiving an equal percentage at 13.2 per cent, other important attributes included risk-taking, strong vision and accomplishment, and high motivation and independence. Together, they constituted 57.9 per cent of all responses from these 28 family members. But, non-family members or intrapreneurs tended to cite 'proactive adaptability to different environments' as the most important attribute (18.4 per cent) of transnational entrepreneurship. Other important attributes were similar to those family members.

Based on these empirical observations, transnational intrapreneurs are much more concerned with adaptability issues than owner entrepreneurs who are more opportunity-driven in their entrepreneurial behaviour. This observation should not be surprising because most trusted professional managers may be sent abroad to manage foreign operations. They have often been chosen because of their excellent adaptability to different business environments. Their performance is assessed on the basis of their success in managing and developing these foreign operations (see case studies in Yeung, 2002a, 2002d). Owner entrepreneurs, however, are less concerned with management issues, since they can entrust their transnational intrapreneurs with management responsibilities. Rather, owner entrepreneurs are keen to expand the overall business activities of the group through capitalizing on business opportunities that may arise in different countries or regions. During its internationalization processes, a typical transformation may occur in an entrepreneurial Chinese family firm when key family members are kept in the home country so that they can be groomed to take over from the founder and/or patriarch when the time is right. Though these family members may be involved directly in the establishment and management of overseas subsidiaries, they are often required to take over more important group strategic management functions (Yeung, 2002a: Chapter 5). This observation brings us to the strategic issue of family succession and the professionalization of management in Chinese family firms, particularly those that engage in transnational operations.

Beyond the three-generation model: transnational entrepreneurship in a global era

Despite my arguments for the professionalization of management in Chinese family firms as a key dimension of hybridizing Chinese capitalism, I do not advocate the complete separation of ownership and management as in Anglo-American corporations and managerial capitalism (Chandler, 1977, 1990; Shleifer and Vishny, 1997; Hamilton, 2000; Redding, 2000).[6] The reality of Chinese capitalism is a messy mixture of the continual domination of Chinese family firms and the rapid transformations and broadening of these family business networks to incorporate increasingly non-Chinese and non-family actors. The complex operating environments in many East and Southeast Asian economies and the historically specific emergence of Chinese capitalism imply that the family-oriented mode of economic organization may continue to enjoy the special advantages of enhancing entrepreneurship and reducing business uncertainty. To reap these competitive advantages embedded in family businesses, nevertheless, the Chinese family firm today needs an explicit strategy for succession, that is, a clear system of promotion to senior executive positions on the basis of some objective and performance-based criteria, even though kinship relations may be one key criterion.

The options for Chinese family firms are thus twofold, either grooming family members (typically sons and nephews) to become successful transnational entrepreneurs or socializing capable professional intrapreneurs into the corporate family in order to become the future heir to top management. For the first option, many Chinese patriarchs are sending their children to be educated in top universities and business schools. They also get their children involved as interns in many leading global corporations before returning to manage family businesses (see Chapter 2). These new-generation successors of Chinese family businesses gain better recognition among bankers, financiers and analysts based in major global financial centres, collectively known as globalizing actor-networks in Chapter 2. But it is true that as the family business empire expands across regions and countries, it will eventually run out of family members to occupy top management positions in the group. There is thus a strong need to develop a professional management system in order to unravel significant entrepreneurialism among managers who can be delegated important management functions (Birkinshaw and Hood, 1998a). Thus, an intrapreneur programme is required in these Chinese family firms so that they can survive beyond the classic dilemma encapsulated in the three-generation model: growth, stagnation and decline associated with each of the three generations of family ownership.

Here, I show how Chinese family firms can grow beyond three generations of family ownership and management through the transnational entrepreneurial activities of key family members and successors. The two case studies of Victor Li from Hong Kong and Richard Y.M. Eu from Singapore demonstrate that internationalization and transnational entrepreneurship may transform the nature of Chinese capitalism beyond the particular culturalist reading of the Chinese family firm: inward-looking in business orientation, closely knit around family members in management and morally hazardous in corporate governance. The transformation happens not because of the demise of the family firm as a mode of economic organization in Chinese capitalism, but because of the continual vitality of the family firm in Chinese capitalism, albeit that the Chinese family firm is no longer exclusively 'Chinese' and 'family'. Chinese capitalism may remain family-oriented in form, but increasingly diverse and hybridized in substance. Globalization tendencies, expressed via the enrolment in globalizing actor-networks, help to revitalize the family firm in Chinese capitalism and in the process transform its very nature and organization. The dominant discourse in the literature on Chinese capitalism in relation to the inherent limits to the growth of Chinese family firms (see also Chapter 1) is briefly summarized below.

Growing beyond three generations? Limits to Chinese family firms

Intra-firm organization of control and coordination is an important nexus for understanding the nature of the Chinese family firm and therefore

Chinese capitalism itself. Redding and Wong (1986: 272) defined organization structure as 'the relatively enduring pattern of relationship among units of individuals inside an organization'. Existing studies have identified several key features of intra-firm Chinese organizational structures (Redding and Wong, 1986; Wong, 1988; Redding, 1990, 1995; Whitley, 1992).

1　The centralization of power through the domination of family ownership and control.
2　The small size and relatively simple organizational structuring.
3　The normal focus on one product or market.
4　Lack of vertical integration and a low level of specialization.
5　Less standardization of activities and less routine procedures – 'management by persons' rather than 'management by rules'.
6　A relative lack of ancillary departments, e.g. R&D and marketing.
7　Strong overlap between ownership and control.
8　Links to the environment with personalized networks.
9　Great sensitivity to cost and financial efficiency.
10　Common linkage, strong but informal, with related and legally independent organizations handling key functions such as parts supply or marketing.
11　Weakness in terms of creating large-scale market recognition for own brands, especially international brand names.
12　Limitations of growth and organizational complexities.
13　A high degree of strategic adaptability.

Given these 'universal' characteristics of the structure and management of Chinese family firms, some researchers have argued that these culturally-specific firms cannot grow beyond a certain size because of the inherent limits to their growth which originate in their organizational structures and management processes (Hamilton, 2000; Yeung, 2000g). To Redding (1990: 3–4: 2000), for example, the Chinese family firm is a special organizational entity because:

it retains many of the characteristics of small scale, such as paternalism, personalism, opportunism, flexibility, even to very large scale. It does not follow the Western pattern of professionalization, bureaucratization, neutralization to anywhere near the same extent. Nor does it follow the Japanese pattern of the powerful but informal transorganizational bonding found in the *sogo-shosha* or *keiretsu*. It is capable of extending its transactions and influence by complex external networking, but the basis and mechanisms of this process seem quite distinct. It is its own animal, and seemingly unique … For the Overseas Chinese [*sic*], the personalized organization, run paternalistically and with ownership overlapping normally onto one or two families, is still perfectly normal, and it is the neutral bureaucracy under public ownership and professional management which is the deviant and almost nonexistent case ... The first professionally managed and publicly owned Chinese multinational is still waiting somewhere in the shadows, and may, in any case, be a fantasy of minds which assume all enterprises contain the same essential dynamics, and are not really cultural artifacts.

(Redding, 1990: 116, 176)

Some scholars (e.g. Kao, 1993; M. Chen, 1995; Fukuyama, 1995; Carney, 1998) have argued that it is very difficult for Chinese family firms to be transformed from family businesses (based on traditional moral reciprocity) to the modern, impersonal and professionally managed corporation (based on contracts and property rights). It is even more inconceivable to expect these family firms to become large TNCs with extensive networks of foreign subsidiaries and affiliates.

Their pessimistic assessment is predicated on four alleged weaknesses in the management processes of Chinese family firms: paternalism, nepotism, personalism and fragmentation (see Redding, 1990; Chau, 1991; M. Chen, 1995; Kets de Vries, 1996). First, paternalism reinforces organizational rigidity in Chinese family firms when the patriarch of the family takes up full control of the firm. Consider a culturalist assessment by Silin (1976: 9–10) that '[i]n Chinese society leaders have a marked preference for hearing only information that supports their point of view. Negative information or alternative methods are not valued. This preference, because it hinders a rapid flow of information, constitutes a cultural impediment'. The decision-maker of the family firm is assumed to be unable or unwilling to delegate authority to professional managers outside the core family, thus deterring the expansionary path of the family firm. In reality, however, we often find a hybrid mixture of management styles with varying degrees of control among Chinese family firms, as the empirical evidence and case studies of this book show. Second, nepotism is a well-known obstacle to the growth of Chinese family firms. The replacement of the retired or deceased founder by family members is arguably not the optimal long-term solution to the crisis of succession because able and competent professional managers, who aspire to the top echelon of the family firm, will be discouraged. There is an upper limit to their promotion and upward mobility within the family firm. The consequence of both tendencies is that the family firm will be depleted of good-quality managers. Instead, it will rely on incompetent personnel who are employed not on the basis of their qualification and performance, but on the basis of their kin relationships to the family.

Third, researchers consider personalism in the management and transactional processes of Chinese family firms to be another critical limit to growth. As suggested in the literature reviewed in Chapter 1, the personalization of business is a defining characteristic of Chinese capitalism. It is also an antithesis to the Weberian style of rational bureaucracy that is based on formalized rules, contracts and professionalism. Accordingly, rules and regulations in Chinese management are often made to be implicit and subject to interpretation under different circumstances (Tang and Ward, 2003). Personalism is particularly relevant to the formation and evolution of informal inter-firm relationships among Chinese firms. Most of these firms activate personal relationships, or *guanxi*, in their business transactions (Tong and Yong, 1998). This personalization inhibits growth because ultimately the sheer complexity of running very large-scale businesses requires the decentralization of decision-making and the formalization of contracts. Personalism and ad hoc decisions make it impossible to institutionalize formal organizational structures and clearly defined lines of authority (Redding, 1990, 2000; Whitley, 1992, 1999). Finally, the role of inheritance in Chinese family business proves to be prohibitive to growth beyond a certain size because it promotes fragmentation. It is true, however, that many Chinese family firms do experience a downsizing effect when they are broken down into separate business units, each headed by a son or a nephew. Moreover, even without this element of fragmentation, some family firms may face dilution of their family control during growth because more capital needs to be raised than the family can afford. Corporate takeovers of Chinese family firms, as a consequence of internal struggles among family members or public listing, sometimes happen.[7] Fragmentation of control and ownership represents, therefore, another important limit to the growth of Chinese family firms.

To conceptualize the temporal dynamics of Chinese family firms, Wong (1985, 1988) proposed a developmental model of four phases in their evolution (see Table 4.4). He argued that '[t]hese phases tend to coincide with generational shifts inside the *jia* [family] so that the profit, management, and estate of the family enterprise are progressively fragmented' (Wong 1988: 152). During the emergent phase, the founder patriarch–entrepreneur is usually involved in a joint venture with several partners. Once a shareholder is successful in securing a majority shareholding of

Table 4.4 A three-generation model of the Chinese family firm

Phases	Estate	Aspect of family firm management	Profit
I Emergence	+	+	+
II Centralization	+	+	−
III Segmentation	+	−	−
IV Disintegration	−	−	−

Sources: Wong (1985: Table 1; 1988: Table 6.5).

Notes
+ means unity.
− means division.

the partnership or in accumulating enough capital from that venture to set up on his own, the family firm is considered as entering the second phase of centralization. Leadership and decision-making are didactic, that is, directive and authoritarian. Put in rather exaggerated terms, Silin (1976: 60; my emphasis) found that the

> emphasis on the intention of actors and on the didactic role of leadership means that *all* authority holders are held personally responsible for initiating *all* actions for which they hold authority and for supervising subordinates once an action is taken. Holders of authority expect to be fully informed on *all* activities within the scope of their responsibilities. They alone make *all* decisions necessary to the unit's functioning. This breadth of scope calls for a high frequency of decision-making.

According to this interpretation, decision-making is highly centralized in the hands of the patriarch, a centripetal authority around founders or core family members (Tong, 1991). It is a kind of entrepreneurial familism in which the family serves as the basic unit of economic competition and organization.

Succession by second-generation family members often takes place in the third phase when the family firm begins to be segmented through equal inheritance. Most Chinese family firms have an internal regulation that if any family member wants to sell his/her shares of the company, he/she must first offer to existing shareholders who are usually family members. This measure has been established to secure the control of the firm in the hands of the family. Over time, tensions begin to build up around the competitive relations or incompatible expectations among siblings and family members. Centralized decision-making becomes untenable, and this in turn reduces the role of the leadership in the growth of the family firm. Sometimes one branch of the family may be able to build up a majority stake in the family firm that will then re-enter the second phase (see the case of Eu Yan Sang below). If this process of rejuvenation does not take place, the family firm then enters into the final phase of disintegration. This often happens in the third generation when rivalries among siblings become intensified and, eventually, detrimental to the very existence of the firm. In the following two case studies, I show that the model has only limited applicability to Chinese family firms that participate in internationalization and globalizing actor-networks.

Succession through internationalization: Victor Li from Hong Kong

As argued on pages 120–1, an internationalization strategy can be a good testing ground for family members to gain experience in management and deal-making. It helps to train high-quality future successors to the Chinese family firm and contributes to overcoming the limits to growth. In general, the patriarch will identify a good business opportunity and have his successor take charge. Overseas projects are sometimes preferred because any potential problems can be hushed up before the reputation and trust of the successor in the 'home' economies are damaged badly. This method of grooming a future heir to the family business assumes that if the successor can establish in a foreign land, he should be able to take over the family business in the 'home' economy where the patriarch is around to socialize the successor into the local business networks. Internationalization has become a strategy for investing in future successors rather than immediate growth *per se.* This distinguishes a Chinese family firm from a professionally managed firm, since the latter cannot afford such investments because of its public accountability. Pursuing an internationalization strategy, Chinese family firms can achieve long-term growth through good-quality successors (with solid business acumen and track records) and control of business within the family (see also the case of Kwek Leng Beng in Chapter 5).

The cross-border property investment of Li Ka-shing, a leading business patriarch in the Hong Kong business community (see Tables 1.5 and 1.6), and his elder son, Victor Li, in Vancouver's former Expo '86 site in 1988 illustrates how the senior Li exposed Victor to different business environments and expanded his own property businesses beyond the limits of the Hong Kong market (Mitchell, 1995; Olds, 2001: Chapter 4). Victor Li was part of the transnational elite who worked and lived in several global locations and was involved in the control of capital and information between these sites (Mitchell, 1993; Sklair, 2000). He was thus well enrolled in globalizing actor-networks. As a Canadian citizen, Victor Li graduated from Stanford University in 1987 with a BA and an MA in civil engineering. He was well placed to participate in the family business of the senior Li. In addition to his role in Concord Pacific, Victor was also a director of Husky Oil of Calgary, one of the first infrastructural development projects 95 per cent owned by his father (see Table 1.6). To Victor Li, the Canadian involvement represented a natural extension of the family business because '[t]here is no difference between my father's personal investments versus my personal investment. It's one. It is called family investment and that's it. The only separation is between family and public companies' (quoted in Mitchell, 1995: 377). Victor Li also found more comfort and excitement in doing business and enrolling in local actor-networks in Canada, particularly Vancouver. He recalled that '[o]ne of the best things about Canada is the way it treats new people. The cultural diversity makes the investor feel comfortable. There's also political stability. Canada is one of the most comfortable places to do business compared to a lot of Western countries' (quoted in Olds, 2001: 115).

The main rationale for purchasing and developing the Expo site was to use this high-profile project as a vehicle for the extension of Victor Li's social networks into Canada. Olds (1995: 14, 2001: 123–6) identified four objectives of the Pacific Place project. First, it permitted Victor Li (at the age of 22 years in 1988) to gain some solid experience in international property development that had been the main source of business and profits for his father in Hong Kong. He could also gain accolades in a more distant locale from Hong Kong so that any problems or failures could be covered up. Second, the project enabled Victor Li to be lifted to the top of Vancouver's social network and hierarchy, a move more or less impossible in such established old boys' network cities as New York and London. Third, Victor Li could build a strong base in Canada, both personally and financially, to prepare him for future business involvement back in Hong Kong. True enough, he returned to Hong Kong as deputy managing director of Cheung Kong Holdings, the flagship firm of the Li family, in 1993. Since 1994, he has been deputy chairman of the family firm. In 1999 he took over from his father as the managing director of Cheung Kong Holdings (http://www.cheungkong.com.hk; accessed on 18 March 2003). Finally, the project could be a pilot for large-scale property development in a non-Chinese setting. The senior Li could learn valuable lessons from intermingling different methods of property development in Hong Kong and Canada. These lessons might be important to Li for making decisions about whether to venture further into the global property market. In short, the Pacific Place project was a beachhead strategy for Li Ka-shing and his son to prepare for the future growth of the family business.

While developing Pacific Place in Vancouver, the senior Li not only provided an opportunity for Victor Li to learn, but also participated actively in establishing business networks and informal ties, a process of developing and enrolling in globalizing actor-networks (see also the case study of Li Ka-shing in Chapter 5). William Shurniak, a senior executive responsible for setting up the Canadian Imperial Bank of Commerce's (CIBC) merchant bank operation in Hong Kong in 1974, was an executive director and group finance director for Li Ka-shing's Hutchison Whampoa when the Pacific Place project was launched (Olds, 2001: 65). Shurniak clearly served as the bridgehead between Canadian financial networks and Li Ka-shing's vast and diversified actor-networks in Asia and beyond. Indeed, Li Ka-shing held approximately 10 per cent of the CIBC, giving him both credibility and financial backing for the Pacific Place project. Li Ka-shing also brought into the Pacific Place project two other influential property magnates from Hong Kong: Cheng Yu-tung (New World Development) and Lee Shau-kee (Henderson Land Development). As indicated in Table 1.6, both tycoons are from leading Chinese business families in Hong Kong. In fact, they had cooperated with Li Ka-shing in many other property development projects (e.g. the Suntec City project in Singapore; see Yeung, 1998a, 188–91). Victor Li once discussed the importance of informal relationships and trust among these Hong Kong property tycoons in the formation of the project: 'When we drew up the original thing, after we got the site, there was no formal agreement more than two pages between all the shareholders. With all these shareholders, their word is their bond' (quoted in Mitchell, 1995: 377).

The diverse actor-networks in which Victor Li was embedded in Vancouver enabled him to overcome grave difficulties in developing the prominent site. As Olds (2001: 90) noted,

> the developers have managed to manoeuvre through Vancouver's local system with sophistication and subtle power. While this development process certainly attests to the skills of Concord officials [developer of the Pacific Place] in working the system to achieve their goals, they were (and are) strongly supported by a labyrinthine 'infrastructure' of institutions, individuals, state policies, and restructuring processes which are constructing Vancouver into the archetypal 'Pacific Rim' metropolis.

In particular, Victor Li was able to tap into Stanley Kwok, a former emigrant from Hong Kong in 1968 and president of Pendero Development Co., who in 1981 was brought on to the ten-person board of directors of BC Place, the development company preceding Pacific Place in Vancouver. Kwok subsequently became the president and CEO of BC Place in 1984, following the death of its former chairman Alvin Narod (Olds, 2001: Box 4.2). He also served on the board of directors of the Expo '86 until 1986. After the provincial government of British Columbia abandoned plans to redevelop the Expo '86 site into BC Place in April 1987, Kwok was hired by Li Ka-shing and Victor Li as director and senior vice-president of Concord Pacific Developments Ltd, the developer that eventually secured the former Expo '86 site for C\$320 million in May 1988. The actual cost, factoring in payment schedules and the government's absorption of clean-up costs, amounted to closer to C\$145 million (Olds, 2001: 108). Drawing upon Kwok's 'excellent connections with all of Vancouver's key political and business elites, as well as with the provincial cabinet and the BCEC board [BC Enterprise Corporation – the contract awarding organization]' (Olds, 2001: 128), Victor Li was able to gain significant credits from his five years of work at Concord Pacific until his return to join the family's flagship firm in Hong Kong in 1993. In short, internationalization is serving the Li family well in grooming the next generation successor to the family business. This phenomenon is less appreciated in the literature on Chinese capitalism, but it is not too different from the experience of some leading business families in advanced industrialized economies, for instance the Murdoch family from Australia, the Wallenberg family from Sweden and the Ford family from the US. The most obvious commonalty among these family businesses is their family ownership and control that coexists with the selective incorporation of non-family members into professionalizing management. Professionalizing the Chinese family firm is even more apparent in the case study below of Eu Yan Sang from Singapore.

Transforming the Chinese family firm across borders: Eu Yan Sang from Singapore

The growth and transformation of Eu Yan Sang from a traditional Chinese medicine retail shop founded in 1879 to a professionally managed modern transnational Chinese medicine and healthcare business group provides another important exception to the three-generation model of Chinese family firms (Yeung, 2001, 2002a). In 2002 Eu Yan Sang International Ltd had under its corporate umbrella over 64 retail outlets in Hong Kong, Singapore and Malaysia (http://www.euyansang.com.sg; accessed on 18 March 2003). It controlled modern manufacturing facilities in Hong Kong and Malaysia and exported over 150 products under the Eu Yan Sang brandname worldwide to some 5,000 supermarkets, retail shops and pharmacies in Australia, Canada, China, Hong Kong, Indonesia, Malaysia, New Zealand, Singapore, Taiwan, the UK and the US. Instead of falling prey to the infamous three-generation trap, Eu Yan Sang has grown from strength to strength since the direct involvement in management by fourth-generation family members.[8] It has also been transformed from a fairly loose group of Chinese herbal medicine shops in different locations into a modern business enterprise with consolidated corporate structures and professionalized management led by family members. This section starts with the historical development of family ownership in Eu Yan Sang.[9] This is followed by a discussion of different ownership and management structures in Eu Yan Sang's transnational operations, emphasizing the role of professional managers. Finally, some recent events are described, that herald the consolidation and internationalization of the Eu Yan Sang Group in the hands of the fourth-generation family members. This evolutionary process has revitalized the family firm and prepared it for its future challenge as the leading transnational producer and retailer of traditional Chinese herbs and medicines in Asia (see Figure 4.1).

The formative years of Eu Yan Sang: 1879–1973

The pioneer Eu Kong founded Eu Yan Sang in 1879 as Yan Sang Medical Shop in Gopeng, a small town in Perak, then British Malaya. This first-generation entrepreneur had left his village in southern China to seek his fortune in Malaya (Chung, 2002). This is the first phase of emergence in Wong's developmental mode of Chinese family firms (see Table 4.4). Upon Eu Kong's untimely death in 1890 at the age of 38, his son, Eu Tong Sen (1877–1941), succeeded his father's business at the age of 20 and diversified it from a Chinese medicine shop into property, tin mining and other businesses. By the turn of the twentieth century, Eu Tong Sen had become one of the two wealthiest Chinese in the field (the other was Loke Yew) (Yoshihara, 1988: 203). He invested some of his fortune from tin mining in rubber plantations, banking, real estate and trading. Under his reign, Eu Yan Sang

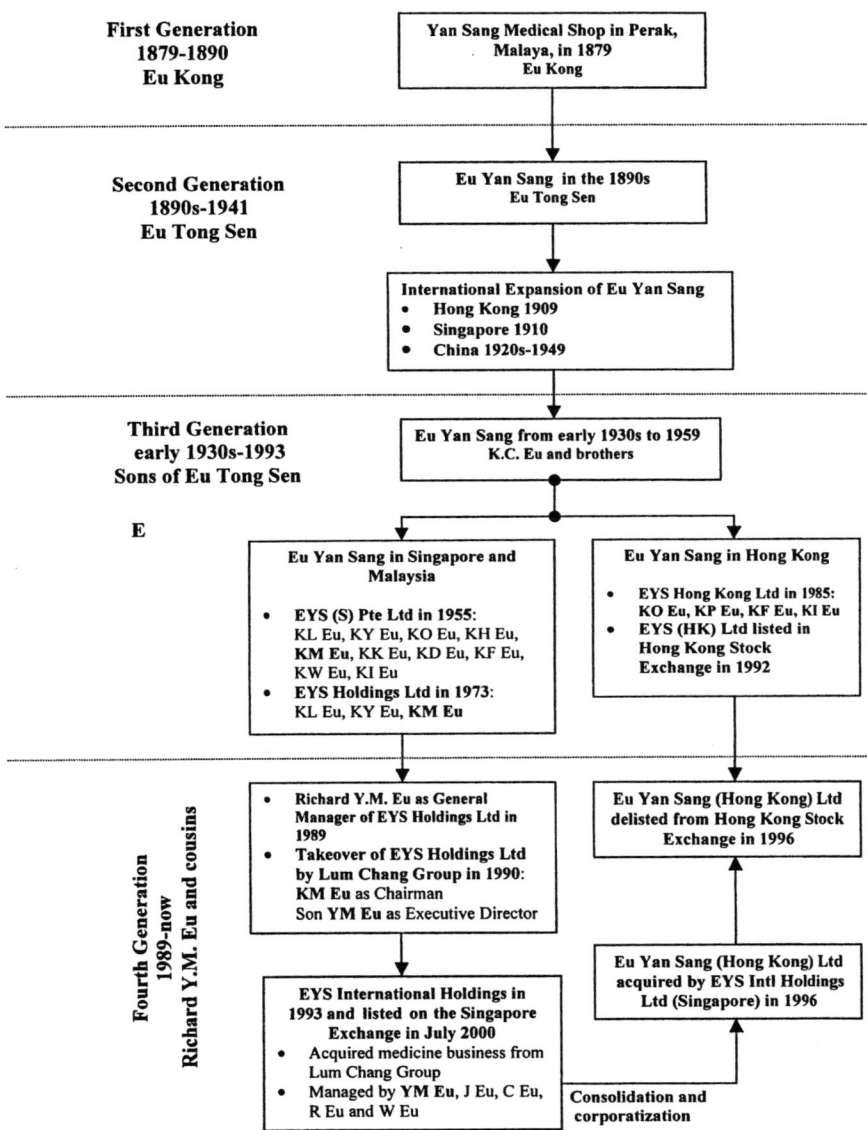

First Generation
1879-1890
Eu Kong

Yan Sang Medical Shop in Perak,
Malaya, in 1879
Eu Kong

Second Generation
1890s-1941
Eu Tong Sen

Eu Yan Sang in the 1890s
Eu Tong Sen

International Expansion of Eu Yan Sang
• Hong Kong 1909
• Singapore 1910
• China 1920s-1949

Third Generation
early 1930s-1993
Sons of Eu Tong Sen

E

Eu Yan Sang from early 1930s to 1959
K.C. Eu and brothers

Eu Yan Sang in Singapore and Malaysia
• EYS (S) Pte Ltd in 1955: KL Eu, KY Eu, KO Eu, KH Eu, KM Eu, KK Eu, KD Eu, KF Eu, KW Eu, KI Eu
• EYS Holdings Ltd in 1973: KL Eu, KY Eu, KM Eu

Eu Yan Sang in Hong Kong
• EYS Hong Kong Ltd in 1985: KO Eu, KP Eu, KF Eu, KI Eu
• EYS (HK) Ltd listed in Hong Kong Stock Exchange in 1992

Fourth Generation
1989-now
Richard Y.M. Eu and cousins

• Richard Y.M. Eu as General Manager of EYS Holdings Ltd in 1989
• Takeover of EYS Holdings Ltd by Lum Chang Group in 1990: KM Eu as Chairman Son YM Eu as Executive Director

Eu Yan Sang (Hong Kong) Ltd delisted from Hong Kong Stock Exchange in 1996

EYS International Holdings in 1993 and listed on the Singapore Exchange in July 2000
• Acquired medicine business from Lum Chang Group
• Managed by YM Eu, J Eu, C Eu, R Eu and W Eu

Eu Yan Sang (Hong Kong) Ltd acquired by EYS Intl Holdings Ltd (Singapore) in 1996

Consolidation and corporatization

Figure 4.1 The historical evolution of family ownership in Eu Yan Sang, 1879–2003.

Sources: Interviews with Richard K.M. Eu and Richard Y.M. Eu, company reports and other materials.

expanded rapidly within Malaya and across borders. The family firm entered into the second phase of centralization in Wong's model (see Table 4.4). During the early 1900s he opened branches in Kuala Lumpur, Seremban and Ipoh. In 1909 the first overseas branch was opened in Hong Kong. In 1910 the Singapore branch was established. Another branch was also set up in China during the 1920s. Eu Tong Sen put all Yan Sang Medical Shops under his sole proprietorship, sowing the early seeds of a transnational business group. In 1911 he was appointed Chinese representative at the Federal Council of Malaya. In 1920 he started a very successful anti-opium smoking campaign. He continued to build his father's herbal business, working hard to promote the health values of Chinese herbs and medicines. Later Eu Tong Sen changed the name of the shop from Yan Sang Medical Shop to Eu Yan Sang Medical Shop. This addition of the family name 'Eu' was in order to reinforce the fact that Eu Yan Sang is a family business to be handed from one generation to another.

True enough, Eu Tong Sen chose to keep his businesses in the family by passing them on into the hands of the third generation (Figure 4.1). During the early 1930s he retired to live in Hong Kong and appointed his eldest son, Keng Chee Eu, as the successor of his vast business empire (author's interview with Dr Richard K.M. Eu).[10] K.C. Eu came back from England to Singapore in 1925 after qualifying as a chartered accountant. Within the next ten years he took over the management and control of the family's various companies. Before his death in Hong Kong in 1941, Eu Tong Sen founded a huge holding company, Eu Tong Sen Ltd, to hold all his properties and plantation estates (Chung, 2002: 606–7). Interestingly, the only business left out of control by this holding company was Eu Yan Sang (and Eu Tong Sen's tin mines). Eu Tong Sen Ltd had 14 shares and Eu Tong Sen gave one share to each of his 13 sons, K.C. Eu, was given two shares. None of his five wives and 11 daughters (one adopted) were the beneficiaries of his businesses. This patriarchal succession pattern followed closely the equal-inheritance system common in most Chinese family firms (see above). Eu Yan Sang remained a sole proprietorship with 13 shares, each held by one of Eu Tong Sen's sons. In the early 1930s, the third-generation family members succeeded to the ownership and control of Eu Yan Sang (see Figure 4.1).

The archetypical Chinese family firm thus entered into the third phase of segmentation in Wong's model (see Table 4.4). Table 4.5 provides a genealogy of the Eu family and the involvement of Eu Tong Sen's 13 sons in Eu Yan Sang. Though having substantial ownership and control of Eu Yan Sang, the third-generation Eu family members did not participate actively in its day-to-day management, which was handled by trusted employees. We might conceptualize this early process of incorporating trusted employees who had been socialized into Eu Yan Sang's corporate family as powers of attorney. These 'attorneys' were professional managers who took care of Eu Tong Sen's vast business activities in Malaysia and Singapore. They would be

Table 4.5 A genealogy of four generations of family members in Eu Yan Sang

First generation: Eu Kong (1879–90)

Second generation: Eu Tong Sen (1877–1941)

Third generation

	(1) Keng Chee Eu (b. 1900)	(2) Keng Loon Eu (b. 1916)	(3) Keng Ngo Eu (b. 1917)	(4) William Keng Yuet Eu (b. 1920)	(5) Edward Keng Oi Eu (b. 1921)	(6) Henry Keng Hong Eu (b. 1923)	(7) Richard Keng Mun Eu (b. 1923)	(8) Charles Keng Pang Eu (b. 1926)	(9) Alex Keng Kee Eu (b. 1927)	(10) John Keng Dean Eu (b. 1927)	(11) Fred Keng Fai Eu (b. 1930)	(12) Andrew Keng Wai Eu (b. 1931)	(13) Roy Keng Iu Eu (b. 1934)
Role		Chairman of EYS Holdings Ltd		Executive Director of EYS Holdings Ltd	Chairman of EYS HK Ltd		Director and later chairman of EYS Holdings Ltd; Executive director of EYS HK	Executive director of EYS HK Ltd		Director of EYS Holdings Ltd	Executive Director of EYS HK Ltd		Executive Director of EYS HK Ltd

Fourth generation

- **Son Joseph William Yee Eu** (under 1): Chairman: EYS Intl Holdings Pte Ltd; Non-executive chairman: EYS Intl Ltd, 2002
- **Son Winston Yee Shun Eu** (under 3): Executive Director: EYS Intl Holdings Pte Ltd
- **Sons Richard Yee Ming Eu** (under 7) (brothers: David Y.T. Eu and Geoffrey Y.K. Eu; sister: Helna M.Y. Eu): Executive director: EYS Holdings Ltd; Managing director: EYS Intl Holdings Pte Ltd; Group CEO: EYS Intl Ltd, 2002
- **Sons Clifford Yee Fong Eu** (under 10) (brother: Laurence Yee Lye Eu; sister: Vicky Eu): Executive director: EYS Intl Holdings Pte Ltd; Managing director: EYS Intl Ltd, 2002
- **Sons Robert James Yee Sang Eu** (under 12) (brother: Douglas Eu and Philip Eu; sister: Anne Eu): Executive director: EYS Intl Holdings Pte Ltd; Non-executive director: EYS Intl Ltd, 2002

Sources: Annual reports, published documents of Eu Yan Sang; personal communications with Richard K.M. Eu and Richard Y.M. Eu.

equivalent to today's chief executive officers who report to the board of directors of a highly professionalized family firm, comprising the patriarch as the chairman and some family members as directors (for instance Ford and Murdoch's News Corp. in the US). During the 1940s and the 1950s, Dr Eu recalled, one of the family members was living in Kuala Lumpur to manage the real-estate business in the then British Malaya. Another was residing in Kampar/Gopeng to manage the tin mines. These two key 'attorneys' in turn reported directly to the head of the Eu family, first Eu Tong Sen and subsequently K.C. Eu until his death in 1959. Within Eu Yan Sang's loose sole proprietorship structure, each shop had its own full-time manager and they reported to the two 'attorneys'. There appeared to be a clear division of labour in the management of Eu Yan Sang and other businesses of Eu Tong Sen. As recalled by Richard Y.M. Eu,

> There was no formal corporate structure for these branches [of Eu Yan Sang]. So they were like proprietorships. Each branch would have been an individual proprietorship because they were not corporatized. So the employees were only responsible for the branch. After the second World War, because this was only one of the businesses that he [K.C. Eu] had, most of the businesses, the decision making, was probably made in Singapore, although they had companies which were incorporated in Malaysia, Hong Kong and Singapore.
>
> (Interviewed in Singapore, 24 November 1998)

The pattern of sole proprietorship in Eu Yan Sang lasted until 1955. In that year Eu Yan Sang's operations in Malaysia and Singapore were converted from sole proprietorship to a limited company, with the establishment of Eu Yan Sang (Singapore) Pte Ltd on 13 October 1955 (see Figure 4.1). On 26 August 1959 Eu Yan Sang (1959) Sdn Bhd was established in Malaya to consolidate the retail shops in Kuala Lumpur, Ipoh, Penang, Seremban and Kampar. During 1955–73, the limited company continued to follow the management pattern that had prevailed during the early years when the shops were under sole proprietorship. On 30 June 1973 Eu Yan Sang Holdings Ltd was listed on the Stock Exchange of Singapore, incorporating both Malaysia and Singapore operations. The main reason for the public listing was to cash in some shares. Dr Eu noted that 'we wanted liquidity. Here you inherit a business, but it's a partnership; and we don't want to get stuck together' (author's interview in Singapore, 15 April 1999). The public offer therefore signals the possible beginning of the fourth phase of disintegration in Wong's model when division and rivalry among family members often happen with a public offering (see Table 4.4). After the public listing the Eu family continued to hold a majority share of 75 per cent in Eu Yan Sang Holdings Ltd. Seven companies, including Eu Yan Sang (Singapore) Pte Ltd, were put under the control of the holding company (see Table 4.6). Meanwhile, Eu Yan Sang

Table 4.6 Subsidiaries of Eu Yan Sang Holdings Ltd, 1973

Name	Date and place of incorporation	Shares issued and capital fully paid	Principal activities
1 Eu Yan Sang (Singapore) Private Ltd	13 October 1955 Singapore	S$234,000	Distribution and sale of traditional
2 Eu Yan Sang (1959) Sendirian Bhd	26 August 1959 Malaya	S$1,107,210	Chinese and other medicines
3 Eu Realty (Singapore) Private Ltd	13 October 1955 Singapore	S$827,400	Property investments
4 Eu Realty (Malaya) Sendirian Bhd	9 September 1959 Malaya	S$785,400	Property investments
5 Eu Court Realty Private Ltd	14 June 1973 Singapore	S$1,902,700	Property investments
6 Empress Realty Private Ltd	14 June 1973 Singapore	S$796,000	Property investments
7 Nam Tin Realty Private Ltd	14 June 1973 Singapore	S$589,200	Property investments

Source: Eu Yan Sang (1973: 5).

Hong Kong Ltd was essentially a dormant shell company managed as a sole proprietorship under the responsibilities of the trustees of the estate of Eu Tong Sen. Both companies used the same registered trademark inherited from Eu Tong Sen. But there were clear differences in the management, growth and evolution of these two family entities in Hong Kong and Singapore.

The public listing of Eu Yan Sang Holdings Ltd in 1973 also led to some mindset changes among family members who were directly involved in managing the company. In particular, they were much more aware of the interests of minority shareholders. They realized that they could not put family interests above those of other non-family shareholders. Between 1973 and 1988–9, Eu Yan Sang Holdings Ltd was effectively managed by William K.Y. Eu, its executive director, and Dr Eu, its chairman (see Table 4.5). As shown in Figure 4.2, the holding company was generally quite profitable except in 1985 when Malaysia and Singapore experienced their worst postwar recessions. After William K.Y. Eu's retirement from the holding company in 1988, the fourth-generation members of the Eu family first entered the top management positions of the family business. In late 1989 Richard Y.M. Eu, the elder son of Dr Eu, was appointed as the general manager of Eu Yan Sang Holdings Ltd (see Table 4.5). This succession process also heralds the beginning of the dramatic transformation of Eu Yan Sang from a then predominantly Chinese family firm to today's leading TNC in traditional Chinese medicines. Before we examine the entrepreneurial role of Richard Y.M. Eu and his cousins in this transformation, it is important to revisit the role of professional managers and 'power attorneys' in managing the cross-border operations of Eu Yan Sang in Singapore, Malaysia and Hong Kong.

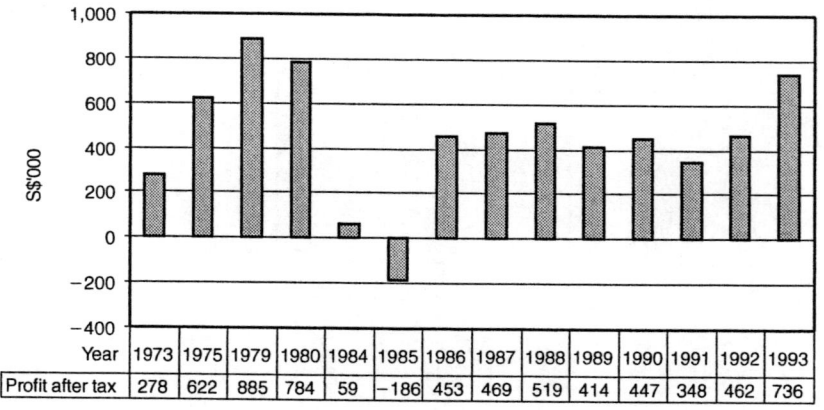

Figure 4.2 After-tax profits of Eu Yan Sang Holdings Ltd, 1973–93.

Power attorneys and professional managers

During much of the reign by the third generation of the Eu family from the early 1930s to 1993, Eu Yan Sang's retail shops in Singapore and Malaysia and manufacturing facilities in Hong Kong had a common ownership. However, their management and business operations were never operated as a single group. Managing across borders in Eu Yan Sang during this era of management by 'attorneys' was in the hands of several key professional managers, a phenomenon uncommon among Chinese family firms at that time. One of these managers in Eu Yan Sang was Yeung Chi Po who first joined the Eu Yan Sang business in Guangzhou, China, in 1946 and was subsequently posted to Hong Kong in 1948 (Eu Yan Sang, 1992: 12). According to Dr Eu, Yeung's father was also a general manager of Eu Yan Sang in Hong Kong. He reported directly to Eu Tong Sen. After Eu Tong Sen passed away, Yeung's father carried on and reported instead to K.C. Eu, who was the overall trustee of the family business. Because of the strong trust he had gained over the years by serving Eu Tong Sen, K.C. Eu gave Yeung's father much autonomy in managing Eu Yan Sang in Hong Kong. Meanwhile, he brought his son Yeung Chi Po into Eu Yan Sang's business in Hong Kong during the 1940s. At his retirement in 1989, Yeung Chi Po had served Eu Yan Sang for over 40 years, first as the financial controller and subsequently as the general manager from 1973 to 1989. After his retirement, he was appointed as a consultant to the holding company. In Singapore and Malaysia, Lum Kai Poh, another professional general manager, was in charge of Eu Yan Sang's operations. As a bilingual manager, he was a powerful 'attorney' to the trustees of Eu Tong Sen. Lum used to work closely with Eu Tong Seng as a senior manager of Eu Yan Sang. In recognition of his service to Eu Yan Sang, Eu Tong Seng gave one nominal share of Eu Tong Seng Ltd to Lum in 1939 as a symbolic gesture, shortly before his death in 1941 (Chung, 2002: 606).

These professional managers in Eu Yan Sang have made very important contributions to its growth and development across borders. First, their abilities in consolidating the company's diverse operations in Singapore, Malaysia and Hong Kong were a key to the subsequent expansion of the company worldwide. In 1958 Yeung was transferred to the Chinese medicinal division of Eu Yan Sang in Hong Kong. During the 1970s he helped reorganize Eu Yan Sang's businesses in Hong Kong. The main aspect of his reorganization exercise was to centralize the purchasing activities of Eu Yan Sang. Prior to that, each shop manager made their own purchasing decisions. Yeung subsequently centralized these decisions in Hong Kong. Though the exercise had started in the 1970s, its implementation was facilitated by the opening of Weng Li Sdn Bhd in Malaysia on 5 January 1980. Weng Li Sdn Bhd was a new venture established under the auspices of third-generation Eu family members and Yeung. It was originally formed as a sole proprietorship (and later a wholly owned subsidiary of Eu Yan Sang Holdings Ltd after its public listing in Singapore) mainly to handle the central purchasing of Chinese herbs and traditional medicines from mainland China and Hong Kong for local market needs in Malaysia and Singapore. When a manufacturing factory was established in Malaysia later, the factory's operations were put under Weng Li Sdn Bhd. This rationalization exercise through central purchasing and backward integration indeed contributed to greater efficiency and profitability in Eu Yan Sang Holdings Ltd. In its 1980 annual report, Weng Li Sdn Bhd was credited as having contributed to 'improved inventory and case flow control' (Eu Yan Sang, 1980: 5). By the mid-1990s, Weng Li had diversified into the manufacturing of traditional pills, capsules, powders and packaging of soups, teas and Bak Kut Teh because of regulations imposed by the Malaysian health authorities. Eu Yan Sang Holdings Ltd saw these new regulations as an opportunity, because it would mean that other imported traditional medicines (i.e. their competitors) were not allowed in Malaysia. Other existing manufacturers in Malaysia might not have the capital base to build factories that would meet the good manufacturing practice (GMP) standard. In fact, Weng Li Sdn Bhd was awarded GMP certification on 15 September 1997, an international recognition of its commitment to maintaining the highest standards in manufacturing traditional medicines. With its GMP certificate, Weng Li Sdn Bhd was able not only to sell within Malaysia, but also to export its products worldwide.

Second, professional managers continued to help manage the disparate operations of Eu Yan Sang throughout almost all the 1980s. This was clearly a difficult task because of different ownership structures and management control in both Singapore/Malaysia and Hong Kong operations. In terms of ownership structures, the operations in Singapore and Malaysia had been consolidated under Eu Yan Sang Holdings Ltd since 1973 (see Figure 4.1). Despite the establishment of Eu Yan Sang Hong Kong Ltd in 1985, little group-level consolidation of business activities took place. The limited company remained dormant, as no assets were put into it. Hong Kong operations remained separated from Eu Yan Sang Holdings Ltd in Singapore, although Yeung managed both operations in Hong Kong and reported to Dr Eu (chairman) and William K.Y. Eu (executive director) in Singapore. According to Dr Eu, Eu Yan Sang Hong Kong Ltd was still managed like a partnership because all 13 sons of Eu Tong Sen were partners. They did not really make use of the limited liability company (i.e. Eu Yan Sang Hong Kong Ltd), since no assets were injected into that company. In terms of management control, Yeung had full control over Eu Yan Sang in Hong Kong and concurrently managed Eu Yan Sang's operations in Singapore. As noted by Dr Eu, managers in Eu Yan Sang Singapore technically should have reported to William K.Y. Eu, but actually they also reported concurrently to Yeung in Hong Kong. As chairman of Eu Yan Sang Holdings Ltd and a partner in Eu Yan Sang Hong Kong Ltd, Dr Eu was involved in policy matters. All other directors depended on him and William K.Y. Eu. The role of Yeung was critical because both the chairman and the executive director of Eu Yan Sang Holdings Ltd in Singapore depended on him for business proposals and decisions. Two main problems confronted the third-generation Eu family. The first problem was a lack of interest among the brothers to manage Eu Yan Sang directly. Those involved had to depend on professional managers such as Yeung. The second problem was the lack of a sufficient number of professional managers to expand Eu Yan Sang into different parts of the Asian region. Yeung was capable of overcoming some of these managerial constraints to overseas expansion by recognizing good staff and their potential and by shifting them around different operations in Singapore, Malaysia and Hong Kong to accumulate business experience. But the number of capable managers was still small. For example, when Eu Yan Sang Holdings Ltd advertised for management positions in 1982, only two candidates turned out to be suitable (Lok Eng Hock and Lui Win Soong). In 2003 these two managers were still with Eu Yan Sang International Ltd: Lok as managing director of EYS (1959) Sdn Bhd and Lui as general manager of Weng Li Sdn Bhd.

Third, Yeung made special marketing efforts to promote the brand name of Eu Yan Sang, which has become one of the most famous brands of Chinese medicines throughout the world today. According to Dr Eu, Mr Yeung was particularly good at building up publicity for Eu Yan Sang through the media. He would even design the commercials for local television channels. In short, professional managers and power attorneys in Eu Yan Sang Hong Kong and Singapore have made a significant contribution to the steady consolidation and rationalization of its retail and manufacturing businesses under the reign of the third-generation Eu family members. This step proves exceptionally important for the eventual return of the fourth-generation family members and the revitalization of the group to become a true TNC headquartered in Singapore.

The fourth generation in Eu Yan Sang: from 1989 to today

As mentioned above, significant transformations in Eu Yan Sang have taken place under the current leadership of the fourth-generation Eu family members, comprising Richard Y.M. Eu, son of Dr Eu, and his four cousins: Joseph Eu, Winston Eu, Clifford Eu and Robert Eu (see Figure 4.1 and Table 4.5). As early as 1985, Richard Y.M. Eu was appointed to Eu Yan Sang Holdings Ltd's board of directors as an alternative director to his father. Among all the directors as at 21 January 1986, Richard Y.M. Eu held the largest number of shares at 604,971 through his family's investment arm, Ridalege Investments Pte Ltd (Eu Yan Sang, 1985: 20–1). In 1989 Richard Y.M. Eu was formally appointed as general manager of Eu Yan Sang Holdings Ltd, signalling the first entry of a fourth-generation family member into executive positions of the family firm. Looking again at Wong's (1985) model in Table 4.4, it seems that instead of going through the fourth phase of disintegration, the family firm has now experienced a rejuvenation and revitalization process (see revisions of the model below). Through this process, Richard Y.M. Eu and his four cousins have regained the ownership and control of part of the family firm and consolidated the entire business operations of Eu Yan Sang in Singapore, Malaysia and Hong Kong into one single corporate umbrella, Eu Yan Sang International Holdings Pte Ltd. This process of privatizing Eu Yan Sang's operations would not have happened without the entrepreneurial spirits and skills embodied in these fourth-generation family members. The revitalization of Eu Yan Sang and its subsequent professionalization clearly implies a significant departure from Wong's model. None of the four phases can adequately capture the highly dynamic nature of this evolutionary process, which I prefer to term the 'corporatization' of the family firm, meaning the simultaneous coexistence of family ownership and control and the adoption of a consolidated corporate structure and a professional management team.

How did this process of corporatization come about? Two key events show the entrepreneurial role of Richard Y.M. Eu and his four cousins in overcoming all odds to revitalize the ailing family firm. The first event was the takeover of Eu Yan Sang Holdings Ltd by the Lum Chang Group on 29 March 1990 and the successful acquisition of the medicine business from L.C. Development Ltd by Eu Yan Sang International Holdings Pte Ltd on 25 August 1993. The takeover bid came from Lum Chang Holdings Ltd controlled by two brothers, David and Raymond Lum. The main purpose of the publicly listed Lum Chang Group acquiring Eu Yan Sang Holdings Ltd was to give them a listed vehicle to develop their property business and to capitalize on some of the properties owned by Eu Yan Sang Holdings Ltd. The acquisition was controversial because the then chairman of Eu Yan Sang Holdings Ltd, Dr Eu, was not informed when some of his brothers and their families decided to sell their shares to the Lum Chang Group. The successful takeover by Lum Chang, another Chinese family firm in Singapore, almost led to the demise of Eu Yan Sang Holdings Ltd as a family business. This fits almost perfectly into the fourth phase of disintegration in Wong's (1985) model (see Table 4.4).

The disintegration of Eu Yan Sang Holdings Ltd as a family firm, however, did not take place. This was because of extraordinary efforts made by Dr Eu, his son and several family members. In fact, Richard Y.M. Eu noted that since 1973 his immediate family had been buying back some of the shares of Eu Yan Sang Holdings Ltd, so that by 1990 he and his father were the largest single shareholder after Lum Chang Holdings, with up to 10 per cent of the shareholding (author's interview in Singapore, 24 November 1998). Both of them agreed to stay on the board of directors as chairman and executive director. In fact, the Lum brothers kept both Dr Eu and his son as well as a non-executive director, Cheong Wing, on Eu Yan Sang Holdings Ltd's board of directors after the takeover. They thought that the public might feel positively about having some family members to continue managing Eu Yan Sang Holdings Ltd. In 1993 Dr Eu and his son engineered a reverse takeover of their traditional medicine business from the Lum Chang-controlled Eu Yan Sang Holdings Ltd. To do that, Dr Eu and his son first set up Eu Yan Sang International Holdings Pte Ltd and Richard Y.M. Eu became its first managing director (group CEO in 2003). In August 1993 the Lum Chang Group renamed Eu Yan Sang Holdings Ltd as L.C. Developments Ltd in order to dispose of the former medicine and related businesses of Eu Yan Sang Holdings Ltd to Eu Yan Sang International Holdings Pte Ltd (led by Richard Y.M. Eu). This acquisition cost the Eu family S$21 million (*The Straits Times*, 5 July 2000). From Lum Chang's point of view, the medicine business was irrelevant to their main business in property development. The sell-off would be a win-win solution to both the Lum brothers and the Eu family. This corporate manoeuvre resulted in the repossession of the traditional Chinese medicine business by fourth-generation Eu family members.

In 1996 further consolidation of Eu Yan Sang took place through the acquisition of Eu Yan Sang (Hong Kong) Ltd by Eu Yan Sang International Holdings Pte Ltd, the holding company based in Singapore (see Figure 4.1). The successful acquisition at HK$230 million led to the delisting of Eu Yan Sang (Hong Kong) Ltd from the Stock Exchange of Hong Kong. This ended the long separation of Eu Yan Sang's business operations in Hong Kong and Singapore/Malaysia. Since then all Eu Yan Sang's operations in Hong Kong, Singapore and Malaysia had been fully owned and managed by Eu Yan Sang International Holdings Pte Ltd. The holding company was subsequently renamed Eu Yan Sang International Ltd after its listing on the Stock Exchange of Singapore (now Singapore Exchange) in July 2000. This process has completed the full cycle of corporatization and Eu Yan Sang has now been returned to the hands of the fourth-generation Eu family based in Singapore. Three specific reasons explain the acquisition of Eu Yan Sang's Hong Kong business by Richard Y.M. Eu and his four cousins. First, there was a serious dispute between the Eu Yan Sang operations in Singapore and in Hong Kong over the use of trademarks after Eu Yan Sang (Hong Kong) Ltd's public listing in Hong Kong in 1992 (see Figure 4.1). A takeover bid by Eu Yan Sang International Holdings ended this trademark saga by merging all Eu Yan Sang's operations in Hong Kong and Singapore/Malaysia under one central holding company that would naturally own all Eu Yan Sang's registered trademarks. Second, the acquisition of Eu Yan Sang (Hong Kong) Ltd means that the Eu family can repossess Eu Yan Sang, a traditional family business handed from one generation to another. As Richard Y.M. Eu reflected,

The three of us [cousins] were in agreement with the principle of doing it, keeping it within the family. It's tied up with the business reason. We wouldn't do this if it didn't make sense. But we could see that there were certain inefficiencies with the Hong Kong operations. We felt that, since we had some experience in operating the business here [Singapore], we could help Hong Kong out by translating our experiences into the business there.

(Author's interview in Singapore, 24 November 1998)

Third, the acquisition of Eu Yan Sang (Hong Kong) Ltd represents the first step in the globalization drive of Eu Yan Sang International Holdings. It reflects the vision and ambition of the fourth-generation Eu family members led by Richard Y.M. Eu, who made this comment on the implications of the acquisition:

That's a by-product. We want to grow the company. You need a certain base and by plugging into Hong Kong, our company base is so much bigger. So the next step in our globalization would obviously have been much easier. Otherwise, we would be competing with the Hong Kong company all over the place, spending more time fighting with them than expanding the business.

(Author's interview in Singapore, 24 November 1998)

After the acquisition, Eu Yan Sang in Hong Kong/China began to contribute over 50 per cent of the group's turnover. In 2002, for example, it accounted for 57 per cent of the group's S$97.2 million turnover and 36 per cent of the group's S$85.7 million assets (Eu Yan Sang, 2002: 73).

By August 1996 the consolidation of Eu Yan Sang's worldwide operations into one business group was complete. Richard Y.M. Eu and his cousins now made another entrepreneurial move to expand further Eu Yan Sang's business operations domestically in Singapore and elsewhere in the Asian region. They restructured the ownership and management of Eu Yan Sang International Holdings Pte Ltd by ensuring that only the fourth-generation family members would be involved in managing the group's operations, bringing in an external shareholder to improve the financial standing of the group and consolidating the management control of the group into the hands of Richard Y.M. Eu and Clifford Eu. The entrepreneurial drive by Richard Y.M. Eu and his cousins led to several important transformations in Eu Yan Sang's transnational business operations. First, the group's product developments and marketing improved substantially, with a significant amount of capital investment being put into this expansion. This investment was not forthcoming during the early 1990s when the Lum Chang Group was controlling Eu Yan Sang Holdings Ltd. New investment was put into product development and marketing. As noted in Eu Yan Sang's corporate website (accessed on 20 November 1998),

> a new generation of managers had been at the helm of Eu Yan Sang. They are qualified professionals, brimming with new ideas and burning with enthusiasm to make the traditional business of Chinese herbs more scientific and contemporary, more relevant to the lifestyle of this generation.

For example, the presentation of traditional herbs has been revolutionized. Instead of preparing the herbs manually for consumption, Eu Yan Sang now packs them as ready-to-consume capsules, pills or powders. These innovations in packaging and products have made traditional Chinese health food and herbs more accessible and easier to use for the younger generation, opening up a huge and relatively untapped consumer market for Eu Yan Sang's products. Though marketing continues to be done locally at the subsidiary level, there is a group marketing manager who works on a consulting basis in Singapore to ensure brand consistency, product development and packaging design.

Second, the involvement of more fourth-generation family members apparently has resolved some of the key problems associated with the lack of competent family members sufficiently interested in reviving the family business. As Dr Eu remarked, '[t]he calculated risk is always there. One of my problems in the past against expansion was the lack of proper personnel. If they [the fourth generation] can cope with that, by all means' (author's interview in Singapore, 15 April 1999). Finally, a consolidated corporate management structure also facilitates the implementation of a common corporate vision and strategy. This is a particularly important consideration for Eu Yan Sang's operations in Hong Kong. Dr Eu noted that 'there shouldn't be any problem for the Hong Kong employees. What they want is really clear-cut management directions. If we can have that, it doesn't matter whether we are from Singapore or Hong Kong. To them, that [common vision] is more important'. As the Group CEO, Richard Y.M. Eu said that his preference was 'to see a professionally run company' and 'to find the best person for the job, whether it's family or not' (author's interview in Singapore, 24 November 1998). In 2002 none of the fourth-generation family members owned more than 25 per cent of the shares. Approximately 30 per cent of the shares were held by the public. Two non-family members were also appointed as independent directors: David C.W. Yeh and Jennifer G.C. Lee (CEO of K.K. Hospital in Singapore). Lee also serves as chairman of both audit and compensation committees. As reported in its 2002 annual report (Eu Yan Sang, 2002: 13), Richard Y.M. Eu led an executive management team comprising 17 senior executives in the Eu Yan Sang group worldwide (Singapore, Hong Kong, Malaysia, Australia and the US). With the exception of both Richard Eu and Clifford Eu, all these senior executives are professional managers hired for their experience, knowledge and competencies. According to Richard Y.M. Eu, most of the business and management decisions are based on the consensus of this executive management team. Local general managers abroad report to Richard Y.M. Eu directly and local financial controllers report to Leslie Mah, the group chief financial officer based in Singapore. The control and reporting system has thus been streamlined to facilitate better corporate governance and intra-group communication and coordination.

By the end of 1998 the Eu Yan Sang group had become the single largest Chinese medicine retail chain in Hong Kong and Southeast Asia, with a turnover exceeding S$60 million, fixed assets of over S$30 million and worldwide employment of about 600. In 2002 the group's turnover increased to S$97.2 million, net profit to S$6.1 million and fixed assets to S$38.6 million (Eu Yan Sang, 2002: 37–8). It remains a Chinese family firm with significant regional operations in the Asia-Pacific region and a vision to promote Chinese values and medicine (see Table 4.7). Building on its immense heritage, Eu Yan Sang's corporate vision is clear. It wants to 'promote herbal healthcare in order to reinforce family values and moral education' and hopes that 'every member in every family will be able to benefit from Chinese herbal healthcare' (http://www.euyansang. com, accessed on 20 November 1998). This vision has not changed since the founding of Eu Yan Sang over 120 years ago by the pioneer Eu Kong. With the Asian region recovering from its worst economic crisis in the late 1990s, Eu Yan Sang is well positioned to expand further into the region and beyond and to transform itself from a traditional Chinese family firm to a modern TNC with a family touch. The entrepreneurial vision of Richard Y.M. Eu and his cousins in revitalizing the 120-year-old Chinese herbal medicine business is apparent. Without that, Eu Yan Sang would not have been transformed into a modern business enterprise managed by both family members and professional managers. Through this process of corporatization and professionalization, Richard Y.M. Eu has successfully moved away from traditional practices in Chinese capitalism in which conservatism and ethnic closure are maintained.

Conclusion: some lessons for Chinese capitalism

A revised model will account for transnational entrepreneurship and dynamic transformations in Chinese capitalism in a global era. The model in Figure 4.3 shows that while Wong's (1985) four developmental phases are generally valid in analysing the rise and fall of Chinese family firms in their domestic settings (typically over three generations), there are other possible developmental trajectories associated with internationalization that may account for both the diversity of organizational outcomes and the hybridized nature of Chinese capitalism. First, the segmentation of

Table 4.7 Subsidiaries of Eu Yan Sang International Ltd, 2002

Name of company	Place of incorporation	Paid-up capital (S$'000)	Principal activities
Wholly-owned subsidiaries			
1 Eu Yan Sang (Singapore) Pte Ltd	Singapore	$3,185	Distribution and sales
2 Eu Yan Sang (Hong Kong) Ltd	Hong Kong	$731	Manufacturing and sales
3 Eu Yan Sang (1959) Sendirian Bhd	Malaya	$4,381	Distribution and sales
4 Eu Realty (Singapore) Pte Ltd	Singapore	$12,366	Property investments
5 Weng Li Sdn Bhd	Malaysia	$50	Manufacturing and sales agent
6 Eu Yan Sang Heritage Sdn Bhd	Malaysia	$57	Property investments
7 Eu Yan Sang Marketing Pte Ltd	Singapore	$10	Distribution
8 Applied Biomedical Intl Pte Ltd	Singapore	$100	Lab testing services
Other subsidiaries and associated companies			
9 Eu Yan Sang Australia Pte Ltd (80%)	Australia	$2,019	Investment holding
10 Chengdu Hua ShengEe Enterprise Co. (50%)	China	$96	R&D of herbal medicine
11 Botanical Health Resources Inc. (48.5%)	United States	$1,060	Distribution and sales
Significant companies held by subsidiaries	% equity held by group		
1 EYS Venture Pte Ltd	Singapore	100	Remittance commission agent
2 Synco (HK) Ltd	Hong Kong	100	Manufacturing and sales
3 Eu Yan Sang (Properties) Ltd	Hong Kong	100	Property investments
4 YourHealth Group	Australia	50	Medical services

Source: Eu Yan Sang (2002: 57–8).

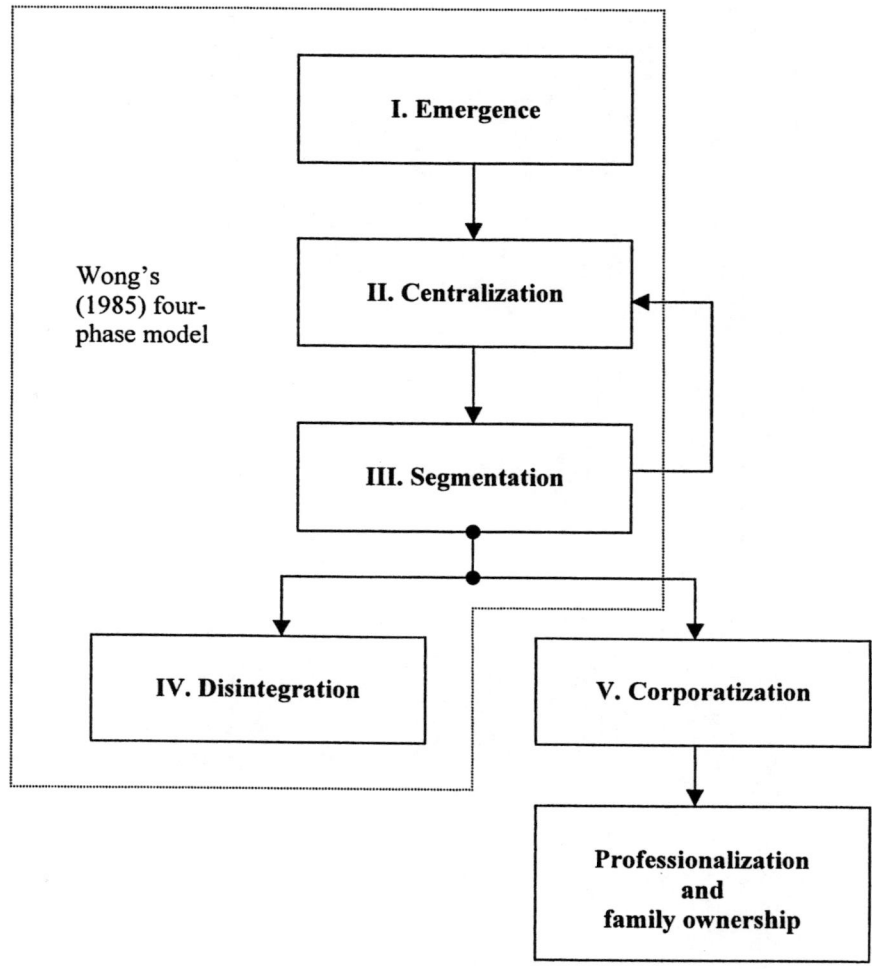

Figure 4.3 A dynamic model of Chinese family firms.

family ownership (phase III) does not necessarily lead to disintegration (phase IV). In some cases, one branch of the family may acquire a controlling stake in the family firm and recentralize its ownership and management, although no significant transformations may occur in its management practices and business strategies. Second, if such a process of acquisition and recentralization takes place together with significant transformations in strategic management and corporate governance, then a Chinese family firm is deemed to have entered a fifth phase of corporatization in which family ownership overlaps with a significant degree of professionalization in corporate management and organizational structures.

This process of corporatization combines the strengths of both entrepreneurship through the direct involvement of family members in management and professionalism through organizational change to incorporate non-family managers in key corporate decision processes. Whereas the presence of family members ensures continuity and heritage, professionalization brings in new business ideas and corporate change that may result in a very different breed of Chinese family firms. The case of Eu Yan Sang, for example, shows that a traditional Chinese family firm can not only operate across borders successfully, but also transcend the three-generation trap to become a professionalized modern business enterprise. Its success clearly contradicts the culturalist expectations that all Chinese family firms remain traditionally managed and conservative in their outlook, *even if* they are increasingly globalizing themselves (cf. Redding, 2000).

What then are the implications of this revised model and the case studies in this chapter for our understanding of hybrid transformations in Chinese capitalism? One implication is clearly concerned with the issue of succession, which remains a thorny issue for many Chinese family firms today (Chau, 1991; Yeung, 1999b; see also Chapter 7). The role of professional managers in sustaining the development of Chinese family firms is another critical implication. The future success of these firms rests with the capability and competencies of their successors rather than the fact that they are family members *per se.* A final and related point is that these firms are increasingly undergoing dynamic transformations to meet the challenges of globalization. Many Chinese family firms from East and Southeast Asia, for example, are internationalizing their operations across borders. This chapter has plainly shown that to manage successfully across borders, a Chinese family firm needs both professional managers and corporatized organizational structures. As global competition becomes increasingly unavoidable in the Asia-Pacific region, these firms need to prepare themselves through the professionalization of management and governance, the consolidation of core competencies and better access to global capital markets. Meeting these serious challenges of globalization requires both entrepreneurial capabilities in family owners and professional competence of managers. In a global era, then, we are beginning to witness significant transformations in the social organization and corporate governance of Chinese firms. These twin dimensions are highly important to our understanding of the change of Chinese capitalism towards a form of hybrid capitalism. The following two chapters examine these dimensions on the basis of empirical case studies and detailed analyses of survey data.

5 Transformations in social organization

Chinese capitalism and access to global finance

This chapter examines how globalizing actor-networks, particularly those associated with international business and finance, are engaging with, reshaping and being reshaped by Chinese capitalism. I argue that although familism and *guanxi* relationships continue to constitute the social organization of Chinese capitalism, the concept of an exclusive and inward-oriented Chinese capitalism needs to be reconfigured to recognize the constitutive nature of a wide range of non-Chinese actors and their powerful networks within and outside the Asia-Pacific region. As discussed in Chapter 2, this transformation occurs primarily because globalizing actor-networks increasingly play fundamental (albeit uneven) roles in shaping the social organization and economic practices of key actors in Chinese capitalism (Olds and Yeung, 1999; Yeung 2000a). The search for new sources of capital beyond the Asia-Pacific region, for example, has brought with it many opportunities as well as tensions; tensions generated by the ever-shifting interaction of ethnic Chinese and non-Chinese actor-networks. As ethnic Chinese business groups accept the tension between losing personal or family control and acquiring access to critical financial resources, they become enrolled in a diverse range of international business actor-networks that have no significant Chinese dimension to them (see Chapter 2). Conversely, international business actors and institutions also seek to generate knowledge about Chinese capitalism as this knowledge benefits them materially when their recommendations and investments generate good profits and returns for their shareholders all over the world. International financial firms need to know whether to invest in specific ethnic Chinese firms, international credit-ratings firms need to know what rating to recommend in relation to the economic potential of specific firms and the international business media need to develop and disseminate knowledge about these firms via texts that are attractive to the global business community. The interactive engagement of such overlapping international business actor-networks generates further interest from additional globalizing actor-networks (such as those running through credit-ratings agencies and, more diffusely, supra-state institutions), as well as other types of actor-networks that run through government research arms, academic institutions and the popular media. These latter types of actor-networks are more interested in the analysis and representation of Chinese capitalism than in the direct satisfaction of their material goals. Irrespective of their intentions though, all these non-Chinese globalizing actor-networks generate products (e.g. books, reports, quotes, concepts, press releases, policy statements, contracts) that circulate via technology information on Chinese capitalism in a variety of geographical scales (see Chapter 1).

Although these globalizing actor-networks all play a significant role in reshaping Chinese capitalism, it is important to recognize their uneven sources of power and influence. As argued in Chapter 2, actor-networks involving international finance and international credit-ratings agencies have the greatest capacity to exert power, because analysts for financial services firms and credit-ratings agencies make judgements and recommendations on specific ethnic Chinese firms (see case studies below) that in turn enrol these Chinese actors into their actor-networks. Supplying this information by key Chinese actors thus becomes a major precondition to their successful access to global financial flows. Moreover, decisions over opening up access to flows of capital ultimately depends upon these actors in Chinese capitalism who in turn will be proposing and implementing changes in their business strategy and economic practices that might be deemed rational and profitable according to the financiers and the analysts in these globalizing actor-networks. As noted in Chapter 2, the majority of these changes entail moving towards more accountable business practices (including audited balance sheets) and professionalized decision-making processes. Given this situation, economic practices and social norms in Chinese capitalism are effectively (re)shaped by the criteria developed by those global financiers and analysts representing the gatekeepers of the global space of financial flows. The case studies below represent some simple, but somewhat linked, empirical narratives to illustrate the main aspects of this argument for conceptualizing Chinese capitalism as hybrid capitalism in a global era (see also Figure 1.2).

In the context of globalization (identified in Chapter 2) and the desire to access large-scale flows of capital to fund development projects, many of the largest Chinese business groups in Asia are faced with new challenges. Indeed, the goal of securing large-scale financial resources becomes one of the most critical factors in reshaping Chinese capitalism into a mode of hybrid capitalism. As Asian economies have leapfrogged in their technological and economic development during the past 20 years, many of the leading Chinese groups have conceivably jumped out of their cultural mould and adopted new management and financial practices that were previously unthinkable. Such transformations in Chinese capitalism do not happen only in such international financial centres as Hong Kong and

Singapore (Wu and Duk, 1995; Chiu *et al.*, 1997; Yeung, 2002a), but also increasingly in such emerging financial markets as Taiwan, Malaysia and Thailand. In many of these economies, there is an interesting juxtaposition of old and new financial practices among ethnic Chinese firms. Some of these new financial practices include tapping into non-Chinese international financial institutions for term loans and equity funds, raising capital through public share offerings and international bond listing, and attracting international equity investors.

An increasing number of Chinese firms are now seeking capital resources beyond their immediate social and ethnic networks to finance their development objectives (Yeung, 2003a). Shikatani's (1995) study provided some very important insights into the corporate financial requirements of 13 large Chinese business groups from Asia during the early 1990s (see Table 5.1). All these corporate groups were controlled by ethnic Chinese and listed on the Hong Kong Stock Exchange, except Hong Leong Industries. Several of them also belonged to much larger family business groups originated from Southeast Asia. (For example, Sino Land belonged to Ng Teng Fong, father of Robert Ng, from Singapore; CP Pokphand to Dhanin Chearavanont from Thailand; First Pacific to Liem Sioe Liong from Indonesia and Hong Leong Industries to Quek Leng Chan from Malaysia.) As indicated in Table 1.6, these Southeast Asian Chinese were highly prominent in their domestic economies. Other than Sino Land, Wharf Holdings and Wheelock, the rest were run by the founding Chinese entrepreneurs with strong individual personalities. Most of their assets were held in publicly owned companies. It is clear that all of them enjoyed good growth rates during the 1988–93 period. Based on an analysis of net profits, total assets, return on equity and interest coverage, Shikatani (1995) divided the 13 companies into three separate groups:

1   The well-balanced type: excelled in rates of growth, profitability and financial stability. They had the greatest capacity to finance their own capital requirements because of their abundant internal funds and their less reliance on short- and long-term debt and paid-in capital.
2   The growth/financial stability type: had strong rates of growth and good financial strength, but could still improve their profitability. The long-term capital requirements of these companies rose rapidly in the 1990s because of skyrocketing prices in Hong Kong's real-estate market.
3   The profitability-oriented type: appeared to place the greatest priority on profitability. A heavy reliance on debt was a distinguishing characteristic of these companies that raised potential questions about their financial stability.

Because many of these 13 companies had their main businesses in Hong Kong's real-estate sector, they had been riding on escalating

Table 5.1 Corporate financial statistics of large ethnic Chinese conglomerates from Asia, 1993

	Cheung Kong	Henderson Land	Sun Hung Kai Properties	Hang Lung Dev't	Hysan Dev't	New World Dev't	Sino Land	Wharf Holdings	Wheelock	Hutchinson Whampoa	CP Pokphand	First Pacific	Hong Leong Industries
Country/economy of ultimate origin	HK	HK	HK	HK	HK	HK	Singapore	HK	HK	HK	Thailand	Indonesia	Malaysia
Chairman	Li Ka-shing	Lee Shau-kee	Kwok Ping-sheung	Chan Chi-chun	Lee Hon-chiu	Cheng Yu-tung	Robert Ng Chee Siong	Woo Kwong-ching	Woo Kwong-ching	Li Ka-shing	Dhanin Chearavanont	Liem Sioe Liong	Quek Leng Chan
Total assets (US$ billion)	6.7	3.8	10.2	4.3	4.6	6.9	2.3	12.9	3.8	10.5	0.6	2.0	0.5
Market capital (US$ billion)	10.0	9.9	16.8	2.1	2.6	4.9	2.4	8.0	4.2	15.9	0.6	1.3	0.7
Equity ratio (%)	68.1	59.6	72.9	45.6	84.2	67.6	76.9	78.4	80.4	59.9	47.2	20.3	38.9
5-year net profits (%)	36.2	31.9	29.5	16.3	33.4	25.4	22.6	19.6	8.0	11.7	20.9	32.2	52.3
Payout ratio (%)	22.5	83.7	49.3	45.2	60.1	39.5	39.0	68.6	39.8	39.0	56.8	31.7	8.5
Working capital (months) 1986–9	8.83	21.21	7.25	5.40	-0.54	3.00	-0.83	-0.36	1.85	2.31	1.14	2.78	2.13
1990–3	7.83	17.76	4.50	10.66	-0.54	1.81	16.19	-2.34	3.74	-0.33	1.40	2.09	0.64
Overall grouping[1]	W	W	W	G	G	G	G	G	G	P	P	P	P

Source: Compiled from tables in Shikatani (1995).

Notes
1 W = well-balanced type
   G = growth/financial stability type
   P = profitability-oriented type (see text for explanations).

real-estate prices in Hong Kong during the late 1980s and the early 1990s to improve their financial positions. Their long-term financial strategy, however, could be too dependent on such a volatile and localized property market (see Table 1.6 for the dramatic decline in their net worth after the 1997–8 Asian economic crisis). Most of them were diversifying into peripheral areas and entering new growth markets, such as telecommunications and infrastructure. To acquire working capital to finance their new investment projects, many used a variety of financial mechanisms including bank loans and the issuance of bonds and securities on local and international financial markets.

Access to such massive flows of global finance is increasingly available in Asian cities and there is a mutually constitutive relationship between world or global city formation in Asia and the transformation of these very large Chinese business groups. Asian-centred financial networks are bound through social and technological networks to global fund managers in global cities such as London and New York. These managers make decisions about investing in equity and bond markets in key Asian cities like Hong Kong, Singapore and Kuala Lumpur, that act as source points for the global financial system. Hong Kong and Singapore, for example, have long served as the twin capitals for ethnic Chinese firms (Wu and Duk, 1995; Enright *et al.*, 1997; Wu, 1997). As reported in La Porta *et al.*'s (1999: Table 2; 492) study of corporate ownership around the world, both Hong Kong and Singapore have better than median shareholder protection despite the large number of Chinese family firms listed on their stock exchanges. In 1994 Chinese family firms controlled 123 companies listed on the Hong Kong Stock Exchange that had an aggregate market capitalization of US$155 billion and total assets of US$173 billion (Wu and Duk, 1995: Table 3; Au *et al.*, 2000). Another estimate reported in the *Far Eastern Economic Review* (10 February 2000: 42) showed that about 70 per cent of all publicly listed firms in Hong Kong in 2000 were family-controlled. In my earlier study reported in Yeung and Soh (2000), we identified 157 Chinese family firms listed on the Stock Exchange of Singapore in 1996, representing some 44.2 per cent of all 355 listed companies (see also Chapter 6).

In the loan syndication business, the two financial centres have catered to customers from different geographic regions. The US$117.5 billion-worth of syndicated loans arranged by Hong Kong-based financial institutions between 1992 and mid-1996 were more than double that of Singapore, but 71.7 per cent of this was accounted for by borrowers from East Asia, many of whom were ethnic Chinese entities. In Singapore the borrowers were mainly from Southeast Asia; these, together with local borrowers, took up 88.5 per cent of Singapore's total syndicated lending of US$54.6 billion during the same period (Wu, 1997: 13–15). Between 1993 and 1994 financial institutions in Hong Kong and Singapore arranged US$6.5 billion-worth and US$8.6 billion-worth of syndicated loans respectively for Indonesian and Thai companies. Of the total US$38.4 billion-worth of funds in the custody of Singapore's fund managers at the end of 1993, some 40 per cent originated in Southeast Asian countries. The bulk of these funds may have come from high net-worth ethnic Chinese and their cash-rich corporate entities (Wu and Duk, 1995: 26). These twin capitals are more than just the berth for ethnic Chinese capital; they also serve as an intermediary to match state-owned enterprises (SOEs) from mainland China and their eager regional and global investors. Indeed, Hong Kong is now the leading financial centre for red-chip SOEs to obtain access to global capital. Just before the Asian economic crisis in July 1997, total Chinese investments in the territory amounted to US$25 billion, the second largest after the UK (*The Straits Times*, 18 March 1997: 36; see also Fung, 1996). There were 1,802 wholly owned mainland companies with total assets of US$5.4 billion in Hong Kong. Well-known red-chip companies (e.g. CITIC and China Resources) also accounted for 8 per cent of the Hong Kong Stock Exchange's total market capitalization. Since the mid-1990s several SOEs from mainland China have made public offerings in the Singapore Exchange or acquired listed companies in Singapore for access to global capital markets and/or other strategic purposes. For example, in 1995, China Merchants Shekou Port Service Co. Ltd became the first public listed company from mainland China to have a secondary listing in Singapore.

The first half of the 1990s was indeed an incredibly fortuitous period for ethnic Chinese business groups in East and Southeast Asia seeking new sources of capital to finance their global expansion of business activities. From Table 5.2 it is clear that global flows of capital into Asia increased very substantially from an average of around US$16 billion during 1977–82 and 1983–9 to over US$40 billion during 1990–4. By 1996, the annual flow had exceeded US$110 billion. Though the inflow was temporarily interrupted by the 1997–8 Asian economic crisis, the amount of capital inflows into Asia in 1998 and 1999 remained comparable with the pre-crisis period. Among the various financial institutions intermediating global financial flows in these Asian economies, banks have occupied a particularly important position, not least because many of them are owned and controlled by Chinese families. Table 5.3 shows that the shares of banks in financial intermediation in Singapore, Taiwan, Indonesia, Malaysia and Thailand during 1994–5 were particularly high compared with their counterparts from the US and South Korea. Foreign banks were also very significant in Hong Kong and Singapore, accounting for 78–80 per cent of total assets in the banking sector. In terms of their net interest margins, banks in most of these East and Southeast Asian economies appeared to be highly profitable during the same period. By the late 1980s and the early 1990s global finance had clearly made significant inroads into the heartland of Chinese capitalism and facilitated the enormous growth and development of its leading business groups. Some empirical

Table 5.2 Global capital flows to emerging economies, 1977-99 (annual averages, US$ billion)

	1977–82	1983–9	1990–4	1995	1996	1997	1998	1999
All emerging economies								
Total net capital flows	30.5	8.8	120.8	192.0	240.8	173.7	291.2	264.3
Net foreign direct investment	11.2	13.3	46.2	96.0	114.9	138.2	170.9	192.0
Net portfolio investment	−10.5	6.5	61.1	23.5	49.7	42.9	15.6	27.6
Other (includes bank lending)	29.8	−11.0	13.5	72.5	76.2	−7.3	104.7	44.7
By region								
Asia	15.8	16.7	40.1	95.8	110.4	13.9	90.7	96.3
Western hemisphere	26.3	−16.6	40.8	35.7	80.5	91.1	188.4	144.5
Other	−11.6	8.7	39.9	60.5	50.0	68.8	12.1	23.5

Sources: Grenville (2000: Table 2.1; based on IMF, 1995: 33; 1998: 13); World Bank (2000: 188).

Note
1977-89 figures exclude transitional economies and some Middle Eastern emerging economies.

Table 5.3 The nature of banks in selected Asian and developed economies, 1994–5

Economy	Bank share in financial intermediation[1]	State-owned banks (% of total assets)	Foreign banks (% of total assets)	Non-interest operating costs[2]	Net interest margins[2]
Hong Kong	–	0	78[3]	1.5	2.2
Singapore	71	0	80	1.4	1.6
Indonesia	91	48	4	2.4	3.3
Malaysia	64	8	16	1.6	3.0
Taiwan	80	57	5	1.3	2.0
Thailand	75	7	7	1.9	3.7
South Korea	38	13	5	1.7	2.1
Japan	79	0	2	0.8	1.1
Germany	77	50[3]	4	1.1	1.4
United States	23	0	22	3.7	3.7

Source: Guillén (2001a: Table 7.1; 185).

Notes
1 Assets as a percentage of the assets of banks and non-bank financial institutions.
2 As a percentage of total assets, averaged over the 1990–4 period.
3 Not directly comparable with percentages for other countries.

narratives follow, to showcase how the social organization of Chinese capitalism has been gradually transformed by the enrolment of key Chinese actors in these globalizing actor-networks in the arena of international business and finance.

Actor-networks in international business and finance: restructuring beyond the family and the bamboo network

The first case study focuses on the ways in which Li Ka-shing and his son, Richard Li, have successfully enrolled in globalizing actor-networks in international business and finance, which simultaneously reduces their dependence on traditional network capital among ethnic Chinese business networks (as described in Chapter 1) and enhances their financial capacity to globalize their business operations. The case also shows the critical importance of non-Chinese actors in ensuring the success of Chinese capitalism. Although this case points to the gradual transformation in the *modus operandi* of financing the growth and expansion of leading Chinese business groups, it does not mean the complete withering away of traditional Chinese business practices either. Interestingly, some non-Chinese actors (e.g. financial analysts and the media) have discursively reconstructed some of these cultural practices in Chinese capitalism (e.g. *guanxi* networks) to entice the appetite of global financial investors. The transformations in the social organization of Chinese capitalism are therefore by no means one-way and unidirectional, but take a hybrid route through which some cultural elements of Chinese capitalism are eroded. However, other dimensions are accentuated for practical reasons very different from their historical and institutional formations. There is thus no permanent fixity in the social organization of Chinese capitalism; change and transformation are endemic in this reshaped form of capitalist economic organization.

On 10 March 1997 Li Ka-shing's multi-billion-dollar corporate empire, the Cheung Kong Group, completed a major shareholding and organizational restructuring (Olds and Yeung, 1999). The group comprised Cheung Kong (Holdings) Ltd which held shares in and controlled Hutchison Whampoa Ltd (acquired in 1977), Cheung Kong Infrastructure Holdings Ltd and Hong Kong Electric Holdings Ltd. As noted in Table 1.5, both Hutchison Whampoa (1st) and Hong Kong Electric (44th) were ranked among the top 50 TNCs from emerging economies in 2000. The corporate reorganization essentially involved a significant transformation in the shareholding structure of the Cheung Kong Group from a three-tier shareholding structure of Cheung Kong (Holdings) Ltd and its three direct subsidiaries (Figure 5.1) to a four-tier shareholding structure that was still in place in March 2003 (see Figure 5.2). It involved the disposal of Cheung Kong (Holdings) Ltd's entire 70.7 per cent shareholding in Cheung Kong Infrastructure Holdings Ltd to a subsidiary of

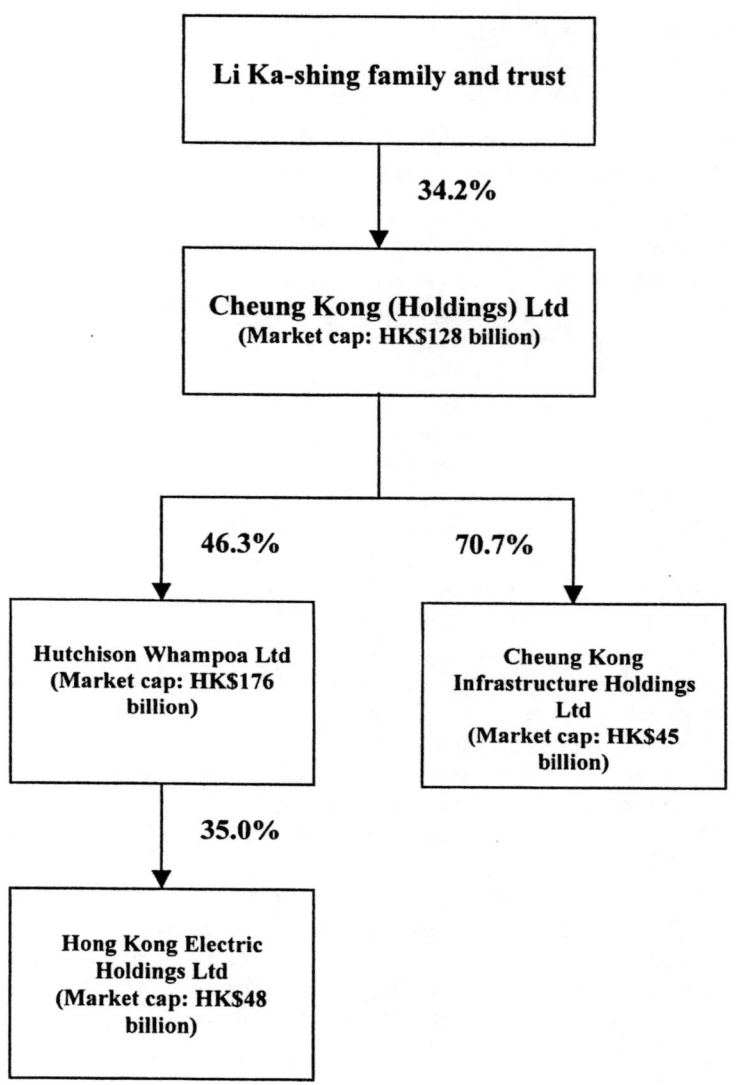

Figure 5.1 Li Ka-shing and the Cheung Kong Group before reorganization on 10 March 1997.

Sources: Cheung Kong (Holdings) Ltd (1998), Cheung Kong Infrastructure Holdings Ltd (1997) and Hong Kong Stock Exchange (1996).

Note
Market capitalization values were as at 30 June 1996.

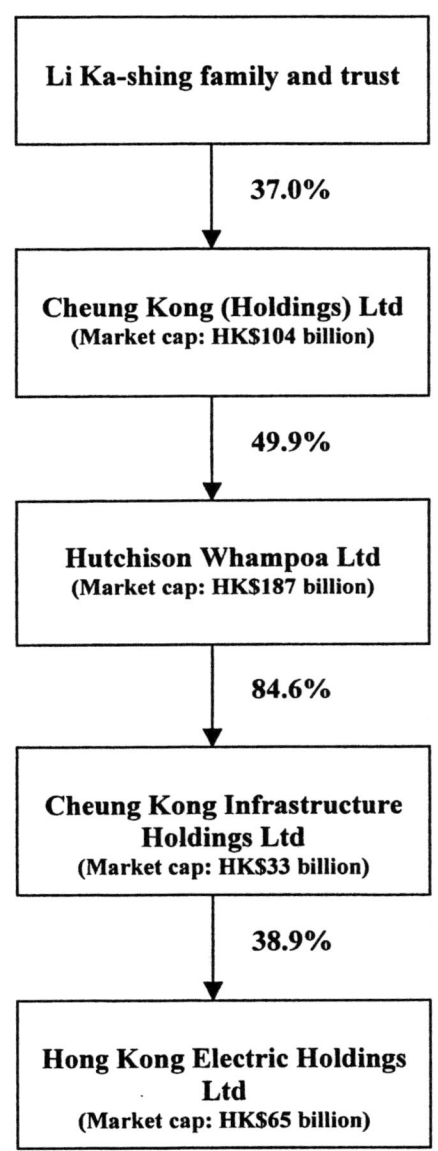

Figure 5.2 Li Ka-shing and the Cheung Kong Group as at 15 March 2003.

Source: http://www.ckh.com.hk/eng/about_group.htm, accessed on 20 March 2003.

Hutchison Whampoa Ltd in consideration for HK$5.6 billion in cash and 254 million ordinary shares of $0.25 each issued by Hutchison Whampoa Ltd. As a result of the share issue, Cheung Kong (Holdings) Ltd's interest in Hutchison Whampoa Ltd was increased by approximately 3.6 per cent to 49.9 per cent (Cheung Kong Holdings Ltd, 1998). Hutchison Whampoa Ltd became the majority shareholder (84.6 per cent) of Cheung Kong Infrastructure Holdings Ltd. The reorganization exercise also involved the acquisition of approximately 35 per cent shares of Hong Kong Electric Holdings Ltd by Cheung Kong Infrastructure Holdings Ltd. The completed organizational structure of the Cheung Kong Group (see Figure 5.2) illustrates a somewhat pyramid-like shareholding structure that allows the Li family to have control rights (i.e. voting rights) in subsidiaries well in excess of their cash flow rights (i.e. ownership of shares). It also enables the direct participation of the Li family members in the management of these subsidiaries.

What was the role of globalizing actor-networks in this major restructuring of the largest Chinese family business group in Hong Kong? About two months earlier on 6 January 1997, writers and reporters representing the global business media were grappling with a complex proposal for the reorganization of Li Ka-shing's multi-billion-dollar corporate empire, in particular his flagship conglomerate, the Cheung Kong Group. A press release was faxed out to them without warning, though those in the know, especially journalists like John Ridding from the *Financial Times*, would clearly have known what was developing in Li's corporate base (Hong Kong) for some time. The channels of gossip in Hong Kong's local business community were simply too quick and dense for Ridding, one of the *Financial Times*' most influential and well-connected journalists based in Hong Kong, to have been caught unaware. Ridding's analysis (written with Louis Lucas), nearly three-quarters of a page long, was published one day later (7 January) in the *Financial Times*, the distinctive pink pages of the world's financial elite (Ridding and Lucas, 1997). This daily newspaper plays a powerful role in disseminating and trading ideas on various geographical scales (from local to global) between three broadly defined communities: the firm, the investor and the fund manager.[1] The *Financial Times* therefore had a significant role in contributing to (though not determining) the rapid formation of opinion in the world's financial centres about the potential effectiveness of the Cheung Kong Group's restructuring.

By 10 January (four days later), global securities firms such as Goldman Sachs, Morgan Stanley and Nomura had released reports on the proposed reorganization of the Cheung Kong Group. These semi-private texts were speedily distributed round the world to qualified institutional buyers. An extract from one of these reports is given in Figure 5.3. Detailed financial analysis from personnel based in Hong Kong was presented in the reports. Many different aspects of the restructuring process were evaluated and

---

CHEUNG KONG GROUP
Proposed Reorganization

* Reiterate BUY Rating on Hutchison Whampoa; Cheung Kong Upgraded to Market Outperformer; Cheung Kong Infrastructure and Hongkong Electric Downgraded to Market Performer.

* Structural Change has no Direct Impact on Hongkong Electric's Earnings or Fundamentals but Coincident with Strategy Change to Pursue IPP Opportunities.

* Dilution of CKI's Long-term Earnings Growth will Likely Dampen Price Performance Before a Strategic Buyer of Hongkong Electric Surfaces.

* Potential Exceptional Gain Will Boost Otherwise Sluggish Reported Profit Growth for Hutchison in Fiscal 1997; Gaining Control of CKI Boosts Earnings Growth Over a Longer Term.

* Bargain Purchase of 5% of Enlarged Hutchison at P/E of 17x Results in Tighter Control for Cheung Kong; Total Attributable Exceptional Gain of HK$5 Billion in Fiscal 1997 Provides Cushion for Earnings Management.

Figure 5.3 A financial report on the Cheung Kong Group's proposed reorganization, 10 January 1997.

Source: Adapted from a confidential company report, dated 10 January 1997.

assessments were made about the short- and long-term prospects for all four publicly listed members of the Cheung Kong Group. The more insightful of these reports addressed the changing nature of the Cheung Kong Group's management structure, as the world's most famous ethnic Chinese patriarch continued to prepare his two sons (Victor Li, the eldest, Cheung Kong's managing director; and Richard Li, Hutchison Whampoa's vice-chairman) for steadily increasing corporate responsibilities (see also Chapter 4). The benefits that can be generated by enrolling in non-Chinese actor-networks are obvious. In this case, the proposed restructuring of the Cheung Kong Group was viewed favourably for the most by globalizing actor-networks in international business and finance. According to London's *Sunday Times* (12 January 1997), this favourable judgement consequently left the patriarch of the empire 'more firmly in control of his four listed companies, shifted value to his personal holdings and increased his group's market value by £2 billion in two days'. Moreover, the proposed restructuring was expected to register 'exceptional gains' of HK$1.9 billion for Hutchison Whampoa Ltd and HK$4.9 billion for Cheung Kong Holdings in fiscal year 1997 (Goldman Sachs, 1997).

How then did these exceptional gains happen? In its 1997 annual report, Cheung Kong (Holdings) Ltd (1998) reported a turnover of only HK$7.9 billion for the calendar year 1997, a 40 per cent decrease from the previous year's turnover at HK$13.2 billion. This result reflected the rapidly deteriorating economic and market conditions in Asia during the second half of 1997 that adversely affected the sales of Cheung Kong's properties. But its profit attributable to shareholders in 1997 recorded a historical high at HK$17.6 billion (HK$7.7 billion alone from the disposal of Cheung Kong Infrastructure), 28 per cent higher than its 1996 profit of HK$13.8 billion. The 1997 profit also doubled its meagre turnover, and earnings and dividend per share registered their respective historical highs. These were substantial gains that enhanced the prices and relative performances of all of the Cheung Kong Group of companies in the volatile Hong Kong stock market, a market perceived by global finance to be a less risky vehicle for investing in Asia (and mainland China in particular). The March 1997 corporate restructuring thus led to a substantial increase in the combined market capitalization of the Cheung Kong Group. Before the restructuring, the Cheung Kong Group, comprising Cheung Kong (Holdings) Ltd, Hutchison Whampoa Ltd and Hong Kong Electric Holdings Ltd, had a combined market capitalization of HK$352 billion as at 30 June 1996 (Cheung Kong Infrastructure Holdings Ltd was listed in July 1996 with a market capitalization of HK$45 billion). After the reorganization, the Group's four listed companies had a combined market capitalization of HK$442 billion as at 28 April 1997. Even in the middle of the Asian economic crisis, the restructured group's total market capitalization remained at HK$433 billion as at 15 April 1998 (http://www.ckh.com.hk, accessed on 12 June 1998). In May 2000 Li Ka-shing's family, including Richard Li's Pacific Century CyberWorks Ltd (see pages 172–5), controlled more than a third of Hong Kong's stock market capitalization (up from 12.7 per cent in 1988), and a large chunk of its economy, ranging from container ports to telecommunications, supermarkets and property (*The Economist*, 3 May 2000). As at 15 March 2003, the combined market capitalization of Li's Cheung Kong Group stood at HK$405 billion, slightly less than 13 per cent of Hong Kong's stock market capitalization (http://www.ckh.com.hk, accessed on 20 March 2003).

Clearly, the willing enrolment of these key actors in Chinese capitalism in globalizing actor-networks can give access to flows of significant financial resources. The massive increase in the Cheung Kong Group's market value would not have materialized without the thumbs-up of powerful non-Chinese actors in these globalizing actor-networks. The anticipated need for this approval from actors in globalizing actor-networks in turn prompted Li Ka-shing to reorganize his family-controlled group in ways that family control remained undiluted, and yet economic efficiency and shareholder benefits must be seen as forthcoming by public shareholders and financial analysts. After all, institutional investors could simply sell off their massive holdings in all Cheung Kong companies if they were unconvinced by the proposed reorganization or if the exercise attracted very critical assessments from most financial analysts and business reporters. In short, the rapid accumulation of capital by leading actors in Chinese capitalism in a global era depends not only on their entrepreneurial tendencies and *guanxi* networks (as described in the literature reviewed in Chapter 1), but also increasingly on their success in enrolling in globalizing actor-networks and enticing favourable support from (non-Chinese) actors in these networks. The recognition of this need has prompted key actors in Chinese capitalism to reconsider the continued relevance of their culturally specific norms and economic practices.

Although it is important to recognize this point about changing social organization, this does not imply that all characteristically Chinese business practices and social norms are deemed to be a constraint upon business growth and that they are destined to dissolve (see also Chapter 4). Such an assumption by those ultra-globalists who believe in full-scale convergence in global capitalist norms and conventions are too simplistic and naïve. Quite on the contrary, while key actors in Chinese capitalism are gradually socialized into globalizing actor-networks, their traditional economic practices and cultural norms have apparently achieved a new lease of life too, albeit this time through the discursive reconstructions of international business actors. Indeed, ethnic business networks and familism appear to be recognized in most international financial circles as the key mechanisms through which Chinese capitalism develops and expands (ING Barings, 1997). The effective management of business networks is perceived to be a critical source of significant profits in socialist developing countries like mainland China and Vietnam. For example, the Union Bank of Switzerland's Hong Kong Equities team put this point bluntly when they recommended in 1994 that global institutional investors should 'buy' Cheung Kong Holdings stocks (a 'big gun loaded with firepower'):

Cheung Kong is one of our favorite China plays, not because of its direct investment there but because of its *well-established connections and goodwill*. We believe the group is poised to ride the crest of robust economic growth in China over the next 10 years through its diversified investment in companies which have substantial mainland exposure. We estimate Cheung Kong's actual investment in China at less than $1.0b; however, through its holdings in Hutchison, Hopewell and some other red-chip companies, it will maintain a substantial exposure in China with little direct risk.

At the moment, risk and return analysis would not justify an aggressive investment in China's property market, since the quality of earnings is still low due to unpredictable market conditions and government controls. We thus favour companies with a more prudent China investment strategy. Once the environment becomes clearer, we expect Cheung Kong will easily match the commitments of other big investors in China, thanks to its *well-maintained connections*. The group enjoys *excellent relationships* with some powerful state enterprises and companies managed by siblings of influential officials.

(UBS Global Research, 1994: 3; my emphasis)

Although the Cheung Kong Group and Li Ka-shing are very well-known in Asia, similar sentiments may be found in other texts about much smaller Chinese family firms and less famous ethnic Chinese businesspeople (East Asia Analytical Unit, 1995; Backman, 1999).

Moreover, investment flows in the Asia-Pacific region are heavily dependent upon the management of networks of social relations that reach across space, with a strong ethnic (and especially Chinese) component. In turn, flows of capital into publicly listed ethnic Chinese firms facilitate the regional expansion of Chinese business networks, and (by proxy) the Asia-Pacific reach of global fund managers. Equity and bond markets in global financial centres are effectively used to tap into capital from around the world. The waves of capital provide the economic resources that support and propel the exploitation of social connections through the initiation of action or the acceptance of inclusion in action initiated by others. Obviously, the *guanxi* element of the investment equation is not the only element financial firms take into account. But it is an important one, as evidenced in another UBS (1995) report on Cheng Yu-tung's New World Development, a powerful property development company that was ranked 6th among the top 50 TNCs from emerging economies in 2000 (see Table 1.5). In the minds of UBS's Hong Kong analysts, New World's success in managing the various stages of its massive investment flows into mainland China was due to its well-connected and appropriate investment style; its investment in government high-priority projects; and its successful spin-off of investment projects. On the first point, UBS (1995: 34) made this clarification: 'The NW China team is well-connected with municipal government officials and has developed solid mutual trust, which is cultivated through long-term commitment and co-operation'.

On 24 March 1998, right in the middle of Asia's worst ever economic crisis, the international credit-rating agency, Moody's, released a rather favourable analysis of New World Development's separately listed infrastructure arm, New World Infrastructure (see Figure 5.4). Moody's assignment of a Ba1 grade to NWI's US$300 million convertible bonds no doubt facilitated its floating in major global financial markets. This positive assessment was offered even though Moody's recognized the project participation of New World Infrastructure Ltd in subsidiaries that carried 'a substantial amount of debt' and the 'structurally subordinating' role of NWI's bondholders because '[t]he creditors to such NWI subsidiaries and projects generally have a priority claim over the cash flows that they generate' (quoted in the text in Figure 5.4). These texts, along with various forms of media reports and the accounts created by financial analysts in firms such as UBS, play a significant role in creating greater consensus in the international finance sphere about the existence and utility of ethnic (particularly Chinese) networks in a global era. This consensus, at least in some of these political-economic circles, underlies political support at a

MOODY'S ASSIGNS Ba1 TO NEW WORLD INFRASTRUCTURE
LIMITED'S SENIOR CONVERTIBLE BONDS DUE 2003

Amount of Debt Rated is up to US$300 Million

Tokyo, March 24, 1998 -- Moody's Investors Service has assigned a Ba1 senior unsecured rating to New World Infrastructure Limited (NWI) up to US$300 million convertible bonds due 2003. The rating reflects NWI's diversified cash flow from a portfolio of infrastructure projects in Hong Kong and the People's Republic of China (PRC), *its close relationship with project hosting localities*, and the company's relatively low debt levels. Negative factors incorporated in the rating include NWI's increasing reliance on less predictable cash flow from PRC toll road projects, the company's aggressive growth strategy, and its holding company structure. The proposed debt issue has been designated for resale under rule 144A of the Securities Act of 1933.

NWI was established in 1995 to acquire from its parent, New World Development Co. Ltd (NWD), infrastructure projects including road, bridge, power generation and airport-related projects in Guangdong Province and Wuhan in the PRC, and tunnel and seaport-related interest in Hong Kong. NWI has aggressively added, or committed to, more than thirty infrastructure projects, mainly in the PRC, with support from its parent; New World is one of the largest foreign investors in PRC and has a *close relationship with many local governments*. Moody's acknowledges that NWI's participation in an increasing number of projects continue to create positive portfolio effects and add stability to its overall cash flow. Nonetheless, to a large extent, the performance of NWI's investments depends on the PRC's continued economic health and sustained local government support. Moody's will also continue to assess the sustainability of NWI's existing projects and the quality of its future investments under PRC's rapidly evolving economic system. NWI's interest in port-related services in Hong Kong should continue to provide a stable source of cash flow, although the importance of such contributions to the company's overall performance shall diminish in the intermediate term.

NWI is expected to substantially increase its reliance on cash flow from PRC's road projects which in Moody's opinion possess a higher degree of demand risk compared to the company's other investments in power generation and port-related services. Although NWI has been able to negotiate favorable joint venture terms to reduce investment risks, the stability and predictability of the company's overall cash flow and debt protection measurements may deteriorate because of its increased dependence on toll road contributions. Uncertainties also exist in securing future toll and tariff hikes from relevant local government agencies in the PRC.

While NWI's balance sheet is relatively unleveraged, Moody's will continue to monitor the management's willingness and ability to maintain a conservative financial profile in pursuing its aggressive growth strategy. The company also participates in various projects through subsidiaries, which carry a substantial amount of debt. *The creditors to such NWI subsidiaries and projects generally have a priority claim over the cash flows that they generate, thus structurally subordinating NWI's bondholders.*

New World Infrastructure Limited is headquartered in Hong Kong.

Tokyo
Takahiro Morita
Senior Vice President
Ratings
Moody's Japan K.K.
(03) 3593-0922

Hong Kong
Julia Turner
Managing Director
Asia Ratings
Moody's Asia Pacific Ltd
Telephone: 852-2509-0200

Figure 5.4 Moody's credit rating of New World Development's convertible bonds, March 1998.

Source: http://www.moodys.com/repldata/ratings/actions/pr.18206.html, accessed on 28 March 1998; my emphasis.

variety of levels to facilitate the spread of Chinese capitalism across space and the desire among some to hook into these globalizing actor-networks, be it directly through a joint venture or indirectly via investment practices (Mitchell, 1993, 1997; Olds, 2001). In turn, flows of capital into listed ethnic Chinese firms facilitate the regional and global expansion of key actors in Chinese capitalism.

In another instance of Li Ka-shing family's strategic enrolment into actor-networks in global finance, one of the hottest corporate manoeuvres in Asia in recent years was the US$29 billion mega-merger deal completed on 17 August 2000, which involved Singapore Telecom (SingTel), Hong Kong's Cable & Wireless HKT (C&W HKT), 54.4 per cent owned by Cable & Wireless plc based in London and renamed from Hong Kong Telecom in 1999, and Hong Kong's Pacific Century CyberWorks Ltd (PCCW). SingTel was a telecommunications monopoly in Singapore. Despite its privatization in the mid-1990s, SingTel was still 76 per cent owned by the Singapore government's official holding company, Temasek Holdings (*The Straits Times*, 15 February 2000: 68). Its CEO and president, 42–year-old Lee Hsien Yang, was the second son of Singapore's former prime minister Lee Kuan Yew (senior minister in 2000). His elder brother, Lee Hsien Loong, was then deputy prime minister of Singapore and named by the prime minister, Goh Chok Tong, as his successor by 2005. In a very similar kinship way, PCCW was founded on 18 August 1999 by the 33-year-old Richard Li (second son of Li Ka-shing) after his Pacific Century Group (founded in October 1993) acquired a controlling stake in Tricom Holdings Ltd, a public company listed on the Hong Kong Stock Exchange, and renamed it PCCW (http://www.pccw.com, accessed on 20 March 2003). By the time PCCW made the US$29 billion counter-offer to Cable & Wireless plc in February 2000, the ten-month-old internet set-up certainly had no specific ownership and control relationships with the Hong Kong government or the mainland Chinese government. It only wanted to set its sights on becoming the largest internet company in Asia.

The prey, C&W HKT (formerly Hong Kong Telecom), had more than 100 years of experience in providing telecommunications services in Hong Kong. It was a colonial set-up by the UK parent company in London, Cable & Wireless plc. It was now being disposed of because Cable & Wireless plc wanted to refocus on the internet and corporate data segments in Europe and to sell off all its non-core assets in Asia. Although the merger talk first started between SingTel and Cable & Wireless plc in November 1999 and a deal was almost sealed in early February 2000, Richard Li and his PCCW surprised the industry by announcing plans to merge with C&W HKT on 11 February 2000. A merger bidding war was initiated. By 29 February 2000, the verdict was out. The board of directors of Cable & Wireless plc held an extraordinary meeting in London on 28 February 2000 and PCCW got the deal to take over their 54.4 per cent of C&W HKT shares (*The Straits Times*, 29 February 2000). The US$29 billion deal, completed in August 2000, involved a combination of US$11.3 billion in cash and the rest in PCCW shares. As at 31 December 2000, Richard Li held about 40.4 per cent of PCCW and Cable & Wireless (Far East) Ltd held another 14.9 per cent (PCCW, 2001a: 61). By 30 June 2002, Richard Li's stake in PCCW had been reduced to 36.8 per cent, whereas Cable & Wireless (Far East) Ltd continued to hold about 14.1 per cent of PCCW shares (PCCW, 2003: 35). Almost two years after the acquisition, Richard Li remained at the helm of PCCW as its controlling shareholder, chairman and CEO.

This story of Richard Li's acquisition of C&W HKT offers some important clues to our analysis of the dynamic evolution and transformation of Chinese capitalism. Contrary to the conventional wisdom portrayed in the literature on Chinese capitalism (see Chapter 1), members of leading Chinese family groups are clearly capable of venturing into high-tech sectors that require much more than deal-making abilities. In fact, Richard Li single-handedly built STAR TV, Asia's first satellite-delivered cable-TV service in 1990, and sold it for US$525 million to Rupert Murdoch's News Corp. in 1993 (Olds, 2001: 120). The US$400 million profit in turn provided the capital to launch the Pacific Century Group in October 1993 and its subsequent agreement to acquire Tricom Holdings for HK$145 million on 3 May 1999 (CCW, 2001b: 191). Richard Li's inroads into telecommunications and the internet business made sense in view of his education in computer engineering and economics at Stanford, University, California (though he never completed his degrees, unlike his elder brother Victor Li). In 1986, he worked as an investment banker for Gordon Investment Corp., a Toronto-based investment bank in which Li Ka-shing owned 5 per cent, and became its youngest executive director and partner (Olds, 2001: 120). Given this technical and financial experience, Richard Li managed to enrol successfully in actor-networks in global finance that allowed him to tap into an unprecedented scale of financial resources required to acquire the giant C&W HKT. In December 1994 Hong Kong Telecom was the second largest listed company ranked by market capitalization (just after HSBC Holdings, the holding company of Hong Kong's largest bank, the Hongkong and Shanghai Banking Corporation). Capitalized at HK$165 billion then, it accounted for 7.9 per cent of the total market capitalization of the Hong Kong Stock Exchange. To finance his US$29 billion acquisition of C&W HKT, Richard Li secured a US$12 billion short-term bridging loan on 29 February 2000 that was drawn down in August 2000. Despite its short-term and bridging nature (the first US$3 billion repayable within 90 days and the rest within 180 days or before 29 February 2001), this loan was still extremely substantial in view of the fact that Richard Li's PCCW was then merely a start-up company with little experience in managing a land-based telecom operator and with few substantial assets as collaterals for the massive loan.[2] The US$12 billion loan syndicate comprised a wide range of international banks and financial institution (PCCW, 2001b: 108).

1   BOCI Capital Ltd (as paying agent);
2   HSBC Investment Bank Asia Ltd (as facility agent and security trustee);
3   Banque National de Paris, Hong Kong Branch;
4   Barclays Capital Asia Ltd (as coordinating arrangers);
5   Bank of China, Hong Kong Branch;
6   Barclays Bank plc;
7   HSBC Bank plc and The Hongkong and Shanghai Banking Corporation Ltd; and
8   Hang Seng Bank Ltd and Hang Seng Finance Ltd (as underwriters).

Although Richard Li's father, Li Ka-shing, might have helped his second son to secure this bridging loan, it must be emphasized that the senior Li and his Cheung Kong Group did not have any direct or deemed interest in PCCW and its acquisition of C&W HKT. Richard Li's almost exclusive reliance on international banks and capital markets to finance the deal certainly contradicted the culturalist prediction that the family patriarch would help his children's ventures financially. Indeed, the senior Li did not offer his second son any financial support to repay his bridging loan either, despite Richard Li's rumoured financial difficulties towards the end of 2000. In its filing of the 2000 annual report with the US Securities and Exchange Commission on 2 July 2001, PCCW (2001b: 94) acknowledged openly that:

> Our Executive Chairman and controlling shareholder, Li Tzar Kai, Richard is the son of Li Ka-shing, who is the Chairman, an Executive Director and the controlling shareholder of Hutchison Whampoa Limited ('HWL') and its associated company, Cheung Kong (Holdings) Limited (together with their subsidiaries and affiliates, the 'Hutchison Whampoa Group').

The filing made a clear distinction between PCCW and Li Ka-shing's corporate empire: 'we do not consider Li Ka-shing and the companies he controls, including the Hutchison Group, to be related parties of ours, and any transactions with the Hutchison Group are not being reported as related party transactions' (PCCW, 2001b: 94). By the end of 2000 Richard Li had managed to repay US$4.3 billion through a combination of internal funds and issuing new rights (HK$4.1 billion) and convertible bonds (US$1.1 billion). By February 2001 PCCW had repaid the entire bridging loan after disposing of Telstra, and held a cash reserve of over US$1 billion (PCCW, 2001a: 6; 40). It also managed to arrange another US$4.7 billion medium- to long-term bank loans with maturity spreads of three years (US$1.5 billion), five years (US$2.3 billion) and seven years (US$0.9 billion) (PCCW, 2001b: 115). These loans were syndicated on 23 November 2000 by five major international banks, comprising Barclays

Capital Asia Ltd, BOCI Capital Ltd, Chase Manhattan Asia Ltd, the Fuji Bank (Mizuho Finance Group) and HSBC Investment Bank Asia Ltd (as coordinating arrangers) (PCCW, 2001b: 110). Interestingly, three of these financial institutions had been involved in syndicating the earlier US$12 billion bridging loan, which indicated their continuing confidence in refinancing Richard Li's rather risky project. In January 2002 PCCW succeeded in issuing another US$450 million of convertible bonds to repay part of its US$4.7 billion bank loans. By September 2002 its wholly owned subsidiary, PCCW-HKT Telephone Ltd (HKTC), was enjoying improved credit ratings from Standard & Poor's (BBB) and Moody's (Ba1) (PCCW, 2003: 11).

Although the senior Li did not offer much direct financial help to Richard Li, it does not mean that all was wrong in the Li family. Despite his youth and relative inexperience, Richard Li's membership of Li Ka-shing's family has presumably enabled him to take advantage strategically of the social capital his father has accumulated over the years, particularly his political connections with mainland China. The end result was apparent: the business family (Li) in Hong Kong won over the political family (Lee) in Singapore. Although the Singapore government denied any political motives for the deal and sent a high-level official delegation to Hong Kong to explain to the chief executive, Tung Chee Hwa, and his senior government officials (*The Straits Times*, 4 February 2000), the dissociation of the Singapore government from the merger talk was not convincing, particularly given the ownership and management links between SingTel, the Singapore government and the Lee family. On 13 and 14 February 2000, both the Hong Kong and the Chinese governments denied reports that they were trying to influence the outcome of merger talks between SingTel and C&W HKT for 'political reasons'. Given the close personal links between Li Ka-shing and the highest level of authority in mainland China, it is hard to believe that the latter did not intervene in the merger process. In fact, the Beijing-controlled newspaper, *Wenhui Daily*, reported on 13 February 2000 that China had 'indirectly expressed its disapproval' of the proposed merger between SingTel and C&W HKT. This intervention from mainland China did not come as a surprise, for several reasons (quoted in the *The Straits Times*, 28 February 2000: 56–7). First, a successful merger between SingTel and C&W HKT would give Singapore a significant stake in one of Hong Kong's oldest and most respected companies. Second, there was fear that Hong Kong's position as a key regional telecommunications hub would be compromised, given the intense rivalry between the two global cities. In this regard, Singapore further liberalized its telecommunications industry to welcome global competition (*The Straits Times*, 22 January 2000). Third, China Telecom, the state monopoly in China, held a 10 per cent indirect stake in C&W HKT. It would clearly like someone closer to Beijing to take over C&W HKT, rather than a rival government-linked company from Singapore.

To sum up, ethnic networks and *guanxi* have sometimes been viewed as merchandisable commodities in the Asia-Pacific region because the key actors in some globalizing actor-networks represent them to be so. My judgement on the hybridization of Chinese capitalism does not deny the significance of ethnic networks and *guanxi* relationships to ethnic Chinese themselves. What it does try to get across is that such a distinctive element of Chinese capitalism can be reinforced and validated by powerful non-Chinese actors who have their own objectives, which are often pragmatic rather than cultural and ethnic. Actor-networks in international business and finance thus (re)shape and sometimes reinforce the dominant forms and norms of economic organization in Chinese capitalism through their judgements and recommendations, particularly in relation to ethnic Chinese actors accessing global finance. In similar ways, key actors in Chinese capitalism seek to gather support and favourable assessments from globalizing actor-networks. In doing so, they may no longer be exclusively Chinese in their social practices and economic behaviour, underscoring the high propensity towards the hybrid form of economic organization known as Chinese capitalism.

Actor-networks in international business and finance: capitalizing on international acquisitions

While the case studies of Li Ka-shing's family in Hong Kong have focused specifically on their corporate activities on their *home* ground, the follow-ing case study of Kwek Leng Beng and his Hong Leong Group from Singa-pore goes beyond the home-base advantage to examine his involvement in acquiring a major international hotel chain that was subsequently listed on the London Stock Exchange. The story of Kwek Leng Beng is equally telling in terms of how key actors in Chinese capitalism are capitalizing on the globalization process and thus becoming increasingly enrolled in glob-alizing actor-networks. Kwek's transnational entrepreneurship (see also Chapter 4), as manifested in his meticulous capitalization on family net-works and linkages at a regional scale, has contributed to his successful international business operations (Yeung, 2000d, 2002a: 159–68). The founder of the Hong Leong Group was the late Kwek Hong Png who came to Singapore from Fujian province in China in 1928. Over a period of five years he built up a vast business empire starting with trading and expanding into property, finance and hotels. The group's Malaysian branch started up in 1963 when his brother Kwek Hong Lye went to Malaya (from which Singapore was soon to separate) to extend the family's operations there (East Asia Analytical Unit, 1995: 332; Brown, 2000: 20–7, 175–87). The Malaysian family branch has grown substantially into one of the largest conglomerates in Malaysia, with an annual turnover of US$1.3 billion. It used to have a strong foothold in Hong Kong's finan-cial industry through its subsidiary, the Guoco Group that had controlled

Dao Heng Bank, the fifth largest local bank in Hong Kong, until its acquisition by Singapore's Development Bank of Singapore in April 2001. When Kwek Hong Lye died in 1996, his son, Quek Leng Chan, took over the Malaysian business. In 2000 Quek's Hume Industries was ranked 50th among the top 50 TNCs from emerging economies (Table 1.5). He was also consistently placed on the *Forbes* list of the world's richest billionaires during 1997–2003 (see Table 1.6).

Singapore's Kwek Leng Beng, son of the late Kwek Hong Png, took charge of the Hong Leong Group in Singapore after his father's death in 1994. Joining his father's business after finishing his law degree in the UK in 1963, Kwek initiated the takeover of a loss-making listed company, City Developments Ltd, in the late 1960s and successfully turned it round to become a leading property developer in Singapore. The Hong Leong Group (see Figure 5.5) is now one of the largest Chinese business groups in Singapore. By 1997 it had a market capitalization value of US$16 billion, an employment strength of 30,000 worldwide and a stable of 300 companies, including 11 listed on various bourses in Singapore, Hong Kong, New Zealand, Manila, New York and London (*Sunday Times*, 2 February 1997). Through its private property arm (Hong Leong Holdings) and its industrial company (Hong Leong Corporation), Kwek controls China's largest refrigerator manufacturer (Xin Fei Electric) and the New York-listed diesel engine maker China Yuchai International (*The Straits Times*, 9 August 1997: 10).

Since taking over from his father in late 1994, Kwek has developed a voracious appetite for major acquisitions abroad. As reported in the *Sunday Times* in Singapore (2 February 1997: 3):

> Just as the 'old man' [the late Kwek Hong Png] was famous for sniffing out good real estate deals, his son [Kwek Leng Beng] has been credited with an astute eye for choice hotels at bargain prices, often picking them up at rock-bottom prices from receivers. In international hotel circles, Mr Kwek is known as 'a business-cycle bottom fisher' and is reputed to be a decisive and fast buyer.

The Hong Leong Group has since globalized into the hotel business through its property development arm, City Developments Ltd (CDL). Until a major corporate reorganization in January 1999, its CDL Hotels International Ltd, majority-controlled by City Developments Ltd and listed on the Hong Kong Stock Exchange (renamed City e-Solutions Ltd in 2000), managed the group's hotel interest. From the late 1980s CDL Hotels International had grown tremendously from owning only five hotels in 1989 to 117 in 2000. In June 1999 CDL Hotels International Ltd sold all its 43 hotels in Asia and Australasia to its 52.4 per cent owned subsidiary listed on the London Stock Exchange, Millennium & Copthorne (M&C) Hotels plc, for £556 million (CDL Hotels International Ltd,

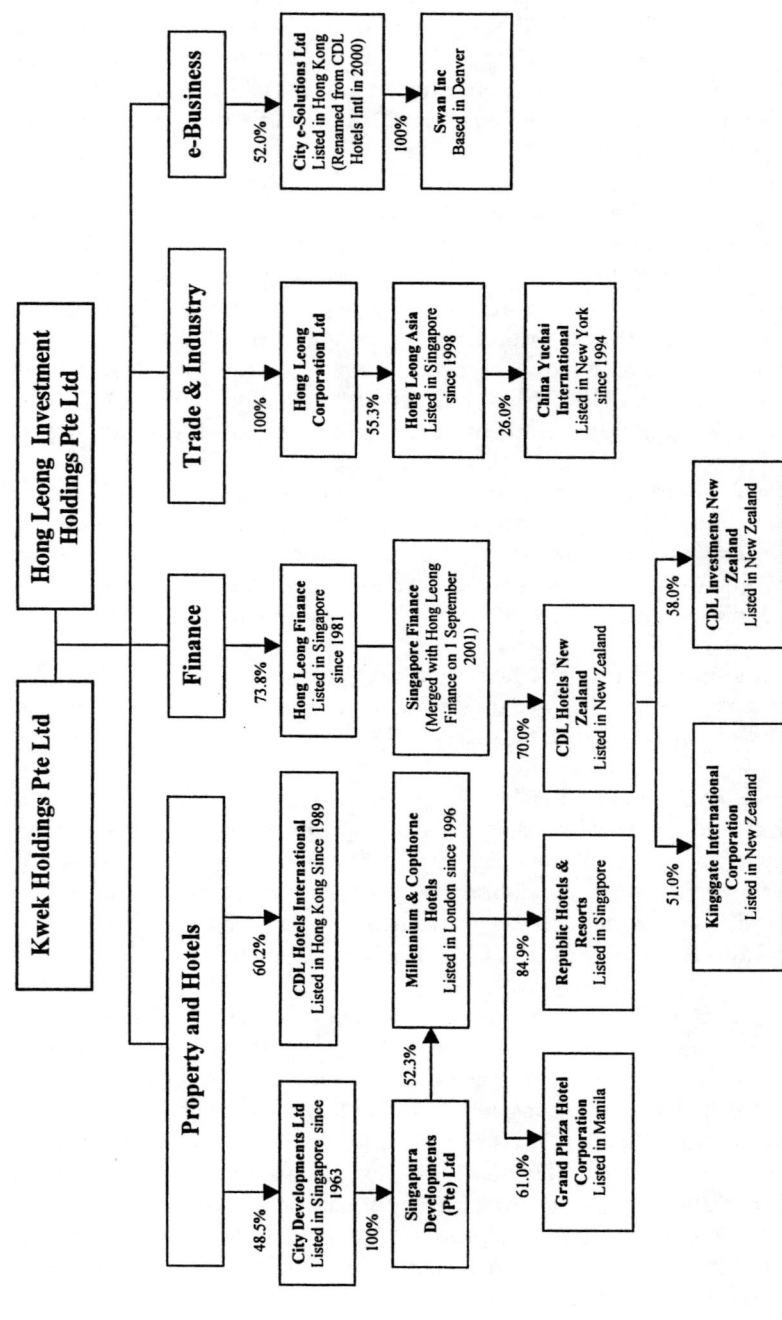

Figure 5.5 Kwek Leng Beng and the Hong Leong Group of companies, 2001.

Sources: Various Annual Reports of the Hong Leong Group of companies.

2000: 8). On 14 August 2000 it also sold its entire shareholding in M&C Hotels plc to its parent company, CDL, and changed its name to City e-Solutions Ltd to focus on providing e-solutions to the hotel industry (http://www.millenniumhotels.com, accessed on 21 March 2003). According to its 1999 annual report, the main rationale for the restructuring was to 'consolidate all our hotel businesses under one internationally recognized hotel group to meet the challenges of an increasingly concentrated competitive environment' (CDL Hotels International Ltd, 2000: 8). Unlike Li Ka-shing's reorganization of his Cheung Kong Group to consolidate family ownership and control (see pages 163–8), this major restructuring of Kwek Leng Beng's hotel operations was initiated in order to enhance product branding (Millennium) and operational efficiency to compete with other major global hotel chains. After completing the restructuring exercise, M&C Hotels plc operated 91 hotels in 17 countries around the world and was ranked as the 34th-largest hotel group in the world by the end of 2002. Its 2002 annual turnover was £567.5 million and its after-tax profit was £38 million (M&C Hotels plc, 2003: 13). Its fixed assets stood at £2.3 billion at the end of 2002.

In many ways, Kwek's success in acquiring hotels on a global scale rests not only with his excellent business acumen and transnational entrepreneurship (see Yeung, 2002a: 159–68), but also more importantly with the sheer financial muscle of the Hong Leong Group, a tangible outcome of Kwek's relentless efforts to enrol in actor-networks in global finance. Kwek's London-listed subsidiary, Millennium & Copthorne (M&C) Hotels plc, was the group's star performer in 1998. M&C Hotels plc was listed on the London Stock Exchange on 25 April 1996, slightly more than a year before the Asian economic crisis. The listing attracted some £1.2 billion investor funds worldwide. Kwek commented a day before the listing that '[w]e are very happy with the timing. It could not have been more perfect from the beginning up to the flotation' (quoted in the *The Straits Times*, 24 April 1996). Indeed, this comment could not have been more appropriate in the context of the crisis. The listing of M&C Hotels plc not only generated net proceeds of £174.5 million to relieve both M&C Hotels plc and its parent company CDL Hotels International Ltd from debt obligations, but also significantly raised the investment profile of Kwek in major global capital markets. This latter point proved to be important when Kwek needed to tap into capital markets during the Asian economic crisis in 1997 and 1998. In brief, what was initially an egg-spreading diversification strategy turned out to be the key ingredient shielding the group from the severe impact of the Asian economic crisis (see pages 234–6). Reflecting on his successful pre-crisis acquisition strategy, Kwek commented that '[w]e have earned the distinction of being the first to export a British hotel brand [Copthorne chain] to countries outside Europe. I think it is also safe to say that this export is being done for the first time by a Singapore company' (press release by the Hong Leong Group, 24 November 1998).

Kwek's strategies of tapping into global capital markets had two critical components. First, he could transfer his goodwill, extensively developed in the 'home' economy of Singapore, that enabled him to list many of his hotel businesses in stock exchanges in Hong Kong, London and New Zealand (see Figure 5.5). His successful placement of M&C Hotels plc on the London Stock Exchange not only brought him immediate financial gains, but also energized the London capital market for hotel investments (*The Straits Times*, 24 April 1996). In 1997 Prudential Client (MSS) Nominees Ltd became a substantial minority shareholder of M&C Hotels plc (1998: 23). As at 1 March 2002, Prudential plc remained a substantial shareholder (5.9 per cent), after City Developments Ltd (M&C Hotels plc, 2002: 21). Kwek's CDL Hotels International Ltd, listed on the Hong Kong Stock Exchange since 1989, also received very good financing support from major banks in Hong Kong (author's interview with a key Kwek family member in Hong Kong, 11 June 1998). As early as March 1993, CDL successfully raised S$305 million through a bond issue (Brown, 2000: 184).

Second, Kwek hedged his long-term borrowings and diversified his bankers through his enrolment in actor-networks in global finance. In 1994 CDL had debts of S$2.4 billion, of which only S$359 million was short-term debt (Brown, 2000: 184). In the case of CDL Hotels International Ltd, hedging of funds was always used as an important instrument to minimize foreign-exchange exposure (author's interview with a key Kwek family member in Hong Kong, 11 June 1998). Its Annual Report in 1997 stated that:

> Care is exercised to ensure that borrowing facilities do not carry onerous or restrictive covenants, and that the terms of the facilities fulfil the underlying requirements. The Group's long-term debt consists of bank debts denominated in various currencies. As part of the hedging policy of the Group, the foreign net currency investments were hedged by borrowing funds in the currencies of the countries where the Group operates.
>
> (CDL Hotels International Ltd, 1998: 19)

A breakdown of CDL Hotels International Ltd's long-term borrowings as at 31 December 1997 shows that its HK$5.9 billion borrowings were denominated in the domestic currencies of the US, the UK, New Zealand, Malaysia, Singapore and Taiwan. Some 60 per cent of these borrowings were denominated in sterling alone, indicating the importance of London-based financial institutions and actor-networks in supporting the globalization of Kwek's business activities in general and his CDL Hotels International Ltd in particular. After selling all its hotels to M&C Hotels plc in June 1999, CDL Hotels International Ltd enjoyed a cash balance of HK$2.9 billion as at 31 December 1999. Its long-term borrowings reached

HK$8.9 billion denominated in nine currencies: 47.2 per cent in US dollars and 23.6 per cent in sterling (CDL Hotels International Ltd, 2000: 20). Some 87 per cent of these borrowings was on floating-rate terms. After completing the entire restructuring exercise in August 2000, M&C Hotels plc became the main vehicle to manage Kwek's worldwide hotel operations. As at 31 December 2001, its total debts amounted to £774.4 million (a 6.5 per cent reduction from £828 million in 2000), denominated in nine currencies: 48.3 per cent in US dollars, 18.2 per cent in sterling and 13.8 per cent in Singapore dollars (M&C Hotels plc, 2002: 45). Some 60.6 per cent of these debts was on floating-rate terms.

In addition to hedging its long-term borrowings through global capital markets, Kwek has enjoyed a highly diversified portfolio of principal banks for both his CDL Hotels International Ltd and M&C Hotels plc. This not only illustrates their strong financial support for Kwek's ambition to globalize his hotel business, but also reduces his risk of a liquidity squeeze in times of economic crisis. For example, CDL Hotels International Ltd's principal banks are from the UK, France, Japan, Hong Kong, Switzerland, Australia and New Zealand. Its former subsidiary, M&C Hotels Plc, has also gained strong support from four major British banks: National Westminster Bank, Midland Bank, ING Barings, HSBC and Lloyds Bank. As at 1 March 2002, its three principal banks were Royal Bank of Scotland plc, HSBC and ING Barings (M&C Hotels plc, 2002: 21). With diversified sources of capital, it is not surprising that both CDL Hotels International Ltd and M&C Hotels plc were able to weather major financial constraints in the Asian economic crisis. The case demonstrates that globalizing in different capital markets can be a key proactive strategy for the long-term expansion of ethnic Chinese transnational entrepreneurs across borders. In turn, these processes of enrolment in globalizing actor-networks have contributed to the transformations of the dominant form and organization of Chinese capitalism.

In the middle of the 1997–8 Asian economic crisis, Kwek's transnational entrepreneurship and globalization strategy paid off very well. All three major listed arms of his Hong Leong Group achieved significant net profits in 1998, a year in which most listed companies in Singapore suffered large losses (see Table 5.4). CDL, which controlled CDL Hotels International Ltd, was ranked the seventh-most profitable listed company in Singapore in 1998, with a net profit of S$123.7 million. Hong Leong Finance, Singapore Finance and Hong Leong Asia pocketed a net profit of S$53.2 million, S$32.8 million and S$17 million respectively. The performance of CDL was way ahead of other listed property developers in Singapore. As shown in Table 5.4, of the top five loss-making listed companies in 1998, four belonged to property developers (Keppel Land, DBS Land, Orchard Parade Holdings and MCL Land). Four other property developers in Singapore also suffered losses in 1998 (Tuan Sing, United Overseas Land, Wing Tai and First Capital). This observation contradicts

Table 5.4 Performance of selected publicly listed companies in Singapore, 1997 and 1998

Ranking	Company	Net profit/(loss) (S$ million)		Turnover (S$ million)	
		1997	1998	1997	1998
Profitable					
1	OCBC Bank	581.1	425.3	4,079.1	4,747.1
2	UOB Bank	502.0	367.8	3,331.2	3,561.5
3	DBS Bank	436.4	222.7	3,689.0	5,407.3
4	OUB Bank	254.8	180.4	2,723.6	2,944.0
5	ST Engineering	120.8	154.7	1,476.7	1,661.7
6	Asia Food & Properties	45.2	140.9	1,432.8	954.9
7	**City Developments**	**409.2**	**123.7**	**2,470.4**	**2,043.3**
15	**Hong Leong Finance**	**72.9**	**53.2**	**374.9**	**422.8**
22	**Singapore Finance**	**34.8**	**32.8**	**135.9**	**153.1**
37	**Hong Leong Asia**	**(34.8)**	**17.0**	**616.0**	**456.3**
Loss-Making					
1	NOL	(297.3)	(438.2)	2,672.5	6,485.3
2	Keppel Land	104.6	(350.6)	621.2	317.9
3	DBS Land	182.3	(239.0)	1,083.2	1,419.8
4	Orchard Parade Holdings	21.6	(196.2)	491.2	193.9
5	MCL Land	19.5	(188.5)	297.0	297.0
9	Tuan Sing	31.6	(83.9)	646.3	575.9
43	United Overseas Land	52.6	(4.1)	357.6	425.5
–	Wing Tai[1]	46.0	(99.8)	–	–
–	First Capital[1]	6.3	(17.8)	–	–

Sources: *The Straits Times* (24 March 1999: 58; 2 April 1999: 86).

Note
1 Data refer to six months ended December 1997 and 1998.

Brown's (2000: 186) pessimistic assessment of the excessive dependence on capital markets and offshore banks of Kwek Leng Beng's CDL:

> The property collapse of 1997 was predictable in view of the dramatic development in the financing of property and the scale and pace of property development. The rapid increase in the exploitation of capital markets as well as offshore banks to finance this expansion added to the risks that were already high in property development. This is clear even from the case study of CDL, which was a property company operating largely in the highly regulated environment of Singapore.

Quite contrary to her observation, CDL and Kwek Leng Beng benefited precisely from his exploitation of global capital markets and offshore financing, that in turn shielded his corporate empire from significant losses.

One of the major contributing factors to the superior performance of

CDL was the net income from its global hotel operations, which exceeded those from its core property development business (see Table 5.5). In 1997 its hotel business in the UK and the US were the most profitable operations and contributed to some 71.8 per cent of profit before taxation of CDL Hotels International Ltd (1998: 75, 85). In 1998 and 1999, CDL Hotels International Ltd (2000: 49) reported respectively HK$1.2 billion and HK$1.3 billion profits before taxation. Once again, the combined profits from operations in the UK and the US accounted respectively for 74.4 per cent and 71.9 per cent of these profits. In 1998 CDL's hotel business turned in profit before taxation of S$171.7 million, not far behind the S$186.2 million from both property development and rental income from investment properties. In 2000 its hotel business again contributed S$288.4 million to its total pre-tax profit of S$578.4 (see Table 5.5). For the first time in the 37 years history of CDL, profits from the hotel exceeded those from property development (S$255.7 million) and rental incomes (S$26.7 million). Kwek Leng Beng pointed out that '[t]his reflects the success of our group's strategy of diversification into international hotels embarked in the early 1990s to ensure a wider spread of earnings' (quoted in the *The Straits Times*, 24 March 1999: 58). My interview with a key Kwek family member in Hong Kong (11 June 1998) indicates that the Hong Leong Group had been prepared for cyclical fluctuations in the property markets well before the Asian economic crisis. All foreign projects of the Hong Leong Group were run as a financially independent unit and hedging was extensively used to reduce foreign-exchange risks. He also said that Kwek Leng Beng had been emphasizing that 'the market is not going up every day. We must also be prepared for the worst'.

Table 5.5 Profits before taxation of Kwek Leng Beng's property development and hotel operations, 1997–2001

Name of listed company	1997	1998	1999	2000	2001
CDL (S$ million)	717.0	347.3	513.1	578.4	138.9
Hotels	179.8	171.7	168.1	288.4	78.2
Property development	503.6	154.7	267.8	255.7	59.7
Rental	49.9	31.5	60.9	26.7	22.4
CDL Hotels International Ltd (HK$ million)[1]	–	1,226.6	1,332.3	–	–
UK	–	517.3	538.0	–	–
US	–	304.8	304.8	–	–
Millennium & Copthorne Hotels plc (£)	48.0	58.4	83.5	129.1	54.2

Sources: Various annual reports.

Note
1 Data for 2000 and 2001 are unavailable because CDL Hotels International Ltd sold all its hotels to M&C Hotels plc in June 1999 and all its shares in M&C Hotels plc in August 2000. Data for 1997 are missing because of unavailability of its annual report.

Actor-networks and international organizations: dismantling 'crony capitalism'

Although the positive, albeit utilitarian, views of globalizing actor-networks shown above characterize the international business and finance sphere, more critical perspectives of Chinese capitalism as a form of crony capitalism also exist in actor-networks related to international organizations (see Chapter 2). These views, expressed via actor-networks running through multilateral institutions, conceive *guanxi* networks and more broadly Chinese capitalism as closed, opaque or outright corrupt, leading to irrational decision-making at various levels (see the Weberian view in Chapter 1). Multilateral institutions, such as the International Monetary Fund and the World Bank, may be able to reshape Chinese capitalism in a thorough yet diffuse manner by encouraging and/or requiring the restructuring of the institutions and power structures in Asia that large Chinese businesses (especially the conglomerates) engage with in reciprocal relations of interdependence. By enrolling other actors (the nation-state) and the necessary codes, procedural frameworks, regulations, material incentives and so on that are required to effect the activation of power, multilateral institutions transform the nature and operation of Chinese capitalism. This involvement of international organizations does not necessarily mean the replacement of Chinese capitalism by 'real' (i.e. Anglo-American) capitalism (Whitley, 1999: 188), but it does facilitate the gradual hybridization of Chinese capitalism, a kind of actor-driven transformation that does not conform to a pre-existing model or system of capitalism (see Chapter 1).

The 1997–8 Asian economic crisis (see also Chapter 7), for example, led to the reworking of state-business relations in Indonesia, leading some analysts to note that 'Indonesia's Chinese conglomerates . . . may soon be relegated to becoming bit players in the new economic landscape' (*Business Times*, 5 October 1998: 1). The severing of network ties between the state and key actors in Chinese capitalism occurred largely in the context of economic crisis, the IMF's stringent bailout and reform package and the linked demise of the Suharto regime. In effect, this externally driven agent significantly challenged the constituency of pre-existing structures of Chinese capitalism in Indonesia. After the former president, Suharto, announced on 15 January 1998 that Indonesia was committed to the IMF's conditionality and economic reforms in exchange for the US$43 billion bailout package, several key actors in Chinese capitalism were severely affected. Among these Chinese Indonesian actors, the case of Mohammad 'Bob' Hasan best illustrates the powerful working of global actor-networks in reshaping Chinese capitalism, because the Washington-based IMF effected change at a distance, leading to his loss of valuable monopoly rights in timber production and trade in Indonesia (Olds and Yeung, 1999: 26–30).

Born in Semarang, Indonesia, in 1931, 'Bob' Hasan is an ethnic Chinese Indonesian who changed his name from The Kian Seng. He was the adopted son of Gatot Subroto who was reported to have saved Suharto after he was dismissed by General Nasution for his involvement in smuggling in the late 1950s (Yoshihara, 1988: 226). Hasan made good use of his adoptive father's relations with Suharto and became a key Suharto ally and friend. This sort of approach to business is evident in some Southeast Asian countries, where actors representing large ethnic Chinese firms need to be strongly embedded in political-economic alliances to generate profits, while politicians benefit through the milking of franchise fees and other rents (McVey, 1992; Gomez, 1999; see literature review in Chapter 1). Before the onset of the Asian economic crisis in July 1997, Hasan controlled a vast empire of timber production and trade in Indonesia because of a profitable monopoly granted by Suharto himself. Sometimes known as 'the king of the forest' because of his many logging concessions, Hasan's personal fortune was estimated by *Forbes* to be worth US$3 billion in 1997, placing him as the 106th richest billionaire in the world (see Table 1.6). In the middle of the Asian crisis Hasan's timber business became a direct casualty when Suharto struck a formal agreement with the IMF managing director, Michel Camdessus, on a series of harsh reforms to be implemented by 1 February 1998. A key reform was the abolition of monopolies and cartels controlled by the former president's family and friends (*The Straits Times*, 19 January 1998: 46). According to a World Bank report in 1996, subsidiaries and other financial favours for firms in the lucrative forestry sector by the Suharto government caused US$750 million lost revenues annually for the state. Suharto was also supposed to chair personally a council to ensure the IMF programme's implementation with a senior adviser from the IMF attached to the reform body.

The IMF structural reform was significant in several aspects. First, it gave the global financial watchdog unprecedented access to policymaking in Indonesia. In a move to appease demands from the IMF for clean government, for example, Suharto instructed on 17 March 1998 all ministers, governors and high-ranking officials to report their private wealth, much of which was expected to have originated from political-economic alliances with the Chinese business community. Second, Hasan's loss of profitable timber monopoly concessions had obvious implications for his business empire, both directly through reduced streams of income and indirectly through reduced ability to borrow capital from international financial markets. For example, the South Korean and Japanese banks that lent Hasan money to finance one of his projects, a US$1.3 billion Kiani Kertas pulp mill project in east Borneo, were forced to reassess their relations with him (*The Straits Times*, 19 January 1998: 46). Third, whereas his firms suffered from the loss of timber concessions, Hasan enjoyed a short period of rising political fortune when he was appointed as the new trade and industry minister in March 1998 and became Indonesia's first ethnic Chinese minister (*The Straits Times*, 15 March 1998: 4). Though he subsequently lost his ministerial appointment under the post-Suharto governments (Suharto stepped down after the May 1998 riots), Hasan's brief stint in Suharto's last cabinet was significant because it was a high-profile attempt to breach the global reach of the IMF into the Indonesian political-economic apparatus, creating actor-networks in effect. The obvious irony of Hasan, as both the beneficiary of a timber cartel and the minister implementing IMF reforms, was not lost on the IMF nor the international business media (http://dte.gn.apc.org/38Has.htm, accessed on 29 March 2003). Hasan's economic fall is similar to that being experienced by many other leaders of Chinese conglomerates in Indonesia, which are suffering because of huge international debt loads, drastically reduced capitalization levels and strong associations with the now discredited Suharto family (*Business Times*, 5 October 1998: 1; see also the case of Peregrine in Chapter 7). In the context of economic crisis and uncertainty under the reworking of global capitalism, Chinese capitalism and its key actors, while being some of the most economically powerful in the region, simply cannot escape from the agendas and influences of globalizing actor-networks in international business and international politics that manage and shape the articulation of regional (i.e. Asia-Pacific) and global economic systems.

Reflections

In the context of the reworking of global capitalism and the reshaping of subglobal capitalism, my analytical framework sheds some light on the networks that bind different actors – Chinese and non-Chinese, family and non-family – together over time and space in uneven (albeit evolving) relations of interdependence (see Figure 1.2). This empirical chapter has demonstrated that key actors in Chinese capitalism are increasingly embedded in an array of globalizing actor-networks that have the capacity to shift flows of information and capital round the world on a rapid basis. These actor-networks (re)shape the dominant forms and norms in Chinese capitalism in such complex and multi-dimensional ways that a hybrid mixture emerges in the reshaped Chinese capitalism. This process (which could also be defined as describing and constituting) plays a significant, though difficult to determine, role in facilitating the international expansion of Chinese capitalism and its leading firms. This is because these ethnic Chinese actors are embedded in a capital-rich and increasingly fluid global financial system, a material context in which elite translators of knowledge on listed (public) firms shift flows of capital round the world's financial centres. Action at the global level subsequently shapes the capacity of listed ethnic Chinese (family) firms to operate on various geographical scales, sometimes global and often regional and local. It also affects the resources, particularly financial, available to the many unlisted firms that are connected to the controlling ethnic Chinese families. The changing structure and organization of Chinese capitalism today are therefore the product of many forces of change, the majority of which – both internal and external to Chinese capitalism – reflect the forces of globalization.

The case studies in this chapter serve as an analysis of these complex changes and transformations in the social organization of Chinese capitalism. Although the subjects may be powerful and influential elites in their domestic economies, I have not used these ethnic Chinese families to represent universally the diverse range of transformative possibilities opening up to ethnic Chinese in East and Southeast Asia. I have showcased how some significant changes are currently happening in certain sectors of Chinese capitalism, particularly those associated with globalizing actor-networks, that might bring about long-term transformations. These case studies are not meant to be conclusive and definitive because the snapshot stories themselves are incomplete. More broad-based evidence is needed to substantiate the theories in this chapter, in order to represent a general picture of Chinese capitalism as a form of hybrid capitalism.

6 Changing corporate governance and strategic management

Introduction

In this chapter the corporate governance, organizational structures and strategic management of leading Chinese firms will be examined in greater depth. This analysis is imperative because globalization and the rise of the so-called 'new economy' have raised serious questions about the continuing viability of traditional governance and practices in Chinese capitalism. As *The Economist* reported in a special issue on 29 April 2000, 'Asia's tycoons are coming under pressure to adopt a more "western" style of business. The change is gradual, but Asia's companies have started to shift away from their old patriarchal cultures and towards those prevailing in America or Britain' (http://www.economist.com, accessed on 3 May 2000). Although the validity of this observation is an empirical issue, the direction of change is by no means clear. Although there is no doubt that Chinese capitalism has been (re)shaped and transformed by globalization, the shift in its forms of corporate governance and management structures does not necessarily converge towards the dominant model of Anglo-American capitalism. Instead, such a shift opens up new possibilities for a strategic (re)combination of both old and new norms and practices, a process leading to the emergence of what may be termed hybrid capitalism (see Chapter 1).

Here the changing nature of corporate governance and management structures among Chinese family firms in both Singapore and Hong Kong is examined. Chinese family firms are the main analytical focus primarily because of their crucial role in defining Chinese capitalism (see Chapter 1). Recent studies of corporate finance have confirmed that family firms are not necessarily the antithesis of the continuing existence and viability of contemporary capitalism (La Porta *et al.*, 1999; Franks *et al.*, 2003), but it is useful to point out again that the family firm constitutes the very core of organizing Chinese capitalism (see Hamilton, 2000; Redding, 2000). As shown in Table 6.1, a large proportion of public companies in East and Southeast Asian economies remains in the hands of families, most of which are ethnic Chinese. These families also play key roles as both con-

Table 6.1 Mechanisms of family control of public companies in East and Southeast Asian economies, 1996

Country/Economy	Total no. of listed companies	No. of companies in sample (% of total)	% owned by families (20% cut-off)	Average % equity to control 20% vote	Pyramids with ultimate owners (%)	Cross-holdings (%)	Controlling owner alone (%)	Management (%)
Hong Kong	583	330 (56.6)	66.7	19.71	25.1	9.3	69.1	53.4
Taiwan	382	141 (36.9)	48.2	19.61	49.0	8.6	43.3	79.8
Indonesia	253	178 (70.4)	71.5	19.17	66.9	1.3	53.4	84.6
Malaysia	621	238 (38.3)	67.2	19.14	39.3	14.9	40.4	85.0
Philippines	216	120 (55.6)	44.6	18.71	40.2	7.1	35.8	42.3
Singapore	266[1]	221 (83.1)	55.4	20.00	55.0	15.7	37.6	69.9
Thailand	454	167 (36.8)	61.6	19.82	12.7	0.8	40.1	67.5

Source: Claessens *et al.* (2000: Tables 2–3).

Note
1 Main board listing only.

trolling shareholders and top management. Any credible argument for the hybridization of Chinese capitalism must include a detailed empirical analysis of the changing corporate governance and strategic management of these firms. This analysis, nevertheless, must go beyond simply offering a few case studies of highly visible Chinese family firms in East and Southeast Asia and assuming their universal representation of Chinese capitalism, a discursive strategy often found in the literature on Chinese capitalism (see Chapter 1). In this chapter three large sets of empirical data on Chinese family firms from Singapore and Hong Kong (see Appendix for methodology) are marshalled together to substantiate my ideas on Chinese capitalism. These originate from an analysis of the annual reports of 157 Chinese family firms listed on the Singapore Exchange (1996, 1998 and 2001) and two separate surveys of 73 ethnic Chinese TNCs from Hong Kong in 1994 (36 of them controlled by families) and another 204 ethnic Chinese TNCs from Singapore in 1998 (54 controlled by families). This analysis aims to provide some solid empirical evidence of the changing corporate governance and management practices in Chinese capitalism and to debunk some common myths in the existing literature on Chinese capitalism.

I have also chosen to analyse Chinese family firms in Hong Kong and Singapore because of their critical importance as representing Chinese capitalism. In many ways Hong Kong and Singapore are the twin capitals of Chinese capitalism (Wu and Duk, 1995; Wu, 1997; Meyer, 2000). Any analysis of the changing nature of Chinese capitalism must therefore address Chinese firms in both these economies. The leading firms are significant not only in terms of their economic prowess (see Tables 1.5 and 1.6). But more importantly, according to the claims of both culturalist and business system perspectives reviewed in Chapter 1, these firms are assumed to be so well embedded in such ideal or typical ethnic Chinese economies that their dominant forms of organizational structures and management practices are unlikely to change. Very few previous studies (Zang, 1999, 2000; Carney and Gedajlovic, 2002a), however, have examined systematically misleading claims championed by these perspectives. To unravel the central dynamics of Chinese capitalism in a global era, a detailed analysis of the changing nature of Chinese family firms in Hong Kong and Singapore is necessary. Despite their exhibition of the dominant norms and cultures of Chinese capitalism, both these economies are especially prone to globalization because of their well-developed articulation in the global economy (Chiu *et al.*, 1997; Yeung, 2002a). Thus Chinese family firms in Hong Kong and Singapore are looked at here both for their alleged representations of Chinese capitalism and, interestingly, for their greater propensities for change and transformations in relation to globalization.

Large and often publicly listed Chinese family firms in Hong Kong and Singapore are focused on for a variety of reasons (see also Chapters 1 and

2). These large firms are much more likely to be the movers and shapers that bring about dynamic changes to Chinese capitalism. In a global era, these firms are increasingly succumbing to the pressures of seeking external capital and finance in order to fund their enormous business growth and development (see case studies in Chapters 3–5). In this process of opening up what has always been closely knit Chinese capitalism and its business networks, such firms are more and more compelled to adopt international standards of corporate governance in their banking and accounting practices. This argument is particularly applicable to firms that are trying to access global finance through such capital markets as stock exchanges and international bond placements (see also Coffee, 2002). To a certain extent, of course, the reshaping of their corporate governance and management structures is also institutionalized in the formal requirements by those stock exchanges and their regulatory authorities. In view of these globalizing processes, it might be argued that publicly listed Chinese family firms are more likely to experience dynamic changes and transformations in their corporate governance and strategic management practices precisely because they are becoming more involved in the global economy than the larger numbers of small-scale Chinese family firms in the domestic economies. As key actors in Chinese capitalism, their changing governance and management behaviour are in turn symptomatic of the broader changes in Chinese capitalism itself.

In my examination of the corporate governance structures of 157 Chinese family firms listed on the Singapore Exchange, my main empirical concern is with their shareholding arrangements, principal banks and auditors. Through an analysis of data for 1996, 1998 and 2001, it is clear that despite the continual importance of family ownership, these firms are seeking global finance by diversifying their principal banks. Their corporate governance and market credibility also improve over time through using major international accounting firms as their auditors. There follows a discussion of key strategic management issues in ethnic Chinese TNCs from Hong Kong and Singapore. Analysing the ownership structures, control mechanisms and sources of technology and capital in their foreign operations, it is shown that there are no significant differences between family- and non-family-controlled TNCs from either Hong Kong or Singapore. These findings challenge the existing literature on Chinese capitalism in which family firms are assumed to be hierarchically structured, centripetal in control and authority systems and inwardly oriented in sourcing for expertise and capital (see Chapter 4).

Global convergence in corporate governance? Publicly listed Chinese family firms in Singapore

There is a major paradox in those glorified examples of the unprecedented success of Chinese capitalism in the literature (see Chapter 1). It is a widely circulated myth that Chinese family firms rely exclusively on kinship ties and network capital to finance their domestic and international operations. If the economic prowess of these Chinese families has become so significant and pervasive today, how is it that they managed to grow from small family businesses to giant TNCs in such a short period of time (often in one or two generations)? Even more paradoxical is the fact that most of this growth has taken place in developing economies in East and Southeast Asia that have weakly developed financial markets and banking systems. To unlock this mystery, we must identify not only the sources of their first 'pots of gold', so to speak, that enabled their early establishment and proliferation in domestic economies. But also, more importantly, we must explain the fundamental basis of their successful transformations from small-scale family businesses to transnational corporate giants. In this quest, we need to link the growth and development of Chinese family firms to financial markets, domestic and international. This linking is necessary because no matter how cooperative the family network is, there is a limit to the extent in which the network can provide capital and finance at the huge scale required for dominating the domestic and regional economies.

Here two key propositions in relation to the changing corporate governance of Chinese family firms are examined. First, these large firms are increasingly engaging with financial markets on a global scale. In order to finance their transnational business activities, these firms require financial services from banks beyond their domestic economies, resulting in a growing number and geographical spread of their principal banks. While these firms are diversifying their principal banks beyond a narrow confinement to other Chinese family-owned banks and financial institutions, their corporate performance will improve over time. This argument is particularly relevant for the 1997–8 Asian economic crisis, because the collapse of several leading Chinese family firms was explained by their excessive reliance on so-called network capital or – as Krugman (1998) argued – crony capitalism (see also Chapter 7). Second, these firms need greater credibility and legitimacy since they are enrolling in actor-networks in global finance. Although many of them continue to be family owned and controlled, these firms seek consciously to improve their corporate governance through engaging major international accounting firms to audit their accounts. This potential improvement in corporate governance is particularly significant in developing economies in which many Chinese family firms thrive and shareholder protection and judicial efficiency are deemed inadequate. Klapper and Love (2002), for example, found that good corporate governance matters a lot more in countries with weak shareholder protection and poor judicial efficiency. The quest for credibility – perceived or real – through the adoption of international accounting standards would certainly be unthinkable among small-scale Chinese family firms that are domestically oriented and reliant primarily on network capital. The use of international accounting standards in improving the corporate governance process of these firms represents a significant change that in turn disturbs the unruly and opaque nature of Chinese capitalism.

Industrial specialization, shareholding arrangements and family control

The data for this section originate from a study of 157 Chinese family firms listed on the Singapore Exchange (formerly the Stock Exchange of Singapore) in 1996 (see Appendix; Yeung and Soh, 2000). The industrial activities of these firms were grouped according to guidelines provided by the *Singapore Standard Industrial Classification, 1990* (Department of Statistics, 1991b). This exercise produced 13 business categories shown in Table 6.2. Manufacturing accounted for more than one-third of them. Four interrelated sectors (property, investment holding, hotel and construction) also constituted an important cluster of sectors in which these firms operated. These four sectors contributed another third of all 157 firms in my sample. If we compare the sectoral distribution in Table 6.2 with earlier studies of the main business concentration of ethnic Chinese in Asia (e.g. East Asia Analytical Unit, 1995), a number of interesting observations emerge. First of all, most Chinese family firms tend to engage in the property, hotel, investment holding and construction sectors because they are seen as long-term cash cow industries (Yoshihara, 1988; Redding, 1990, 1995; Lim, 2000). The importance of these sectors in Singapore is further reinforced by the significant presence of Chinese family firms in some sectors reported in *Singapore 1000*, an annual publication

Table 6.2 Industrial sector of Chinese family firms listed on the Singapore Stock Exchange, 1996

Business sector	No.	%	Cumulative %	Ranking
Manufacturing	58	36.9	36.9	1
Property	17	10.8	47.7	2
Investment-holding	15	9.6	57.3	3
Hotel	13	8.3	65.6	4
Construction	9	5.7	71.3	5
Shipping	9	5.7	77.0	6
Finance	8	5.1	82.1	7
Retailing	8	5.1	87.2	8
Retail trade	8	5.1	92.3	9
Banking	5	3.2	95.5	10
Securities investment	4	2.5	98.0	11
Insurance	2	1.4	99.4	12
Transport	1	0.6	100.0	13
Total	157	100.0	–	–

Source: Author's compilation from annual reports of companies.

that ranks the top 1,000 companies in Singapore in terms of their sales performance, total assets and shareholder's funds (Datapool, 1999a). In the hotel sector in the 1999 edition of *Singapore 1000*, Chinese family firms made up three of the top five ranked companies and 46.7 per cent of all companies in the sector. In real estate, Chinese family firms constituted five of the top ten companies and 37 per cent of all companies in the sector.

Second, in the East Asia Analytical Unit's (1995) sample, manufacturing was estimated to account for about one-third of the core companies. This percentage is relatively similar to the case of Singapore. Third, a difference in the importance of the banking sector is notable. Banking had a low representation at 3.2 per cent in the Singapore data, but it was placed second (6.5 per cent) in the East Asia Analytical Unit study. This difference does not, however, negate the importance of listed Chinese family banks in Singapore. Indeed, they made up more than half (55.6 per cent) of all establishments in the banking sector in *Singapore 1000* (Datapool, 1999a). The Overseas-Chinese Banking Corporation (OCBC), United Overseas Bank (UOB) and Overseas United Bank (OUB; acquired by UOB in October 2001) constitute three of Singapore's big four banks (the other being the government-owned Development Bank of Singapore, DBS), with each tracing its origins to financing trade among the Chinese community in Singapore and the rest of the world (Sender, 1991).

Table 6.3 presents the distribution of family shareholdings among these 157 Chinese family firms in 1996, 1998 and 2001. In 1996, about 51.3 per cent (n = 77) of them had a majority shareholding above the 50 per cent threshold. If we take a 20 per cent shareholding as the yardstick

Table 6.3 Distribution of family shareholdings among Chinese family firms listed on the Singapore Stock Exchange, 1996, 1998 and 2001

Family shareholdings (%)	No. (%)			% change between 1996 and 2001
	1996	*1998*	*2001*	
1–10	0 (0.0)	3 (2.1)	6 (4.4)	4.4
11–20	10 (6.7)	14 (9.7)	15 (11.0)	4.3
21–30	23 (15.3)	24 (16.7)	20 (14.7)	−0.6
31–40	13 (8.7)	14 (9.7)	11 (8.1)	−0.6
41–50	27 (18.0)	19 (13.2)	15 (11.0)	−7.0
51–60	30 (20.0)	28 (19.4)	29 (21.3)	1.3
61–70	23 (15.3)	21 (14.6)	18 (13.2)	−2.1
71–80	16 (10.7)	13 (9.0)	10 (7.4)	−3.3
81–90	7 (4.7)	6 (4.2)	11 (8.1)	3.4
91–100	1 (0.6)	2 (1.4)	1 (0.7)	0.1
Total	150 (100)	144 (100)	136 (100)	–
NA	7	13	21	–

Source: Author's compilation from annual reports of companies.

for family control (La Porta *et al.*, 1999; Zang, 1999, 2000), then an over-whelming majority of Chinese families (n = 140; 93 per cent) had a sub-stantial stake in these publicly listed firms. Interestingly, this pattern of family shareholding had not changed very much by 2001. Some 50.7 per cent (n = 69) of them had a majority stake controlled by various families, although only 84.5 per cent (n = 115) had a substantial stake of over 20 per cent shareholding in these firms. This reduction occurred mainly in the 41–50 per cent category (7 per cent decrease from 18 per cent in 1996 to 11 per cent in 2001), indicating that corporate restructuring and manoeuvres during the 1997–8 Asian economic crisis had taken their toll on some publicly listed firms in which Chinese families did not hold a majority stake. Overall, data in Table 6.3 point to the relative stability in the shareholding structures of Chinese family firms in Singapore during the 1996–2001 period. Apart from direct shareholding, the appointment of family members in such key positions as chairmen, chief executive offi-cers and managing directors represents another important way through which control of the publicly listed firm is maintained in the family (compare family firms in the UK; see Franks *et al.*, 2003). More than 90 per cent of the listed Chinese family firms had family members holding key executive positions and/or sitting on the boards of directors. The remaining 8.3 per cent employed professionals to manage their family firms, in which, however, the controlling family normally had a majority shareholding. This ownership and management pattern ensures that the authority and importance of the family in the firm is not compromised. For example, about half of this 8.3 per cent of all Chinese family firms had shareholdings in the range of 54.7–83.3 per cent.

Substantial shareholdings and appointment of family members to key executive positions are thus two major mechanisms through which an ethnic Chinese family can assume ownership and control over publicly listed firms in Singapore. This general finding indicates continuity in one key dimension of Chinese capitalism: the important role of the Chinese family firm in a global era. The two variables (substantial shareholdings and holding key executive positions) are, more often than not, inter-related. Of the 157 firms, 84.7 per cent had family members holding key executive positions as chairmen, chief executive officers and managing directors. The leading families also held majority stakes (i.e. more than 50 per cent) in 49.7 per cent (n = 78) of all 157 listed Chinese family firms. Some 67 of them (42.7 per cent) therefore embraced both ownership and control mechanisms in their corporate governance (Shleifer and Vishny, 1997). The remaining group of firms at the other end of the spectrum, i.e. firms with minority shareholdings (no controlling stakes) and firms with no family members holding key executive positions (but sitting on boards of directors), constituted only a small presence of 6.4 per cent of all 157 firms. Generally, these 157 firms can be categorized into three main groups: having strong family control, moderate family control and weak family control. The first group consists of firms in which the family has a majority shareholding and holds key executive positions. The second group comprises firms in which the family has either a majority shareholding without family members holding key executive positions, or a minority shareholding with family members holding key executive positions in the firm. In the third group, the firm has family members holding neither key executive positions nor substantial shareholdings.

In contrast to earlier studies that found strong family control among listed Chinese family firms in Singapore during the early 1990s (Zang, 1999, 2000), my study has identified the category with moderate family control as the dominant group (n = 77; 49.0 per cent). With the strong family control category (42.7 per cent), they made up just over 92 per cent of all 157 listed Chinese family firms. Interestingly, an overwhelming majority (86 per cent) of the 77 firms in the moderate family control group had minority shareholdings belonging to family members who held key executive positions. This pattern indicates that as these firms gain access to global finance via listing on stock markets, they are more willing to accept a dilution of family shareholdings with public offerings. This finding broadly conforms to the evolution of family ownership and control among listed companies in the UK (Franks *et al.*, 2003). Next will be discussed the reality of listed Chinese family firms in Singapore being linked to the globalizing world economy through actor-networks such as international principal banks and accounting firms. Reconstituted through these globalizing actor-networks, Chinese capitalism is no longer as closed or inwardly oriented as it used to be. It is in fact situated and (re)shaped in a global web of actor-networks that is constantly evolving and changing in such ways that a mode of hybrid capitalism is being produced.

Principal banks and corporate governance

Principal banks are often indicated in the corporate data section of annual reports. By examining their global geography and country of origin, we can infer much in terms of a Chinese family firm's core activities, corporate governance and global spread. This is because if a firm's operations are globalizing, it needs to employ principal banks beyond its home country. In particular, the pattern of principal banks used by the 157 listed Chinese family firms reveals some interesting insights into the changing nature of Chinese capitalism. In Table 6.4, the majority of these firms had between one and five principal banks. In absolute numbers, the DBS, a government-linked bank, topped the list with 56 citations by the 157 firms. Three other big four Singapore banks, the OCBC, UOB and OUB, were respectively in the second, third and fourth positions. Since Singapore is the ultimate origin of more than 90 per cent of these 157 firms, this finding is hardly surprising because these firms were more

Table 6.4 Chinese family firms listed on the Singapore Stock Exchange and their principal banks, 1996, 1998 and 2001

No. of principal banks	No. (%)			% change between 1996 and 2001
	1996	1998	2001	
1–5	84 (75.7)	77 (78.6)	72 (82.8)	7.1
6–10	19 (17.1)	16 (16.3)	12 (13.8)	−3.3
11–15	6 (5.4)	3 (3.1)	2 (2.3)	−3.1
16–20	1 (0.9)	1 (1.1)	0 (0.0)	−0.9
21–25	0 (0.0)	0 (0.0)	0 (0.0)	0.0
26–30	1 (0.9)	1 (1.1)	1 (1.1)	0.2
Subtotal	111 (100)	98 (100)	87 (100)	−15.3
No. indicated principal banks	46 (29.3)	59 (37.6)	70 (44.6)	15.3
Total	157 (100)	157 (100)	157 (100)	–

Source: Author's compilation from annual reports of companies.

likely to use Singapore banks when doing business in Singapore and abroad. Moreover, all big four Singapore banks had extensive presences in the Asia-Pacific region. During 1996 and 2001, however, there was a significant decrease in the number of principal banks used by Chinese family firms (see Table 6.4). In 1996, about 75.7 per cent (n = 84) of Chinese family firms had between one and five principal banks. But this figure increased to 82.8 per cent (n = 72) in 2001. During the same period, the proportion of these firms having six or more principal banks decreased. This reduction reflects the slowdown in corporate expansion among these firms in the post-crisis era, the mergers and acquisitions in the domestic banking sector (Keppel-Tat Lee Bank in 1998 and its acquisition by OCBC in 2001 and UOB-OUB in 2001; see Chapter 7) and the reserved attitude of non-Singapore banks towards the short-term growth of these family firms.

Reconsidering the culturalist perspective on Chinese capitalism (Chapter 1), it follows that Chinese family firms should be more inclined to use network capital to finance their domestic and international operations. Among SMEs, this network capital often comes from pooling together investments and savings among family members and an inner circle of close friends. In the largest Chinese family firms, so the culturalist literature proposed, the founders and/or family patriarchs often attempt to use their personal relationships with other Chinese bankers to secure access to capital and finance (see case studies in Chapter 5). In Singapore's banking sector before 1998, only two domestic banks were government-linked (DBS and Keppel Bank).[1] According to my interviews with ethnic Chinese entrepreneurs in Singapore (Yeung, 2002a), these government-linked banks were notoriously reluctant to extend loans and equity financing to Chinese family firms. In fact, a local entrepreneur wrote to

Singapore's most read newspaper and openly complained that 'all of them [banks in Singapore] were only interested in property business and trading – all heavily secured transactions. They had no desire to support a technical enterprise. The local banks also have limited experience in small- and medium-sized enterprise (SME) operations and venture funding' (*The Straits Times*, 7 July 1999). All other domestic banks and finance houses in Singapore before 1998 were owned and controlled by leading Chinese families: Hong Leong Finance (the Kwek family; see Chapter 5), Industrial and Commercial Bank (the Wee family), OCBC (the Lee and the Tan family), OUB (the Lien family), Singapore Finance (the Kwek family), Tat Lee Bank (the Goh family) and UOB (the Wee family).

Given this predominance of Chinese family-owned banks and finance houses in Singapore's banking sector, we would expect more Chinese family firms listed on the Singapore Exchange to use them as their principal banks, particularly those firms with higher shareholdings owned by Chinese families. This is because majority-owned family firms are more likely to develop strong personal relationships with ethnic Chinese banks. The culturalist perspective would like us to believe in the positive relationship between family shareholding of family firms and their use of ethnic Chinese banks. Table 6.5 presents results from a simple correlation analysis of the relationship between percentages of family shareholding and the number of Singapore banks as principal banks. The assumption is that greater family shareholding should correspond with more use of

Table 6.5 Correlation between percentages of family shareholding and the number of Singapore banks as principal banks of Chinese family firms listed on the Singapore Stock Exchange, 1996, 1998 and 2001

Independent variables		*No. of Singapore banks as principal banks*		
		1996	*1998*	*2001*
Family share percentage, 1996	Pearson correlation	-0.270[1]	-0.306[1]	-0.146
	sig. (2-tailed)	0.005	0.003	0.190
	n	107	92	82
Family share percentage, 1998	Pearson correlation	–	-0.352[1]	-0.181
	sig. (2-tailed)	–	0.001	0.102
	n	–	93	83
Family share percentage, 2001	Pearson correlation	–	–	-0.220[2]
	sig. (2-tailed)	–	–	0.042
	n	–	–	86

Source: Author's compilation from annual reports of companies.

Notes
1 Correlation is significant at the 0.01 level (2-tailed).
2 Correlation is significant at the 0.05 level (2-tailed).

Singapore banks (as a proxy for ethnic Chinese banks). Ironically, the correlation analysis does not support the culturalist perspective on the alleged positive relationship between family shareholding and the use of ethnic Chinese banks as principal banks. Indeed, there are consistently negative relationships for the three years 1996, 1998 and 2001 (statistically significant in four out of six cases). This finding indicates that the higher the family share of a listed Chinese family firm, the less is its number of Singapore (ethnic Chinese) banks as principal banks. It firmly refutes the culturalist interpretation of network capital as the dominant source of financing Chinese capitalism (Yeung, 2003a).

So what sort of banks did these Chinese family firms use as their principal banks? Tables 6.6 and 6.7 summarize the geographical origins of principal banks of Chinese family firms by country and by region. Two observations may be made. First, the majority of principal banks are from outside Singapore. In 1996 only 14 out of 76 principal banks (18.5 per cent) were from Singapore (Table 6.6) and this figure decreased by 50 per cent to only seven Singapore banks in 2001, an outcome of the mega-mergers and acquisitions during the 1998–2001 period. In Table 6.7, however, this small number of Singapore banks accounted for a disproportionately higher number of citations as the principal banks of Chinese family firms. In 1996 the 14 Singapore banks made up 45.1 per cent (n = 222) of total citations (n = 492) by the 111 Chinese family firms that

Table 6.6 Country of origin of principal banks of Chinese family firms listed on the Singapore Stock Exchange, 1996, 1998 and 2001

Origin of principal banks	No. (%)			Change between 1996 and 2001 (%)
	1996	1998	2001	
Canada and US	11 (14.5)	11 (15.3)	5 (8.3)	–54.5
Australia and New Zealand	3 (3.9)	3 (4.2)	4 (6.7)	33.3
France	3 (3.9)	5 (6.9)	5 (8.3)	66.7
Germany	7 (9.2)	7 (9.7)	6 (10.0)	–14.3
Luxembourg and Switzerland	4 (5.3)	4 (5.6)	2 (3.3)	–50.0
Netherlands	4 (5.3)	3 (4.2)	4 (6.7)	0.0
UK	5 (6.6)	5 (6.9)	5 (8.3)	0.0
China	3 (3.9)	4 (5.6)	4 (6.7)	33.3
Hong Kong SAR	4 (5.3)	4 (5.6)	4 (6.7)	0.0
Japan	7 (9.2)	4 (5.6)	4 (6.7)	–42.9
Malaysia	7 (9.2)	7 (9.7)	6 (10.0)	–14.3
Singapore	14 (18.5)	12 (16.7)	7 (11.7)	–50.0
Others	4 (5.4)	3 (4.2)	4 (6.7)	0.0
Total	76 (100)	72 (100)	60 (100)	–21.1

Source: Author's compilation from annual reports of companies.

Table 6.7 Regional origins of principal banks and their citations by Chinese family firms listed on the Singapore Stock Exchange, 1996, 1998 and 2001

Origin of principal banks	No. of citations (%)			Change between 1996 and 2001 (%)
	1996	1998	2001	
Southeast Asia	268 (54.5)	235 (55.0)	199 (55.7)	−25.7
Western Europe	140 (28.5)	123 (28.8)	99 (27.7)	−29.3
North America	45 (9.1)	40 (9.4)	30 (8.4)	−33.3
East Asia	34 (6.9)	24 (5.6)	23 (6.4)	−32.4
Australasia	5 (1.0)	4 (0.9)	5 (1.4)	0.0
Other regions	0 (0.0)	1 (0.2)	1 (0.3)	−
Total	492 (100)	427 (100)	357 (100)	−27.4
Singapore	222 (45.1)	199 (46.6)	162 (45.4)	−27.0
Outside Singapore	270 (54.9)	228 (53.4)	195 (54.6)	−27.8

Source: Author's compilation from annual reports of companies.

indicated principal banks in their annual reports. Following the decline in the number of Singapore banks available as principal banks in 2001, the citation of Singapore banks also decreased by 27 per cent to 162 in 2001, whereas its relative share of citations remained stable at 45.4 per cent. This shows that during the period 1996–2001 fewer Singapore banks were available as principal banks for listed Chinese family firms, though they continued to enjoy a relatively higher share of the citations than non-Singapore banks.

Second, the geographical scope of principal banks is highly diverse, ranging from the more obscure banks in South Africa (Amalgamated Banks of South Africa) and the Middle East (Arab Banking) to such globalized banks as Citibank (the US) and HSBC (the UK). What is particularly interesting in Table 6.6 is the fact that Chinese family firms have tapped into banks from North America and Western Europe as their principal banks. In 1996 11 banks from North America and 23 from Western Europe accounted for 43.4 per cent of the total pool of principal banks (n = 76). The two regions made up 37.6 per cent (n = 185) of total citations (see Table 6.7). These findings confirm my earlier argument that listed Chinese family firms were increasingly linked to actor-networks in global finance through their principal banks during the 1990s, an observation certainly not anticipated in the existing literature on Chinese capitalism (see Chapters 2 and 5). To establish a large number of subsidiaries in different regions of the global economy, these family firms need to tap into the vast international networks of global financial institutions to service their fund transfer, acquisition of foreign currencies and even the most basic business need of issuing cheques. Their linkages with other major banks around the world also induce these principal banks to establish branches in East and Southeast Asia. Before the 1997–8 Asian economic crisis, banks from North America and Western Europe were highly active in financing and servicing both the domestic and international operations of Chinese family firms from Singapore. Together with banks from East Asia, Australasia and other regions, non-Singapore banks contributed to almost 55 per cent of total citations as principal banks of Chinese family firms (Table 6.7). For example, HSBC, a London-headquartered bank, served as a principal bank for 36 listed Chinese family firms. Today, HSBC Holdings plc is one of the largest banking and financial services organizations in the world. Being one of the most accessible banks in terms of its global reach may explain its popularity among globalizing Chinese family firms. As compared with Citibank (more than 600 offices in 40 countries), HSBC's international network comprises more than 8,000 offices in 80 countries, operating under well-established names in the Asia-Pacific region, Europe, America, the Middle East and Africa (http://www.hsbc.com, accessed on 29 March 2003).

By 2001, however, there were some major changes to the geographical patterns of principal banks. The number of banks available as principal banks decreased by 21.1 per cent from 76 in 1996 to only 60 in 2001 (Table 6.6). The decline occurred primarily among banks from North America (from 11 in 1996 to five in 2001), Japan (from seven in 1996 to four in 2001) and Singapore (from 14 in 1996 to seven in 2001). To a certain extent, this decrease correlates with the 15.3 per cent decline in the number of Chinese family firms indicating their principal banks (Table 6.4). It also reflects the adverse impact of the Asian economic crisis on the Asian operations of American and Japanese banks, and the tendency among Chinese family firms to use fewer principal banks as they streamlined their operations and restructured their core business activities. In terms of citations in 2001 (Table 6.7), banks from all regions except Australasia experienced a dramatic reduction in their citations as principal banks of Chinese family firms, although their relative percentage shares remained unchanged. The decline ranged from 25.7 per cent for banks from Southeast Asia to 33.3 per cent for banks from North America. Banks from Singapore and outside Singapore experienced a similar decline in their citations (around 27 per cent). These figures are all well above the 15.3 per cent decrease in Chinese family firms that indicated principal banks in their annual reports, pointing to a general tendency among these firms to use fewer principal banks during the 1996–2001 period.

To understand the dynamic relationships between Chinese family firms and the global financial system through their principal banks, the role played by these banks in the shareholdings of Chinese family firms should be considered. More insights are offered on how the financial system (via overseas banks) is intermeshed with the increasingly globalizing actor-networks of Chinese family firms in Singapore. This analysis also provides more depth than the usual one-way relationship in which

Chinese family firms are linked to the international networks by the engagement of international banks. Among the 157 listed Chinese family firms in Singapore, banks are often found to be substantial shareholders. In 1996 banks accounted for the highest shareholding in about 21 per cent of the 157 firms (n = 33). Among these banks, the OCBC held substantial shareholdings in about 12 listed Chinese family firms, such as Focal Finance, Fraser & Neave Ltd, Great Eastern Life Assurance, Harimau Investments Ltd, Hotel Negera, United Engineers Ltd and WBL Corporation Ltd. This shows that banks can have great influence on Chinese family firms, a finding similar to the corporate governance and financing behaviour among German firms (Pauly and Reich, 1997; Shleifer and Vishny, 1997; Lane, 2000; Lazonick and O'Sullivan, 2000). German banks usually play a leading supervisory role on the management boards. They also effectively control voting rights through Germany's proxy voting system.

This bank-centred pattern of corporate governance, does not automatically lead to an implied direct correspondence between banks as substantial shareholders and their adoption as principal banks. Substantial shareholdings by banks in Chinese family firms do not necessarily determine their choice of principal banks. The percentage of double coincidence in my sample (i.e. a bank as both substantial shareholder and principal bank) is rather low. For example, among all listed Chinese family firms that used OCBC as a principal bank, only 8.5 per cent had OCBC as a substantial shareholder. I also found low percentages of double coincidence for DBS (8.8 per cent) and UOB (10.8 per cent). Such banks as Chase Manhattan, Standard Chartered and OUB had no coincidence at all between their shareholdings and their role as principal banks of listed Chinese family firms in Singapore. The HSBC case is again revealing here. Its huge interests in Asia may be manifested through its shareholdings in many listed Chinese family firms in Singapore. My data show that in 1996 HSBC was featured very prominently as one of the top ten shareholders of many listed Chinese family firms. In some 65 of all 157 firms (41.4 per cent) the HSBC was one of their top ten shareholders. Its shareholding percentages ranged from 0.27 per cent in Bonvests Holdings Ltd to 21.77 per cent in Hwa Hong Corporation Ltd. These shareholdings held by HSBC, however, did not guarantee its role as their principal bank. In fact, HSBC only served as a principal bank for about one-third of these 65 firms in which it had shareholdings. This lack of direct correspondence between banks as one of the top ten shareholders in Chinese family firms and their role as principal banks helped to avoid potential conflicts of interest and ensure proper corporate governance among Chinese family firms. Contrary to the literature on Chinese capitalism (see Chapter 1), there is a seemingly clear division between ownership and service (as a principal bank) by leading banks for listed Chinese family firms in Singapore.

Principal auditors and corporate governance

According to McKee and Garner (1996), economic expansion in a nation is to some extent dependent on the adequacy and sophistication of its accounting services. Standish (1990) has surveyed the historical evolution of accounting in advanced capitalist economies and its role as subservient to private interests shaped by the historical conditions of laissez-faire capitalism. In a highly globalized financial world in which corporate governance standards must be maintained for equity and transparency purposes, full and fair disclosure in financial reports is of utmost importance, particularly to Chinese family firms seeking to issue shares and stocks to attract both private and institutional investors from outside their 'home' economies. Adopting international accounting standards may also ensure the proper governance of these firms and thereby increase their likelihood of generating a higher return on investments. For example, Mitton (2002: 227) recently found that among 398 firms from the five crisis-struck countries (Indonesia, South Korea, Malaysia, the Philippines and Thailand), firms with big six auditors had, on average, an additional higher return of 8.1 per cent over the crisis period. Brown (2000: 60) offered a case study of how the appointment of the Dutch accounting firm, A.L. Vrijberg, as the chief accountant of PT Astra International in 1970 persuaded the controlling family, William Soeryadjaya and his children, to move closer to a multi-division structure. The new organizational structure consisted of the board of commissioners constituted of family members and the board of directors constituted of *pribumi* friends and professional managers. PT Astra International subsequently grew from one firm in 1957 to 125 firms in 1995. To Brown (2000: 60),

> [t]his separation of ownership from management and the creation of managerial hierarchies that co-existed within a more centralized decision-making structure, was unique for a Chinese family firm. The divisional system of management coincided with divisions in production, finance and marketing.[2]

Indeed, the growth of international accounting firms is directly related to the globalization of capital markets because 'as investors worldwide increasingly invest in foreign securities, more comprehensive financial statements will be required, resulting in an increased demand for the auditing and other services of international accounting firms' (Bavishi, 1991: 428). The globalization of accountancy standards also allows financial management from a distance (see Sassen, 1999; Clark *et al.*, 2001). Finance and accountancy services are arguably two of the most globalized sectors in the world. By situating my analysis of listed Chinese family firms in Singapore within global actor-networks of finance and accountancy (incorporating actors like banks and auditors), we can approximate better to at least one key dimension of corporate governance in Chinese capitalism, accountability and credibility. There are international linkages among the 157 listed Chinese family firms through their principal auditors. Table 6.8 offers observations on the corporate governance of Chinese family firms in Singapore. In the first place, the big six international accounting firms such as Ernst & Young, Coopers & Lybrand (merged with Price Waterhouse to become PricewaterhouseCoopers in 1998), Deloitte & Touche, KPMG Peat Marwick, Price Waterhouse and Arthur Andersen topped the list of principal auditors for these listed firms. In 1996 they constituted 89.2 per cent of all auditors employed by them. In 2001 their share increased slightly to 90.2 per cent. The 1998 merger between Coopers & Lybrand and Price Waterhouse enabled PricewaterhouseCoopers to become the leading auditor for these firms, accounting for 27.7 per cent of the share in 2001.

To a large extent, my findings correspond well with Bavishi's (1991) study of global accounting and auditing trends that shows the predominance of the big six (see also Clark *et al.*, 2001). The need for listed Chinese family firms to have transparency and reliability in the eyes of the public and the shareholders makes it necessary for them to employ internationally renowned and reputable accounting firms. This finding challenges the crony capitalism argument that assumes illicit and insider dealings. As Brown (2000: 16) noted in her study of leading Chinese firms in Southeast Asia,

> the most important feature was the constant revaluation of assets to exaggerate their value in order to raise offshore loans using overvalued assets as collateral. There was, therefore, a detectable logic in misrepresentation; but to brand all Chinese corporations as indulging in fake accounting is not only inaccurate but also sensationalist.

In fact, my finding supports the key argument in this book that in an era of global finance, Chinese family firms, particularly those seeking public listing in Asia, the US and the UK, are compelled to set higher standards of corporate governance in order to attract global capital and investment (see also Coffee, 2002). This trend for greater transparency and accountability underscores a fundamental shift in Chinese capitalism away from a closed and family-oriented mode of economic organization towards more diversified modes of governance and structures. Even when local accountancy firms were used, for example, 16 per cent of the Chinese family firms in my sample still preferred a joint auditing arrangement by naming one local firm and one big six firm as their auditors.

The employment of international accounting firms thus reinforces the international linkages listed Chinese family firms have with globalizing actor-networks. This interdependence is, however, built on uneven grounds of power relations. These firms are basically subjected to two

Table 6.8 Chinese family firms listed on the Singapore Stock Exchange and their auditors, 1996, 1998 and 2001

Auditor	1996			1998			2001		
	No.	%	Cumulative %	No.	%	Cumulative %	No.	%	Cumulative %
PricewaterhouseCoopers	–	–	–	–	–	–	39	27.7	27.7
Ernst & Young	33	21.0	21.0	32	21.5	21.5	30	21.3	49.0
Coopers & Lybrand	30	19.1	40.1	27	18.1	39.6	–	–	–
Deloitte & Touche	28	17.8	58.0	26	17.4	57.0	28	19.9	68.9
KPMG Peat Marwick	25	15.9	73.9	23	15.4	72.4	18	12.8	81.7
Price Waterhouse	16	10.2	84.1	16	10.7	83.1	–	–	–
Arthur Andersen	8	5.1	89.2	10	6.8	89.9	12	8.5	90.2
Foo, Kon & Tan	5	3.2	92.4	5	3.4	93.3	4	2.8	93.0
Ng, Lee & Associates	2	1.3	93.6	2	1.3	94.6	1	0.7	93.7
Soh, Wong & Partners	2	1.3	94.9	2	1.3	95.9	–	–	–
Others	8	5.1	100.0	6	4.1	100.0	9	6.3	100.0
Total	157	100.0	–	149	100.0	–	141	100.0	–

Source: Author's compilation from annual reports of companies.

levels of constraints and governance that influence the transformation of Chinese capitalism. The first level is in the international arena where the firms are linked to the international system of accounting and finance. They have to adopt a more compliant position because of the transparency involved in the process of external auditing by international accountancy firms. Gone are the days when financial information was the most closely guarded secret of the controlling families (see the literature reviewed in Chapter 1). Instead, it is now replaced by stricter adherence to international accounting rules and regulations, such as the standards set by the International Auditing Standards Committee. The second level of governance refers to the specific national accounting rules and regulations. Chinese family firms listed on the Singapore Exchange have to adhere to a mandatory semi-annual auditing practice specified by the Singapore Exchange. The Singapore government also plays a role as a regulator through its ruling in the Singapore Accountants Act of 1987 that all accountants must be publicly certified. Publicly listed Chinese family firms are truly linked up, locally and internationally.

Strategic management across borders: Chinese family firms from Hong Kong and Singapore

This section examines the strategic management and organization of Chinese family firms from Hong Kong and Singapore in their international context. Two research questions provide a guide to this section. What are the key organizational strategies of these firms when they go transnational? Do they necessarily conform to the conventional views of Chinese capitalism and its family firms, as reviewed in Chapter 1? One important dimension of these complex questions is the role of strategic control and coordination of the transnational operations of Chinese family firms (Yeung, 2000j). These are prime organizational issues in sustaining the competitive advantage of TNCs and their overseas operations because of the inherent difficulties in transferring competitive advantage from home countries to host economies. If appropriate strategic control and coordination are not exercised in the management of foreign affiliates, a TNC may eventually find its firm-specific advantages being eroded in an era of intensified global competition. Research in international business and strategic management has shown that as a consequence of transnational operations, national firms have the disadvantage of being 'foreigners' or 'outsiders' (Hymer, [1960] 1976; Hu, 1995; Zaheer, 1995; Matsuo, 2000). This competitive disadvantage arises from a lack of local knowledge of social, political and economic conditions in the host country. The ability to control and coordinate foreign subsidiaries and/or affiliates has become one of the core capabilities for TNCs to compete in foreign markets (Bartlett and Ghoshal, 1989; Hamel and Prahalad, 1994).

As reviewed in Chapter 1, previous research into Chinese capitalism has informed us that Chinese family firms are particularly prone to tighter control and centralized coordination under the fingertips of the patriarchs. These patriarchs exercise control and coordination over their foreign affiliates through several strategies. First, they can hold majority equity shares and establish wholly owned subsidiaries abroad. These organizational forms and ownership structures result from a process of internalizing foreign operations within the core family. Second, indirect control and coordination can be achieved through special connections and privileges enjoyed by the patriarchs and their associates during the processes of establishing foreign operations (see also Chapter 4). Third, the family-ization of transnational operations can be accomplished by sending family members from home countries as foreign expatriates to manage their overseas operations. Fourth, these patriarchs can control their foreign operations through frequent personal visits, keeping key marketing and sourcing activities and technology within parent family firms and controlling the finance of foreign affiliates. As a whole, this aspect of strategic management in Chinese capitalism, that is, highly centralized control and coordination, was seen in the literature as both a defining attribute of Chinese capitalism and a potential source of competitive advantage for its family firms when they operate internationally (Redding, 1990; Kotkin, 1992; Kao, 1993; Weidenbaum and Hughes, 1996; Haley *et al.*, 1998; M.-J. Chen, 2001).

Here I show that the nature of strategic control and coordination in the transnational operations of Chinese family firms is indeed changing. My empirical materials are grounded in two separate studies of ethnic Chinese TNCs from Hong Kong (n = 73) and Singapore (n = 204) (see Appendix). These two samples are divided into those TNCs that are family-controlled and non-family-controlled. The nature of strategic control and coordination between these two variants of Chinese firms is compared: those owned and managed by family members (defined as family-controlled), and those owned by diverse shareholders and managed by professional managers (defined as non-family-controlled). In the literature on Chinese capitalism, strategic control and coordination have been assumed to be much tighter among these firms because these are allegedly the foundational characteristics of Chinese capitalism. The autonomy of their overseas subsidiaries is a function of personal trust and particularized relationships between the patriarchs and their overseas managers. Lack of trust in the foreign subsidiaries managed by non-family members often results in tighter control and coordination by the headquarters. But strategic control and coordination may not be so tight in professionally managed firms because they may have adopted international management practices and decentralized their decision-making power. By virtue of their professionalism, the managers may be more open to sharing power and control; they may also be more willing to engage in strategic partnerships and other sorts of cooperative alliances with non-Chinese actors (see Chapter 5).

If my argument on the changing corporate governance of these firms in a global era is valid at all, we should expect some kind of convergence in strategic management between family- and non-family-controlled firms. Couched in such terms, my empirical proposition is that we should not find any significant differences in the strategic management behaviour of such firms in relation to their family ownership. In other words, if Chinese capitalism is indeed being hybridized when its key actors participate in globalizing actor-networks, the reality of these firms should not be as neatly dichotomized into family and non-family variants as suggested in the literature. Rather it may be quite messy in that family ownership (vis-à-vis other contextual factors) may not play a determining role in shaping the strategic management of these firms. If there were any difference in the strategic management of these firms from Hong Kong and Singapore, the key explanatory variable should likely be their different economies of origin (Yeung, 2002a). Such differences are more likely to account for major discrepancies in the strategic management behaviour of the respective Chinese firms. In short, the operating context might be a more significant factor than family ownership *per se* in explaining the different strategic managements. The second proposition is therefore that two ethnic Chinese TNCs from the same home economy, one family-controlled and another non-family-controlled, may exhibit similar strategic management behaviour when they operate across borders.

Table 6.9 provides a summary of the key characteristics of 73 ethnic Chinese TNCs from Hong Kong (HKTNCs) and 204 from Singapore (SINTNCs). Out of the total 73 Chinese HKTNCs, some 36 of them were owned, managed and operated by at least two generations of immediate family members. The other 37 Chinese HKTNCs were owned by diverse public shareholders and managed by professional managers. In the case of the 204 SINTNCs, about 26.5 per cent (n = 54) can be defined as Chinese family firms. In the sample of HKTNCs, the only statistically significant difference between family- and non-family-controlled variants was their employment size. Interestingly, significantly more family-controlled HKTNCs had more than 1,000 employees, indicating the dominance of large Chinese family groups in the Hong Kong economy (see Table 1.6 and case study of Li Ka-shing in Chapter 5). Among the 204 SINTNCs, the opposite pattern was statistically significant when fewer family-controlled firms were listed. These family-controlled SINTNCs were also significantly smaller than their non-family-controlled counterparts in terms of employment size, turnover and assets. This significant difference in size among my sample of SINTNCs can be explained by the domination of very large government-linked companies in the Singapore economy (see Table 6.1; Yeung, 2002a).

Figures 6.1 to 6.3 show the extent of intra-firm control, integration and

Table 6.9 Characteristics of ethnic Chinese transnational corporations from Hong Kong and Singapore

Characteristics	Hong Kong TNCs			Singapore TNCs		
	Family-controlled (%)	Non-family-controlled (%)	Total (%)	Family-controlled (%)	Non-family-controlled (%)	Total (%)
Economic sector						
Manufacturing	22 (61)	15 (41)	37 (51)	28 (52)	65 (43)	93 (45.6)
Services	14 (39)	20 (54)	34 (47)	24 (44)	83 (55)	107 (52.5)
Construction	0 (0)	2 (3)	2 (3)	2 (4)	2 (2)	4 (2)
Total	36 (100)	37 (100)	73 (100)	54 (100)	150 (100)	204 (100)
Public listing[1]						
Yes	17 (47)	18 (49)	35 (48)	6 (11)	50 (33)	56 (27)
No	19 (53)	19 (51)	38 (52)	48 (89)	100 (67)	148 (73)
Employment size[1,2]						
Less than 200	3 (8)	11 (30)	14 (19)	35 (65)	67 (45)	102 (50)
200–999	7 (19)	10 (27)	17 (23)	15 (28)	43 (29)	58 (28)
More than 1,000	26 (72)	16 (43)	42 (58)	4 (7)	40 (26)	44 (22)
Turnover (HK/S$ million)[1]						
1–9	0 (0)	1 (3)	1 (1)	17 (32)	29 (20)	46 (23)
10–49	2 (6)	0 (0)	2 (3)	25 (48)	45 (32)	70 (36)
50–99	1 (3)	4 (11)	5 (7)	5 (10)	16 (11)	21 (11)
100 or more	33 (92)	32 (86)	65 (89)	5 (10)	53 (37)	58 (30)
Assets (HK/S$ million)[1]						
1–9	2 (6)	5 (14)	7 (10)	22 (41)	47 (34)	69 (36)
10–49	4 (11)	3 (8)	7 (10)	23 (43)	33 (24)	56 (29)
50–99	1 (3)	0 (0)	1 (1)	4 (8)	12 (8)	16 (8)
100 or more	26 (72)	27 (73)	53 (73)	4 (8)	48 (34)	52 (27)
Not available	3 (8)	2 (5)	5 (7)	–	–	–

Sources: Author's surveys.

Notes
1 SINTNCs: Statistically significant at p < 0.05; chi-square = 9.8/10.1/15.2/16.1; d.f. = 1; 2; 3.
2 HKTNCs: Statistically significant at p < 0.05; chi-square = 7.5; d.f. = 2.

HKTNCs (n = 73)

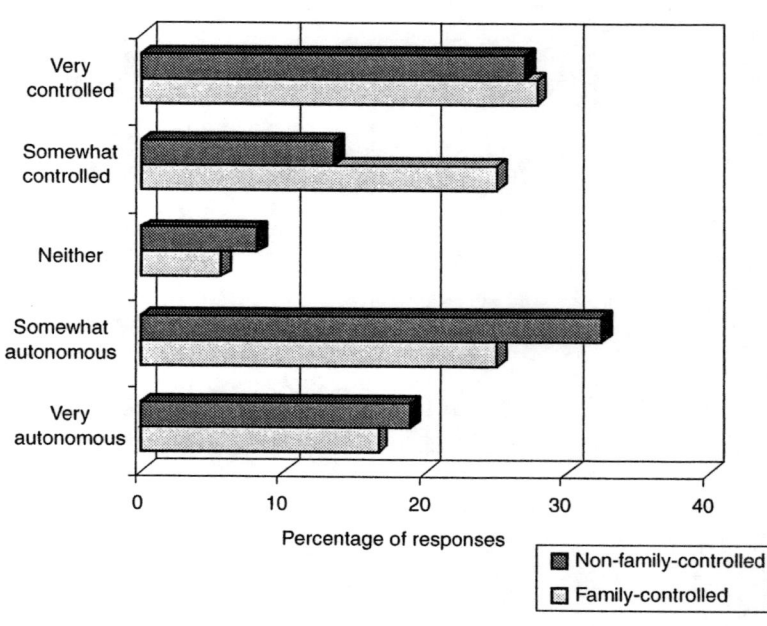

SINTNCs (n = 202)

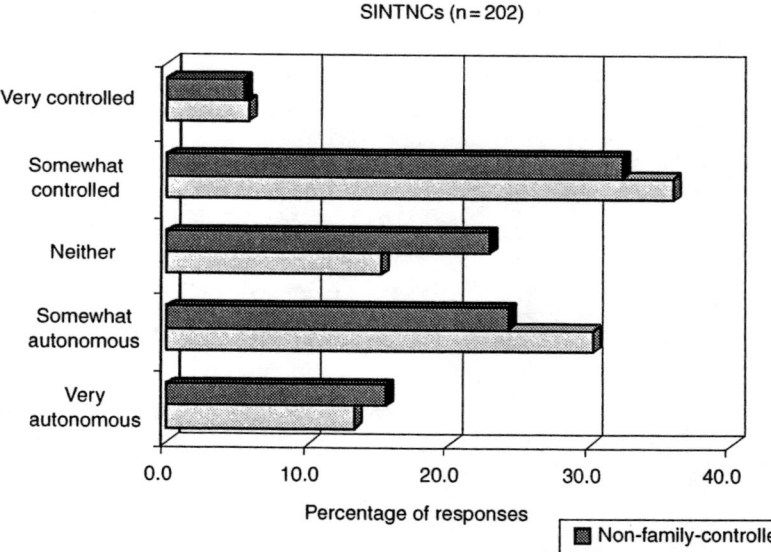

Figure 6.1 Intra-firm control among ethnic Chinese transnational corporations from Hong Kong and Singapore.

Sources: Author's surveys.

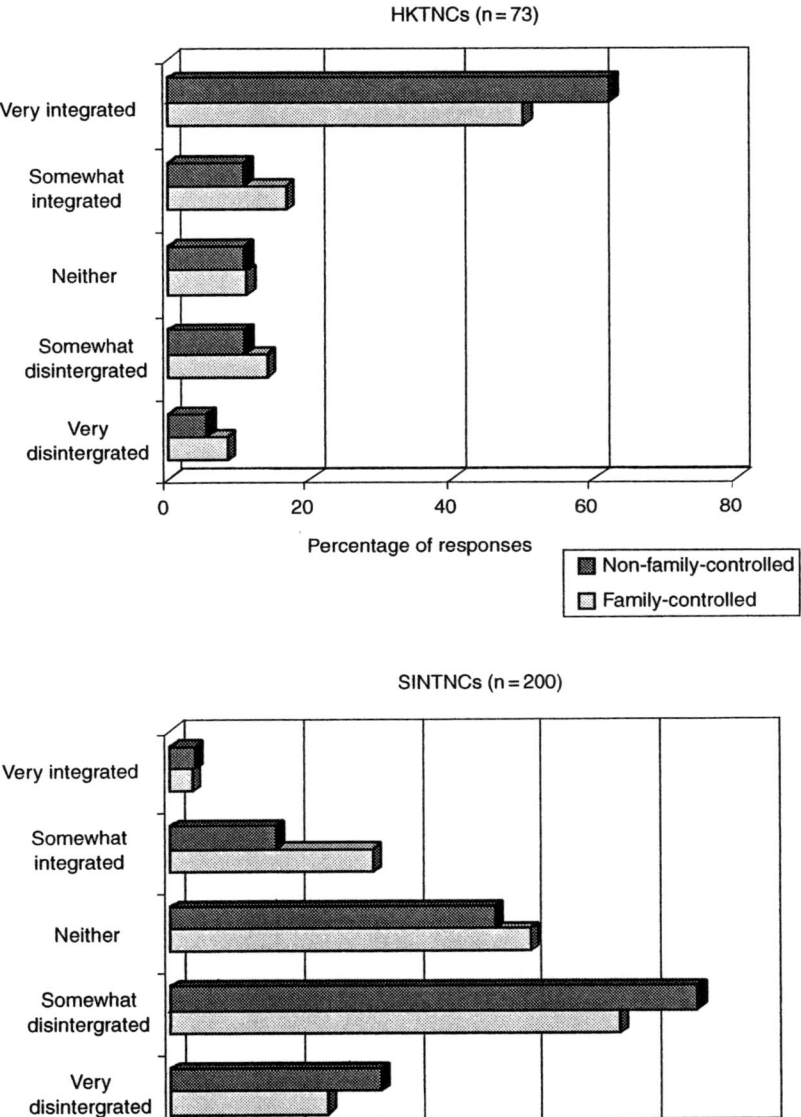

Figure 6.2 Intra-firm integration among ethnic Chinese transnational corporations from Hong Kong and Singapore.

Sources: Author's surveys.

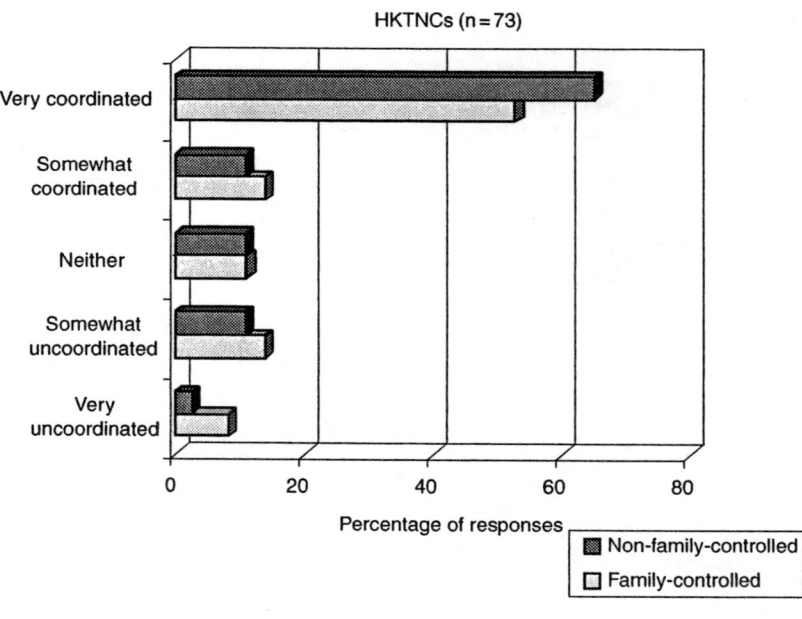

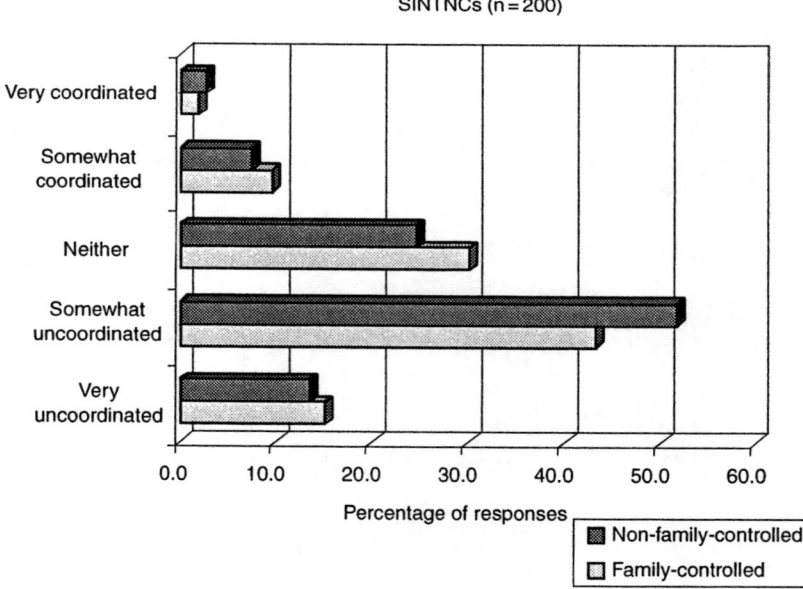

Figure 6.3 Intra-firm coordination among ethnic Chinese transnational corporations from Hong Kong and Singapore.

Sources: Author's surveys.

coordination among HKTNCs and SINTNCs in their foreign operations.[3] In Figure 6.1 there is no obvious difference in the extent of control exercised by either HKTNCs or SINTNCs. There are almost as many HKTNCs and SINTNCs exercising tight control over their foreign operations as those granting substantial autonomy to their foreign subsidiaries. Controlling for sectoral and country differences, this observation implies that in general, Chinese firms from Hong Kong and Singapore are not necessarily exercising tight control over their foreign subsidiaries. If we pay closer attention to family- and non-family-controlled firms, there is also no significant difference in the extent of controlling foreign operations. In other words, these firms from Hong Kong and Singapore do not conform to the conventional stereotype in the literature in which family ownership is assumed to imply a tighter control over their foreign operations. In fact, as many as half of HKTNCs and SINTNC actually granted substantial autonomy to their foreign subsidiaries. The key explanatory factor (i.e. independent variable) seems to be the specific contexts of these foreign operations, not family ownership *per se*. For example, there may be sectoral specificity in that strategic control and coordination are more critical in manufacturing operations because substantial capital and technology are invested. The issue of asset specificity (Williamson, 1975, 1985) in foreign manufacturing affiliates may also be significant. These manufacturing operations may require careful control and closer supervision to ensure sufficient returns on investment. Service operations abroad normally require less capital input and involve lower risks. Less control and more autonomy will be expected for foreign service affiliates of these HKTNCs and SINTNCs. Figures 6.2 and 6.3 also reveal some interesting differences in the extent of integration and coordination among Chinese HKTNCs and SINTNCs. HKTNCs tended to be much more integrated and coordinated in their foreign operations than their counterparts from Singapore. There are, however, no statistically significant differences ($p < 0.05$) in the extent of integration and coordination between family- and non-family-controlled Chinese firms from either Hong Kong or Singapore. This finding again indicates that the operating contexts or country of origin (Hong Kong or Singapore) matter a great deal more than family ownership in explaining the differential extent of integration and coordination in the foreign operations of HKTNCs and SINTNCs. It confirms similar findings in recent studies of the effects of home countries on the competitive strategies of transnational corporations (e.g. Murtha and Lenway, 1994; Anand and Delios, 1997; Erramilli *et al.*, 1997; Pantzalis, 2001).

What then are the key strategies of control and coordination implemented by ethnic Chinese HKTNCs and SINTNCs in their international operations? Table 6.10 shows that there is no clear pattern of differences in structures of ownership and equity shareholding between family- and non-family-controlled TNCs from either Hong Kong or Singapore. The

Table 6.10 Ownership percentages of ethnic Chinese transnational corporations from Hong Kong and Singapore

Characteristics	Hong Kong TNCs			Singapore TNCs		
	Family-controlled (%)	*Non-family-controlled* (%)	*Total* (%)	*Family-controlled* (%)	*Non-family-controlled* (%)	*Total* (%)
Indonesia						
Less than 50%	2 (40)	1 (14)	3 (25)	0 (0)	13 (28)	13 (23)
50–99%	0 (0)	6 (86)	6 (50)	6 (60)	17 (36)	23 (40)
100%	3 (60)	0 (0)	3 (25)	4 (40)	17 (36)	21 (37)
Total	5 (100)	7 (100)	12 (100)	10 (100)	47 (100)	57 (100)
Malaysia						
Less than 50%	3 (20)	2 (12)	5 (16)	2 (7)	17 (23)	19 (18)
50–99%	3 (20)	5 (29)	8 (25)	11 (38)	19 (25)	30 (29)
100%	9 (60)	10 (59)	19 (59)	16 (55)	39 (52)	55 (53)
Total	15 (100)	17 (100)	32 (100)	29 (100)	75 (100)	104 (100)
Singapore/Hong Kong						
Less than 50%	2 (8)	2 (7)	4 (7)	1 (8)	9 (20)	10 (17)
50–99%	7 (29)	2 (7)	9 (17)	2 (15)	9 (20)	11 (19)
100%	15 (63)	26 (86)	41 (76)	10 (77)	28 (60)	38 (64)
Total	24 (100)	30 (100)	54 (100)	13 (100)	46 (100)	59 (100)
Thailand						
Less than 50%	5 (33)	7 (47)	12 (40)	2 (33)	10 (48)	12 (45)
50–99%	3 (20)	3 (20)	6 (20)	1 (17)	5 (24)	6 (22)
100%	7 (47)	5 (33)	12 (40)	3 (50)	6 (28)	9 (33)
Total	15 (100)	15 (100)	30 (100)	6 (100)	21 (100)	27 (100)

The Philippines

Less than 50%	2 (40)	2 (33)	4 (36)	1 (20)	8 (33)	9 (31)
50–99%	1 (20)	1 (17)	2 (18)	1 (20)	5 (21)	6 (21)
100%	2 (40)	3 (50)	5 (46)	3 (60)	11 (46)	14 (48)
Total	5 (100)	6 (100)	11 (100)	5 (100)	24 (100)	29 (100)

Mainland China[1]

Less than 50%	2 (8)	4 (14)	6 (11)	3 (8)	29 (31)	32 (24)
50–99%	7 (29)	5 (17)	12 (23)	17 (45)	37 (39)	54 (41)
100%	15 (63)	20 (69)	35 (66)	18 (47)	28 (30)	46 (35)
Total	24 (100)	29 (100)	53 (100)	38 (100)	94 (100)	132 (100)

Western Europe

Less than 50%	0 (0)	0 (0)	0 (0)	1 (100)	3 (27)	4 (33)
50–99%	2 (15)	4 (33)	6 (24)	0 (0)	2 (18)	2 (17)
100%	11 (85)	8 (67)	19 (76)	0 (0)	6 (55)	6 (50)
Total	13 (100)	12 (100)	25 (100)	1 (100)	11 (100)	12 (100)

North America

Less than 50%	1 (4)	0 (0)	1 (2)	1 (20)	5 (20)	6 (20)
50–99%	5 (23)	2 (10)	7 (17)	0 (0)	5 (20)	5 (17)
100%	16 (73)	17 (90)	33 (81)	4 (80)	15 (60)	19 (63)
Total	22 (100)	19 (100)	41 (100)	5 (100)	25 (100)	30 (100)

Sources: Author's surveys.

Notes
Figures for the total reflect two samples of 73 HKTNGs and 204 SINTNGs.
1 SINTNCs: Statistically significant at p < 0.05; chi-square = 8.5; d.f. = 2.

only statistically significant exception is the mainland China operations of SINTNCs that registered less likelihood of non-family-controlled SINTNCs to exercise control through majority or 100 per cent shareholdings. At the group level, however, there seem to be some differences in ownership shareholdings between HKTNCs and SINTNCs, particularly in their mainland China, European and North American operations. HKTNCs were more likely to wholly own their operations in mainland China (n = 35; 66 per cent), Europe (n = 19; 76 per cent) and North America (n = 33; 81 per cent) than SINTNCs: mainland China (n = 46; 35 per cent), Europe (n = 6; 50 per cent) and North America (n = 19; 63 per cent).

Second, the extent of strategic control and coordination can be assessed by looking at the diverse ways in which HKTNCs and SINTNCs established their foreign operations (Table 6.11). Quite clearly, both HKTNCs and SINTNCs made use of a variety of mechanisms, ranging from highly controlled (e.g. sending expatriates) to little controlled (e.g. reliance on local partners or branching out from existing operations abroad), to establish their foreign operations. In general, HKTNCs preferred four mechanisms of establishing foreign operations that collectively accounted for 84 per cent of all 68 responses. Two of these, relying upon suitable local partners (n = 20; 29 per cent) and seeking assistance from host-country government authorities (n = 13; 19 per cent), imply a low level of control by parent firms in Hong Kong (see also Chapter 4). The reliance on local partners, for instance, is peculiar to many Southeast Asian countries because of host-country government regulations and the extensive presence of Chinese business networks (see Chapter 3). Control is therefore shared among different actors in the network, rather than internalized within the family in Hong Kong. There are also a number of HKTNCs that relied on personal relations in establishing and managing their cross-border operations (n = 14; 21 per cent). Only a small number of HKTNCs (n = 10; 15 per cent) explicitly relied on direct means of establishing overseas operations by the transfer of expatriates from Hong Kong. In the case of SINTNCs, Table 6.11 shows five mechanisms that contributed to 87 per cent of all 145 responses. In contrast to the HKTNCs, three of these were particularly prominent: branching out from existing operations abroad (n = 32; 22 per cent), well-developed corporate procedures (n = 31; 21 per cent) and suggestions from major clients (n = 24; 17 per cent). These mechanisms imply a low level of direct control of foreign operations by parent companies in Singapore, a phenomenon explained by the highly corporatized nature of SINTNCs (see also Chapter 4). Interestingly, there are no statistically significant differences ($p < 0.05$) in the ways that family- and non-family-controlled TNCs from either Hong Kong or Singapore established foreign operations. This pattern implies that the two different sets of mechanisms were important for both family and non-family firms to operate abroad. Their difference rests in the geographical origins of HKTNCs and SINTNCs, not their family ownership.

Table 6.11 Different ways of establishing international operations by ethnic Chinese transnational corporations from Hong Kong and Singapore

Way of establishment	Hong Kong TNCs			Singapore TNCs		
	Family-controlled (%)	Non-family-controlled (%)	Total (%)	Family-controlled (%)	Non-family-controlled (%)	Total (%)
1 Able to find a suitable local partner/person to set up the operation	8 (25)	12 (33)	20 (29)	3 (8)	18 (16)	21 (15)
2 Personal relations, important in establishing overseas operations	5 (16)	9 (25)	14 (21)	7 (19)	11 (10)	18 (12)
3 Stimulation, guidance and assistance from local government institutions	9 (28)	4 (11)	13 (19)	2 (6)	5 (5)	7 (5)
4 Sent someone over to set up the operation	5 (16)	5 (14)	10 (15)	0 (0)	9 (8)	9 (6)
5 A well-developed corporate procedure to set up overseas operations	1 (3)	2 (6)	3 (4)	5 (14)	26 (24)	31 (21)
6 Decision or suggestions from major clients	0 (0)	2 (6)	2 (3)	8 (22)	16 (15)	24 (17)
7 Long history of operation	2 (6)	0 (0)	2 (3)	0 (0)	0 (0)	0 (0)
8 Direct merger or acquisition	1 (3)	1 (3)	2 (3)	0 (0)	3 (3)	3 (2)
9 Branch out from existing operations elsewhere in the host region	1 (3)	1 (3)	2 (3)	11 (31)	21 (19)	32 (22)
Total	32 (100)	36 (100)	68 (100)	36 (100)	109 (100)	145 (100)

Sources: Author's surveys.

Note
Because of non-responses, the total number of responses is smaller than the total size of samples for both HKTNCs (n = 73) and SINTNCs (n = 204).

Third, Table 6.12 shows that the control strategies of HKTNCs and SINTNCs represent both direct and indirect control. Three major strategies were commonly employed by both HKTNCs and SINTNCs: periodic reports, periodic inspection and cost control, accounting for respectively 60 per cent and 62 per cent of all control strategies of HKTNCs (n = 146) and SINTNCs (n = 548). These three strategies are very similar to those of TNCs headquartered in North America and Western Europe (Doz and Prahalad, 1981; Baliga and Jaeger, 1984; Prahalad and Doz, 1987; Bartlett and Ghoshal, 1989; Gupta and Govindarajan, 1991; Birkinshaw and Hood, 1998b; Harzing, 1999). Periodic reports are normally expected from foreign subsidiaries. The frequency of reporting varies between different subsidiaries and parent firms. The reports usually contain financial and inventory statistics. The frequency of visits by top executives is likely to be once a month or once every six months. These visits are infrequent, considering the geographical proximity of Asian countries in which HKTNCs and SINTNCs primarily operate. In terms of family ownership, there are again no statistically significant differences ($p < 0.05$) in the use of different control practices between family- and non-family-controlled TNCs from either Hong Kong or Singapore. Further examination of Table 6.12 shows that the employment of expatriate managers and operational controls (e.g. inventory and production) was less important in the strategic management of foreign operations by both HKTNCs (n = 8; 5 per cent) and SINTNCs (n = 58; 11 per cent). The local subsidiaries were often given power to make decisions in production and marketing planning as well as in inventory and quality of products. Few respondents (less than 11 per cent) noted that decision-making came from the parent firms in Hong Kong or Singapore. These findings indicate that the control strategies of HKTNCs and SINTNCs are becoming similar to the strategies employed by TNCs headquartered in North America and Western Europe, which enable the decentralization of decision-making and management by delegation and responsibility. There is less evidence, at least in so far as family ownership is concerned, to support a distinctively ethnic Chinese approach to strategic management. On the contrary, there seems to be a broad trend towards some convergence in management and control strategies.

Fourth, survey data on channels of marketing and sourcing suggest that the Southeast Asian affiliates of both HKTNCs and SINTNCs were fairly autonomous. Table 6.13, shows how marketing and sourcing activities among these affiliates were conducted at the local level. For those Southeast Asian affiliates of HKTNCs having marketing and sourcing activities, at least 50 per cent of them were empowered to make decisions without referring to their parent firms in Hong Kong. There is a slight difference between family- and non-family-controlled HKTNCs. The Southeast Asian affiliates of the former group relied relatively less on local marketing and sourcing channels, though the difference is not statistically significant

Table 6.12 Control strategies of ethnic Chinese transnational corporations from Hong Kong and Singapore

Control practices	Hong Kong TNCs			Singapore TNCs		
	Family-controlled (%)	Non-family-controlled (%)	Total (%)	Family-controlled (%)	Non-family-controlled (%)	Total (%)
1 Periodic report of local managers to headquarters	12 (16)	20 (27)	32 (22)	29 (20)	102 (25)	131 (24)
2 Periodic inspection by top management executives from headquarters	14 (19)	15 (21)	29 (20)	38 (27)	92 (23)	130 (24)
3 Cost control by headquarters	12 (16)	14 (19)	26 (18)	25 (17)	50 (12)	75 (14)
4 Production and marketing planning from headquarters	6 (8)	7 (10)	13 (9)	4 (3)	10 (2)	14 (3)
5 Provision of broad guidelines by corporate groups	6 (8)	6 (8)	12 (8)	7 (5)	60 (15)	67 (12)
6 Centralized decision-making from headquarters	5 (7)	5 (7)	10 (7)	24 (17)	34 (8)	58 (11)
7 Inventory and quality control by headquarters	6 (8)	2 (3)	8 (5)	3 (2)	3 (1)	6 (1)
8 Employment of expatriate managers and/or executives	7 (10)	1 (1)	8 (5)	11 (8)	47 (12)	58 (11)
9 Mutual exchange of information	3 (4)	3 (4)	6 (4)	2 (1)	7 (2)	9 (2)
10 Annual meetings	2 (3)	0 (0)	2 (1)	0 (0)	0 (0)	0 (0)
Total	73 (100)	73 (100)	146 (100)	143 (100)	405 (100)	548 (100)

Sources: Author's surveys.

Note
The total number of responses from both HKTNCs and SINTNCs is larger than the two-sample size (n = 73 and n = 204) because up to three answers were allowed from each respondent.

Table 6.13 Channels of marketing and sourcing among Southeast Asian operations of ethnic Chinese transnational corporations from Hong Kong and Singapore

Channels	Hong Kong TNCs			Singapore TNCs		
	Family-controlled (%)	Non-family-controlled (%)	Total (%)	Family-controlled (%)	Non-family-controlled (%)	Total (%)
Marketing						
1 Through central marketing department in headquarters	3 (8)	1 (3)	4 (5)	10 (28)	32 (27)	42 (27)
2 Through local marketing department in subsidiaries/affiliates	20 (56)	26 (70)	46 (63)	21 (58)	73 (61)	94 (60)
3 Through subcontracting independent marketing services in Hong Kong	0 (0)	1 (3)	1 (1)	–	–	–
4 Through subcontracting independent marketing services in Southeast Asia	4 (11)	6 (16)	10 (14)	–	–	–
5 No such marketing activities	9 (25)	3 (8)	12 (16)	–	–	–
6 Through overseas offices	–	–	–	5 (14)	15 (13)	20 (13)
Total	36 (100)	37 (100)	73 (100)	36 (100)	120 (100)	156 (100)
Sourcing[1]						
1 Through central corporate sourcing from headquarters	7 (19)	2 (5)	9 (12)	21 (58)	37 (33)	58 (39)
2 Through local production and supply department in subsidiaries/affiliates	14 (39)	16 (43)	30 (41)	13 (36)	64 (57)	77 (52)
3 Through subcontracting independent suppliers in Southeast Asia	3 (8)	4 (11)	7 (10)	–	–	–
4 No such sourcing activities	12 (33)	15 (41)	27 (37)	2 (6)	11 (10)	13 (9)
Total	36 (100)	37 (100)	73 (100)	36 (100)	112 (100)	148 (100)

Sources: Author's surveys.

Notes

Because of non-responses, the total number of responses is smaller than the total size of samples for both HKTNCs (n = 73) and SINTNCs (n = 204).

1 SINTNCs: Statistically significant at $p < 0.05$; chi-square = 7.3; d.f. = 2. Data on East Asian operations were not statistically significant, $p = 0.285$; chi-square = 5.0; d.f. = 2.

(p < 0.05). The case of SINTNCs, however, offers a very different picture from that of HKTNCs. In contrast to HKTNCs, the Southeast Asian operations of SINTNCs were much more tightly controlled via central marketing and sourcing activities from the headquarters in Singapore. I found statistically significant differences (p < 0.05) in the sourcing behaviour between family- and non-family-controlled SINTNCs. Some 58 per cent (n = 21) of family-controlled SINTNCs sourced centrally for their Southeast Asian operations, but only 33 per cent (n = 37) of non-family-controlled SINTNCs did so. This finding tentatively supports the literature on Chinese capitalism that Chinese family firms often exercise more control over their foreign subsidiaries. An additional analysis of the unreported data on the East Asian operations of these SINTNCs, however, reveals no statistically significant differences (p < 0.05) between these two groups of SINTNCs. This analysis of marketing and sourcing channels seems to confirm the fairly insignificant role of family ownership in determining the marketing and sourcing behaviour of HKTNCs and SINTNCs.

Table 6.14 shows the main sources of technology and management expertise in the international operations of HKTNCs and SINTNCs. Almost 50 per cent of HKTNCs' Southeast Asian subsidiaries developed their own technology and expertise, although caution is needed in interpreting this finding. In fact, most of the technology and expertise of these operations were either transferred or locally adapted from parent HKTNCs, at least at the beginning phase of their operations. This is particularly the case for family-controlled HKTNCs. In Indonesia, Malaysia, Thailand and the Philippines, the majority of the affiliates of family-controlled HKTNCs relied on the direct transfer of technology and management expertise from their parent firms in Hong Kong. But the majority of their non-family-controlled counterparts relied on local development in technology and the accumulation of management expertise. Other than technology transfer applicable mostly to manufacturing operations, family-controlled HKTNCs also transferred managerial expertise to local Southeast Asian affiliates. As noted earlier, however, the Southeast Asian operations of non-family-controlled HKTNCs retained one key area of management expertise that was particularly important for service industries: local marketing expertise. There appears to be relatively little intra-firm control of Southeast Asian operations by non-family-controlled HKTNCs through marketing, sourcing or technology. The case of SINTNCs is more straightforward because there are no significant differences (p < 0.05) in the sourcing of technology and/or expertise between family- and non-family-controlled Chinese firms. Some 53 per cent (n = 85) of their East Asian operations and 68 per cent (n = 106) of their Southeast Asian operations relied on direct transfer from parent companies in Singapore. However, only 39 per cent (n = 12) and 33 per cent (n = 10) of the subsidiaries in Western Europe and North America depended on direct transfer from parent companies. The majority of

Table 6.14 Sources of technology and expertise among international operations of ethnic Chinese transnational corporations from Hong Kong and Singapore

Sources	Hong Kong TNCs			Singapore TNCs		
	Family-controlled (%)	Non-family-controlled (%)	Total (%)	Family-controlled (%)	Non-family-controlled (%)	Total (%)
	Indonesia	Indonesia	Indonesia	–	–	–
Direct transfer from parent	5 (83)	2 (29)	7 (54)	–	–	–
Local development	1 (17)	5 (71)	6 (46)	–	–	–
Total	6 (100)	7 (100)	13 (100)	–	–	–
	Malaysia	Malaysia	Malaysia	East Asia	East Asia	East Asia
Direct transfer from parent	10 (67)	7 (39)	17 (52)	24 (55)	61 (52)	85 (53)
Local development	5 (33)	11 (61)	16 (48)	18 (41)	51 (43)	69 (43)
Global sharing	–	–	–	2 (4)	6 (5)	8 (5)
Total	15 (100)	18 (100)	33 (100)	44 (100)	118 (100)	162 (100)
	Singapore	Singapore	Singapore	SE Asia	SE Asia	SE Asia
Direct transfer from parent	7 (29)	12 (40)	19 (35)	28 (78)	78 (65)	106 (68)
Local development	15 (63)	17 (57)	32 (60)	6 (17)	38 (31)	44 (28)
Global sharing	2 (8)	1 (3)	3 (6)	2 (5)	5 (4)	7 (4)
Total	24 (100)	30 (100)	54 (100)	36 (100)	121 (100)	157 (100)

	Thailand	Thailand	Thailand	W Europe	W Europe	W Europe
Direct transfer from parent	9 (60)	8 (47)	17 (53)	2 (50)	10 (37)	12 (39)
Local development	6 (40)	9 (53)	15 (47)	2 (50)	12 (44)	14 (45)
Global sharing	–	–	–	0 (0)	5 (19)	5 (16)
Total	15 (100)	17 (100)	32 (100)	4 (100)	27 (100)	31 (100)

	Philippines	Philippines	Philippines	N America	N America	N America
Direct transfer from parent	4 (80)	2 (29)	6 (50)	1 (25)	9 (35)	10 (33)
Local development	1 (20)	5 (71)	6 (50)	3 (75)	14 (54)	17 (57)
Global sharing	–	–	–	0 (0)	3 (11)	3 (10)
Total	5 (100)	7 (100)	12 (100)	4 (100)	26 (100)	30 (100)

Sources: Author's surveys.

Note
Because of non-responses, the total number of responses is smaller than the total size of samples for both HKTNCs (n = 73) and SINTNCs (n = 204).

them either developed their own capabilities locally or engaged in global sharing of technology and/or expertise. There is thus no clearly identifiable pattern in the sources of technology and expertise among the foreign subsidiaries of these HKTNCs and SINTNCs. Rather, the host region seems to be an important determinant of the extent of reliance on parent companies for direct transfer of technology or expertise.

Of all the strategic control mechanisms, finance is perhaps the most likely area in which significant differences between family- and non-family-controlled HKTNCs and SINTNCs may be found. This is because the family patriarchs are supposedly much more careful with their investment funds than public shareholders. In Table 6.15, it is clear that an overwhelming majority of both HKTNCs and SINTNCs used internal capital reserve to finance their foreign operations. The role of family ownership matters only in the case of the Southeast Asian operations of SINTNCs, though the statistical significance is relatively weak at $p < 0.10$. As predicted in the literature, more family-controlled SINTNCs ($n = 36$; 95 per cent) used internal reserves to finance their Southeast Asian operations, thereby maintaining tighter control within families. In general, however, there is no significant difference in the sourcing of capital between family- and non-family-controlled firms from either Hong Kong or Singapore, indicating some extent of convergence in the financing of international operations by the two variants of Chinese firms. These findings also lend some support to my claim that the sources of capital for large Chinese business conglomerates are increasingly diversified beyond the controlling families and their immediate networks (see also Chapter 5).

Conclusion

In this empirical chapter I have assembled and analysed in detail three sets of quantitative data to support my core proposition that corporate governance and strategic management among Chinese family firms are indeed changing and moving away from traditional practices of reliance on network capital and hierarchical control and authority systems. In particular, I have demonstrated that Chinese family firms listed on the Singapore Exchange are increasingly adopting international standards in their corporate governance. Using principal banks and auditors as surrogates for corporate governance practices, I have shown that these Chinese family firms are compelled to adopt international standards of corporate governance through the role played by their global banks and auditing firms. The institutional requirements of these global banks and auditing firms suggest that Chinese family firms have moved beyond traditional closely knit family networks in both capital and management practices. In an era of global finance, it is clearly possible that Chinese family firms are capable of professionalizing their governance systems in order to gain credibility and legitimacy in the international business and finance community through their enrolment in globalizing actor-networks.

While some of their governance and management characteristics continue to conform to those found in the literature on Chinese capitalism (e.g. substantial shareholdings and occupation of key management positions), an emerging trend of dilution in family control occurs, possibly as a result of the increasing listing of Chinese family firms on various stock exchanges. In the literature on Chinese capitalism, family firms are widely recognized as tightly controlled on the basis of centripetal authority exercised by the patriarchs. To a certain extent, these observations may be true in the domestic context of Chinese capitalism in East and Southeast Asia, because the family can serve as a basic platform of economic competition against outsiders by providing trusted personnel and by pooling capital and resources. It also facilitates rapid decision-making and flexibility in strategic orientations. But all these acknowledged attributes and competitive advantages may be inapplicable when they venture abroad or confront globalization. The rapid emergence of ethnic Chinese TNCs (see also Chapter 3) implies that they may not be able to transfer their family-based competitive advantage to an international context characterized by global competition and local variations mediated through state regulations. These family firms are thus left with two strategic choices. First, they can maintain strict control over and tight coordination of their foreign operations to avoid leakage of competitive advantage and to internalize their core capabilities within the family. Second, they can adapt their organizational structures to allow for more local autonomy and decision-making. They can also take in more local expertise through local partners and joint ventures, thereby building up new sources of competitive advantage to compete in the regional and global economy.

The analysis of the survey data on 73 ethnic Chinese HKTNCs and 204 SINTNCs shows that family ownership does not necessarily play a significant role in determining strategic management behaviour. In most of its dimensions I found no statistically significant differences between family- and non-family-controlled Chinese firms from either Hong Kong or Singapore. In line with my arguments pursued through case studies in the previous chapters, my empirical analysis in this chapter has confirmed that we simply do not have a convincing case for using family ownership and control to define the distinctiveness of Chinese capitalism in its international context (Hamilton, 2000; Redding, 2000). Rather, management practices of Chinese family firms are increasingly converging towards those found among non-family-controlled Chinese firms from the same home economies. My analysis has also suggested that there is nothing uniquely family about the organization and management of transnational operations among Chinese family firms from Hong Kong and Singapore. Indeed, the management practices of Chinese family firms are not too different from major TNCs from North America and Western Europe. Taken

Table 6.15 Sources of finance among international operations of ethnic Chinese transnational corporations from Hong Kong and Singapore

Sources	Hong Kong TNCs			Singapore TNCs		
	Family-controlled (%)	Non-family-controlled (%)	Total (%)	Family-controlled (%)	Non-family-controlled (%)	Total (%)
	Indonesia	Indonesia	Indonesia	East Asia	East Asia	East Asia
Reserve from parent firm	5 (83)	7 (100)	12 (92)	37 (90)	93 (80)	130 (82)
Host-country capital market	0 (0)	0 (0)	0 (0)	1 (2)	10 (8)	11 (7)
International capital market	1 (17)	0 (0)	1 (8)	3 (7)	14 (12)	17 (11)
Total	6 (100)	7 (100)	13 (100)	41 (100)	117 (100)	158 (100)
	Malaysia	Malaysia	Malaysia	SE Asia[1]	SE Asia	SE Asia
Reserve from parent firm	14 (93)	15 (83)	29 (88)	36 (95)	95 (80)	131 (83)
Host-country capital market	0 (0)	3 (17)	3 (9)	2 (5)	10 (8)	12 (8)
International capital market	1 (7)	0 (0)	1 (3)	0 (0)	14 (12)	14 (9)
Total	15 (100)	18 (100)	33 (100)	38 (100)	119 (100)	157 (100)
	Singapore	Singapore	Singapore			
Reserve from parent firm	19 (79)	28 (93)	47 (87)			
Host-country capital market	4 (17)	2 (7)	6 (11)			
International capital market	1 (4)	0 (0)	1 (2)			
Total	24 (100)	30 (100)	54 (100)			

	Thailand	Thailand	Thailand	W Europe	W Europe	W Europe
Reserve from parent firm	14 (93)	15 (94)	29 (94)	3 (75)	19 (73)	22 (73)
Host-country capital market	0 (0)	1 (6)	1 (3)	0 (0)	5 (19)	5 (17)
International capital market	1 (7)	0 (0)	1 (3)	1 (25)	2 (8)	3 (10)
Total	15 (100)	16 (100)	31 (100)	4 (100)	26 (100)	30 (100)

	Philippines	Philippines	Philippines	N America	N America	N America
Reserve from parent firm	4 (80)	6 (86)	10 (84)	4 (100)	21 (75)	25 (78)
Host-country capital market	0 (0)	1 (14)	1 (8)	0 (0)	4 (14)	4 (13)
International capital market	1 (20)	0 (0)	1 (8)	0 (0)	3 (11)	3 (9)
Total	5 (100)	7 (100)	12 (100)	4 (100)	28 (100)	32 (100)

Sources: Author's surveys.

Notes

Because of non-responses, the total number of responses is smaller than the total size of samples for both HKTNCs (n = 73) and SINTNCs (n = 204).

1 SINTNCs: Statistically significant at p < 0.10; chi-square = 5.6; d.f. = 2.

together, the evidence presented in this chapter indicates that the nature of Chinese capitalism is more characterized by multiplicity and complexity, rather than the static caricatures often found in the existing literature, which has substantially exaggerated the extent of unique governance and management practices associated with family ownership and control. The reality of Chinese capitalism is blessed with a mixture of uniquely cultural norms and internationally acknowledged economic practices; it is subject to the specificity of institutional contexts and globalizing actor-networks in which Chinese firms operate. The complex interpenetration of globalization has therefore led to a much more diversified and hybridized mode of economic organization in Chinese capitalism. This hybridization indicates that Chinese capitalism is itself changing, although its direction and trajectory are by no means clear and unidirectional.

7 The future of Chinese capitalism

Reinterpreting Chinese capitalism in a global era

Since the beginning of the 1980s, globalization has significantly intensified, a phenomenon driven primarily by the champions of market mechanism, technological change and time-space compression (Olds *et al.*, 1999; Dicken, 2003a; Peck and Yeung, 2003). In this increasingly global economy, it is claimed that the convergent effects of globalization and cross-border organizational learning have rapidly outpaced the divergent effects of cultures, national institutions and social systems (Mueller, 1994; Guillén, 2001a). In this book I have argued that local modes of capitalism serve as an institutional mechanism to mediate the tantalizing effects of globalization. These distinct modes of economic-organizational norms and practices provide the institutional links among cultures, polities and economies. Despite its uncertain and often contested effects on capitalism, globalization exerts an important contingent influence on the advance and expansion of capitalism in different regional economies (see Figure 1.2). In many East and Southeast Asian economies where Chinese capitalism has been a dominant institutional form of capitalist economic organization, although globalization and its associated crisis-laden tendencies have posed serious challenges to the organization and dynamics of Chinese capitalism, they have also triggered multiple and transformative responses from key actors in Chinese capitalism, that is, firms and their close political-economic allies (Yeung, 1999b, 2000c). As globalization extends its reach into the Asia-Pacific region, Chinese capitalism no longer remains as a set of static cultural artefacts. Instead, globalization and its transformative forces have been contested and negotiated vigorously by means of the dynamic strategies of key actors in Chinese capitalism. In this sense, Chinese capitalism is highly dynamic and capable of meeting the challenges of globalization. And yet in meeting these challenges Chinese capitalism itself undergoes significant transformations and changes in its dominant norms and structures that in turn lead to the emergence of a metamorphosized form of economic organization known as hybrid capitalism.

In the earlier chapters of this book I presented both theoretical arguments and empirical evidence to showcase these significant changes and transformations. In theoretical terms, I have developed an actor-network perspective on the dynamics of Chinese capitalism that relates the reconfiguration of capitalist norms and structures to the strategic enrolment of key capitalist actors in globalizing actor-networks (see Chapter 2). This perspective avoids the methodological pitfall of taking an either all-change or no-change view in its analysis of the interaction between contemporary capitalism and globalization. Contrary to the claims by ultra-globalists that all economic actors are subordinated to ruthless globalization (e.g. Ohmae, 1990, 1995), the perspective addresses both the contestation and participation of key actors in globalization. Unlike the pervasive focus on enduring capitalist structures and social systems in most comparative analyses of capitalism, this actor-oriented analysis allows for both contingencies and evolutionary change. I have not set up stringent a priori conditions in order just to negate all possible changes and transformations that might occur in any particular capitalist mode of economic organization. My view on the dynamics of Chinese capitalism runs contrary to Whitley's (1999: 134; my emphases) conclusion that

> the conditions required for significant changes to take place in the nature and behaviour of firms as a result of their expanding their operations abroad are so *stringent* that late-twentieth-century patterns of internationalization are *unlikely* to generate qualitative step changes in the characteristics and strategies of leading firms in most economies.

In Chapter 2 I developed this actor-network perspective to account for three main mechanisms through which key actors in Chinese capitalism might be enrolled in globalizing actor-networks: engaging with actor-networks in international business and finance; gathering knowledge and experience through international educational institutions; and connecting with international organizations and multilateral institutions. These actor-specific processes are conceived as critical mechanisms through which dynamic changes and transformations in Chinese capitalism may be facilitated.

Chapters 3 to 6 shed light on different, but interrelated, dimensions of these changes and transformations. In Chapter 3 some empirical evidence was presented on the internationalization of Chinese capitalism, with an analysis of its interaction with changing operating contexts on various geographical scales ranging from global and regional to national and local. My evidence and analysis point to the recent participation of key actors in Chinese capitalism in globalization, since the 1980s and the 1990s. The focus on the internationalization is important for two reasons. First, much of the existing literature reviewed in Chapter 1 examines Chinese capitalism in its domestic contexts and therefore conveniently ignores transformations brought about through actor-specific processes embedded in different international contexts. Second, significant changes and transformations in capitalist norms and practices are unlikely to be induced through domestic pressures. Instead, they are facilitated both by the new experience and knowledge that key actors have gathered through their international operations and by their strategy of blending this new learning with the existing norms in their domestic contexts. There followed an analysis of some qualitative case studies of Chinese family firms in different Asian economies and quantitative data on Chinese firms in Singapore and Hong Kong. Chapter 4 showed that a large number of Chinese family firms from Singapore and Hong Kong no longer rely exclusively on family and kinship linkages to sustain their international operations. Their transnational business networks have been broadened to include non-family members such as professional managers and business associates. Two case studies, of Victor Li from Hong Kong and Eu Yan Sang from Singapore, clearly illustrated the growing involvement of non-family members in the entrepreneurial activities of key actors in Chinese capitalism. They also showed that dynamic transformations in Chinese family firms (e.g. professionalization and corporatization) can propel these ethnocentric firms to survive beyond the three-generation trap infamously popularized in the literature on Chinese capitalism.

In Chapter 5 the argument was taken a step further by offering three detailed case studies of how Chinese business networks are no longer exclusively limited to ethnic Chinese actors. In particular, the strategic enrolment of these ethnic Chinese in actor-networks in global finance necessitates a reciprocal process of enrolling non-Chinese elites in Chinese business networks, thereby effectively broadening their ethnic composition and reshaping the social organization of Chinese capitalism into a less ethno-centric mode of economic organization. The detailed case studies of Li Ka-shing and his family (Hong Kong) and Kwek Leng Beng (Singapore) challenge the caricatured notion of bamboo networks that assumes network exclusivity in terms of both ethnicity (Chinese) and social units (family). What has been shown here, then, is the key role played collectively by such non-Chinese elites in international media, credit-rating agencies and financial institutions in broadening the membership of actor-networks and enacting dynamic transformations in Chinese capitalism.

In Chapter 6 two strategic analytical moves were made to strengthen the core argument on the dynamics of Chinese capitalism. First, three large sets of quantitative data were drawn on to substantiate the more qualitative claims in the earlier chapters. This was necessary since much of the literature on Chinese capitalism builds its arguments on the basis of a few glamorous examples of well-known Chinese businessmen. As noted by Nonini (1997: 222):

> The triumphalist narratives of legendary Chinese tycoons and their family enterprises spanning the Asia Pacific nation-states should certainly continue to be grist for our theoretical mill as we seek to understand the transnationalization of overseas Chinese capitalism. Yet capitalism cannot be identified solely with a form of economic organization, nor Asian capitalism only with a family form of organization ... Nor should diasporic Chinese throughout the Asia Pacific be reduced to being represented metonymically by a very few, spectacularly successful capitalist exemplars.

This rather journalistic approach to such a complex and multi-faceted phenomenon as Chinese capitalism is dangerously close to a form of sensational essentialism, sensational in terms of its exaggerations and stigmatization and essentialism in terms of its universal reification of ethnic Chinese and Chinese capitalism. Second, firm-level organizational processes are focused on as a proxy of broader structural changes in Chinese capitalism. This analysis is legitimate because most comparative analyses of capitalism and business systems in economic sociology and international political economy have emphasized corporate governance and organizational structures as the distinguishing criteria of different varieties of capitalism (Whitley, 1992, 1999; Hall and Soskice, 2001a). More specifically, the empirical analysis of quantitative data on 157 Chinese family firms listed on the Singapore Exchange showed that the substantial involvement of international banks (as principal banks) and big six accounting firms has significantly strengthened the corporate governance of these family firms. My analysis of data on 73 TNCs from Hong Kong and 204 from Singapore also demonstrates the insignificance of family ownership as a key variable in explaining the differences, if any, in the strategic management of their international operations.

To conclude, theoretical arguments have been developed and a variety of empirical evidence has been marshalled to offer a reinterpretation of the nature and dynamics of Chinese capitalism in a global era. I have identified family ownership as a major nexus of continuity in Chinese capitalism, a quite common phenomenon in the global economy today (Franks *et al.*, 2003). More importantly, I have found significant changes and transformations in the socio-economic organization of Chinese capitalism into the greater inclusion of non-family members through professionalization, the broadening of Chinese business networks through actor-specific processes, and the enrolment of key Chinese elites into increasingly non-Chinese actor-networks in international business and global finance (see also Figure 1.2). Although these changes may be seen by some observers of Chinese capitalism as rather limited (e.g. Whitley, 1999; Redding, 2000), they represent a very important step towards the hybridization of Chinese capitalism in a global era. This does not necessarily entail a complete negation of distinctive nationally-based business systems that are presumably enduring and hard to change. I take a more modest view of Chinese capitalism, in favour of dynamic change towards hybridization rather than a complete transformation towards a dominant mode of capitalist economic organization, say the Anglo-American model.

Indeed, many of these transformations in Chinese capitalism occur at the level of actors and firms and their strategic behaviour, rather than structures and institutions. As such, I do not claim a total change and transformation of Chinese capitalism and its business system towards some pre-defined model of global capitalism. The domestic realm of Chinese capitalism may well remain dominated by many of the core characteristics identified in the literature (see Chapter 1), although this domination is itself highly differentiated among different East and Southeast Asian economies. I believe that Chinese capitalism is evolving and the evolution in the role of familism and ethno-centric business networks has been described and explained in this book in relation to globalization. Although business-state relations, financial systems and labour processes and management in the 'home' economies of these ethnic Chinese actors may not change as rapidly as their own business strategies and economic behaviour, this should not negate the gradual transformation occurring at the level of actors and firms, particularly those that actively engage in and are (re)shaped by globalization.

Chinese capitalism and the aftermath of the Asian economic crisis

Given my key argument and the empirical evidence presented here, does it mean that Chinese capitalism will be unequivocally dissolved and disembedded by the challenges of globalization tendencies? This pessimistic view is premature, for although it is undergoing dynamic changes and transformations, Chinese capitalism continues to persist in East and Southeast Asia. The 1997–8 Asian economic crisis presented a very clear challenge to the traditional practices and social organization of Chinese capitalism. But we are not witnessing the wholesale demise of Chinese capitalism as a dominant form of economic organization in East and Southeast Asia. In fact, I would argue that the crisis has speeded up transformations in Chinese capitalism that otherwise might not have happened; these transformations in turn serve to enhance the viability of Chinese capitalism in the global economy. On the one hand, some key actors in Chinese capitalism were undoubtedly besieged by the crisis because their very mode of economic practices overexposed them to excessive risks and crony capitalism. On the other hand, other key Chinese actors embraced the difficult challenges of the crisis by broadening their actor-networks across and beyond the Asian region in order to consolidate their international operations. This process of reorganizing and transforming Chinese capitalism has important implications for its future in East and Southeast Asia.

Before dismissing the idea of actors in Chinese capitalism who fiercely contest globalization, it is useful to briefly review the nature and extent of the 1997–8 Asian economic crisis and its relation to globalization. Starting with the devaluation of the Thai baht in August 1997, the crisis seriously disrupted the expanding economies of Indonesia, Thailand and South Korea. All three NIEs, albeit in different generations of their evolutionary trajectories, resorted unwillingly to the IMF for financial bailouts (see also Chapter 5, footnote 2). During the second half of 1997 and first half of 1998, many Asian economies saw their currencies depreciating rapidly against the US dollar,[1] their stock markets tumbled, their banks and other non-bank financial institutions were in serious trouble and their annual growth rates plummeted downwards (see Table 7.1). In the words of Mahathir Mohamad, then prime minister of Malaysia, the economic turmoil caused by the devaluation of Asian currencies 'reduced the [Asian] tigers to whimpering kittens and forced them to seek help from international agencies' (*The Straits Times*, 3 March 1998). To some neoliberal observers (e.g. Krugman, 1998; Montes, 1998), the crisis was an inevitable outcome of economic globalization as global financial integration had made capital flows much more mobile and the regional impact of a local crisis much more rapid and serious. As shown in Table 5.2, global capital inflows to Asia in 1995 and 1996 were extremely high at US\$95.8 billion and US\$110.4 billion respectively, compared with US\$40.1 billion during 1990–4 and US\$16.7 billion during 1983–9. In this reading of the crisis, little power and autonomy was given to the domestic actors in these Asian economies, that is, firms and states. Instead, the crisis was seen as an externally driven disciplinary action imposed by economic globalization on what otherwise might be deemed corrupt and crony Asian capitalist economies. To neoliberal believers in the 'Washington consensus', excessive exposure to economic globalization brought an end to the Asian miracle in which Chinese capitalism was and still is an integral component. The opaque and closely-knit nature of Asian capitalism (and, by inference, Chinese capitalism) became the natural culprit responsible for the crisis (see Hamilton, 1999d).

There were, however, other interpretations of the crisis that emerged to challenge the crony capitalism argument. A key explanation was linked to the excessive deregulation of domestic financial markets in the first instance, that allowed Asian firms to engage in massive foreign borrowing (Higgott, 1998; Wade and Veneroso, 1998; Ariff and Khalid, 2000; Noble and Ravenhill, 2000a; Chang *et al.*, 2001). Clifford and Engardio (2000: 9) argued that it is unfair to blame crony capitalism as the fundamental cause of the crisis:

Table 7.1 Exchange rates per US dollar and real GDP growth rates of Asian economies, 1991–2001

Economy	1991-6	1997	1998	1999	2000	2001
Indonesia (rupiah)						
Exchange rate	–	2,393	12,900	9,322	7,300	9,370
Real GDP growth	6.0	5.0	–13.2	0.9	4.8	3.3
Thailand (baht)						
Exchange rate	–	25.81	54.22	36.98	37.15	42.99
Real GDP growth	8.2	–1.4	–10.8	4.2	4.3	1.8
South Korea (won)						
Exchange rate	–	855	1,725	1,177	1,124	1,274
Real GDP growth	7.4	5.0	–6.7	10.9	8.8	3.0
Hong Kong[1] (HK$)						
Exchange rate	–	7.74	7.74	7.75	7.78	7.80
Real GDP growth	5.2	5.0	–5.32	3.0	10.5	1.0
Taiwan (New Taiwan $)						
Exchange rate	–	27.44	33.71	32.35	30.81	32.57
Real GDP growth	6.6	6.9	4.3	5.6	6.4	–2.2
Singapore (Singapore $)						
Exchange rate	–	1.41	1.76	1.69	1.68	1.73
Real GDP growth	8.4	8.5	0.1	5.9	9.9	–2.4
Malaysia[2] (ringgit)						
Exchange rate	–	2.49	4.50	3.80	3.80	3.80
Real GDP growth	8.9	7.3	–7.4	5.8	8.5	0.4
Philippines (peso)						
Exchange rate	–	26.33	42.16	38.85	40.46	49.25
Real GDP growth	2.7	5.2	–0.6	3.4	4.0	3.4

Sources: Hamilton-Hart (2002: Tables 7.1 and 7.2) and 2001 GDP data from http://www.worldbank.org/data/countrydata/countrydata.html, accessed on 31 March 2003.

Notes
1 Hong Kong's exchange rate against the US dollar has been pegged at US$1 to HK$7.8 since 1984.
2 Malaysia introduced capital control in September 1998 and fixed the exchange rate against the US dollar at US$1:RM$3.80.

Western finger-pointing at Asia's crony capitalism and lack of transparency rings just as hollow. The shaky foundations of East Asia's financial architecture, which were at the heart of the meltdown, were there for all to see. The foreign banks, investment houses, and portfolio managers knew these flaws intimately because they had thousands of experts on the ground. Yet they still priced their debt at rates that treated even shaky Asian corporations as rock-solid risks ... To be a politically well-connected businessman or, better yet, the son of a top leader in Jakarta or Beijing, was as good as an investment-grade bond rating for the go-go investment bankers at even some of the West's most elite financial houses.

In the absence of effective government control of domestic companies, banking supervision or even any policy coordination on borrowings and investment, excessive foreign borrowings gave rise to the real problem of illiquidity rather than insolvency in times of severe exchange-rate fluctuations (Radelet and Sachs, 1998; Webber, 2001). The massive increase in foreign debt since the early 1990s and the rush of foreign financial institutions to call in short-term loans led to the rapid escalation of the economic crisis. In other words, what started off as a local currency crisis in Thailand due to excessive borrowing of short-term foreign loans and 'bubble' tendencies eventually led to an Asia-wide economic crisis. The process seriously undermined the high debt model of Asian development that has often been referred to in the international press as crony capitalism. The Asian economic miracle first legitimized by the World Bank (1993) thus came to an abrupt end on 25 June 1997 when Thailand's new finance minister discovered the true state of his country's foreign-exchange reserves and the problems of its financial system (*The Straits Times*, 15 January 1998; see also Garnaut, 1998).

Governing Chinese family firms: corporate performance and the Asian economic crisis

In order to examine the validity of this alleged relationship between crony capitalism and the Asian economic crisis, I return to my time-series data on 157 Chinese family firms listed on the Singapore Exchange (see also Chapter 6). The notion of crony capitalism is premised on poor corporate governance arising from either excessive family ownership of the corporate sector (Johnson *et al.*, 2000; Mitton, 2002) or cozy state-business relations (infamously known as the 'moral hazard'; see Chang, 2000). As reviewed in Chapter 1, the commonly alleged nature of Chinese capitalism in the various crisis-struck economies (except South Korea) seems to conform to these premises: highly concentrated family ownership and excessive reliance on network capital. It is thus postulated that Chinese capitalism in East and Southeast Asia should be highly prone to crisis. As shown in Table 7.2, the 1997–8 Asian economic crisis has adversely affected the profitability of the 157 Chinese family firms listed on the Singapore Exchange. In 1996 they collectively enjoyed a combined after-tax profit of S$4.8 billion. In 1998, however, the figure declined very significantly by 62.5 per cent to S$1.8 billion. Data presented in Table 7.2 reveal clearly that while 144 (91.7 per cent) of these 157 Chinese family firms enjoyed after-tax profits in 1996, only 95 (60.5 per cent) of them did so in 1998. There is thus no question that a large number of these publicly listed firms suffered serious losses from the 1997–8 Asian economic crisis.

The more significant question is whether there is a direct relationship between family ownership and corporate profitability. The answer can possibly inform our understanding of a critical perspective on Asian financial

Table 7.2 Profit and loss among Chinese family firms listed on the Singapore Stock Exchange, 1996, 1998 and 2001

Profit and loss	No. (%)		
	1996	1998	2001
Profits after tax	144 (91.7)	95 (60.5)	101 (64.3)
Loss after tax	13 (8.3)	54 (34.4)	39 (24.8)
NA	0 (0.0)	8 (5.1)	17 (10.8)
Total	157 (100)	157 (100)	157 (100)

Source: Author's compilation from annual reports of companies.

markets where Chinese family firms participate as both providers and recipients of financial capital. For it might be argued, as the critics of crony capitalism would certainly have, that the more a publicly listed firm is owned and controlled by a family, the more likely it would be to suffer from major losses during the Asian economic crisis. This is because, so the argument goes, family control could result in unwieldy diversification and irrational investment decisions made by the founders and/or the patriarchs in their own personal or family interests rather than in the interests of minority shareholders and the public companies in which they have invested. Tightly coupled family ownership and control also tends to generate poorer corporate governance and a greater likelihood of the expropriation of minority shareholders in the event of financial difficulties and crises. This argument against family control of public companies was extremely influential during the post-crisis restructuring of many Asian financial markets. In Table 7.3 family shareholding is used as a proxy to measure the extent of family ownership and control and correlate the percentage of family shareholding with after-tax profits.[2] The results seem to support the crony capitalism argument since in all three years under examination (1996, 1998 and 2001), there are negative correlations between family shareholding and after-tax profits. The results for these three cases are also statistically significant ($p < 0.05$). In brief, higher family shareholdings in a Chinese family firm seem to correlate with lower after-tax profits or higher losses during the 1996–2001 period.

My evidence also lends some support to the conclusions in several recent studies on the relationship between family ownership and corporate performance. In a study of 106 Chinese family firms listed on the Hong Kong Stock Exchange in 1993, Carney and Gedajlovic (2002a: 137) identified statistically significant positive relationships between the tighter coupling of family ownership and control and dividends payouts, and negative relationships between the tight coupling of ownership and control and investment in fixed assets. Their findings suggested that tighter family ownership and control leads to a lower likelihood of

Table 7.3 Correlation between percentages of family shareholding and profits after tax of Chinese family firms listed on the Singapore Stock Exchange, 1996, 1998 and 2001

Independent variables		Profits after tax		
		1996	1998	2001
Family share percentage, 1996	Pearson correlation	-0.203^1	-0.132	-0.170^1
	sig. (2-tailed)	0.013	0.116	0.050
	n	150	142	133
Family share percentage, 1998	Pearson correlation	–	-0.115	-0.188^1
	sig. (2-tailed)	–	0.170	0.028
	n	–	144	136
Family share percentage, 2001	Pearson correlation	–	–	-0.093
	sig. (2-tailed)	–	–	0.278
	n	–	–	137

Source: Author's compilation from annual reports of companies.

Note
1 Correlation is significant at the 0.05 level (2-tailed).

corporate profitability due to higher dividend payouts and lower investment in fixed assets. Claessens *et al.*'s (2000) World Bank study of over 5,500 East Asian firms in nine economies during the 1988–96 period also showed that family control helps explain the negative relationship between control rights and market evaluation. In another study of the 1997–8 performance of 398 firms from the five crisis countries (Indonesia, South Korea, Malaysia, the Philippines and Thailand), Mitton (2002: 229) suggested that blockholders of shares who are also involved with management could have more opportunity or incentive for the expropriation of minority shareholders. Claessens *et al.* (1999) also observed that family ownership tends to reduce the likelihood of an East Asian firm filing for bankruptcy possibly at the expense of minority shareholders. This relationship thus explains the survival of some family firms despite their lower or negative profitability during the crisis.

Reconsidering my observations in Chapter 6 on changing corporate governance in Chinese capitalism, it might be useful to speculate on the relationship between the use of principal banks by Chinese family firms and their profitability. My proposition is that a Chinese family firm using more and geographically diversified principal banks before the crisis is more likely to make profits and less susceptible to losses arising from the crisis. This positive relationship can be explained on two grounds. First, different principal banks may offer different financial services and investment knowledge to a Chinese family firm. From the perspective of the recipients of credits and funds, this risk diversification and thus a diversified base of principal banks, allowed the recipients to make a more effective assessment of the global investment climate and credit availability before the onset of the crisis. An excessive reliance on a single or a few principal banks may reduce the potential repertoire of market information and financial knowledge available among a diverse pool of principal banks. Second, the role of personal relationships and relationship banking is less likely to be effective when the number of principal banks increases, which reduced the propensity for expropriation and fraud before the crisis. Principal banks may have divergent credit requirements and risk-assessment procedures that put significant constraints on both the corporate governance and investment strategies of a Chinese family firm. We can thus infer that through diversifying principal banks, a firm wants to tap into the financial strength and knowledge of the chosen principal banks rather than to secure capital and credits through personal relationships. This kind of firm is also more likely to engage in professional management, impersonal decision-making and sound corporate governance.

In Table 7.4 the total number of principal banks of Chinese family firms and their after-tax profits in 1996, 1998 and 2001 is correlated. The

Table 7.4 Correlation between the use of principal banks and profits after tax of Chinese family firms listed on the Singapore Stock Exchange, 1996, 1998 and 2001

Independent variables		*Profits after tax*		
		1996	*1998*	*2001*
Total no. of principal banks, 1996	Pearson correlation	0.567[1]	0.211[2]	−0.059
	sig. (2-tailed)	0.000	0.032	0.560
	n	111	104	99
Total no. of principal banks, 1998	Pearson correlation	–	0.288[1]	−0.044
	sig. (2-tailed)	–	0.004	0.673
	n	–	98	93
Total no. of principal banks, 2001	Pearson correlation	–	–	−0.055
	sig. (2-tailed)	–	–	0.612
	n	–	–	87
No. of non-Singapore principal banks, 1996	Pearson correlation	0.586[1]	0.293[1]	−0.021
	sig. (2-tailed)	0.000	0.003	0.835
	n	111	104	99
No. of Singapore banks as principal banks, 1996	Pearson correlation	0.288[1]	−0.058	−0.121
	sig. (2-tailed)	0.002	0.558	0.232
	n	111	104	99

Source: Author's compilation from annual reports of companies.

Notes
1 Correlation is significant at the 0.01 level (2-tailed).
2 Correlation is significant at the 0.05 level (2-tailed).

positive and statistically significant correlations between the number of principal banks and after-tax profits in 1996 and 1998 support my proposition that a larger number of principal banks before the crisis might have led to a higher propensity for profitability in a Chinese family firm during the crisis. There is apparently a difference between the use of Singapore and non-Singapore banks as principal banks. Although both types of principal banks are positively correlated with the after-tax profits of these firms in 1996, the number of non-Singapore principal banks remains positively correlated with after-tax profits in 1998. The negative correlation between the number of Singapore principal banks and after-tax profits in 1998 seems to imply that the direct involvement of Chinese family banks in Singapore's corporate sector has a negative impact on profitability during the crisis. The statistically insignificant (negative) results for after-tax profits in 2001 imply that the relationship between principal banks and corporate performance tends to be less straightforward during non-crisis periods. Still, these findings establish the significant role of a diversified pool and geographical origin of principal banks in ensuring the profitability and good corporate governance of Chinese family firms. To a certain extent, it explains why many Chinese family firms have moved away from the traditional model of financing their business activities through network capital. There are clear benefits for those Chinese family firms that rely less on the culture of familism and more on the practice of professionalism and sound governance structures through their diversification of principal banks beyond other Chinese family banks. To ensure sound corporate governance and credibility, many listed Chinese family firms have increasingly opted for international accounting firms as their principal auditors (see Chapter 6). As seen in Table 7.5, more loss-making Chinese family firms experienced changes in their auditors in 1996, 1998 and 2001 (statistically significant in 1998). In all three years, 20.5–27.3 per cent of loss-making Chinese family firms changed their auditors, compared with 10–13.8 per cent of profitable firms.

Chinese capitalism under siege: a case of network failure

The analysis on pages 236–7 lends some support to the crony capitalism argument, although the extent of the negative impact of family ownership on corporate performance during the Asian economic crisis was mediated both by the number and the geographical spread of their principal banks and by their use of big six auditors. How then did the crisis put some key actors in Chinese capitalism under siege and yet open up new possibilities for others? There follows some case studies of how ethnic Chinese firms and nation-states in East and Southeast Asia negotiated the crisis. The first concerns the overexposure of a Hong Kong-based investment bank in Indonesia and its subsequent collapse. It is a typical case of Chinese capitalism that went wrong when the network failed. The next two are

Table 7.5 Relationships between change of auditor and profits after tax of Chinese family firms listed on the Singapore Stock Exchange, 1996, 1998 and 2001

	Auditor change		
	Yes (%)	*No (%)*	*Total (%)*
1996			
Loss	3 (27.3)	8 (72.7)	11 (100.0)
Profit	18 (13.8)	112 (86.2)	130 (100.0)
Total	21 (14.9)	120 (85.1)	141 (100.0)
1998[1]			
Loss	12 (24.0)	38 (76.0)	50 (100.0)
Profit	9 (10.0)	81 (90.0)	90 (100.0)
Total	21 (15.0)	119 (85.0)	140 (100.0)
2001			
Loss	8 (20.5)	31 (79.5)	39 (100.0)
Profit	12 (12.0)	88 (88.0)	100 (100.0)
Total	20 (14.4)	119 (85.6)	139 (100.0)

Source: Author's compilation from annual reports of companies.

Note
1 Chi-square = 4.9; d.f. = 1 ($p < 0.05$).

about the role of nation states as an intervening factor in transforming Chinese capitalism. Together, these case studies show how key actors in Chinese capitalism might take advantage of new opportunities arising from diverse national responses to the crisis.

On 12 January 1998, Peregrine Investment Holdings Ltd, Asia's leading home-grown investment bank with 1,700 employees, announced that it was filing for liquidation, making it a major casualty of Asia's economic meltdown (*The Straits Times*, 14 January 1998; see also Yeung, 1999b: 16–18). On the very same day, the Hong Kong Stock Exchange fell by 8.7 per cent in one day. The collapse of the Hong Kong investment house was the first major bankruptcy in Hong Kong since the territory had reverted to mainland Chinese rule on 1 July 1997. Peregrine fell victim to a single massive bad loan in Indonesia and it was undone by the very practices it came to personify and the international media often celebrated: highly risky ventures, questionable partners and reliance on personal, often political, connections. The story of Peregrine's collapse involves a highly suspicious bond issue and a key political mover, Mrs Rukmana, who was the daughter of the former Indonesian president Suharto and the vice-chairman of the then ruling Golkar Party in Indonesia. Among other business interests, Mrs Rukmana controlled an Indonesian toll company and when she decided to lend her name and patronage to a local taxicab entrepreneur as part of an equity swap, Peregrine's doomed fate began.

The taxicab franchise holder was Yopie Widjara, an ethnic Chinese Indonesian educated in Australia with grandiose plans and a reputation, among those who knew him, as a smooth-talking wheeler-dealer. Peregrine agreed to loan him US$260 million in the form of an unsecured bridging loan (a third of Peregrine's capital) as the cost of underwriting bonds in his PT Steady Safe taxicab company. He had big dreams of becoming a transportation czar by creating a series of car ferries linking the islands of Indonesia's sprawling archipelago. For Peregrine, the situation began to spin out of control when the economic crisis hit Asia in the summer of 1997. Peregrine was stuck with bonds no one wanted to buy, as its traditional Asian investors turned away. The devastating devaluation of the Indonesian rupiah in July 1997 (see Table 7.1) further aggravated the situation, when PT Steady Safe stock became almost worthless overnight. From a high of 3,240 rupiah per share before the economic crisis in 1997 to about 300 rupiah per share in dollar terms in January 1998. Peregrine, as a result, could never expect PT Steady Safe – no longer so 'steady' and 'safe' now – to repay its bridging loan.

On 18 November 1997, Peregrine announced that Zurich Centre Investments (ZCI), an arm of the Zurich Group, would take a 24.1 per cent stake (US$200 million) in Peregrine, making it its largest shareholder. Philip Tose, chairman of Peregrine, said that the Swiss investment 'not only strengthens our substantial capital base but also deepens our relationship with a well-respected multinational company that brings to Peregrine extensive financial services knowledge and technical expertise' (quoted in *The Business Times*, 18 November 1997). On 9 January 1998, however, the deal with the Zurich Group fell apart as the depth of Peregrine's problems became apparent. The pull-out by the Zurich Group and Peregrine's failure to find a new buyer meant that Peregrine became insolvent just about one decade after making its first debut in the Asian financial market. The Peregrine case serves to demonstrate the inherent risk of engaging in globalization and the limits to Chinese capitalism. Because of its 18 founding shareholders and reputable local partners, it was able to build up significant relationships with existing and potential clients that gave rise to its distinctive competitive advantage (see Yeung, 1998a: 220–3). It exploited network capital concept from both fronts. First, it managed to establish its regional network of operations to serve clients from existing networks and potential customers in host countries. The strength of the Peregrine Group was predicated on its local presence through extensive networks of partnership.

Second, the Peregrine Group developed extensive networks of personal and business relationships that formed its core competencies. The ability to develop the group's activities in the major countries of Asia was considerably enhanced by its core strategy of establishing partnerships with prominent industrial and business entities. The group's Asian partners provided an important understanding of local markets and allowed for rapid market penetration. These partners often assisted in the development of local businesses and participated in certain of the group's investments. This network gave the group its strength and breadth that few other regional investment banks could match. From an equity base of US$38 million in 1988 when Peregrine was established, it ballooned to US$864 million by the end of 1996. This huge success enabled Peregrine to leapfrog Jardine Fleming Securities to become Asia's largest independent investment bank in 1996 (Clifford and Engardio, 2000: 77). One senior staff member from Peregrine once commented that they had 'serious, deep relationships throughout Asia' with such key figures as Li Ka-shing, Gordon Wu, CITIC Pacific managers and the generals who ruled Myanmar. When CITIC decided to buy a stake in Hong Kong Telecom (renamed Cable & Wireless HKT in 1999) in 1993, it called Morgan Stanley for advice on the financing. However, CITIC's stake in Peregrine automatically qualified the latter to have a role in the deal, ending Morgan Stanley's hope for an exclusive role (*Far Eastern Economic Review*, 9 May 1996: 72).

Tose once professed proudly that the Peregrine way was to 'sit down over a cup of tea with the top guy; there isn't documentation; the deal is done' (quoted in *The Economist*, 12 November 1994: 24). In another interview, he complained that American investment firms were too slow and unresponsive to compete in Asia, particularly in mainland China. He further boasted that 'we are prepared to look at anything and can commit significant sums of money very quickly. At the end of the day, two people make the decisions – myself and Francis [Leung, managing director]. We don't run this company by committee' (quoted in Clifford and Engardio, 2000: 77). For example, when Li Ka-shing's Cheung Kong Holdings decided to do a huge share placement in Hong Kong in early 1996, the proposed plan was declined by Morgan Stanley after 20 minutes of evaluation. But when Li Ka-shing went to Peregrine (Li was a large shareholder of Peregrine), the smaller but much more aggressive Hong Kong brokerage found its match. Without any hesitation, Peregrine stepped in to assume the risk and lead-manage the US$679 million deal (*Far Eastern Economic Review*, 9 May 1996: 70). Tose's huge confidence in Cheung Kong and relationship with Li Ka-shing went all the way back to the late 1970s when Tose served as a broker for the London firm Vickers da Costa (Clifford and Engardio, 2000: 76–7). After Li Ka-shing's Cheung Kong successfully absorbed Hutchison Whampoa in 1977, in one of the earliest ethnic Chinese takeovers of a major British *hong* in Hong Kong, Li asked Tose to place a 20 per cent share of the Cross Harbour Tunnel and the deal was concluded in 30 minutes, in a way not too dissimilar from the 1996 placement of Cheung Kong shares. According to Clifford and Engardio (2000: 76–7), '[t]hanks to Tose, Cheung Kong won a huge following of institutional investors, enabling Li to raise the low-cost equity capital he needed to expand more aggressively' (see also the case study of Li Ka-shing in Chapter 5).

Yet it is clear that Peregrine's too great a reliance on network relationships and crony capitalism eventually brought down the whole group. The point here is that the reliance on *guanxi* or network relationships and political-economic alliances, a defining feature of Chinese capitalism in East and Southeast Asia, did not always give Peregrine advantages. After its failed ventures in Myanmar and Vietnam, Tose admitted that 'We got a little too big-headed. We thought we could do anything in Asia, and Myanmar and Vietnam were mistakes. We were in businesses that we didn't really understand. We thought we had people who knew those businesses that we backed. And when they began to go wrong, of course we didn't have any expertise to put them right' (quoted in *Asia, Inc.*, December 1997/January 1998: 31). Global financial integration and the Asian economic crisis indeed put Peregrine under siege to the extent of no return. What is equally amazing is that Peregrine's powerful actor-networks within Chinese capitalism failed to save its untimely demise, thereby signalling the end of an era of Chinese capitalism that is defined by cultural specificity and family orientation in business practices and economic behaviour.

Transforming Chinese capitalism: the state as an intervening actor

The Asian economic crisis not only exposed the inherent instability of globalization as a complex set of dynamic countervailing tendencies, but also shifted our attention away from the Asian miracle to the structural weaknesses of Asian economies. As far as Chinese capitalism in East and Southeast Asia is concerned, one of the most significant transformative forces comes from the dissipation of what Yoshihara (1988) called 'ersatz capitalism' a term that refers to the rent-seeking behaviour of Southeast Asian Chinese capitalists through political-economic alliances with dominant ruling elites (see also Chapter 1). This structural transformation in the political economy of Southeast Asian countries is likely to increase competition within and between ethnic Chinese and non-Chinese business communities (Yeung, 2000c). Several concurrent movements in the aftermath of the crisis have heralded the imminent demise or at least significant transformations of ersatz capitalism in East and Southeast Asia. In particular, social movements towards greater democratic participation by the people in the political process and a much more transparent governance system have been organized in Indonesia and Malaysia. In Indonesia, student movements in early 1998 not only brought down the Suharto regime, but also led to an early parliamentary election on 7 June 1999, after which the opposition party Democratic Party-Perjuangan (Struggle), led by Megawati Sukarnoputri, emerged as the winner. For the first time in its history, Indonesia has a democratically elected president. In Malaysia, the sacked former deputy prime minister Anwar Ibrahim, his wife and his supporters have established the Parti Keadilan Nasional and reorganized the opposition to contest the dominant ruling party. These social and political movements have raised the political awareness of people in Southeast Asia in their quest for the political and economic reforms necessary if these countries are to reap the full benefits of globalization and development. These movements have also challenged the long existence of ersatz capitalism and called for the demolition of unjust monopolies and special privileges held by certain ethnic Chinese and indigenous people.

This brings us to another type of movement that is primarily concerned with economic reforms in post-crisis Southeast Asia countries. The new reform movements have important ramifications for Chinese capitalism because of the loss of monopolistic positions and the collapse of political-economic alliances, two pre-crisis strategies aggressively pursued by ethnic Chinese in the economic realm of East and Southeast Asia (see Chapter 1). The structural reforms imposed by the IMF on Indonesia and Thailand have led to the loss of many monopolistic positions long held by ethnic Chinese elites (see Chapter 5 for the case of Mohammad 'Bob' Hasan and IMF conditionality). The reworking of Chinese capitalism in Indonesia explains why the net worth of several leading ethnic Chinese actors in Indonesia decreased so significantly after 1999 (see Table 1.6). By 2003, none of the ethnic Chinese elites in Indonesia were making it to the *Forbes* list of the world's richest billionaires.

Political shake-ups in some Southeast Asian countries have also contributed to the collapse of certain political-economic alliances between ethnic Chinese rent-seekers and their political patrons. This phenomenon is best seen in Malaysia. As discussed in Chapter 3, the Malaysian government has been pursuing an ethnic-biased *bumiputra* policy, since the New Economic Policy inaugurated in 1971, to enable indigenous Malays to take control of the Malaysian corporate sector. Its logic rests on attempts at an 'ethnic bypass' through which the *bumiputra* can collaborate with foreign partners in order to avoid excessive dependence upon ethnic Chinese in Malaysia (Jomo, 1997; Gomez, 1999). Under the *bumiputra* policy there is a 30 per cent ceiling on shareholdings by foreigners, whereas a minimum of 30 per cent of any local company's stake must be owned by the *bumiputra* Malays. This policy is unpopular particularly among the Malaysian Chinese who see the *bumiputra* policy as a political instrument to contain their continuing expansion in commerce and industry. It has also been highly contested by foreign companies operating in Malaysia. For example, the issue surfaced in 1998 and threatened to scuttle World Trade Organization talks on trade liberalization. The US was upset that Malaysia would not allow the insurance giant American International Group to retain 100 per cent control over its long-established local subsidiary in Malaysia. Despite sustained pressure from the US, Malaysia refused to budge (*The Straits Times*, 11 February 1998). As a consequence of the *bumiputra* policy, many Malaysian Chinese have made good use of political patronage by *bumiputra* Malay politicians to gain privileged access to state contracts and licences (Jesudason, 1989, 1997; Hara, 1991; Heng, 1992; Gomez and Jomo, 1997; Gomez, 1999). In return, these political patrons are given company directorships and shares to compensate for their 'contributions' to corporate development. Ethnic Chinese capital was, and still is, subservient to Malay *bumiputra* hegemony, as Gomez (1999: 192–3) observed in his analysis of political patronage among nearly 40 Malaysian Chinese-controlled companies listed on the Kuala Lumpur Stock Exchange.

The Asian economic crisis and the stock-market plunge, however, crippled many Malaysian companies, particularly those owned by Malay *bumiputra* entrepreneurs. This unintended consequence of Malaysia's participation in the global economy forced the National Economic Action Council (NEAC), a high-powered council established by the prime minister to get the Malaysian economy back on track to high growth rates, to consider what previously was unthinkable – allowing non-*bumiputra* Malaysians and foreigners to own larger shares in local companies (*The Straits Times*, 21 February 1998, 24 July 1998). Although Malaysia suffered from the downside of global financial integration when it saw the ringgit and local stock market plunging heavily in October 1997 (see Table 7.1), the state continued to contest globalization by engaging in stronger regional cooperation to promote mutual financial stability (Higgott, 1999). Malaysia also resisted the temptation of asking the IMF for financial assistance. The opening of the Malaysian corporate sector can thus be seen as a pragmatic response by the state to meet the challenges of globalization. To ruling Malay politicians, there was no way out of the crisis but to relinquish the indigenous control of certain companies for the good of the larger economy. The move would signal to the world that Malaysia was willing to take the most politically sensitive move to turn the economy round. It must be noted, however, that this was not the first time Malaysia had liberalized its economy (Jomo, 1997). The deep crisis of the mid-1980s also accelerated economic liberalization first started by Prime Minister Mahathir, who came to power in 1982. In 1986, the Malaysian government discreetly suspended its New Economic Policy and inaugurated a range of measures to liberalize its investment climate and to attract foreign investors, in particular those from Japan and Taiwan. This liberalization movement, however, was not quite as radical as the one in 1997–8 because Malaysia, like many other Asian countries, was badly affected by the Asian economic crisis.

By the late 1990s, the fundamental problem confronting many local *bumiputra* companies in Malaysia was that the ringgit devaluation and stock-market plunge led to high costs of importing materials and intermediate products for production and financial strain because of the lack of working capital. As revealed by Tun Daim Zainuddin, then the head of the NEAC and Minister with Special Functions, the crisis impacted more on *bumiputra* companies than others. The market value of equity held by these companies dropped by 54 per cent between July 1997 and February 1998. The overall *bumiputra* equity ownership in public companies at market value fell from 29 per cent in June 1997 to 27 per cent in February 1998 (*The Straits Times*, 24 July 1998). To resolve the problem of capital shortage, he initiated a bold move in early 1998 that allowed non-*bumiputra* Malaysians to inject new capital into ailing *bumiputra* companies in order to save them from bankruptcy. In certain strategic industries (e.g. banking, automobiles, aerospace and shipping industries), the 30 per cent ceiling on foreign ownership remained effective. Otherwise, the 30 per cent *bumiputra* corporate ownership requirement was to be calculated on an economy-wide basis, rather than on the basis of individual firms. In the manufacturing sector, the government lifted equity and export conditions on all new manufacturing projects after 1 August 1998, including those meant for expansion and diversification. Before this policy change, only industries exporting over 80 per cent of their products were given the flexibility of 100 per cent equity ownership. With some exemptions, local Malaysians and foreigners were allowed to engage in wholly owned new manufacturing projects established before 31 December 2000 (*Sunday Times*, 2 August 1998). This relaxation of equity ownership restrictions effectively opened up new economic opportunities for cash-rich Malaysian Chinese firms to acquire and take control, at much lower costs now, of many local companies previously majority-owned by *bumiputra* Malays. Although some critics regarded the ownership relaxation as a political statement rather than a real policy change, the NEAC did promise that non-Malays and foreign investors who took stakes in ailing local companies would not be pressured to give up their shares once the economy recovered (*The Straits Times*, 28 February 1998, 24 July 1998).

The Asian economic crisis also severed political-economic alliances in other ways. Tun Daim Zainuddin, then NEAC executive director, compelled some Malaysian Chinese who had previously benefited from political-economic alliances to take over ailing companies controlled by politically well-connected *bumiputra* Malays. This was part of the state's recapitalization programme through which it, represented by the NEAC, intended to reflate the economy in order to jump-start economic recovery under conditions of foreign-exchange control and restricted global capital flows. Several well-connected Malaysian Chinese actors were specifically asked by Daim to bail out debt-ridden companies. Among them were Francis Yeoh, the beneficiary of the highly profitable power-generating licence (YTL Group), and Lim Goh Tong who depended heavily on the renewal of his lucrative casino licence to sustain his Genting casino and resort businesses (Gomez, 1999). Other Malaysian Chinese elites well connected to the sacked former deputy prime minister Anwar Ibrahim, however, suffered badly from the demise of their political patron. Some of them stumbled to identify themselves with such new political patrons as

Daim Zainuddin. Others failed to relinquish their association with Anwar and became subjects of politically inspired corporate investigations. In the general assembly of the ruling party in 1999, Prime Minister Mahathir provided details of all individuals, ethnic Chinese and *bumiputra* Malays, who had benefited from Anwar's reign as deputy prime minister and finance minister. In July 1999, Malaysia experienced the biggest-ever corporate clean-up. It was rumoured that a witch-hunt was on against Anwar's businessmen cronies (again both ethnic Chinese and *bumiputra* Malays) after the Securities Commission decided to charge a top stockbroker, Tony Tiah, with abetting another businessman to defraud Omega Securities of RM$425 million (*The Straits Times*, 6 August 1999, 13 August 1999). The economic crisis therefore opened up new opportunities for Malaysian Chinese to venture into business sectors previously closed to non-*bumiputra* participation. These opportunities, however, were complicated by political favours to bail out ailing state and/or Malay companies and internal political struggles.

Challenging Chinese capitalism: the liberalization of domestic economies

In other Southeast Asian countries, ethnic Chinese actors are facing much greater competition emanating from the growing liberalization of domestic economies to foreign investors. Although the excessive liberalization of short-term foreign borrowing in many Southeast Asian economies was at least partially responsible for the Asian economic crisis, many real sectors of these economies were highly regulated and remained closed to foreign investors. Banks and other financial institutions in Southeast Asia, for example, were well protected against foreign competition. In Indonesia, Malaysia and Thailand, state agencies or cronies of political patrons often controlled major financial institutions (Backman, 1999; Hamilton-Hart, 2002). Many of these cronies were ethnic Chinese and their family members. In Indonesia alone, for example, there were more than 200 private banks before the crisis. These banks were often part of large non-banking conglomerates engaging in the property and manufacturing sectors. In consequence, Backman (1999: 84) remarked that 'Indonesia's banking sector is the most compromised of all Asia's banking sectors'. The performance of these banks was often evaluated not on the basis of their operational efficiency and competitiveness, but rather on their political connections and loyalty.

The crisis contributed to the major restructuring of the banking and finance industry in Southeast Asian economies. More foreign ownership had been allowed in view of the imminent prospect of major bankruptcy among banks in ailing Southeast Asian countries. In Indonesia and Thailand, foreign financial institutions made significant corporate inroads and acquired several domestic banks and related financial institutions. On 16 October 1998, the Indonesian parliament approved a landmark bill that allowed 100 per cent foreign ownership of banks. The move aimed to attract foreign capital to strengthen its disaster-hit banking sector (*The Straits Times*, 17 October 1998). On 8 June 1999, the Indonesian government put in place regulations to make it easier for ailing companies to swap debt for equity (*The Straits Times*, 12 June 1999). Till then, Indonesian companies had been saddled with over US$60 billion in foreign borrowings. The new laws allowed foreign creditors to take over new holding companies or to fully acquire existing ones, lifting previous restrictions on foreign ownership. Despite these new initiatives put in place by the Indonesian government, foreign investors remained cautious in taking over failed Indonesian banks. In May 2000, for example, the government attracted only lukewarm interest among foreign investors in acquiring a 22.5 per cent stake in Bank Central Asia, formerly the largest private bank in Indonesia, controlled by a powerful ethnic Chinese, Liem Sioe Liong (Hamilton-Hart, 2002: 158).

In Malaysia, the imposition of capital and foreign exchange controls on 1 September 1998 gave domestic banks some breathing space to recapitalize their reserves. But the same measure also backfired because foreign capital hesitated to invest in Malaysia's financial sector. On 29 July 1999, the central bank, Bank Negara, issued a directive to consolidate Malaysia's 21 commercial banks, 25 finance companies and 12 merchant banks into six major banking groups (*The Straits Times*, 31 July 1999). In this restructuring exercise, banks controlled by ethnic Chinese, mostly family-owned, lost their favour with Bank Negara and were absorbed into other banking groups. As Ali A.H. Sulaiman, then Bank Negara governor, said, 'there was no place for family-run banks to survive in the long run in the face of globalization' (*The Straits Times*, 12 August 1999). Indeed, the exercise saw eight Chinese-controlled banks merging into two banking groups led by Public Bank (controlled by Teh Hong Piow) and Southern Bank (controlled by Khoo Kay Peng). Two losers in the merger plan, both ethnic Chinese banking groups, were seen as having links to the former deputy prime minister, Anwar Ibrahim: Hong Leong Bank (controlled by Quek Leng Chan) and PhileoAllied Bank. Two other *bumiputra* losers, RHB-Sime Bank and Arab-Malaysian Bank, were well regarded professionally, but out of favour politically (*The Straits Times*, 3 August 1999). Multi-Purpose Bank, the smallest among the six proposed core banks with only RM$7.2 billion in assets, absorbed three larger financial institutions, including the newly merged RHB-Sime Bank that was eight times larger (*The Straits Times*, 23 August 1999). The central bank later modified this hard-line approach by increasing capital requirements for bank-based groups and leaving the choice of merger partners to the banks. By December 2000, 50 financial institutions had been consolidated into ten major banking groups, representing 94 per cent of the total assets of Malaysia's domestic banking sector (Hamilton-Hart, 2002: 165).

Singapore, as a relatively unscathed Southeast Asian economy (see Table 7.1), moved swiftly to liberalize its financial sector in order to become more competitive in the regional and global financial markets. In May 1999, the Singapore government announced the most comprehensive liberalization programme ever for the banking sector, which had serious implications for three of the four largest local banks controlled by ethnic Chinese families: OUB, OCBC and UOB (see also Chapter 6). The objectives of the programme were to encourage banks in Singapore to be efficient and innovative, to nurture robust local banks which could stand up to leading international banks and to encourage strong foreign banks to take a stake in Singapore's financial system. The deputy prime minister, Lee Hsien Loong (also chairman of the central bank, the Monetary Authority of Singapore), declared that 'the banking environment is being transformed, in the region and globally. Existing franchises and market shares are being challenged. Competition, not protection, is the only way to develop strong local banks which measure up, against the best international players' (quoted in *The Straits Times*, 17 May 1999: 38). In fact, the programme had already begun in 1990 when the Monetary Authority of Singapore (MAS) raised foreign shareholdings of Singapore banks from 20 per cent to 40 per cent. Foreign banks could compete freely with local banks in wholesale domestic banking, offshore banking, and treasury and capital market activities. They accounted for more than one-third of resident deposits, 45 per cent of loans to resident borrowers and about 90 per cent of business with non-residents (*The Straits Times*, 17 May 1999: 38). In 1995, foreign banks made up 80 per cent of total assets in Singapore's banking sector (see Table 5.3). On 17 May 1999, the Singapore government announced that by 2001, six Qualifying Full Banks (QFB) licences would be issued to foreign banks, which would be allowed to set up additional branches and off-premise automated teller machines and to share an ATM network among themselves, practices previously disallowed (*The Straits Times*, 18 May 1999: 51). The MAS would also increase the number of restricted banks from 13 to 18 by 2001 to cater to offshore banks, giving these greater flexibility in the Singapore-dollar wholesale business.

The latest round of liberalizing Singapore's banking sector had significant impact on local banks, particularly Chinese family banks, which had their interest margins squeezed with stiffer competition from 22 full-licence, 13 restricted and 98 offshore foreign banks in Singapore. These local banks had been well protected by the MAS for a long period, since no new licences for full and restricted banks had been granted since 1970 and 1983 respectively. Lee again remarked that:

> Government protection and strict MAS supervision have enabled local banks to grow into sound, well-capitalised institutions ... The present situation is not sustainable. Even if the Government does not liberalize the banking industry, local banks will be unable to maintain the status quo. Globalization and electronic delivery channels have altered fundamentally the competitive landscape. Further rapid devel-

opments in Internet banking will enable foreign banks to reach out extensively to domestic consumers, reducing and eventually neutralising the advantages of an extensive branch network and Government protection.

(Quoted in *The Straits Times*, 18 May 1999: 48)

The long-term impact of the liberalization programme on local banks was to foster mergers and acquisitions, a necessary consolidation process to achieve economies of scale for the continuing expansion and growth of the banking sector. In fact, the Singapore government had already taken the lead on 24 July 1998 by merging the state-owned Post Office of Singapore Bank (POSB) and the Development Bank of Singapore (DBS), a government-linked bank. After the merger, DBS was able to tap into the deposit-rich POSB to become a huge and possibly dominant force in the regional banking industry (*The Straits Times*, 25 July 1998). DBS was already a net lender in the interbank market before the proposed merger. According to its former chairman and CEO, Ngiam Tong Dow, DBS's aim was 'to become a regional bank with a global reach' (*The Straits Times*, 20 April 1998). It was on the prowl for more acquisitions in the Asia-Pacific region. During the crisis, DBS acquired an 85 per cent interest in an Indonesia bank, increased its stake to 50.3 per cent in Thai Danu Bank and took a 60 per cent stake in the Philippines' Bank of Southeast Asia and another 65 per cent stake in Hong Kong's Kwong On Bank (*The Straits Times*, 17 December 1998). Together, these acquisitions cost DBS more than S$330 million. After its merger with POSB, DBS enjoyed total deposits of S$59.3 billion, shareholders' funds of S$9.4 billion and total assets of S$93.4 billion, enabling it to extend its global reach into the region and beyond. Referring to HSBC Holdings, the London-based global player in the banking industry, a financial analyst said that the DBS-POSB merger represented 'the [Singapore] Government's way of forcing the pace on the private sector to re-capitalize and fulfil its wish for a HSBC here [in Singapore]' (*The Straits Times*, 25 July 1998).

What then is the impact of the banking liberalization on Singapore's three Chinese family-controlled local banks (OUB, OCBC and UOB)? Lee expected that '[t]here is room for consolidation, but we hope that there will be at least two Singapore institutions ... If we succeed in building up two such strong local banks, our financial system will have two pillars of strength and stability' (quoted in *The Straits Times*, 17 May 1999: 38, 18 May 1999: 49). Clearly, the Singapore government wanted greater synergy among these three local family banks and favoured consolidation among them into one single banking group (with DBS as the other banking group). The challenge for these three banks controlled by three different families (OUB by the Lien family, OCBC by the Lee family and UOB by the Wee family) was how to deal with strong competitive pressures in the domestic economy. The results were seen in 2001–2 when OCBC bought into Keppel-TatLee Bank (previously owned by the government-linked Keppel Group) and UOB initiated a friendly takeover of OUB to become the largest local bank in Singapore. These two family-controlled banks were also aggressively expanding abroad by opening new branches (UOB in mainland China) and/or through acquisition.

Back to the future: whither Chinese capitalism?

Predicting the future is always fraught with inherent difficulties and problems. Even an assessment of the impact of the Asian economic crisis on the future evolution of Asian capitalism can be extremely difficult, as acknowledged by Noble and Ravenhill (2000b: 33):

> If the crisis persists long enough to break up entrenched bureaucratic and business interests, yet not so long as to devastate the region's economies, it may be recalled as a turning-point, a crucial and possibly salutary node in the punctuated equilibrium of regional development. Even then, it will probably be some years before we can tell if the region is converging, for better or worse, toward an Anglo-American pattern of financial and corporate regulation, or if the world of comparative capitalism will remain as diverse as ever.

Conducting such an exercise on Chinese capitalism, an increasingly hybrid form of economic organization embedded in highly dynamic regional and national contexts, is almost impossible. With this caveat in mind, I want to make a modest attempt in this final section to outline a vision for Chinese capitalism. Instead of predicting what its evolutionary trajectories and organizational outcomes might be, I think it is more fruitful to offer an assessment of some of the critical dimensions that might sustain a viable, albeit continuously evolving and hybridizing, form of Chinese capitalism. This assessment is therefore necessarily contingent and tentative. My first point relates to the need for the continuing professionalization of economic practices in Chinese capitalism. The domination of family ownership and control may mean that Chinese family firms can be locked into the tunnel vision of their founders and/or patriarchs who may take an irrational and opportunistic expansion path to corporate development. The viability of such a culturally embedded organization in a global era is increasingly questionable. This is because '[t]he need to act in an increasingly internationalized business world imposes forms of behavior that erode Chinese exclusivity' (Brook and Luong, 1997: 16). In this sense, I agree with Backman's (1999: 79) assessment that 'in the era of the global marketplace, cultural idiosyncrasies belong anywhere but in the boardroom. Ramshackle corporate structures and patriarchal management might be quaint, but they come at an enormous cost'.

Although, for example, Peregrine had very strong alliances and connections throughout Asia, the activation of these networks and connections came with system risks because of the very nature of its lack of transparency and poor information flows. It becomes very important for Chinese family firms not only to develop and exploit networking, but also to manage networks carefully through a professional management system that assesses risk objectively and effectively. This requires the development of professionalism in management through the horizontal and vertical broadening of capabilities. The head of Peregrine's debt team was an American, Andre Lee, who came to Peregrine from Lehman Brothers. Under his direction, Peregrine won the contract of selling the PT Steady Safe bonds, after agreeing, incredibly, to underwrite them to the tune of a US$260 million bridging loan. Although Lee's superiors in Peregrine most certainly were involved in all his decisions, the case still shows the lack of a corporate management system whereby risk is objectively assessed and handled with professionalism. Of course, in times of good fortune and a world flushed with money, the story is spun to make the greed sound like a good investment. The Peregrine case therefore is an excellent, albeit tragic, reminder to key actors in Chinese capitalism that greed and lack of professionalism can quickly undo the very fortune accumulated through the very same tactics.[3]

Still, many ethnic Chinese firms in Asia will continue to rely on family control and management and this organizational pattern will not wither away in the near future, just like the continual role of family ownership in different varieties of industrial capitalism (Hamilton, 2000). Instead of pushing blindly for a wholesale retreat of family ownership in the corporate sector, I believe it is much more effective to address the investment portfolio and competitiveness of these family firms in the regional and global economy. Learning from the 1997–8 Asian economic crisis, some of these Chinese family firms obviously have too much exposure to financial and property markets, making them highly vulnerable and risky in times of economic and political crises. It becomes vital for them to diversify their investment portfolio in order to reduce this excessive exposure to any single sector. Moreover, tight family control and management can be a potential source of strength in certain sectors in which deal-making and privileged information may be critical (namely banking and finance and property development). Shifts in the global economy, however, are showing up the weaknesses of many Chinese family business groups. Sources of value-added activities are increasingly originating from technology and marketing activities that are mostly associated with professional management and sound corporate governance. While we find many very large Chinese family conglomerates in the financial and property sectors, we find very few world-class manufacturing and producer services firms owned by ethnic Chinese (Hamlin 1998, 2000; Mathews, 2002).[4] Moreover, further liberalization of markets in East and Southeast Asia will likely intensify competition from global corporations that have significant competitive advantages in almost all the segments of the value chains. With the removal of protectionist barriers, in particular non-tariff barriers, Chinese family firms in East and Southeast Asia need to step up their restructuring and reorganization efforts when faced with global competition.

It seems rather unlikely that the future of Chinese capitalism in East and Southeast Asia can continue to be sustained by political-economic alliances with powerful political elites which used to enable ethnic Chinese to accumulate capital rapidly through monopoly and franchising rights. As argued earlier, the Asian economic crisis has not only bankrupted several authoritarian states in Asia, but also seriously threatened pre-existing alliances between ethnic Chinese capitalists and ruling power elites. In Southeast Asia, continual ethnic tensions and political instability imply that coalitions with the ruling elites will no longer provide a sure guarantee to corporate success. Rather, Chinese firms must turn to their core competencies in terms of skills, technology and expertise to compete effectively against global corporations both in Southeast Asia and in the global economy. And yet a contradiction remains that these Chinese firms will face more political pressures from within the regional economies to redistribute wealth for the purposes of national security and racial harmony. This contradiction is likely to be exacerbated by the advent of globalization in Southeast Asia. As it stands, Chinese capitalism, with all its inherent strengths and weaknesses, has a long way to go before it can successfully meet the challenges of globalization. My conclusion, though tentative, is therefore that the future of Chinese capitalism in Southeast Asia cannot be conceived in terms of an exclusively indigenous process of social and institutional change. Globalization has a significant role to play in the process of continuity and change in Chinese capitalism. At the very least, globalization should be seen as a catalyst for the emergence of hybrid capitalism among Chinese business communities in Southeast Asia. Otherwise, it can serve as an active force directly shaping the developmental trajectories of Chinese capitalism in Southeast Asia (e.g. the need for liberalization and its impact on Chinese business communities). These ethnic communities are also participating actively in globalization through their strategic enrolment in globalizing actor-networks.

Elsewhere, in the predominantly ethnic Chinese economies of Hong Kong, Singapore and Taiwan, the future of Chinese capitalism will clearly be linked to the deeper integration of these economies with the burgeoning economy of mainland China and the rapid articulation of China into the global economy through trade and investment flows. While many ethnic Chinese business groups from the three economies have already spearheaded global investment drives into mainland China during the past two decades, the impact of these investment flows on the economic organization of their *home* economies remains unclear. Will Chinese capitalism remain as a viable theoretical category if the current distinction between the economic organizations of ethnic Chinese inside mainland China and those outside in East and Southeast Asia is gradually disappearing? For if mainland China succeeds in moving towards a socialist market economy, the heuristic category 'Chinese capitalism' of the variety described in this book might become a misnomer, because it can no longer occupy a conceptual privilege as a form of capitalism outside mainland China. Its many distinguishing features may cease to be unique to the three economies of Hong Kong, Singapore and Taiwan, because these economies may be increasingly absorbed into the economic organization of mainland China and thereby share the dominant form of capitalist norms and organizational practices emanating from China. Meanwhile, ethnic Chinese actors from these three economies may also transfer their economic-organizational practices to mainland China, further propelling a concurrent process of hybridization in the mainland Chinese form of socialist capitalism. We may therefore witness the emergence of a truly hybridized form of Chinese capitalism, distinguishable not in terms of its ethnic composition, but rather in terms of its geographical reach in East and Southeast Asia.

Though the debate on the future of capitalism and its varieties has not reached its logical conclusion (see Hall and Soskice, 2001a), what is clear is that there are no a priori reasons to expect Chinese capitalism to converge towards a particular model of capitalism. The future of Chinese capitalism and its dominant form of economic organization therefore remain very much an open-ended question. Cognizant of dynamic changes and transformations in the global economy, we need to take an evolutionary and non-essentialist view of Chinese capitalism. We must not repeat the mistake committed by previous studies of Chinese capitalism that made a priori assumptions about certain constant cultural traits and social norms of economic organization and subsequently produced many seriously misleading stereotypes about Chinese capitalism. In a global era, then, Chinese capitalism and its key actors cannot be essentialized as some static forms of cultural artefacts that resist change and transformations irrespective of their discursive and material practices. The course of Chinese capitalism will almost certainly be blessed with a hybrid mixture of families, networks, hierarchies and markets as the core foundations of economic organization among ethnic Chinese within and outside mainland China. Such a non-essentialist and actor-oriented conceptualization of Chinese capitalism as a form of hybrid capitalism, in my view, represents a much more useful approach to grapple with one of the greatest transformations in the complex landscape of political economies in the Asia-Pacific region during the twenty-first century – economic globalization and the reshaping of Chinese capitalism.

Appendix
Methodology of data collection and analysis

Data used in each chapter

This book is based primarily on data and information on a large number of ethnic Chinese family firms in East and Southeast Asia that I collected between 1993 and 2003. The empirical data for the firm-level analysis in Chapters 4 and 6 originate from two separate surveys of the international operations of Chinese family firms from Singapore and Hong Kong. In the first study, I conducted personal interviews with top executives from 54 ethnic Chinese firms in Singapore that own and control foreign operations and over 50 Singaporean entrepreneurs in Hong Kong and China. This empirical dataset is derived from a larger set of detailed firm-level database on the globalization of 204 Singapore-based TNCs (Yeung, 2002a). This database was developed on the basis of a large-scale research project conducted between November 1997 and January 1999. At the initial stage of this project, we entered into our database basic corporate information on some 1,246 Singapore TNCs. This information was gathered from various business directories and company reports between November 1997 and January 1998. Of these 1,246 companies, 340 companies had information only on their correspondence in mainland China, so they could not be used for our survey in Singapore. In addition, the database included 84 foreign TNCs in Singapore that were subsequently discarded in accordance with the requirements of the research project. Together, only 822 companies in our database fulfilled the preliminary requirements of being Singapore-incorporated TNCs. At the end of the survey in Singapore in January 1999, another 34 companies were disqualified because either they had been closed down (n = 11) or had no foreign subsidiaries and investments (n = 23). This left us with an effective sampling population of 788 Singapore TNCs for our corporate survey in Singapore. At the end of our survey, we successfully interviewed 204 parent companies, representing a 25.9 per cent response rate. Some 54 of these 204 parent companies (26.5 per cent) were owned and managed by ethnic Chinese families.

Empirical data in the second study are based on a sample of 73 ethnic

Chinese firms from Hong Kong that engaged in international operations in East and Southeast Asia. The original study of TNCs from Hong Kong was based on field research in Hong Kong and Southeast Asia in 1994 and 1995 (Yeung, 1998a, 2000j). Updates on some sampled companies were also conducted in 1997 to ensure consistency of information on their ownership and control patterns. For the specific purpose of this book, the master sample of 113 TNCs from Hong Kong (HKTNCs) was further subdivided to distinguish those owned and operated by ethnic Chinese. These firms were defined as ethnic Chinese HKTNCs. This subsampling process resulted in 73 ethnic Chinese HKTNCs having operations in at least one Southeast Asian country. Another variable was introduced into the subsampling process: ethnic Chinese family firms, defined here as Hong Kong firms owned and controlled by at least two generations of ethnic Chinese and their immediate family members (e.g. father and son). Family ownership and control was defined as the family having the largest shareholding in and management control of the HKTNC. This family-controlled HKTNC could be listed on the Hong Kong Stock Exchange (e.g. Li & Fung) or incorporated as a private limited company (e.g. Esquel Garment Group). If none of the family members was involved in management control, a HKTNC would be defined as non-family-controlled. This definition might be biased against newly established Chinese firms because their owners and top executives might not have passed down their shareholding and control to family members and these firms might turn into family-controlled firms in future.

In Chapter 6, I have presented a third set of empirical data that originate from a study of 157 Chinese family firms listed on the Stock Exchange of Singapore in 1996 (Yeung and Soh, 2000). Updates for 1998 and 2001 were subsequently completed in late 2002 and early 2003 at the Singapore Exchange (http://www.sgx.com). We collected data from annual reports of all 157 Chinese family firms. We manually went through the entire pool of 355 listed firms. This pool comprised both Mainboard and Sesdaq firms listed in *Companies Handbook 1997,* Parts 1–4, published by the Stock Exchange of Singapore (1998). *Companies Handbook 1997* has relevant information on all public-listed firms from 1 January 1996 to 31 December 1996. We chose 1996 as the beginning year of analysis on the hunch that the 1997–8 Asian economic crisis might have a significant impact on the corporate organization and performance of these listed companies. Since the study was concerned with the corporate governance of Chinese family firms, it would be useful to consider their corporate governance before and after the Asian economic crisis.

How then did we distinguish the archetypical category of the Chinese family firm that was so often discussed synonymously with Chinese capitalism in the literature? In defining the Chinese family firm, we took the term 'family' to mean persons related by blood or marriage. In general, the most commonly found relationships are usually that of father and son/daughter, husband and wife, and brother/sister and brother/sister. This forms the core family unit that consists of husbands, wives and/or their children. Other relationships may include family relatives related by blood or marriage, e.g. cousins, uncles, aunts and so on. We identified all family relationships in sole or substantial shareholding ownership, be it deemed or direct interest, of a particular listed Chinese family firm in Singapore. Broadly, we used three criteria to identify a Chinese family firm listed on the Singapore Exchange. The first and most obvious condition stipulated Chinese ethnicity for the family or the individual in question. The determination of ethnicity was done through two ways, first, by examining the names on the board of directors and substantial shareholdings. If the names were of Chinese origin, for example having a surname of Chen, Tan or Lee, the criterion was therefore satisfied. The second way was to confirm through telephone conversations with personnel in the respective listed firms. Secretaries or personal assistants to the chief executive officer or general manager were approached to obtain information about the relevant board of directors and also to confirm relationships between several members on the board of directors.

Our second criterion, family ownership, was the most important condition without which no evidence could be presented that a listed firm should be constituted as a 'family firm'. Substantial shareholdings listed in annual reports were considered in this case. The family (consisting of at least two individuals related by blood or marriage) had to be the largest substantial shareholder (be it deemed or direct interest) in the respective listed firm. This is a much stricter, but more accurate, definition of family ownership than the one used in recent studies of corporate finance and governance, because at least two family members and substantial shareholders must be identified in each case. In those studies, an individual ownership or blockholder of 10–20 per cent voting rights was often considered sufficient to define a family firm (e.g. La Porta *et al.*, 1999; Zang, 1999, 2000; Claessens *et al.*, 2000). Our third criteria required family members to occupy important executive positions, such as chairman, chief executive officer or managing director. This was not a necessary condition because some listed firms satisfied the second criterion without satisfying the third. In this case, professional managers might be employed to take care of the family's diverse interests.

With the above stated criteria, the pool of publicly listed firms available in the *Companies Handbook 1997* was collated manually and a database was set up to facilitate our empirical analysis. Variables were identified and data collection could be considered as raw and secondary in nature, such as consulting annual reports and making references to *Companies Handbook 1997* (Stock Exchange of Singapore, 1998) and *Singapore's Corporate Family Tree* (Datapool, 1999b). The database yielded substantial data on the internal organization of listed Chinese family firms in Singapore. Although it covered only a certain percentage of the entire population of

Chinese family firms (i.e. excluding privately owned Chinese family firms), the findings and observations gleaned from this kind of analysis can still enrich us about the realities and governance of Chinese family businesses in Singapore (Zang, 1999, 2000). Altogether, our manual exercise of going through 355 listed firms (available from *Companies Handbook 1997*) yielded a total of 157 Chinese family firms, which made up about 44.2 per cent of the total number of firms listed on the Mainboard and Sesdaq of the Stock Exchange of Singapore in 1996. Their combined activities in 1996 amounted to S$37.2 billion (turnover), S$4.9 billion (after-tax profits) and S$27.2 billion (fixed assets). About 91 per cent (n = 143) of these also satisfied all three criteria, indicating the tight coupling of family ownership, control and management. By the end of 2001, some significant corporate transformations had occurred among 45 of these 157 Chinese family firms. Some 18 of them were acquired by other firms, five of which were subsequently delisted from the Singapore Exchange. Another 13 were delisted and 14 experienced significant changes in shareholding (n = 7) and the board of directors (n = 7). These Chinese family firms' combined activities in 2001 totalled respectively S$38.8 billion (turnover), S$4.1 billion (after-tax profits) and S$36.5 billion (fixed assets).

Methods of data analysis

The empirical analysis of data presented in this book is guided by a careful combination of statistical analysis of data from my quantitative surveys of Chinese firms and in-depth case studies of key actors in Chinese capitalism (based on information gathered from qualitative personal interviews and secondary documents in the public domain). I do not purport to search for statistical regularities between abstract properties of such formal organizations as firms in order to develop universal generalizations about Chinese capitalism. As Whitley (1999: 11) pointed out so aptly,

> this style and focus of research was most institutionalized in Anglo-Saxon countries. The development of a generalizing organizational science based on statistical correlations of abstract properties of formal structures was highly consonant with prevailing conceptions of 'science' in such cultures. More significantly, it made much more sense as an intellectual programme in economies where firms combined both units of common ownership and units of authoritative integration and also tended to operate at arm's length from each other in a largely adversarial mode.

If Chinese capitalism is indeed increasingly hybridized, as evident in the empirical focus of this book, it becomes a moot point to identify the ideal-typical type of formalized and integrated firms commonly found in

Anglo-Saxon countries. My empirical analysis of the highly diversified and hybridized nature of dominant agents of economic organization in Chinese capitalism engenders 'messy' data that, with few exceptions, preclude elegant statistical manipulations. Instead, both quantitative and qualitative data are analysed in a complementary manner to tackle the different empirical dimensions of Chinese capitalism as a form of hybrid capitalism. Such a triangulation of data (Yeung, 2003c) represents a much more realistic and, perhaps, accurate depiction of the ongoing and dynamic transformations of Chinese capitalism.

Notes

1 Hybrid capitalism: demystifying Chinese capitalism

1 I use 'home' in inverted commas throughout this book because many East and Southeast Asian economies may not be the birthplace of the first and, sometimes, second generations of many ethnic Chinese people. Unless otherwise specified, the term 'economies' is used throughout this book in lieu of 'countries' because while economies like Hong Kong and Taiwan are populated by the largest concentration of ethnic Chinese outside mainland China, it is hotly debatable whether they can be known as 'countries' in their own right.

2 The term 'overseas Chinese' may be contentious to some scholars of ethnic Chinese who are living outside mainland China. The term is related to the Chinese term *huaqiao* (Chinese national abroad) that has been sharply criticized in Southeast Asia for its implications that Chinese born abroad with status as a citizen in another nation are still Chinese in essence. *Huaren* (ethnic Chinese) has become more politically acceptable. In English, overseas Chinese is usually used to include *huaqiao, huaren* and residents of Taiwan, Hong Kong and Macau (*tong bao*) who are considered to be compatriots living in parts of the territory of China temporarily outside mainland Chinese control. See Wang (1991, 1999), Bolt (2000) and Ma (2003) for the origin and status of ethnic Chinese living outside mainland China. Throughout this book, I will refer to 'ethnic Chinese' or to specific groups (e.g. Hong Kong entrepreneurs) rather than 'overseas Chinese' in my discussions of research materials. But references to the literature sometimes require the term 'overseas Chinese' to be clear. In such cases, I will use inverted commas to illustrate my discomfort with the term.

3 The term 'mainland China' will be used throughout this book to denote the People's Republic of China. Despite the claim of 'red capitalism' in post-reform mainland China (Lin, 1997), the PRC is excluded from this book's analysis mainly because private ownership and individual control of firms is indeed a very recent phenomenon in mainland China. To date, state-owned enterprises (SOEs) and town and village enterprises (TVEs) remain as the organizational backbone of China's transitional economy. The International Finance Corporation (2000: 18) estimated that in 1998 the share of GDP generated by the officially registered self-employed and private businesses amounted to 13 per cent. Another 13 per cent might be added if we make some allowance for enterprises registered as collectives but run as *de facto* private businesses (see also Tang and Ward, 2003: 107). Taken together, private businesses controlled by individual Chinese contributed to roughly one-quarter of China's GDP in 1998. My exclusion of mainland China from the analysis of Chinese capitalism thus follows Redding's (1990: 3) delimitation:

'It is however important to draw a line and make clear that this book is not about China now, and will only make passing reference to what is happening there. There will be more substantial consideration, at the end, of possible implications for, even possibly strong influence on, a notional future China, but our agenda here is the Chinese as capitalists, not as communists or socialists'.

4 I would like to thank David Ley for the origin of this idea.

5 Several detailed case studies have already been published on the globalization of leading Chinese firms from Asia in different sectors: Acer from Taiwan (Hobday, 1998; Mathews and Snow, 1998; Mathews, 2002) and Johnson Electric from Hong Kong (Ellis, 1998) in electronics, Li & Fung from Hong Kong in trading (Fung, 1995; Magretta, 1998), the Charoen Pokphand Group from Thailand in agribusiness (Brown, 1998, 2000; Pananond and Zeithaml, 1998; Goss *et al.*, 2000; Pananond, 2001), Cheung Kong from Hong Kong in property development (2001), the Hong Leong Group from Singapore in hotels (Yeung, 2000d; 2002a), and Eu Yan Sang from Singapore in traditional Chinese medicine (Yeung, 2001; 2002a; Chung, 2002).

6 This summary is based on the predominant representations of the nature of Chinese capitalism. It is structured to reflect the generalities of these arguments. Of course, there are some analysts who do not adopt such a generalist (and perhaps essentialist) perspective, but it is clear that such dissenting voices have had little impact on this field of study.

7 See, for example, Wong (1988), Redding (1990), Hamilton (1991a), Menkhoff (1993), Chan and Chiang (1994), East Asia Analytical Unit (1995), Lever-Tracy *et al.* (1996), Weidenbaum and Hughes (1996), Hefner (1998), Douw *et al.* (1999, 2001), Chan (2000), Gomez and Hsiao (2001), Menkhoff and Gerke (2002) and Yao (2002).

8 Here I support Alan Smart's (1997: 410) response to Dirlik that 'If I can be old-fashioned enough to say that these hegemonic narratives are a mixture of truth and falsity, then we must attend to the truths as well as their deceptions. Chinese local officials and Hong Kong investors alike find elements of Confucian capitalism that work and which can be mobilized to resolve some of their problems'.

9 See, for example, Hamilton (1991a; 1996c), Menkhoff (1993), East Asia Analytical Unit (1995), Redding (1995), Wong (1995), Weidenbaum and Hughes (1996), Yeung (1997a, 1998a), Haley *et al.* (1998), Tong and Yong (1998), Chan (2000) and Peng (2000).

10 Many authors have emphasized that contracts still play the most important role even in cooperative ventures among Western firms (Lewis, 1995; Willcocks and Choi, 1995; Beamish and Killing, 1997; Doz and Hamel, 1998). Having said that, it can also be argued that in a well-functioned market system, formal contracts enable businesses to be conducted among complete strangers, thereby contributing to greater transparency and economic efficiency.

11 See, for example, Limlingan (1986), Cushman and Wang (1988), Yoshihara (1988), Jesudason (1989, 1997), McVey (1992), Hicks (1993), Brown (1994, 1995a, 2000), Suryadinata (1995), Hsing (1998), Gomez (1999) and Gomez and Hsiao (2001).

12 Hsing's (1998) study is an exception in terms of its empirical focus. She examined how Chinese firms from Taiwan managed to establish themselves successfully in mainland China through complicated political-economic alliances with local and provincial authorities.

13 The 1997–8 Asian economic crisis has thrown these practices into serious question. To many neoliberal observers, the evils of the Asian economic crisis were argued to be corruption and cronyism that originated from the self-interested

and utility-maximizing behaviour of state officials and business people (e.g. Lim, 1997; Rosenberger, 1997; Emmerson, 1998; Haggard and MacIntyre, 1998; Yeung, 1999b; Haggard and Mo, 2000). See also Chapter 7.

14 My study runs parallel to other excellent studies of the emerging hybrid forms of economic organizations in transitional economies in mainland China (Nee, 1992; Guthrie, 1999, 2000) and Eastern Europe (Stark, 1996; Grabher and Stark, 1997; Stark and Bruszt, 1998, 2001). Reviewing the diverse pathways to post-socialist capitalism in Eastern Europe, Stark and Bruszt (2001: 1130) argued that 'the new hybrid game was played with institutions cobbled together partly from remnants of the past that, by limiting some moves and facilitating other strategies, gave rise to a bricolage of multiple social logics. If from these coexisting and overlapping principles they are building a distinctively postsocialist capitalism, they share with all modern societies a common feature that the social fabric is woven with multiple, discrepant systems of value'. In a similar study of China's transitional economy, Guthrie (1999: 6) contended that '[c]hanges in [mainland] Chinese organizations are part of a unique Chinese transitional path that will lead to an organizational configuration and market economic system at the end of transition that is distinctively Chinese'.

2 The dynamics of Chinese captialism: globalization and actor-networks

1 See, for example, Mittelman (1996, 2000), Cox (1997), Doremus *et al.* (1998), Held *et al.* (1999), Hirst and Thompson (1999), Olds *et al.* (1999), Guillén (2001b), Dicken (2003a) and Peck and Yeung (2003).

2 See, for example, Berger and Dore (1996), Crouch and Streeck (1997), Hollingsworth and Boyer (1997), Orrù *et al.* (1997), Hefner (1998), Whitley (1999), Guillén (2001a) and Hall and Soskice (2001a).

3 See, for example, Redding (1990), Hamilton (1991a), Gerlach (1992), Whitley (1992, 1999), East Asia Analytical Unit (1995), Weidenbaum and Hughes (1996), Orrù *et al.* (1997), Chu and Wu (1998), McNamara (1999) and Richter (1999).

4 The inverted commas acknowledge the different ways of conceptualizing such an ethnic categorization.

5 Links to regional financial markets during the 1997–8 Asian economic crisis have led the collective net worth of Asia's 57 richest tycoons to fall by US$61 billion from September 1997 to March 1998 (*The Straits Times*, 24 March, 1998: 4; see also Lever-Tracy, 2002). See also Chapter 7.

3 The internationalization of Chinese capitalism

1 This 'network advantage', however, does not necessarily work in all circumstances. See Chapter 7 for a case of 'network failure'.

2 It is useful to situate this manufacturing decline in the context of the emergence of Hong Kong as the coordination centre of cross-border manufacturing activities. Enright *et al.* (1997: 21) estimated that more than 6,000 manufacturing firms in Hong Kong were reclassified into services firms in 1992 and 1993 alone because of the closure of their Hong Kong factories. The Census and Statistics Department (2000: 91) reported that in 1998, some 6,550 trading establishments in Hong Kong had been operated as manufacturing firms before.

4 Transnational entrepreneurship

1 See, for example, Wong (1988), Redding (1990), Whitley (1992, 1999), Brown (1994), Chan and Chiang (1994), Gambe (2000), Gomez and Hsiao (2001) and Menkhoff and Gerke (2002) for over a decade of such domestically-oriented studies of Chinese entrepreneurship.

2 There is a huge literature on management and organization studies on parent-subsidiary relationships. See, for example, Alsegg (1971), Otterbeck (1981), Prahalad and Doz (1987), Bartlett and Ghoshal (1989), Birkinshaw and Hood (1998b), Harzing (1999) and Gupta and Govindarajan (2000).

3 Based on information from author's interviews with Billy Lee, president of Sembawang Marine & Logistics, in Singapore, 18 May 1998 and Ronnie Yuen, deputy general manager of Chiwan Petroleum Supply Base Co Ltd, in Shekou, China, 12 June 1998.

4 Based on information from author's interviews with Jack Teo, managing director of Hock San Yuen Food Manufacturing, in Singapore, 2 October 1998 and Pamela Heng, Operation Manager of Sunwa Construction & Interior (Pte) Ltd, in Singapore, 2 November 1998.

5 Based on information from author's interview with Richard K.M. Eu, managing director of Eu Yan Sang Holdings International, in Singapore, 24 November 1998.

6 See La Porta *et al.* (1999), Sykes (2000) and Franks *et al.* (2003) for very different interpretations of what Anglo-American capitalism should be in relation to corporate ownership and management control. While La Porta *et al.*'s (1999) study demonstrated clearly the incomplete separation between ownership and control in the largest public companies in the US and the UK, Franks *et al.*'s (2003) study showed that the evolution of corporate control among public companies in the UK remains in the hands of founding families through board membership and executive appointments. Of the three studies, Sykes (2000) made the most radical case by arguing for the reunification of corporate ownership and control among British companies to overcome their severe problems of absentee ownership, inadequate management accountability and short-termism. He identified passive absentee ownership as the fundamental weakness in corporate governance in British capitalism because 'shareholders, particularly the 80 per cent of beneficial shareholders, are not in a position to look after their shareholdings properly to reflect fully their own values and long-term interests' (Sykes, 2000: xi). Together, these recent studies of corporate governance point to the hybridized form of managerial capitalism in the US and the UK.

7 The case of Singapore's Yeo Hiap Seng, a well-known food and beverage business in East and Southeast Asia, is perhaps most instructive here. The intense rivalry between two factions of the second generation Yeo family during the early 1990s led to the eventual takeover of the family firm by another powerful family firm, Orchard Parade Holdings controlled by Ng Teng Fong, in 1994 (Brown, 2000: 75–86).

8 In fact, Eu Yan Sang International Ltd is the only company that still bears the family name today. All other companies founded by Eu Tong Sen, the second generation patriarch, have been renamed or consolidated under different holding companies.

9 The information in this section is based on author's interviews with Dr Richard Keng Mun Eu (7th son of Eu Tong Sen and former director and chairman of Eu Yan Sang Holdings Ltd) in Singapore on 15 April 1999 and his son, Richard Yee Ming Eu (Group CEO of Eu Yan Sang International Ltd in 2003) in Singapore on 24 November 1998. I also made use of many unpublished company

documents and reports, and some secondary material from local libraries and archives.

10 See Chung (2002) for a historical analysis of Eu Tong Sen's move to Hong Kong in 1928 and his eventual death in 1941. She noted that Eu Tong Sen shifted his business base from Singapore to Hong Kong because of the exponential growth in Eu Yan Sang's remittance business and the rise of Hong Kong as the powerbase of Eu Yan Sang's remittance business: 'Starting from the 1920s, the most profitable part of Eu's businesses was neither tin mining nor rubber growing, but remittance business between Southeast Asia and Southern China' (Chung, 2002: 604).

5 Transformations in social organization

1 See Clark and Wojcik (2001) for a similar analysis of the discursive construction of the Asian economic crisis through reports published in the the *Financial Times*.
2 To give a sense of the quantum of the US$12 billion bridging loan to PCCW as a set-up company, it is useful to compare with the IMF's rescue packages offered to such troubled nation-states as Indonesia (US$43 billion), Thailand (US$17.2 billion) and South Korea (US$58 billion) in late 1997 (Clifford and Engardio, 2000: Chapter 8).

6 Changing corporate governance and strategic management

1 The third government-linked bank was the Post Office Savings Bank (POSB), which merged with the Development Bank of Singapore in July 1998 (Yeung, 2000h; see also Chapter 7). As a savings bank, the POSB did not involve itself much in corporate loans to Chinese family firms.
2 This separation between ownership and management, however, did not allow Astra to escape the severe impact of the 1997–8 Asian economic crisis. Having incurred debts of US$2 billion since 1996, PT Astra was eventually sold to a consortium led by Singapore's Cycle and Carriage Corporation for US$506 million in March 2000 (Brown, 2000: 72). See Chapter 7 for more evidence and case studies of the impact of the crisis on Chinese family firms.
3 The various levels of control are measured in terms of subjective responses from interviewees along a 5-scale continuum from 'very controlled' to 'not controlled at all'.

7 The future of Chinese capitalism

1 The only exception is Hong Kong where a pegged rate of US$1 to HK$7.8 was defended at the expense of high domestic interest rates and a severe credit crunch. In Southeast Asia, the Indonesian rupiah had depreciated as much as 72 per cent against the US dollar by early 1998. Other Southeast Asian currencies also depreciated about 30–40 per cent (*The Straits Times* 3 March 1998).
2 Correlation analysis is useful here as it tells us about the direction of change between two different variables. Since I am not interested in predicting the causality of the exact change (as in regression analysis), correlation analysis is a sufficient tool for my purpose. Although the corporate finance literature often uses return on assets (ROA) or return on invested capital (ROIC) as the proxy for profitability and performance (e.g. Carney and Gedajlovic, 2002a; Mitton, 2002), I use after-tax profits as a simplified proxy for performance in my correlation analysis.

3 This discussion does not imply that greed and corruptive practices are only found in Chinese capitalism. Indeed, these qualities are associated with capitalism, wherever it is practised. The collapse of Barings Bank, the oldest merchant bank in the UK, in February 1995 serves as a good reminder of the pervasiveness of greed and rogue behaviour in global finance (see http://www.riskglossary. com/articles/barings_debacle.htm, accessed on 26 March 2003; Tickell, 1996; Clark, 1997).

4 To be fair again, some of the world's leading manufacturers and services firms today are still family-owned and controlled, e.g. Ford, Fiat, Porsche and Michelin in the automobile industry, Ericsson in the telecommunications industry, News Corp. in the media industry and Wal-Mart Inc. in the retail industry.

References

Alsegg, Richard J. (1971), *Control Relationships Between American Corporations and Their European Subsidiaries*, New York: American Management Association.

Amsden, Alice H. (1989), *Asia's Next Giant*, New York: Oxford University Press.

Amsden, Alice H. (2001), *The Rise of 'The Rest'*, New York: Oxford University Press.

Amsden, Alice H. and Chu, Wan-Wen (2002), 'Upscaling: recasting old theories to suit late industrializers', in Peter C.Y. Chow (ed.), *Taiwan in the Global Economy*, Westport, CT: Praeger, 23–38.

Anand, Jaideep and Delios, Andrew (1997), 'Location specificity and the transferability of downstream assets to foreign subsidiaries', *Journal of International Business Studies*, 28(3), 579–603.

Andersen, Otto (1993), 'On the internationalization process of firms: a critical analysis', *Journal of International Business Studies*, 24(2), 209–31.

Andreski, Stanislav (ed.) (1983), *Max Weber on Capitalism, Bureaucracy and Religion: A Selection of Texts*, London: Allen & Unwin.

Appelbaum, Richard P. (2000), 'Moving up: industrial upgrading, social networks and buyer-driven commodity chains in East Asian Chinese firms', *International Studies Review*, 3(1), 21–41.

Appelbaum, Richard P. and Henderson, Jeffrey (eds) (1992), *States and Development in the Asian Pacific Rim*, Newbury Park, CA: Sage.

Ariff, Mohamed and Khalid, Ahmed M. (2000), *Liberalization, Growth and the Asian Financial Crisis*, Cheltenham: Edward Elgar.

Asia, Inc. (1996), *The Merchant Mandarins*, Hong Kong: Asia Inc.

Asia, Inc. (December 1997/January 1998), 31. Hong Kong.

Au, Kevin, Peng, Mike W. and Wang, Denis (2000), 'Interlocking directorates, firm strategies, and performance in Hong Kong', *Asia Pacific Journal of Management*, 17(1), 29–47.

Backman, Michael (1999), *Asian Eclipse*, Singapore: John Wiley.

Baer, Werner, Miles, William R. and Moran, Allen B. (1999), 'The end of the Asian myth', *World Development*, 27(10), 1735–47.

Baliga, B. Rajaram and Jaeger, Alfred M. (1984), 'Multinational corporations: control systems and delegation issues', *Journal of International Business Studies*, 15(3), 25–40.

Barlow, Colin (ed.) (1999), *Institutions and Economic Change in Southeast Asia*, Cheltenham: Edward Elgar.

Bartlett, Christopher A. and Ghoshal, Sumantra (1989), *Managing Across Borders*, London: Century Business.

Bavishi, V. (1991), *International Accounting and Auditing Trends*, Princeton. NJ: Centre for International Analysis and Research.

Beamish, Paul W. and Killing, J. Peter (eds) (1997), *Cooperative Strategies*, San Francisco, CA: The New Lexington Press.

Becht, Marco, Betts, Paul and Morck, Randall (2003), "The complex evolution of family affairs', *Financial Times*, 2 February.

Berger, Peter L. (1986), *The Capitalist Revolution*, New York: Basic Books.

Berger, Peter L. (2002), 'Introduction', in Peter L. Berger and Samuel P. Huntington (eds), *Many Globalizations*, 1–16, Oxford: Oxford University Press.

Berger, Peter L. and Huntington, Samuel P. (eds) (2002), *Many Globalizations*, Oxford: Oxford University Press.

Berger, Suzanne and Dore, Ronald (eds) (1996), *National Diversity and Global Capitalism*, Ithaca, NY: Cornell University Press.

Berger, Suzanne and Lester, Richard K. (eds) (1997), *Made by Hong Kong*, Hong Kong: Oxford University Press.

Best, Michael H. (1990), *The New Competition*, Cambridge: Polity Press.

Best, Michael H. (2001), *The New Competitive Advantage*, Oxford: Oxford University Press.

Biggart, Nicole Woolsey and Guillén, Mauro F. (1999), 'Developing difference: social organization and the rise of the auto industries of South Korea, Taiwan, Spain, and Argentina', *American Sociological Review*, 64, 722–47.

Birkinshaw, Julian M. and Hood, Neil (1998a), 'Multinational subsidiary evolution: capability and charter change in foreign-owned subsidiary companies', *Academy of Management Review*, 23(4), 773–95.

Birkinshaw, Julian M. and Hood, Neil (eds) (1998b), *Multinational Corporate Evolution and Subsidiary Development*, London: Macmillan.

Björkman, Ingmar and Kock, Sören (1995), 'Social relationships and business networks: the case of Western companies in China', *International Business Review*, 4(4), 519–35.

Block, Fred (2002), 'Rethinking capitalism', in Nicole W. Biggart (ed.), *Readings in Economic Sociology*, 219–30, Oxford: Blackwell.

Blomstermo, Anders and Sharma, D. Deo (eds) (2002), *Learning in the Internationalization Process of Firms*, Cheltenham: Edward Elgar.

Bolt, Paul J. (2000), *China and Southeast Asia's Ethnic Chinese*, New York: Praeger.

Bond, Michael Harris (ed.) (1986), *The Psychology of the Chinese People*, Hong Kong: Oxford University Press.

Braadbaart, Okke (1995), 'Sources of ethnic advantages: a comparison of Chinese and *pribumi*-managed engineering firms in Indonesia', in Rajeswary Ampalavana Brown (ed.), *Chinese Business Enterprise in Asia*, 177–96, London: Routledge.

Braverman, Harry (1974), *Labor and Monopoly Capital*, New York: Monthly Review Press.

Bridge, Gary (1997), 'Mapping the terrain of time-space compression: power networks in everyday life', *Environment and Planning D: Society and Space*, 15, 611–26.

Brook, Timothy and Luong, Hy V. (eds) (1997), *Culture and Economy*, Ann Arbor: University of Michigan Press.

Brown, Rajeswary Ampalavana (1994), *Capital and Entrepreneurship in South-East Asia*, London: Macmillan.

Brown, Rajeswary Ampalavana (ed.) (1995a), *Chinese Business Enterprise in Asia*, London: Routledge.

Brown, Rajeswary Ampalavana (1995b), 'Introduction', in Rajeswary Ampalavana Brown (ed.), *Chinese Business Enterprise in Asia*, 1–26, London: Routledge.

Brown, Rajeswary Ampalavana (1998), 'Overseas Chinese investments in China', *The China Quarterly*, 155, 610–36.

Brown, Rajeswary Ampalavana (2000), *Chinese Big Business and the Wealth of Asian Nations*, London: Palgrave.

Brush, Candida G. (1995), *International Entrepreneurship*, New York: Garland.

Buck, Daniel (2000), 'Growth, disintegration, and decentralization: the construction of Taiwan's industrial networks', *Environment and Planning A*, 32(2), 245–62.

Buckley, Peter J. (ed.) (1994), *Cooperative Forms of Transnational Corporation Activity*, London: Routledge.

Buckley, Peter J. and Ghauri, Pervez (eds.) (1993), *The Internationalization of the Firm*, London: Academic Press.

Business Times, The, various issues, Singapore.

Callon, Michel (1986), 'Some elements of a sociology of translation', in John Law (ed.), *Power, Action, Belief*, 196–233, London: Routledge.

Callon, Michel (1987), 'Society in the making', in W. Bijker., T. Hughes and T. Pinch (eds), *The Social Construction of Technological Systems*, 83–103, Cambridge, MA: MIT Press.

Cantwell, John (1989), *Technological Innovation and Multinational Corporations*, Oxford: Basil Blackwell.

Carney, Michael (1998), 'A management capacity constraint?', *Asia Pacific Journal of Management*, 15, 137–62.

Carney, Michael and Gedajlovic, Eric (2002a), 'The coupling of ownership and control and the allocation of financial resources', *Journal of Management Studies*, 39(1), 123–46.

Carney, Michael and Gedajlovic, Eric (2002b), 'The co-evolution of institutional environments and organizational strategies', *Organization Studies*, 23(1), 1–29.

Carney, Michael and Gedajlovic, Eric (2003), 'Strategic innovation and the administrative heritage of East Asian family business groups', *Asia Pacific Journal of Management*, 20(1), 5–26.

Castells, Manuel (1996), *The Rise of the Network Society*, Cambridge, MA: Basil Blackwell.

Castells, Manuel, Goh, L. and Kwok, Reginald Yin-Wang (1990), *The Shek Kip Mei Syndrome*, London: Pion.

CDL Hotels International Ltd (1998), *Annual Report 1997*, Hong Kong: CDL Hotels International Ltd.

CDL Hotels International Ltd (2000), *Annual Report 1999*, Hong Kong: CDL Hotels International Ltd.

Chan, Kwok Bun (ed.) (2000), *Chinese Business Networks: State, Economy and Culture*, Singapore: Prentice Hall.

Chan, Kwok Bun and Chiang, See-Ngoh Claire (1994), *Stepping Out: The Making of Chinese Entrepreneurs*, Singapore: Simon and Schuster.

Chan, Wellington K.K. (1982), 'Organizational structure of the transitional Chinese firm and its modern reform', *Business History Review*, 56(2), 218–35.

Chan, Wellington K.K. (1992), 'Chinese business networking and the Pacific Rim', *Journal of American East Asian Relations*, 1(2), 171–90.

Chan, Wellington K.K. (1995), 'The origins and early years of the Wing On Company group in Australia, Fiji, Hong Kong and Shanghai', in Rajeswary

Ampalavana Brown (ed.), *Chinese Business Enterprise in Asia*, 80–95, London: Routledge.

Chan, Wellington K.K. and McElderry, Andrea (eds.) (1998), 'Historical patterns of Chinese business', special issue *Journal of Asian Business*, 14(1), 1–69.

Chandler, Alfred D. Jr (1977), *The Visible Hand*, Cambridge, MA: Harvard University Press.

Chandler, Alfred D. (1990), *Scale and Scope*, Cambridge, MA: Harvard University Press.

Chang, Ha-Joon (2000), 'The hazard of moral hazard', *World Development*, 28(4), 775–88.

Chang, Ha-Joon, Palma, Gabriel and Whittaker, D. Hugh (eds) (2001), *Financial Liberalization and the Asian Crisis*, New York: Palgrave.

Chang, Maria Hsu (1995) 'Greater China and the Chinese "global tribe,"' *Asian Survey*, 35(10), 955–67.

Chau, Theodora Ting (1991), 'Approaches to succession in East Asian business organizations', *Family Business Review*, 4(2), 161–80.

Chen, Che-hung (1986), 'Taiwan's foreign direct investment', *Journal of World Trade Law*, 20, 639–64.

Chen, Homin and Chen, Tain-Jy (1998), 'Network linkages and location choice in foreign direct investment', *Journal of International Business Studies*, 29(3), 445–68.

Chen, Min (1995), *Asian Management Systems*, London: Routledge.

Chen, Ming-Jer (2001), *Inside Chinese Business: A Guide for Managers Worldwide*, Boston, MA: Harvard Business School Press.

Chen, Tain-Jy (1992), 'Determinants of Taiwan's direct foreign investment: the case of a newly industrializing country', *Journal of Development Economics*, 39, 397–407.

Chen, Tain-Jy (ed.) (1998), *Taiwanese Firms in Southeast Asia*, Cheltenham: Edward Elgar.

Chen, Weixing (1998), 'The political economy of rural industrialization in China', *Modern China*, 24(1), 73–96.

Chen, Xiangming (1994), 'The new spatial division of labor and commodity chains in the Greater South China Economic Region', in Gary Gereffi and Miguel Korzeniewicz (eds), *Commodity Chains and Global Capitalism*, 165–86, Westport, CT: Praeger.

Chen, Xiangming (1996), 'Taiwan investments in China and Southeast Asia', *Asian Survey*, 36(5), 447–67.

Cheung Kong (Holdings) Ltd (1998), *Annual Report, 1997*, Hong Kong: Cheung Kong (Holdings) Ltd.

Cheung Kong Infrastructure Holdings Ltd (1997), *Annual Report, 1996*, Hong Kong: Cheung Kong Infrastructure Holdings Ltd.

Chew, Yoke-Tong and Yeung, Henry Wai-chung (2001), 'The SME advantage', *Regional Studies*, 35(5), 431–48.

Chiu, Catherine C.H. (1998), *Small Family Business in Hong Kong*, Hong Kong: Chinese University Press.

Chiu, Stephen W.K., Ho, Kong Chong and Lui, Tai-Lok (1997), *City-States in the Global Economy*, Boulder, CO: Westview.

Chow, Peter C.Y. (ed.) (2002), *Taiwan in the Global Economy*, Westport, CN: Praeger.

Christerson, Brad and Appelbaum, Richard P. (1995), 'Global and local subcontracting', *World Development*, 23(8), 1363–74.

Chryssochoidis, George, Millar, Carla and Clegg, Jeremy (eds) (1997), *Internationalisation Strategies*, London: Macmillan.

Chu, Yen-Peng and Wu, Rong-I. (eds) (1998), *Business, Markets and Government in the Asia-Pacific*, London: Routledge.

Chung, Stephanie P.Y. (1998), *Chinese Business Groups in Hong Kong and Political Changes in South China, 1900–1925*, London: Macmillan.

Chung, Stephanie P.Y. (2002), 'Surviving economic crises in Southeast Asia and southern China', *Modern Asian Studies*, 36(3), 579–617.

Chung, Wai-Keung and Hamilton, Gary G. (2001), 'Social logic as business logic', in Richard P. Appelbaum, William L.F. Felstiner and Volkmar Gessner (eds), *Rules and Networks*, 325–46, Oxford: Hart Publications.

Claessens, Stijn, Djankov, Simeon and Klapper, Leora (1999), *Resolution of Corporate Distress*, Policy Research Working Paper No. 2133, Washington, DC: World Bank.

Claessens, Stijn, Djankov, Simeon and Lang, Larry H.P. (2000), 'The separation of ownership and control in East Asian corporations', *Journal of Financial Economics*, 58 (1–2), 81–112.

Clark, Gordon L. (1997), 'Rogues and regulation in global finance', *Regional Studies*, 31(3), 221–36.

Clark, Gordon L., Mansfield, Daniel and Tickell, Adam (2001), 'Emergent frameworks in global finance', *Economic Geography*, 77(3), 250–71.

Clark, Gordon L. and Wojcik, Dariusz (2001), 'The City of London in the Asian crisis', *Journal of Economic Geography*, 1(1), 107–30.

Clarke, Linda, Yue, Ming and von Glinow, Mary Ann (1999), 'Chinese family business networks and regional economic development in China', in Frank-Jürgen Richter (ed.), *Business Networks in Asia*, 171–207, Westport, CT: Quorum Books.

Clegg, Stewart R. and Redding, S. Gordon (eds) (1990), *Capitalism in Contrasting Cultures*, Berlin: De Gruyter.

Clifford, Mark L. and Engardio, Pete (2000), *Meltdown: Asia's Boom, Bust, and Beyond*, Paramus, NJ: Prentice Hall Press.

Coffee, John C. (2002), 'Racing towards the top?', *Columbia Law Review*, 102(7), 1757–831.

Contractor, Farok J. and Lorange, Peter (eds) (1988), *Cooperative Strategies in International Business*, Lexington, MA: Lexington Books.

Cox, Kevin R. (ed.) (1997), *Spaces of Globalization*, New York: Guilford.

Crawford, Darryl (2000), 'Chinese capitalism', *Third World Quarterly*, 21(1), 68–86.

Crawford, Darryl (2001), 'Globalisation and guanxi', *New Political Economy*, 6(1), 45–65.

Crouch, Colin and Streeck, Wolfgang (eds) (1997), *Political Economy of Modern Capitalism*, London: Sage.

Cushman, Jennifer W. and Wang, Gungwu (eds) (1988), *Changing Identities of the Southeast Asian Chinese Since World War II*, Hong Kong: Hong Kong University Press.

Daly, George G. (1998), 'Entrepreneurship and business culture in Japan and the U.S.', *Japan and the World Economy*, 10, 487–94.

Datapool (1999a), *Singapore 1000*, Singapore: Datapool.

Datapool (1999b), *Singapore's Corporate Family Tree*, Singapore: Datapool.

Deyo, Frederic C. (ed.) (1987), *The Political Economy of the New Asian Industrialism*, Ithaca, NY: Cornell University Press.

Dicken, Peter (2003a), *Global Shift*, 4th edn, London: Sage.

Dicken, Peter (2003b), ' "Placing" firms: grounding the debate on the "global" corporation', in Jamie Peck and Henry Wai-chung Yeung (eds), *Remaking the Global Economy*, 27–44, London: Sage.

Dicken, Peter, Kelly, Philip, Olds, Kris and Yeung, Henry Wai-chung (2001), 'Chains and networks, territories and scales: towards an analytical framework for the global economy', *Global Networks*, 1(2), 89–112.

Dicken, Peter and Yeung, Henry Wai-chung (1999), 'Investing in the future: East and Southeast Asian firms in the global economy', in Kris Olds, Peter Dicken, Philip Kelly, Lily Kong and Henry Wai-chung Yeung (eds), *Globalisation and the Asia-Pacific*, 107–28, London: Routledge.

DiMaggio, Paul J. (ed.) (2001a), *The Twenty-First-Century Firm*, Princeton, NJ: Princeton University Press.

DiMaggio, Paul J. (2001b), 'Introduction', in Paul J. DiMaggio (ed.), *The Twenty-First-Century Firm*, 3–30, Princeton, NJ: Princeton University Press.

DiMaggio, Paul J. and Powell, Walter W. (1983), 'The iron cage revisited: institutional isomorphism and collective rationality in organisational fields', *American Sociological Review*, 48, 147–60.

DiMaggio, Paul J. and Powell, Walter W. (eds) (1991), *The New Institutionalism in Organizational Analysis*, Chicago, IL: University of Chicago Press.

Dirlik, Arif (1992), 'The Asia-Pacific idea', *Journal of World History*, 3(1), 55–79.

Dirlik, Arif (1997), 'Critical reflections on "Chinese capitalism" as paradigm', *Identities*, 3(3), 303–30.

Dixon, Chris (1991), *South East Asia in the World-Economy*, Cambridge: Cambridge University Press.

Doremus, Paul N., Keller, William W., Pauly, Louis W. and Reich, Simon (1998), *The Myth of the Global Corporation*, Princeton, NJ: Princeton University Press.

Douw, Leo M., Huang, Cen and Godley, Michael R. (eds) (1999), *Qiaoxiang Ties*, London: Kegan Paul.

Douw, Leo Huang, Cen and Ip, David (eds) (2001), *Rethinking Chinese Transnational Enterprises*, Richmond, Surrey, UK: Curzon.

Doz, Yves L. and Hamel, Gary (1998), *Alliance Advantage*, Boston, MA: Harvard Business School Press.

Doz, Yves L. and Prahalad, C.K. (1981), 'Headquarters influence and strategic control in MNCs', *Sloan Management Review*, 23(1), 15–29.

Dunfee, Thomas W. and Warren, Danielle E. (2001), 'Is guanxi ethical?', *Journal of Business Ethics*, 32(3), 191–204.

Dunning, John H. (1993), *Multinational Enterprises and the Global Economy*, Reading, MA: Addison Wesley.

Dunning, John H. (1997), *Alliance Capitalism and Global Business*, London: Routledge.

East Asia Analytical Unit (1995), *Overseas Chinese Business Networks in Asia*, Parkes, Australia: Department of Foreign Affairs and Trade.

Economic News, 2 February 1993, Hong Kong.

Economist, The, various issues, London.

Ellis, Paul (1998), 'Johnson Electric', *Asian Case Research Journal*, 2, 53–66.

Emirbayer, Mustafa (1997), 'Manifesto for a relational sociology', *American Journal of Sociology*, 103(2), 281–317.

Emmerson, Donald K. (1998), 'Americanizing Asia?', *Foreign Affairs*, 77(3), 46–56.

Eng, Irene (1997), 'Flexible production in late industrialization: the case of Hong Kong', *Economic Geography*, 73(1), 26–43.

Enright, Michael J., Scott, Edith E. and Dodwell, David (1997), *The Hong Kong Advantage*, Hong Kong: Oxford University Press.

Eriksson, Kent, Johanson, Jan, Majkgård, Anders and Sharma, D. Deo (1997), 'Experiential knowledge and cost in the internationalization process', *Journal of International Business Studies*, 28(2), 337–60.

Erramilli, M. Krishna, Agarwal, Sanjeev and Kim, Seong-Soo (1997), 'Are firm-specific advantages location-specific too?', *Journal of International Business Studies*, 28(4), 735–57.

Eu Yan Sang (1973), *Prospectus of Eu Yan Sang Holdings Ltd*, Singapore.

Eu Yan Sang (1980), *1980 Annual Report of Eu Yan Sang Holdings Limited*, Singapore.

Eu Yan Sang (1985), *1985 Annual Report of Eu Yan Sang Holdings Limited*, Singapore.

Eu Yan Sang (1992), *New Issue of Eu Yan Sang (Hong Kong) Limited*, Hong Kong.

Eu Yan Sang (2002), *Annual Report of Eu Yan Sang International Limited, 2002*, Singapore.

Fan, Ying (2002), 'Questioning guanxi', *International Business Review*, 11(5), 543–61.

Far Eastern Economic Review, various issues, Hong Kong.

Feenstra, Robert C., Yang, Tzu-Han and Hamilton, Gary G. (1999), 'Business groups and product variety in trade', *Journal of International Economics*, 48(1), 71–100.

Fields, Karl J. (1995), *Enterprise and the State in Korea and Taiwan*, Ithaca, NY: Cornell University Press.

Financial Times, various issues, London.

Forbes, August 1992, Hong Kong.

Franks, Julian, Mayer, Colin and Rossi, Stefano (2003), *The Origination and Evolution of Ownership and Control*, ECGI Working Papers No. 09/203, Brussels: European Corporate Governance Institute.

Fukuyama, Francis (1995), *Trust*, London: Hamish Hamilton.

Fung, K.C. (1996), 'Mainland Chinese investment in Hong Kong', *Journal of Asian Business*, 12(2), 21–39.

Fung, Victor (1997), 'Evolution in the management of family enterprises in Asia', in Gungwu Wang and Siu-lun Wong (eds), *Dynamic Hong Kong: Business and Culture*, 216–29, Hong Kong: Hong Kong University Press.

Gabor, Andrea (2000), *The Capitalist Philosophers*, New York: Times Business.

Gambe, Annabelle R. (2000), *Overseas Chinese Entrepreneurship and Capitalist Development in Southeast Asia*, London: Macmillan.

Garnaut, Ross (1998), 'The financial crisis', *Asian-Pacific Economic Literature*, 12(1), 1–11.

Gereffi, Gary (1996), 'Global commodity chains', *Competition and Change*, 1(4), 427–39.

Gerlach, Michael L. (1992), *Alliance Capitalism*, Berkeley: University of California Press.

Gertler, Meric S. (1995), '"Being there": proximity, organization, and culture in the development and adoption of advanced manufacturing technologies', *Economic Geography*, 71(1), 1–26.

Gertler, Meric S. (2003), *Manufacturing Culture*, Oxford: Oxford University Press.

Gertler, Meric S., Wolfe, David A. and Garkut, David (2000), 'No place like home? The embeddedness of innovation in a regional economy', *Review of International Political Economy*, 7(4), 688–718.

Gibson-Graham, J.K. (1996), *The End of Capitalism*, Oxford: Blackwell.

Giddens, Anthony (1992), 'Introduction', in Max Weber, *The Protestant Ethic and the Spirit of Capitalism*, vii–xxiv, London: Routledge.

Gnyawali, Devi R. and Madhavan, Ravindranath (2001), 'Cooperative networks and competitive dynamics', *Academy of Management Review*, 26(3), 431–45.

Go, Frank M. and Pine, Ray (1995), *Globalization Strategy in the Hotel Industry*, London: Routledge.

Godley, Michael R. (1981), *The Mandarin-Capitalists from Nanyang*, Cambridge: Cambridge University Press.

Goldman Sachs (1997), 'Cheung Kong Group: Proposed Restructuring', unpublished report, 10 January.

Gomes-Casseres, Benjamin (1996), *The Alliance Revolution*, Cambridge, MA: Harvard University Press.

Gomez, Edmund Terence (1999), *Chinese Business in Malaysia*, Richmond, Surrey: Curzon.

Gomez, Edmund T. and Jomo, K.S. (1997), *Malaysia's Political Economy*, Cambridge: Cambridge University Press.

Gomez, Edmund Terence and Hsiao, Hsin-Huang Michael (eds) (2001), *Chinese Business in South-East Asia*, Richmond, Surrey: Curzon.

Goss, J., Burch, D. and Rickson, R.E. (2000), 'Agri-food restructuring and Third World transnationals', *World Development*, 28, 513–30.

Grabher, Gernot and Stark, David (eds) (1997), *Restructuring Networks in Post-Socialist Societies*, Oxford: Oxford University Press.

Granovetter, Mark (1991), 'The social construction of economic institutions', in Amitai Etzioni and Paul R. Lawrence (eds), *Socio-Economics*, 75–81, Armonk, NY: M.E. Sharpe.

Granovetter, Mark (1995), 'Coase revisited: business groups in the modern economy', *Industrial and Corporate Change*, 4, 93–130.

Greenhalgh, Susan (1994), 'De-orientalizing the Chinese family firm', *American Ethnologist*, 21(4), 746–75.

Grenville, Stephen (2000), 'Capital flows and crises', in Gregory W. Noble and John Ravenhill (eds), *The Asian Financial Crisis and the Architecture of Global Finance*, 36–56, Cambridge: Cambridge University Press.

Guillén, Mauro F. (2001a), *The Limits of Convergence*, Princeton, NJ: Princeton University Press.

Guillén, Mauro F. (2001b), 'Is globalization civilizing, destructive or feeble?', *Annual Review of Sociology*, 27, 235–60.

Gulati, Ranjay, Nohria, Nitin and Zaheer, Akbar (2000), 'Strategic networks', *Strategic Management Journal*, 21(3), 203–15.

Gupta, Anil K. and Govindarajan, Vijay (1991), 'Knowledge flows and the structure of control within multinational corporations', *Academy of Management Review*, 16(4), 768–92.

Gupta, Anil K. and Govindarajan, Vijay (2000), 'Knowledge flows within multinational corporations', *Strategic Management Journal*, 21, 473–96.

Guthrie, Douglas (1998), 'The declining significance of *guanxi* in China's economic transition', *The China Quarterly*, 154, 254–82.

Guthrie, Douglas (1999), *Dragon in a Three-Piece Suit: The Emergence of Capitalism in China*, Princeton, NJ: Princeton University Press.

Guthrie, Douglas (2000), 'Understanding China's transition to capitalism', *Sociological Forum*, 15(4), 727–49.

Haggard, Stephen and MacIntyre, Andrew (1998), 'The political economy of the Asian economic crisis', *Review of International Political Economy*, 5(3), 381–92.

Haggard, Stephen and Mo, Jongryn (2000), 'The political economy of the Korean financial crisis', *Review of International Political Economy*, 7(2), 197–218.

Haley, George T., Tan, Chin-Tiong and Haley, Usha C.V. (1998), *The New Asian Emperors*, Oxford: Butterworth-Heinemann.

Hall, Peter A. and Soskice, David (eds) (2001a), *Varieties of Capitalism: The Institutional Foundations of Comparative Advantage*, Oxford: Oxford University Press.

Hall, Peter A. and Soskice, David (2001b), 'An introduction to varieties of capitalism', in Peter A. Hall and David Soskice (eds), *Varieties of Capitalism*, 1–68, Oxford: Oxford University Press.

Hamel, Gary and Pralahad, C.K. (1994), *Competing for the Future: Breakthrough Strategies for Seizing Control of Your Industry and Creating the Markets of Tomorrow*, Boston, MA: Harvard Business School Press.

Hamilton, Gary G. (ed.) (1991a), *Business Networks and Economic Development in East and South East Asia*, Hong Kong: Centre of Asian Studies, University of Hong Kong.

Hamilton, Gary G. (1991b), 'The organizational foundation of Western and Chinese commerce: a historical and comparative analysis', in Gary G. Hamilton (ed.), *Business Networks and Economic Development in East and South East Asia*, 48–65, Hong Kong: Centre of Asian Studies, University of Hong Kong.

Hamilton, Gary G. (ed.) (1996a), *Asian Business Networks*, Berlin: De Gruyter.

Hamilton, Gary G. (1996b), 'Overseas Chinese capitalism', in Wei-ming Tu (ed.), *Confucian Traditions in East Asian Modernity*, 328–42, Cambridge, MA: Harvard University Press.

Hamilton, Gary G. (1996c), 'The theoretical significance of Asian business networks', in Gary G. Hamilton (ed.), *Asian Business Networks*, 283–98, Berlin: de Gruyter.

Hamilton, Gary G. (1997), 'The organization of capitalism in South Korea and Taiwan', in A.E. Safarian and Wendy Dobson (eds), *East Asian Capitalism*, 19–44, Toronto: University of Toronto Press.

Hamilton, Gary G. (ed.) (1999a), *Cosmopolitan Capitalists*, Seattle, WA: University of Washington Press.

Hamilton, Gary G. (1999b), 'Introduction', in Gary G. Hamilton (ed.), *Cosmopolitan Capitalists*, 1–13, Seattle, WA: University of Washington Press.

Hamilton, Gary G. (1999c), 'Hong Kong and the rise of capitalism in Asia', in Gary G. Hamilton (ed.), *Cosmopolitan Capitalists*, 14–34, Seattle, WA: University of Washington Press.

Hamilton, Gary G. (1999d), 'Asian business networks in transition: or, what Alan Greenspan does not know about the Asian business crisis', in T.J. Pempel (ed), *The Politics of the Asian Economic Crisis*, 45–61, Ithaca, NY: Cornell University Press.

Hamilton, Gary G. (2000), 'Reciprocity and control', in Henry Wai-chung Yeung and Kris Olds (eds), *Globalization of Chinese Firms*, 55–74, New York: Macmillan.

Hamilton, Gary G. (2004), *Commerce and Capitalism in Chinese Societies*, London: RoutledgeCurzon.

Hamilton, Gary G. and Biggart, Nicole Woolsey (1988), 'Market, culture, and authority', *American Journal of Sociology (Supplement)*, 94, S52–94.

Hamilton, Gary G., Biggart, Nicole Woolsey and Feenstra, Robert (forthcoming), *Comparing Business Networks in East Asia*, Cambridge: Cambridge University Press.

Hamilton, Gary G. and Feenstra, Robert (1995), 'Varieties of hierarchies and markets', *Industrial and Corporate Change*, 4(1), 93–130.

Hamilton, Gary G. and Kao, Cheng-shu (1990), 'The institutional foundations of Chinese business', *Comparative Social Research*, 12, 95–112.

Hamilton, Gary G. and Waters, Tony (1995), 'Chinese capitalism in Thailand', in Edward K.Y. Chen and Peter Drysdale (eds), *Corporate Links and Foreign Direct Investment in Asia and the Pacific*, 87–111, New South Wales, AUS: HarperEducational.

Hamilton-Hart, Natasha (2002), *Asian States, Asian Bankers*, Ithaca, NY: Cornell University Press.

Hamlin, Michael Alan (1998), *Asia's Best*, Singapore: Prentice Hall.

Hamlin, Michael Alan (2000), *The New Asian Corporation*, San Francisco, CA: Jossey-Bass.

Hara, Fujio (1991), 'Malaysia's New Economic Policy and the Chinese business community', *The Developing Economies*, XXIX(4), 350–70.

Harmes, Adam (1998), 'Institutional investors and the reproduction of neoliberalism', *Review of International Political Economy*, 5(1), 92–121.

Harzing, Anne-Wil (1999), *Managing the Multinationals*, Cheltenham: Edward Elgar.

Heenan, David A. and Keegan, Warren J. (1979), 'The rise of third world multinationals', *Harvard Business Review*, January–February, 101–9.

Hefner, Robert W. (ed.) (1998), *Market Cultures: Society and Values in the New Asian Capitalisms*, Singapore: Institute of Southeast Asian Studies.

Held, David, McGrew, Anthony, Goldblatt, David and Perraton, Jonathan (1999), *Global Transformations*, Cambridge: Polity.

Helleiner, Eric (1994), *States and the Reemergence of Global Finance*, Ithaca, NY: Cornell University Press.

Henderson, Jeffrey (1999), 'Uneven crises: institutional foundations of East Asian economic turmoil', *Economy and Society*, 28(3), 327–68.

Henderson, Jeffrey, Dicken, Peter, Hess, Martin, Coe, Neil and Yeung, Henry Wai-chung (2002), 'Global production networks and the analysis of economic development', *Review of International Political Economy*, 9(3), 436–64.

Heng, Pek Koon (1992), 'The Chinese business elite of Malaysia', in Ruth McVey (ed.), *Southeast Asian Capitalists*, 127–44, Ithaca, NY: Cornell University Southeast Asia Program.

Hicks, George L. (ed.) (1993), *Overseas Chinese Remittances from Southeast Asia 1910–1940*, Singapore: Select Books.

Higgott, Richard (1998), 'The Asian economic crisis', *New Political Economy*, 3(3), 333–55.

Higgott, Richard (1999), 'The political economy of globalisation in East Asia', in Kris Olds, Peter Dicken, Philip Kelly, Lily Kong and Henry Wai-chung Yeung, (eds), *Globalisation and the Asia Pacific*, 91–106, London: Routledge.

Hirst, Paul and Thompson, Grahame (1999), *Globalization in Question*, 2nd edn, Cambridge: Polity Press.

Ho, Yin-Ping (1992), *Trade, Industrial Restructuring and Development in Hong Kong*, London: Macmillan.

Hobday, Michael (1998), 'Latecomer catch-up strategies in electronics: Samsung of Korea and Acer of Taiwan', *Asia Pacific Business Review*, 4(2/3), 48–83.

Hodder, Rupert (1996), *Merchant Princes of the East*, Chichester: John Wiley.

Hodgson, Geoffrey M. (1988), *Economics and Institutions*, Cambridge: Polity Press.

Hodgson, Geoffrey M. (2000), *Evolution and Institutions*, Cheltenham: Edward Elgar.

Hollingsworth, J. Rogers and Boyer, Robert (eds) (1997), *Contemporary Capitalism*, Cambridge: Cambridge University Press.

Hong Kong Census and Statistics Department (2000), *Hong Kong Annual Digest of Statistics 1999*, Hong Kong: Government Printer.

Hong Kong Cotton Spinners Association (1988), *Forty Years of the Hong Kong Cotton Spinning Industry*, Hong Kong: Hong Kong Cotton Spinners Association.

Hong Kong Stock Exchange (1996), *The Stock Exchange of Hong Kong, 1986–1996*, CD-ROM, Hong Kong: Hong Kong Stock Exchange.

Horsman, Mathew and Marshall, Andrew (1994), *After the Nation State*, London: Harper Collins.

Hsiao, Hsin-Huang Michael (2002), 'Coexistence and synthesis: cultural globalization and localization in contemporary Taiwan', in Peter L. Berger and Samuel P. Huntington (eds), *Many Globalizations*, 48–67, Oxford: Oxford University Press.

Hsing, You-tien (1996), 'Blood thicker than water: interpersonal relations and Taiwanese investment in Southern China', *Environment and Planning A*, 28, 2241–61.

Hsing, You-tien (1998), *Making Capitalism in China*, New York: Oxford University Press.

Hsing, You-tien (2003), 'Ethnic identity and business solidarity: Chinese capitalism revisited', in Laurence J.C. Ma and Carolyn Cartier (eds), *The Chinese Diaspora*, 221–35, Boulder, CO: Rowman and Littlefield Publishers.

Hsu, Jinn-Yuh and Cheng, Lu-Lin (2002), 'Revisiting economic development in post-war Taiwan', *Regional Studies*, 36(8), 897–908.

Hsu, Jinn-Yuh and Saxenian, AnnaLee (2000), 'The limits of guanxi capitalism', *Environment and Planning A*, 32(11), 1991–2005.

Hu, Yao-Su (1992), 'Global firms are national firms with international operations', *California Management Review*, 34(2), 107–26.

Hu, Yao-Su (1995), 'The international transferability of the firm's advantages', *California Management Review*, 37(4), 73–88.

Huang, Cen (1998), 'The organization and management of Chinese transnational enterprises in South China', *Issues & Studies*, 34(3), 51–70.

Huff, W.G. (1994), *The Economic Growth of Singapore*, Cambridge: Cambridge University Press.

Hwang, Kwang-kuo (1987), 'Face and favour: the Chinese power game', *American Journal of Sociology*, 92(4), 944–74.

Hymer, Stephen H. [1960] (1976), *The International Operations of National Firms*, Cambridge, MA: MIT Press.

ING Barings (1997), 'Hong Kong Stock Market Review', unpublished report, June.

International Finance Corporation (2000), *China's Emerging Private Enterprises*, Washington, DC: IFC.

International Monetary Fund (1995), *International Capital Markets*, Washington, DC: IMF.

International Monetary Fund (1998), *International Capital Markets*, Washington, DC: IMF.

Jesudason, James V. (1989), *Ethnicity and the Economy*, Singapore: Oxford University Press.

Jesudason, James V. (1997), 'Chinese business and ethnic equilibrium in Malaysia', *Development and Change*, 28(1), 119–41.

Johnson, Chalmer (1982), *MITI and the Japanese Economic Miracle*, Stanford, CA: Stanford University Press.

Johnson, Chalmer (1995), *Japan: Who Governs?*, New York: W.W. Norton.

Johnson, Simon, Boone, Peter, Breach, Alasdair and Friedman, Eric (2000), 'Corporate governance in the Asian financial crisis', *Journal of Financial Economics*, 58, 141–86.

Jomo, Kwame Sundaram (1988), *A Question of Class*, New York: Monthly Review Press.

Jomo, K.S. (1997), 'A specific idiom of Chinese capitalism in Southeast Asia', in Daniel Chirot and Anthony Reid (eds), *Essential Outsiders*, 237–57, Seattle: University of Washington Press.

Kao, John (1993), 'The worldwide web of Chinese business', *Harvard Business Review*, March–April, 24–36.

Keister, Lisa A. (2000), *Chinese Business Groups*, Oxford: Oxford University Press.

Kelly, Philip F. (1999), 'The geographies and politics of globalization', *Progress in Human Geography*, 23(3), 379–400.

Kelly, Philip F. (2000), *Landscapes of Globalization*, London: Routledge.

Kenny, Martin and Florida, Richard (1993), *Beyond Mass Production*, New York: Oxford University Press.

Kets de Vries, Manfred F.R. (1996), *Family Business*, London: International Thomson Business Press.

King, Ambrose Yeo-chi (1991), '*Kuan-hsi* and network building', *Daedalus*, 120(2), 63–84.

Klapper, Leora F. and Love, Inessa (2002), *Corporate Governance, Investor Protection, and Performance in Emerging Markets*, Policy Research Working Paper No. 2818, Washington, DC: World Bank.

Koike, Kenji (1993), 'Introduction', special issue, *The Developing Economies*, 31(4), 363–77.

Kotkin, Joel (1992), *Tribes*, New York: Random House.

Kraar, Louis (1993), 'Importance of Chinese in Asian business', *Journal of Asian Business*, 9(1), 87–94.

Krugman, Paul (1998), 'Asia: what went wrong?', *Fortune*, 137(4), 32.

Kwok, Reginald Yin-Wang and So, Alvin (eds) (1995), *The Hong Kong-Guangdong Link*, London: M.E. Sharpe.

La Croix, Sumner, J., Plummer, Michael and Lee, Keun (eds) (1995), *Emerging Patterns of East Asian Investment in China*, Armonk, NY: M.E. Sharpe.

La Porta, Rafael, Lopez-de-Silanes, Florencio and Shleifer, Andrei (1999), 'Corporate ownership around the world', *Journal of Finance*, 54(2), 471–517.

Landa, Janet T. (1994), *Trust, Ethnicity, and Identity*, Michigan: University of Michigan Press.

Lane, Christel (2000), 'Globalization and the German model of capitalism', *British Journal of Sociology*, 51(2), 207–34.

Lane, Christel and Bachmann, Reinhard (eds) (1998), *Trust Within and Between Organizations*, Oxford: Oxford University Press.

Lau, Ho-Fuk (1991), 'Development process of the Hong Kong manufacturing companies', in Edward K.Y. Chen, Mee-Kau Nyaw and Teresa Y.C. Wong (eds), *Industrial and Trade Development in Hong Kong*, 427–44, Hong Kong: Centre of Asian Studies, University of Hong Kong.

Law, John (1994), *Organizing Modernity*, Oxford: Blackwell.

Law, John and Hassard, John (eds) (1999), *Actor Network Theory and After*, Oxford: Blackwell.

Lazonick, William (1991), *Business Organization and the Myth of the Market Economy*, Cambridge: Cambridge University Press.

Lazonick, William and O'Sullivan, Mary (2000), 'Maximizing shareholder value', *Economy and Society*, 29(1), 13–35.

Lee, Ji-Ren and Chen, Jen-Shyang (2003), 'Internationalization, local adaptation, and subsidiary's entrepreneurship', *Asia Pacific Journal of Management*, 20(1), 51–72.

Leung, Chi-kin (1993), 'Personal contacts, subcontracting linkages, and development in the Hong Kong-Zhujiang Delta region', *Annals of the Association of American Geographers*, 83(2), 272–302.

Lever-Tracy, Constance (2002), 'The impact of the Asian crisis on diaspora Chinese tycoons', *Geoforum*, 33(3), 509–23.

Lever-Tracy, Constance, Ip, David and Tracy, Noel (1996), *The Chinese Diaspora and Mainland China*, London: Macmillan.

Lévy, Brigitte (1995), 'Globalization and regionalization', *The International Executive*, 37(4), 349–71.

Lewis, Jordan D. (1995), *The Connected Corporation*, New York: The Free Press.

Lim, Linda Y.C. (1996), 'The evolution of Southeast Asian business systems', *Journal of Southeast Asia Business*, 12(1), 51–74.

Lim, Linda Y.C. (1997), 'The Southeast Asian currency crisis and its aftermath', *Journal of Asian Business*, 13(4), 65–83.

Lim, Linda Y.C. (2000), 'Southeast Asian Chinese business', *Journal of Asian Business*, 16(1), 1–14.

Lim, Linda Y.C. and Gosling, L.A. Peter (eds) (1983), *The Chinese in Southeast Asia*, Singapore: Maruzen Asia.

Limlingan, Victor Simpoa (1986), *The Overseas Chinese in ASEAN*, Manila: Vita Development Corporation.

Lin, George C.S. (1997), *Red Capitalism in South China*, Vancouver: University of British Columbia Press.

Low, Linda (1998), *The Political Economy of a City-State*, Singapore: Oxford University Press.

Low, Linda, Ramstetter, Eric D. and Yeung, Henry Wai-chung (1998), 'Accounting for outward direct investment from Hong Kong and Singapore', in Robert E. Baldwin, Robert E. Lipsey and J. David Richardson (eds), *Geography and Ownership as Bases for Economic Accounting*, 139–68, Chicago, IL: University of Chicago Press.

Lundvall, B.-Å. (ed.) (1992), *National Systems of Innovation: Towards a Theory of Innovation and Interactive Learning*, London: Pinter.

Luo, Qi and Howe, Christopher (1993), 'Direct investment and economic integration in the Asia Pacific', *The China Quarterly*, 136, 746–69.

Lynn, Pann (ed.) (1998), *The Encyclopedia of Chinese Overseas*, Singapore: Archipelago Press.

M&C Hotels plc (1998), *Annual Report 1997*, London: M&C Hotels plc.

M&C Hotels plc (2002), *Annual Report 2001*, London: M&C Hotels plc.

M&C Hotels plc (2003), *Preliminary Report 2002*, London: M&C Hotels plc.

Ma, Laurence J.C. (2003), 'Space, place and transnationalism in the Chinese diaspora', in Laurence J.C. Ma and Carolyn Cartier (eds), *The Chinese Diaspora*, 1–50, Boulder, CO: Rowman and Littlefield Publishers.

Ma, Laurence J.C. and Cartier, Carolyn (eds) (2003), *The Chinese Diaspora*, Boulder, CO: Rowman and Littlefield Publishers.

Mackie, Jamie A.C. (1988), 'Changing economic roles and ethnic identities of the Southeast Chinese', in Jennifer W. Cushman and Gungwu Wang (eds), *Changing Identities of the Southeast Asian Chinese Since World War II*, 217–60, Hong Kong: Hong Kong University Press.

Mackie, Jamie A.C. (1992), 'Overseas Chinese entrepreneurship', *Asian-Pacific Economic Literature*, 6(1), 41–64.

Mackie, Jamie A.C. (1998), 'Business success among Southeast Asian Chinese', in Robert W. Hefner (ed.), *Market Cultures*, 129–46, Singapore: Institute of Southeast Asian Studies.

Magretta, Joan (1998), 'Fast, global, and entrepreneurial: supply chain management, Hong Kong style', *Harvard Business Review*, 76(5), 103–14.

Mahathir Mohamad (1970), *The Malay Dilemma*, Singapore: The Asia Pacific Press.

Mair, Andrew, Florida, Richard and Kenny, Martin (1988), 'The new geography of automobile production: Japanese transplants in North America', *Economic Geography*, 64, 352–73.

Malnight, Thomas W. (1995), 'Globalization of an ethnocentric firm', *Strategic Management Journal*, 16, 119–41.

Martin, Ron (1994), 'Stateless monies, global financial integration and national economic autonomy', in Stuart Corbridge, Ron Martin and Nigel Thrift (eds), *Money, Power and Space*, 253–78, Oxford: Basil Blackwell.

Marton, Andrew M. (2000), *China's Spatial Economic Development*, London: Routledge.

Massey, Doreen (1994), *Space, Place and Gender*, Cambridge: Polity Press.

Mathews, John A. (1997), 'A silicon valley of the east: creating Taiwan's semiconductor industry', *California Management Review*, 39(4), 26–54.

Mathews, John A. (1999), 'A silicon island of the east: creating a semiconductor industry in Singapore', *California Management Review*, 41(2), 55–78.

Mathews, John A. (2002), *Dragon Multinational: A New Model for Global Growth*, Oxford: Oxford University Press.

Mathews, John A. and Cho, D.S. (1998), *Tiger Chips*, Cambridge: Cambridge University Press.

Mathews, John A. and Snow, Charles C. (1998), 'A conversation with the Acer Groups' Stan Shih on global strategy and management', *Organizational Dynamics*, 27(1), 65–74.

Matsuo, H. (2000), 'Liability of foreignness and the uses of expatriates in Japanese multinational corporations in the United States', *Sociological Inquiry*, 70(1), 88–106.

McDougall, Patricia P. and Oviatt, Benjamin M. (1996), 'New venture internationalization, strategic change, and performance: a follow-up study', *Journal of Business Venturing*, 11(1), 23–40.

McDougall, Patricia P. and Oviatt, Benjamin M. (2000), 'International entrepreneurship', *Academy of Management Journal*, 43(5), 902–6.

McDougall, Patricia P., Shane, Scott and Oviatt, Benjamin M. (1994), 'Explaining the formation of international new ventures', *Journal of Business Venturing*, 9(6), 469–87.

McKee, D.L. and Garner, D.E. (1994), *Accounting Services, Growth and Change in the Pacific Basin*, Westport, CT: Quorum Books.

McNamara, Dennis L. (ed.) (1999), *Corporatism and Korean Capitalism*, London: Routledge.

McVey, Ruth (ed.) (1992), *Southeast Asian Capitalists*, Ithaca, NY: Cornell University Southeast Asia Program.

Menkhoff, Thomas (1993), *Trade Routes, Trust and Trading Networks – Chinese Small Enteprises in Singapore*, Saarbrucken, Germany: Verlag Breitenback Publishers.

Menkhoff, Thomas and Gerke, Solvay (eds) (2002), *Chinese Entrepreneurship and Asian Business Networks*, Richmond, Surrey, UK: Curzon.

Meyer, David R. (2000), *Hong Kong as a Global Metropolis*, Cambridge: Cambridge University Press.

Mitchell, Katharyne (1993), 'Multi-culturalism, or the united colors of capitalism', *Antipode*, 25(4), 263–94.

Mitchell, Katharyne (1995), 'Flexible circulation in the Pacific Rim', *Economic Geography*, 71(4), 364–82.

Mitchell, Katherine (1997), 'Transnational subjects', in Aihwa Ong and Donald M. Nonini (eds), *Ungrounded Empires*, 228–56 London: Routledge.

Mittelman, James H. (ed.) (1996), *Globalization*, Boulder, CO: Lynne Rienner.

Mittelman, James H. (2000), *The Globalization Syndrome*, Princeton, NJ: Princeton University Press.

Mitton, Todd (2002), 'A cross-firm analysis of the impact of corporate governance on the East Asian financial crisis', *Journal of Financial Economics*, 64, 215–41.

Mueller, Frank (1994), 'Societal effect, organizational effect and globalization', *Organization Studies*, 15(3), 407–28.

Murtha, Thomas P. and Lenway, Stefanie A. (1994), 'Country capabilities and the strategic state', *Strategic Management Journal*, 15(1), 113–29.

Nathan, Andrew (1993), 'Is Chinese culture distinctive?', *Journal of Asian Studies*, 52(4), 923–36.

Nee, Victor (1992), 'Organizational dynamics of market transition: hybrid forms, property rights and mixed economy in China', *Administrative Science Quarterly*, 37(1), 1–27.

Ng, Linda Fung-Yee and Tuan, Chyau (eds) (1996), *Three Chinese Economies – China, Hong Kong and Taiwan*, Hong Kong: Chinese University Press.

Niosi, Jorge (1999), 'The internationalization of industrial R&D: from technology transfer to the learning organization', *Research Policy*, 28, 107–17.

Noble, Gregory W. and Ravenhill, John (eds) (2000a), *The Asian Financial Crisis and the Architecture of Global Finance*, Cambridge: Cambridge University Press.

Noble, Gregory W. and Ravenhill, John (2000b), 'Causes and consequences of the Asian financial crisis', in Gregory W. Noble and John Ravenhill (eds), *The Asian*

Financial Crisis and the Architecture of Global Finance, 1–35, Cambridge: Cambridge University Press.

Nohria, Nitin and Ghoshal, Sumantra (1997), *The Differentiated Network,* San Francisco, CA: Jossey-Bass.

Nonini, Donald M. (1997), 'Shifting identities, positioned imaginaries', in Aihwa Ong and Donald M. Nonini (eds), *Ungrounded Empires,* 203–27, London: Routledge.

Nonini, Donald M. and Ong, Aihwa (1997), 'Chinese transnationalism as an alternative modernity', in Aihwa Ong and Donald M. Nonini (eds), *Ungrounded Empires,* 3–33, London: Routledge.

O'Brien, Richard (1992), *Global Financial Integration,* New York: Council on Foreign Relations Press.

Ohmae, Kenichi (1985), *Triad Power,* New York: The Free Press.

Ohmae, Kenichi (1990), *The Borderless World,* London: Collins.

Ohmae, Kenichi (1995), *The End of the Nation State,* London: HarperCollins.

Olds, Kris (1995), 'Globalization and the production of new urban spaces', *Environment and Planning A,* 27, 1713–43.

Olds, Kris (2001), *Globalization and Urban Change,* Oxford: Oxford University Press.

Olds, Kris, Dicken, Peter, Kelly, Philip, Kong, Lily and Yeung, Henry Wai-chung (eds) (1999), *Globalisation and the Asia-Pacific,* London: Routledge.

Olds, Kris and Yeung, Henry Wai-chung (1999), '(Re)shaping 'Chinese' business networks in a globalising era', *Environment and Planning D: Society and Space,* 17(5), 535–55.

Ong, Aihwa (1997), 'Chinese modernities: narratives of nation and of capitalism', in Aihwa Ong and Donald M. Nonini (eds), *Ungrounded Empires,* 171–202, London: Routledge.

Ong, Aihwa and Nonini, Donald (eds) (1997a), *Ungrounded Empires,* London: Routledge.

Ong, Aihwa and Nonini, Donald (1997b), 'Toward a cultural politics of diaspora and transnationalism', in Aihwa Ong and Donald M. Nonini (eds), *Ungrounded Empires,* 323–32, London: Routledge.

Orrù, Marco, Biggart, Nicole and Hamilton, Gary G. (1997), *The Economic Organization of East Asian Capitalism,* London: Sage.

Otterbeck, L. (ed.) (1981), *The Management of Headquarters-Subsidiary Relationships in Multinational Corporations,* Aldershot: Gower.

Palanca, Ellen H. (1995), 'Chinese business families in the Philippines since the 1890s', in Rajeswary Ampalavana Brown (ed.), *Chinese Business Enterprise in Asia,* 197–213, London: Routledge.

Pananond, Pavida (2001), 'The making of Thai multinationals', *Journal of Asian Business,* 17, 41–70.

Pananond, Pavida and Zeithaml, Carl P. (1998), 'The international expansion process of MNEs from developing countries', *Asia Pacific Journal of Management,* 15, 163–84.

Pantzalis, Christos (2001), 'Does location matter?', *Journal of International Business Studies,* 32(1), 133–55.

Patel, Pari (1995), 'Localised production of technology for global markets', *Cambridge Journal of Economics,* 19, 141–53.

Pauly, Louis W. and Reich, Simon (1997), 'National structures and multinational corporate behavior', *International Organization,* 51(1), 1–30.

PCCW (2001a), *Annual Report, 2000,* Hong Kong: PCCW Ltd.

PCCW (2001b), *Annual Report On Form 20–F 2000,* Hong Kong: PCCW Ltd.

PCCW (2003), *Interim Report, 2002,* Hong Kong: PCCW Ltd.

Peck, Jamie and Yeung, Henry Wai-chung (eds) (2003), *Remaking the Global Economy,* London: Sage.

Peng, D. (2000), 'Ethnic Chinese business networks and the Asia-Pacific economic integration', *Journal of Asian African Studies,* 35(2), 229–50.

Perlmutter, Howard V. (1969), 'The tortuous evolution of the multinational corporations', *Columbia Journal of World Business,* January–February, 9–18.

Perry, Martin, Kong, Lily and Yeoh, Brenda (1997), *Singapore: A Developmental City State,* London: John Wiley.

Perry, Martin, Poon, Jessie and Yeung, Henry (1998a), 'Regional offices in Singapore', *Review of Urban and Regional Development Studies,* 10(1), 42–59.

Perry, Martin and Tan, Boon Hui (1998), 'Global manufacturing and local linkage in Singapore', *Environment and Planning A,* 30(9), 1603–24.

Perry, Martin, Yeung, Henry and Poon, Jessie (1998b), 'Regional office mobility', *Geoforum,* 29(3), 237–55.

Phillips, Su-Ann Mae and Yeung, Henry Wai-chung (2003), 'A place for R&D? The Singapore Science Park', *Urban Studies,* 40(4), 707–32.

Porter, Michael E. (1985), *Competitive Advantage,* New York: The Free Press.

Porter, Michael E. (1998), *On Competition,* Boston, MA: Harvard Business School Press.

Powell, Walter W. (1990), 'Neither market nor hierarchy: network forms of organization', *Research in Organizational Behaviour,* 12, 295–336.

Prahalad, C.K. and Doz, Yves (1987), *The Multinational Mission,* New York: The Free Press.

Priebjrivat, Vuthiphong and Rondinelli, Dennis A. (1994), 'Privatizing Thailand's telecommunications industry', *Business & the Contemporary World,* 6(1), 70–83.

Pyatt, T. Roger and Redding, S. Gordon (2000), 'Trust and forbearance in ethnic Chinese business relationships in Hong Kong and Thailand', *Journal of Asian Business,* 16(1), 41–64.

Radelet, Steven and Sachs, Jeffrey D. (1998), 'The East Asian financial crisis', *Brookings Papers on Economic Activity,* 1, 1–90.

Redding, S. Gordon (1990), *The Spirit of Chinese Capitalism,* Berlin: De Gruyter.

Redding, S. Gordon (1995), 'Overseas Chinese networks', *Long Range Planning,* 28(1), 61–9.

Redding, S. Gordon (1996), 'The distinct nature of Chinese capitalism', *The Pacific Review,* 9(3), 426–41.

Redding, S. Gordon (2000), 'What is Chinese about Chinese family business?', in Henry Wai-chung Yeung and Kris Olds (eds), *Globalization of Chinese Firms,* 31–54, New York: Macmillan.

Redding, S. Gordon and Wong, Gilbert Y.Y. (1986), 'The psychology of Chinese organisational behaviour', in Michael Harris Bond (ed.), *The Psychology of the Chinese People,* 267–95, Oxford: Oxford University Press.

Reid, Anthony (1997), 'Entrepreneurial minorities, nationalism, and the state', in Daniel Chirot and Anthony Reid (eds), *Essential Outsiders,* 33–71, Seattle: University of Washington Press.

Richter, Frank-Jürgen (1999), *Strategic Networks,* New York: International Business Press.

Ridding, John and Kynge, James (1997), 'Empires can strike back', *The Financial Times*, 5 November, 13.

Ridding, John and Lucas, Louis (1997), 'Li Ka-shing stays ahead of the game', *Financial Times*, 7 January, 20.

Robison, Richard (1986), *Indonesia: The Rise of Capital*, Sydney: Allen & Unwin.

Rodan, Garry (1989), *The Political Economy of Singapore's Industralization*, London: Macmillan.

Rosenberger, Leif Roderick (1997), 'Southeast Asia's currency crisis: a diagnosis and prescription', *Contemporary Southeast Asia*, 19(3), 223–51.

Sabel, Charles F. and Zeitlin, Jonathan (eds) (1996), *Worlds of Possibility*, Cambridge: Cambridge University Press.

Sako, Mari (1992), *Prices, Quality and Trust*, Cambridge: Cambridge University Press.

Sassen, Saskia (1991), *The Global City*, Princeton, NJ: Princeton University Press.

Sassen, Saskia (1996), *Losing Control?*, New York: Columbia University Press.

Sassen, Saskia (1999), 'Servicing the global economy', in Kris Olds, Peter Dicken, Philip Kelly, Lily Kong and Henry Wai-chung Yeung, (eds), *Globalisation and the Asia Pacific*, 149–62, London: Routledge.

Sato, Yuri (1993), 'The Salim Group in Indonesia', *The Developing Economies*, 31(4), 408–41.

Saunders, Peter (1995), *Capitalism*, Minneapolis: University of Minnesota Press.

Saxenian, AnnaLee and Hsu, Jinn-Yuh (2001), 'The Silicon Valley-Hsinchu connection', *Industrial and Corporate Change*, 10(4), 893–920.

Schenk, Catherine R. (2001), *Hong Kong as an International Financial Centre*, London: Routledge.

Schmukler, Sergio and Vesperoni, Esteban (2001), *Globalization and Firms' Financing Choices*, IMF Working Paper WP/01/95, Washington, DC: IMF.

Schumpeter, Joseph A. (1934), *The Theory of Economic Development*, Cambridge, MA: Harvard University Press.

Screpanti, Ernesto (2001), *The Fundamental Institutions of Capitalism*, London: Routledge.

Sender, H. (1991), 'Inside the Overseas Chinese network', *Institutional Investor*, August, 29–45.

Shiba, Takao and Shimotami, Masahiro (eds) (1996), *Beyond the Firm*, Oxford: Oxford University Press.

Shieh, Gwo Shyong (1992), *'Boss' Island: The Subcontracting Network and Micro-Entrepreneurship in Taiwan's Development*, New York: Peter Lang.

Shikatani, Takuya (1995), 'Corporate finances of overseas Chinese financial groups', *Nomura Research Institute Quarterly*, 4(1), 68–91.

Shleifer, Andrei and Vishny, Robert W. (1997), 'A survey of corporate governance', *Journal of Finance*, 52(2), 737–83.

Silin, Robert H. (1976), *Leadership and Values*, Cambridge, MA: Harvard University Press.

Silk, Leonard and Silk, Mark (1996), *Making Capitalism Work*, New York: New York University Press.

Sim, A.B. and Pandian, J. Rajendran (2003), 'Emerging Asian MNEs and their internationalization strategies', *Asia Pacific Journal of Management*, 20(1), 27–50.

Singapore Business, various issues, Singapore.

Singapore Department of Statistics (1991a), *Singapore's Investment Abroad 1976–1989*, Singapore: DOS.

Singapore Department of Statistics (1991b), *Singapore Standard Industrial Classification, 1990*, Singapore: DOS.

Singapore Ministry of Finance (1993), *Interim Report of the Committee to Promote Enterprise Overseas*, Singapore: MOF.

Singh, Kulwant and Ang, Siah Hwee (1998), *The Strategies and Success of Government Linked Corporations in Singapore*, Research Paper Series No. 98–06, Faculty of Business Administration, National University of Singapore, Singapore.

Sit, Victor F.S. and Wong, Siu Lun (1989), *Small and Medium Industries in an Export-Oriented Economy*, Hong Kong: Centre of Asian Studies, University of Hong Kong.

Siu, Wai Sum and Martin, Robert G. (1992), 'Successful entrepreneurship in Hong Kong', *Long Range Planning*, 25(6), 87–93.

Sklair, Leslie (2000), *The Transnational Capitalist Class*, Oxford: Blackwell.

Smart, Alan (1997), 'Capitalist story-telling and hegemonic crises: some comments', *Identities*, 3(3), 399–412.

Smart, Alan and Smart, Josephine (1998), 'Transnational social networks and negotiated identities in interactions between Hong Kong and China', in Michael Peter Smith and Luis Eduardo Guarnizo (eds), *Transnationalism from Below*, 103–29, New Brunswick: Transaction Publishers.

Smart, Josephine and Smart, Alan (1991), 'Personal relations and divergent economies: a case study of Hong Kong investment in South China', *International Journal of Urban and Regional Research*, 15(2), 216–33.

Standish, Peter E.M. (1990), 'Accounting: the private language of business or an instrument of social communication?', in Stewart R. Clegg and S. Gordon Redding (eds), *Capitalism in Contrasting Cultures*, 215–48, Berlin: De Gruyter.

Stark, David (1996), 'Recombinant property in East European capitalism', *American Journal of Sociology*, 101(4), 993–1027.

Stark, David and Bruszt, László (1998), *Postsocialist Pathways: Transforming Politics and Property in East Central Europe*, Cambridge: Cambridge University Press.

Stark, David and Bruszt, László (2001), 'One way or multiple paths: for a comparative sociology of East European capitalism', *American Journal of Sociology*, 106(4), 1129–37.

Stock Exchange of Singapore (1998), *Companies Handbook 1997*, Parts 1–4, Singapore: SES.

Storper, Michael and Salais, R. (1997), *Worlds of Production*, Cambridge, MA: Harvard University Press.

Strange, Susan (1996), *The Retreat of the State*, Cambridge: Cambridge University Press.

Straits Times, The, various issues, Singapore.

Suehiro, Akira (1985), *Capital Accumulation and Industrial Development in Thailand*, Bangkok: Chulalongkorn University Social Research Institute.

Suehiro, Akira (1993), 'Family business reassessed: corporate structure and late-starting industrialization in Thailand', *The Developing Economies*, 31(4), 378–407.

Sunday Times, 12 January 1997, London.

Sunday Times, various issues, Singapore.

Sung, Yun-wing (1991), *The China-Hong Kong Connection*, Cambridge: Cambridge University Press.

Suryadinata, Leo (1988), 'Chinese economic elites in Indonesia', in Jennifer W. Cushman and Gungwu Wang (eds), *Changing Identities of the Southeast Asian Chinese Since World War II*, 261–88, Hong Kong: Hong Kong University Press.

Suryadinata, Leo (ed.) (1995), *Southeast Asian Chinese and China: The Political-Economic Dimension*, Singapore: Times Academic Press.

Suryadinata, Leo (ed.) (1997), *Ethnic Chinese as Southeast Asians*, Singapore: Institute of Southeast Asian Studies.

Sykes, Allen (2000), *Capitalism for Tomorrow: Reuniting Ownership and Control*, Oxford: Capstone.

Taiwan Ministry of Economic Affairs (1996), *Statistics on Outward Investment*, Taipei: MEA.

Tan, Chia Zhi and Yeung, Henry Wai-chung (2000a), 'The regionalization of Chinese business networks', *The Professional Geographer*, 52(3), 437–54.

Tan, Chia-Zhi and Yeung, Henry Wai-chung (2000b), 'The internationalization of Singaporean firms into China', in Henry Wai-chung Yeung and Kris Olds (eds), *Globalization of Chinese Firms*, 220–43, New York: Macmillan.

Tang, Jie and Ward, Anthony (2003), *The Changing Face of Chinese Management*, London: Routledge.

Thompson, Grahame F. (2003) *Between Hierarchies and Markets*, Oxford: Oxford University Press.

Thompson, Paul (1989), *The Nature of Work*, Basingstoke: Macmillan.

Thrift, Nigel (1996), *Spatial Formations*, London: Sage.

Thrift, Nigel (1998), 'The rise of soft capitalism', in Andrew Herod, Gearóid Ó Tuathail and Susan M. Roberts, *An Unruly World*, 25–71, London: Routledge.

Thrift, Nigel (1999), 'The globalisation of business knowledge', in Kris Olds, Peter Dicken, Philip Kelly, Lily Kong and Henry Wai-chung Yeung, (eds), *Globalisation and the Asia Pacific*, 57–71, London: Routledge.

Thrift, Nigel (2000), 'Performing cultures in the new economy', *Annals of the Association of American Geographers*, 90(4), 674–92.

Thrift, Nigel and Leyshon, Andrew (1994), 'A phantom state?', *Political Geography*, 13, 299–327.

Tickell, Adam T. (1996), 'Making a melodrama out of a crisis', *Environment and Planning D: Society and Space*, 14(1), 5–33.

Tiessen, James H. (1997), 'Individualism, collectivism and entrepreneurship', *Journal of Business Venturing*, 12(5), 367–84.

Tong, Chee Kiong (1991), 'Centripetal authority, differentiated networks', in Gary G. Hamilton (ed.), *Business Networks and Economic Development in East and South East Asia*, 176–200, Hong Kong: Centre of Asian Studies, University of Hong Kong.

Tong, Chee Kiong and Yong, Pit Kee (1998), 'Guanxi bases, xinyong and Chinese business networks', *British Journal of Sociology*, 49(1), 75–96.

Tricker, Robert I. (1990), 'Corporate governance: a ripple on the cultural reflection', in Stewart R. Clegg and S. Gordon Redding (eds), *Capitalism in Contrasting Cultures*, 187–213, Berlin: De Gruyter.

Tsang, Eric W.K. (1998), 'Can *guanxi* be a source of sustained competitive advantage for doing business in China?', *Academy of Management Executive*, 12(2), 64–73.

Tsang, Eric W.K. (1999a), 'Internationalization as a learning process', *Academy of Management Executive*, 13(1), 91–101.

Tsang, Eric W.K. (1999b), 'The knowledge transfer and learning aspects of international HRM', *International Business Review*, 8(5/6), 591–609.

Tsang, Eric W.K. (2001), 'Internationalizing the family firm', *Journal of Small Business Management*, 39(1), 88–94.

Tsang, Eric W.K. (2002), 'Learning from overseas venturing experience – the case of Chinese family businesses', *Journal of Business Venturing*, 17(1), 21–40.

Tu, Wei-Ming (ed.) (1996), *Confucian Traditions in East Asian Modernity*, Cambridge, MA: Harvard University Press.

Tuan, Chyau and Ng, Linda Fung-Yee (1995a), 'The turning point of the Hong Kong manufacturing sector', *Journal of International Trade and Economic Development*, 4(2), 153–70.

Tuan, Chyau and Ng, Linda Fung-Yee (1995b), 'Manufacturing evolution under passive industrial policy and cross-border operations in China', *Journal of Asian Economics*, 6(1), 71–88.

UBS Global Research (1994), 'Cheung Kong (Holdings) Ltd. – A Big Gun Loaded with Firepower', unpublished report, April.

UBS Global Research (1995), 'New World Development: Taking the China Road', unpublished report, July.

UNCTAD (1996), *World Investment Report 1996*, New York: United Nations.

UNCTAD (1997), *World Investment Report 1997*, New York: United Nations.

UNCTAD (1998), *World Investment Report 1998*, New York: United Nations.

UNCTAD (2002), *World Investment Report 2002*, New York: United Nations.

Ungson, Gerardo R., Steers, Richard M. and Park, Seung-Ho (1997), *Korean Enterprise*, Boston, MA: Harvard Business School Press.

Wade, Robert (1990), *Governing the Market*, Princeton, NJ: Princeton University Press.

Wade, Robert and Veneroso, Frank (1998), 'The Asian crisis', *New Left Review*, 228, 3–23.

Wang, Gungwu (1981), *Community and Nation: Essays on Southeast Asia and the Chinese*, Singapore: Heinemann.

Wang, Gungwu (1991), *China and the Chinese Overseas*, Singapore: Times Academic Press.

Wang, Gungwu (1999), 'Chineseness: the dilemmas of place and practice', in Gary G. Hamilton (ed.), *Cosmopolitan Capitalists*, 118–34, Seattle: University of Washington Press.

Wang, Gungwu (2000), *The Chinese Overseas: From Earthbound China to the Quest for Autonomy*, Cambridge, MA: Harvard University Press.

Wang, Gungwu and Wong, Siu-lun (eds) (1997), *Dynamic Hong Kong: Business and Culture*, Hong Kong: Hong Kong University Press.

Wang, Jason H.J. and Yeung, Henry Wai-chung (2000), 'Strategies for global competition: transnational chemical firms and Singapore's chemical cluster', *Environment and Planning A*, 32(5), 847–69.

Weber, Max [1930] (1992), *The Protestant Ethic and the Spirit of Capitalism*, translated by Talcott Parsons, London: Routledge.

Weber, Max [1920] (1983a), 'The failure of capitalism in the ancient world', in Stanislav Andreski (ed.), *Max Weber on Capitalism, Bureaucracy and Religion: A Selection of Texts*, 30–58, London: Allen & Unwin.

Weber, Max [1920] (1983b), 'The Confucianist bureaucracy and the germs of capitalism in China', in Stanislav Andreski (ed.), *Max Weber on Capitalism, Bureaucracy and Religion: A Selection of Texts*, 59–84, London: Allen & Unwin.

Webber, Michael (2001), 'Finance and the real economy', *Geoforum*, 32(1), 1–13.

Weidenbaum, Murray and Hughes, Samuel (1996), *The Bamboo Network*, New York: The Free Press.

Weiss, Linda (1998), *The Myth of the Powerless State*, Cambridge: Polity Press.

Wenger, Etienne (1998), *Communities of Practice*, Cambridge: Cambridge University Press.

Wenger, Etienne (2000), 'Communities of practice and social learning systems', *Organization*, 7(2), 225–46.

Westney, D. Eleanor (1987), *Imitation and Innovation*, Cambridge, MA: Harvard University Press.

Whitley, Richard (1992), *Business Systems in East Asia*, London: Sage.

Whitley, Richard (1994), 'The internationalization of firms and markets', *Organization*, 1(1), 101–24.

Whitley, Richard (1996), 'Business systems and global commodity chains', *Competition and Change*, 1, 411–25.

Whitley, Richard (1998), 'Internationalization and varieties of capitalism', *Review of International Political Economy*, 5(3), 445–81.

Whitley, Richard (1999), *Divergent Capitalisms*, New York: Oxford University Press.

Whitley, Richard and Kristensen, Peer Hull (eds) (1996), *The Changing European Firm*, London: Routledge.

Whitley, Richard and Kristensen, Peer Hull (eds) (1997), *Governance at Work*, Oxford: Oxford University Press.

Whyte, Martin King (1996), 'The Chinese family and economic development', *Economic Development and Cultural Change*, 45(1), 1–30.

Willcocks, Leslie and Choi, Chong Ju (1995), 'Co-operative partnership and "total" IT outsourcing', *European Management Journal*, 13(1), 67–78.

Williamson, Oliver E. (1975), *Markets and Hierarchies*, New York: The Free Press.

Williamson, Oliver E. (1985), *The Economic Institution of Capitalism*, New York: The Free Press.

Windolf, Paul and Beyer, Jürgen (1996), 'Co-operative capitalism: corporate networks in Germany and Britain', *British Journal of Sociology*, 47(2), 205–31.

Wong, Siu-lun (1985), 'The Chinese family firm: a model', *British Journal of Sociology*, 36, 58–72.

Wong, Siu-lun (1988), *Emigrant Entrepreneurs*, Hong Kong: Oxford University Press.

Wong, Siu-lun (1991), 'Chinese entrepreneurs and business trust', in Gary G. Hamilton (ed.), *Business Networks and Economic Development in East and South East Asia*, 13–29, Hong Kong: Centre of Asian Studies, University of Hong Kong.

Wong, Siu-lun (1995), 'Business networks, cultural values and the state in Hong Kong and Singapore', in Rajeswary Ampalavana Brown (ed.), *Chinese Business Enterprise in Asia*, 136–53, London: Routledge.

Wong, Siu-lun (2000), 'Transplanting enterprises in Hong Kong', in Henry Wai-chung Yeung and Kris Olds (eds), *Globalization of Chinese Firms*, 153–66, New York: Macmillan.

World Bank (1993), *The East Asian Miracle*, Oxford: Oxford University Press.

World Bank (1999), *World Development Report 1999/2000: Entering the 21st Century*, Oxford: Oxford University Press.

World Bank (2000), *Global Development Finance 2000*, Washington, DC: World Bank.

Wu, Friedrich (1997), 'Hong Kong and Singapore: a tale of two Asian business hubs', *Journal of Asian Business*, 13(2), 1–17.

Wu, Friedrich and Duk, Sin Yue (1995), 'Hong Kong and Singapore: 'twin capitals' for overseas Chinese capital', *Business & the Contemporary World*, 7(3), 21–33.

Yan, Yunxiang (2002), 'Managed globalization: state power and cultural transition in China', in Peter L. Berger and Samuel P. Huntington (eds), *Many Globalizations: Cultural Diversity in the Contemporary World*, 19–47, Oxford: Oxford University Press.

Yang, Mayfair M.H. (2002), 'The resilience of guanxi and its new deployments', *The China Quarterly*, 170, 459–76.

Yao, Souchou (1987), 'The fetish of relationships: Chinese business transactions in Singapore', *Sojourn*, 2, 89–111.

Yao, Souchou (1997), 'The romance of Asian capitalism: geography, desire and Chinese business', in Hank T. Berger and Douglas A. Borer (eds), *The Rise of Asia: Critical visions of the Pacific Century*, pp. 221–40. London: Routledge.

Yao, Souchou (2002), *Confucian Capitalism*, London: RoutledgeCurzon.

Yen, Ching-hwang (2002), *The Ethnic Chinese in East and Southeast Asia*, Singapore: Times Academic Press.

Yeung, Henry Wai-chung (1994a), 'Critical reviews of geographical perspectives on business organisations and the organisation of production: towards a network approach', *Progress in Human Geography*, 18(4), 460–90.

Yeung, Henry Wai-chung (1994b), 'Transnational corporations from Asian developing countries', *Journal of Asian Business*, 10(4), 17–58.

Yeung, Henry Wai-chung (1996), 'The historical geography of Hong Kong investments in the ASEAN region', *Singapore Journal of Tropical Geography*, 17(1), 66–82.

Yeung, Henry Wai-chung (1997a), 'Business networks and transnational corporations: a study of Hong Kong firms in the ASEAN region', *Economic Geography*, 73(1), 1–25.

Yeung, Henry Wai-chung (1997b), 'Cooperative strategies and Chinese business networks', in Paul W. Beamish and J. Peter Killing (eds), *Cooperative Strategies*, 22–56, San Francisco, CA: The New Lexington Press.

Yeung, Henry Wai-chung (1998a), *Transnational Corporations and Business Networks*, London: Routledge.

Yeung, Henry Wai-chung (1998b), 'Capital, state and space', *Transactions of the Institute of British Geographers*, 23(3), 291–309.

Yeung, Henry Wai-chung (1998c), 'The social-spatial constitution of business organisations', *Organization*, 5(1), 101–28.

Yeung, Henry Wai-chung (1998d), 'The political economy of transnational corporations: a study of the regionalisation of Singaporean firms', *Political Geography*, 17(4), 389–416.

Yeung, Henry Wai-chung (1998e), 'Transnational economic synergy and business networks', *Regional Studies*, 32(8), 687–706.

Yeung, Henry Wai-chung (1999a), 'Regulating investment abroad? The political economy of the regionalisation of Singaporean firms', *Antipode*, 31(3), 245–73.

Yeung, Henry Wai-chung (1999b), 'Under siege? Economic globalisation and Chinese business in Southeast Asia', *Economy and Society*, 28(1), 1–29.

Yeung, Henry Wai-chung (1999c), 'The internationalization of ethnic Chinese firms from Southeast Asia', *International Journal of Urban and Regional Research*, 23(1), 103–27.

Yeung, Henry Wai-chung (ed.) (1999d), *The Globalisation of Firms from Emerging Economies*, 2 vols, Cheltenham: Edward Elgar.

Yeung, Henry Wai-chung (2000a), 'The dynamics of Asian business systems in a globalising era', *Review of International Political Economy*, 7(3), 399–433.

Yeung, Henry Wai-chung (2000b), 'Neoliberalism, *laissez-faire* capitalism and economic crisis: the political economy of deindustrialisation in Hong Kong', *Competition and Change*, 4(2), 121–69.

Yeung, Henry Wai-chung (2000c), 'Economic globalisation, crisis, and the emergence of Chinese business communities in Southeast Asia', *International Sociology*, 15(2), 269–90.

Yeung, Henry Wai-chung (2000d), 'Managing crisis in a globalising era: the case of Chinese firms from Singapore', in David Ip, Constance Lever-Tracy and Noel Tracy (eds), *Chinese Businesses and the Asian Crisis*, 87–113, Aldershot: Gower.

Yeung, Henry Wai-chung (2000e), 'The dynamics of the globalization of Chinese firms', in Henry Wai-chung Yeung and Kris Olds (eds), *Globalization of Chinese Firms*, 75–104, New York: Macmillan.

Yeung, Henry Wai-chung (2000f), 'A crisis of industrial and business networks in Asia?', *Environment and Planning A*, 32(2), 191–200.

Yeung, Henry Wai-chung (2000g), 'Limits to the growth of family-owned business? The case of Chinese transnational corporations from Hong Kong', *Family Business Review*, 13(1), 55–70.

Yeung, Henry Wai-chung (2000h), 'State intervention and neoliberalism in the globalising world economy: lessons from Singapore's regionalisation programme', *The Pacific Review*, 13(1), 133–62.

Yeung, Henry Wai-chung (2000i), 'Local politics and foreign ventures in China's transitional economy', *Political Geography*, 19(7), 809–40.

Yeung, Henry Wai-chung (2000j), 'Strategic control and coordination in Chinese firms', *Journal of Asian Business*, 16(1), 95–123.

Yeung, Henry Wai-chung (2001), 'Managing traditional Chinese family firms across borders: four generations of entrepreneurship in Eu Yan Sang', in Leo Douw, Cen Huang and David Ip (eds), *Rethinking Chinese Transnational Enterprises*, 184–207, Richmond, Surrey, UK: Curzon.

Yeung, Henry Wai-chung (2002a), *Entrepreneurship and the Internationalisation of Asian Firms*, Cheltenham: Edward Elgar.

Yeung, Henry Wai-chung (2002b), 'The limits to globalization theory', *Economic Geography*, 78(3), 285–305.

Yeung, Henry Wai-chung (2002c), 'Entrepreneurship in international business', *Asia Pacific Journal of Management*, 19(1), 29–61.

Yeung, Henry Wai-chung (2002d), 'Transnational entrepreneurship and Chinese business networks', in Thomas Menkhoff and Solvay Gerke (eds), *Chinese Entrepreneurship and Asian Business Networks*, 184–216, Richmond, Surrey, UK: Curzon.

Yeung, Henry Wai-chung (2003a), 'Financing Chinese Capitalism', paper presented at the Conference on 'Cultural Approaches to Asian Financial Markets', Cornell Law School, Ithaca, NY, 26 April.

Yeung, Henry Wai-chung (2003b), 'International/transnational entrepreneurship and Chinese business research', in Leo Paul Dana (ed.), *The Handbook of Research on International Entrepreneurship*, Cheltenham: Edward Elgar.

Yeung, Henry Wai-chung (2003c), 'Practicing new economic geographies', *Annals of the Association of American Geographers*, 93(2), 442–62.

Yeung, Henry Wai-chung and Olds, Kris (1998), 'Singapore's global reach', *International Journal of Urban Sciences*, 2(1), 24–47.

Yeung, Henry Wai-chung and Olds, Kris (eds) (2000a), *Globalization of Chinese Firms*, New York: Macmillan.

Yeung, Henry Wai-chung and Olds, Kris (2000b), 'Globalizing Chinese firms', in Henry Wai-chung Yeung and Kris Olds (eds), *Globalization of Chinese Firms*, 1–28, New York: Macmillan.

Yeung, Henry Wai-chung, Poon, Jessie and Perry, Martin (2001), 'Towards a regional strategy: the role of regional headquarters and regional offices in the Asia Pacific', *Urban Studies*, 38(1), 157–83.

Yeung, Henry Wai-chung and Soh, Tse Min (2000), 'Corporate governance and the global reach of Chinese family firms in Singapore', *Seoul Journal of Economics*, 13(3), 301–34.

Yoshihara, Kunio (1988), *The Rise of Ersatz Capitalism in South East Asia*, Singapore: Oxford University Press.

Yoshihara, Kunio (1994), *The Nation and Economic Growth: The Philippines and Thailand*, Singapore: Oxford University Press.

Yu, Fu-Lai Tony (1997), *Entrepreneurship and Economic Development in Hong Kong*, London: Routledge.

Zaheer, Srilata (1995), 'Overcoming the liability of foreignness', *Academy of Management Journal*, 38(2), 341–63.

Zang, Xiaowei (1999), 'Personalism and corporate networks in Singapore', *Organization Studies*, 20(5), 861–77.

Zang, Xiaowei (2000), 'Intercorporate ties in Singapore', *International Sociology*, 15(1), 87–105.

Index

Printed in Singapore
by Markono Print Media Pte Ltd.
R464000001B/R4640PG107647UKSX00002B/2}